PROSE POETRY

PROSE POETRY

AN INTRODUCTION

Paul Hetherington and Cassandra Atherton

PRINCETON UNIVERSITY PRESS
Princeton and Oxford

Copyright © 2020 by Princeton University Press

Requests for permission to reproduce material from this work should be sent to permissions@press.princeton.edu

Published by Princeton University Press
41 William Street, Princeton, New Jersey 08540
6 Oxford Street, Woodstock, Oxfordshire OX20 1TR

press.princeton.edu

All Rights Reserved

Library of Congress Cataloging-in-Publication Data

Names: Hetherington, Paul, 1958– author. | Atherton, Cassandra L., 1974– author.
Title: Prose poetry : an introduction / Paul Hetherington and Cassandra Atherton.
Description: Princeton : Princeton University Press, [2020] | Includes bibliographical references and index.
Identifiers: LCCN 2020012471 (print) | LCCN 2020012472 (ebook) | ISBN 9780691180649 (hardback) | ISBN 9780691180656 (paperback) | ISBN 9780691212135 (ebook)
Subjects: LCSH: Prose poems—History and criticism.
Classification: LCC PN1059.P76 H48 2020 (print) | LCC PN1059.P76 (ebook) | DDC 808.1—dc23
LC record available at https://lccn.loc.gov/2020012471
LC ebook record available at https://lccn.loc.gov/2020012472

British Library Cataloging-in-Publication Data is available

Editorial: Anne Savarese and Jenny Tan
Production Editorial: Ellen Foos
Text and Jacket/Cover Design: Pamela L. Schnitter
Production: Erin Suydam
Publicity: Alyssa Sanford and Amy Stewart
Copyeditor: Cathryn Slovensky

Jacket/Cover Credit: Shutterstock

This book has been composed in Adobe Garamond Pro

Printed on acid-free paper. ∞

Printed in the United States of America

10 9 8 7 6 5 4 3 2 1

Contents

PREFACE   vii

PART 1: BEGINNINGS
Chapter 1. Introducing the Prose Poem   3
Chapter 2. The Prose Poem's Post-Romantic Inheritance   28
Chapter 3. Prose Poetry, Rhythm, and the City   51

PART 2: AGAINST CONVENTION
Chapter 4. Ideas of Open Form and Closure in Prose Poetry   79
Chapter 5. Neo-Surrealism within the Prose Poetry Tradition   102
Chapter 6. Prose Poetry and TimeSpace   128

PART 3: METHODS AND CONTEXTS
Chapter 7. The Image and Memory in Reading Prose Poetry   153
Chapter 8. Metaphor, Metonymy, and the Prose Poem   177
Chapter 9. Women and Prose Poetry   199
Chapter 10. Prose Poetry and the Very Short Form   224

ACKNOWLEDGMENTS   249

NOTES   261

BIBLIOGRAPHY   287

INDEX   329

Preface

This volume introduces and provides wide-ranging perspectives on English-language prose poetry, discussing a broad range of examples. Prose poetry is a highly significant literary form flourishing in most English-speaking countries and it deserves sustained critical attention. Because of the contemporary renaissance in prose poetry, we focus to a considerable degree on works written in the last forty or fifty years. To convey a sense of how the form has evolved, however, we also consider a selection of compelling prose poems from the nineteenth and early twentieth centuries.

English-language prose poetry had a checkered history for most of the twentieth century and only fully emerged as a major poetic form in recent decades. We explore prose poetry's trajectory as a literary form and discuss the emergence of significant key practitioners—some of whose views have strongly influenced the way the form has been received and understood. The views of many scholars and critics of the prose poem are also represented and discussed as we probe the ways in which they have characterized or defined what has often been understood as a contradictory or paradoxical literary form.

Although our focus is on English-language prose poetry, we also provide some examples of prose poetry in translation, mainly to illustrate prose poetry's development in nineteenth-century France, and to give a brief indication of prose poetry's literary antecedents. We are particularly interested in what constitutes, and may be said to define, a prose poem, and in the question of how prose poetry differs from (while using many of the same devices as) lineated lyric poetry and poetic prose. We also trace the social, historical, cultural, and aesthetic contexts that have informed prose poetry's development.

In order to link the history and evolution of prose poetry to contemporary examples of the form, and thereby to contextualize and explicate the practice of contemporary prose poets, we have divided this volume into three parts. Part 1 ("Beginnings," chapters 1 to 3) introduces prose poetry and discusses the periods and contexts from which it grew. Chapter 1 focuses on prose poetry's development in nineteenth-century France and its early reception and subsequent critical views about the form. It defines the prose poem's main features and discusses the challenge prose poetry presents to established ideas of literary genre. Chapters 2 and 3 explore specific historical contexts for understanding prose poetry's development—its relationship to the Romantic fragment in England and Germany, the way fragmentariness is a defining feature of the form, and the connection of many of prose poetry's characteristically diverse rhythms to the urban centers in which it developed. This includes a consideration of both the rhythms of perambulation and—in terms of recent work—prose poetry's suitability for the articulation of postmodern experience.

Part 2 ("Against Convention," chapters 4 to 6) provides different perspectives on the ways in which prose poetry challenges or defies traditional literary assumptions or expresses itself in unconventional ways. Prose poetry may not always be subversive but, as chapter 4 demonstrates, it does not conform to the expectations associated with either conventional, lineated lyric poetry or conventional narrative prose. Importantly, prose poetry is an open form that rarely exhibits the kinds of formal closure associated with the lineated lyric, even in its free verse manifestations. Chapter 5 considers the American neo-surreal as an influential strand of prose poetry, adapting ideas that originated with the surrealists to challenge assumptions about how the world should be understood, and prose-poetic narratives ought to be read. Prose poetry's distortion of space and time is the focus of chapter 6, which explores the effects created by prose poetry's simultaneously condensed and onrushing language.

Part 3 ("Methods and Contexts," chapters 7 to 10) examines how individual prose poems employ particular literary techniques and devices to achieve characteristic effects, and highlights two of the important and particular contexts that strongly influence contemporary practitioners. The use of visual imagery remains a hallmark of prose poetry as the twenty-first century unfolds, and chapter 7 examines how such imagery relates to evocations of memory, and the continuing connection of some of prose poetry's effects to those generated by photographs and ekphrastic responses to a range of art forms. The use of metonymy and metaphor is another central feature of prose poetry, and chapter 8 discusses the importance of such figurative language to reading and interpreting individual works, allowing an understanding of the ways in which many prose poems simultaneously present a variety of possible (often shifting) interpretations. This chapter also looks at prose poetry's resonant employment of intertextuality to enrich its content. The final two chapters (9 and 10) focus on specific contexts for, and features evident in, contemporary prose poetry, especially works written by women—including the strong emergence of feminist themes and ideas in recent decades and the influence of online publishing and social media, in which prose poetry has powerfully established its presence.

Prose poetry is an expansive and rapidly developing field with many strands and numerous practitioners. We thank prose poets everywhere for their help and inspiration, and for the many thousands of prose poems that enriched our lives while we undertook research and wrote this book.

PART 1

BEGINNINGS

CHAPTER 1

Introducing the Prose Poem

Prose Poetry's "Problem" of Definition

The prose poem in English is now established as an important literary form in many countries at a time when the composition and publication of poetry is thriving. While prose poetry is still written and published less often than lineated poetry, notable books of prose poems have been produced—including Mark Strand's acclaimed volume, *The Monument* (1978);[1] Charles Simic's Pulitzer Prize-winning *The World Doesn't End* (1989); Luke Kennard's *The Solex Brothers* (2005), winner of an Eric Gregory Award; Claudia Rankine's multi-award-winning, hybrid work, *Citizen: An American Lyric* (2014); and Eve Joseph's *Quarrels* (2018), winner of the Griffin Prize.

Such books demonstrate prose poetry's capacity to articulate poetic ideas in ways that are conspicuously different from contemporary lineated lyric poetry*—now usually defined as short, sometimes musical forms of poetry that appear to address personal emotions and feelings, often using the first-person voice. However, while poetry generally continues to be recognized as a literary genre highly suited to expressing intense emotion, grappling with the ineffable and the intimate, and while lineated lyric poetry is widely admired for its rhythms and musicality, the main scholarship written about English-language prose poetry to date defines the form as problematic, paradoxical, ambiguous, unresolved, or contradictory. This is despite the fact that a prose poem rarely looks unapproachable, unfinished, or confused. In some instances, the prose poem has even been portrayed as little more than illusory or nonsensical, as in this quotation from poet George Barker:

> Like the Loch Ness monster the prose poem is a creature of whose existence we have only very uncertain evidence. Sometimes it seems to appear, like a series of undulating coils, out of the dithyrambs of Walt Whitman; several French critics claim to have taken photographs of this extraordinary beast, and a great many American poets possess tape recordings of the rhapsodies it chants up from the depths of the liberated imagination.[2]

---

* We are using the term "lineated lyric poetry" as opposed to "lyric poetry" to acknowledge that there are also lyric prose poems.

The common observation that the term "prose poetry" appears to contain a contradiction is not surprising given that poetry and prose are often understood to be fundamentally different kinds of writing. Prose poetry has also been described as "a poem written in prose instead of verse," characterized as a form that "avails itself of the elements of prose . . . while foregrounding the devices of poetry," defined in relation to flash fiction and microfiction, and compared to free verse.[3] In the first issue of *The Prose Poem: An International Journal*, the editor and prose poet Peter Johnson states, "Just as black humor straddles the fine line between comedy and tragedy, so the prose poem plants one foot in prose, the other in poetry, both heels resting precariously on banana peels."[4]

Johnson's analogy is entertaining and instructive, but the prose poem looks robust rather than precarious and, despite critics' vacillations, its literary currency is increasing to the extent that a number of new prose poetry anthologies and critical books about prose poetry have been published in recent years, or are in preparation. These include the *Anthology of Australian Prose Poetry* (2020), edited by Cassandra Atherton and Paul Hetherington; the anthologies *The Valley Press Anthology of Prose Poetry* (2019), edited by Anne Caldwell and Oz Hardwick; *A Cast-Iron Aeroplane that Can Actually Fly: Commentaries from 80 Contemporary American Poets on Their Prose Poetry* (2019), edited by Peter Johnson; and *The Penguin Book of the Prose Poem: From Baudelaire to Anne Carson* (2018), edited by Jeremy Noel-Tod. They also include the essay collections *The Edinburgh Companion to the Prose Poem* (forthcoming), edited by Mary Ann Caws and Michel Delville, and *British Prose Poems: The Poems Without Lines* (2018), edited by Jane Monson, also editor of the 2011 anthology *This Line Is Not For Turning: An Anthology of Contemporary British Prose Poetry*; and, in Australia, a number of small anthologies of prose poetry—including *Tract: Prose Poems* (2017), *Cities: Ten Poets, Ten Cities* (2017), *Pulse: Prose Poems* (2016), and *Seam: Prose Poems* (2015) (various editors)—linked to the International Prose Poetry Group started in 2014 by the International Poetry Studies Institute at the University of Canberra.[5] In this book we will discuss a variety of contemporary prose poems, including some from recent anthologies, because it is instructive to examine diverse examples of the form and we are interested in the way prose poetry continues to develop at a rapid pace.[6]

Prose poetry is flourishing for a variety of reasons, one of them being the late twentieth- and twenty-first-century embrace of apparently hybrid or new literary forms. Apart from the prose poem, there are many other examples, including the lyric essay, novels that largely eschew narrative, fictocritical works, poetic memoir, and epistolary works written as poetry. There are also works that demonstrate a multivalent hybridity, such as graphic novels, which include prose poems. We explore the hybrid nature of some prose poems in more detail in later chapters but, generally speaking, the prose poem is one of a number of kinds of literature that appear to possess the characteristics, or use the techniques, of more than one established genre or form. Many of the significant scholars of prose poetry emphasize this point, including Robert Alexander, Michel Delville, Stephen Fredman, Jonathan Monroe, Steven Monte, Margueritte S. Murphy, and Nikki Santilli.[7]

As some of these critics have acknowledged, the apparently thorny issue about how to define the terms "poetry," "prose," and "prose poetry" may be due partly to the confusion in many people's minds between poetry and verse. Santilli notes how in the twentieth century, Roman Jakobson "is able to shift discussion away from a verse/prose dialectic to a more liberal concept of 'poetry' that may inhabit verse and nonversified work alike."[8] Emmylou Grosser also comments on this distinction with respect to the Hebrew Bible, observing that "the ancient Hebrew poetic texts have been passed down to us in mostly unlineated form."[9] She states, "For those who view poetry as . . . identifiable by the concentration of certain poetic features (most of which can also be found in prose), prose and poetry in the Bible are best viewed as the opposing ends of a continuum . . . [while] prose and verse are best viewed as distinct categories."[10] Such comments provide, in analogical form, a summary of some key features of the contemporary debate about prose poetry.

Disagreement about how to understand the term "poetry" is not new. Wladyslaw Tatarkiewicz discusses contention among the ancient Greeks about this matter, noting that Aristotle questioned whether there was an "expression in the Greek tongue to signify poetry proper."[11] Contemporary debates about how to interpret the term "poetry" are sometimes even more vexed than those of the ancient world. Some people understand "poetry" to mean condensed, highly suggestive, and often imagistic writing composed of lines that do not run to the page's right-hand margin or, if they speak of "verse," they usually invoke the notion that verse is identifiable by such characteristics as meter and rhyme or other aspects of verse's formal patterning of language. When people talk of "prose," they frequently mean something like narrative prose fiction.

Such issues demonstrate how questions of literary genre and form remain slippery and continue to generate much discussion and debate. The early difficulty in categorizing Charles Simic's volume *The World Doesn't End* (1989) provides an example of such slipperiness in practice. The book's success in winning the Pulitzer Prize for poetry helped to legitimate prose poetry as a form but, reportedly, Simic did not write his works with the prose poem form specifically in mind. It was his editor who negotiated with him in order to make the book more marketable:

> I showed [my manuscript] to my editor, who, to my surprise, offered to publish it. Oddly, it was only then that the question of what to call these little pieces came up. "Don't call them anything," I told my editor. "You have to call them *something*," she explained to me, "so that the bookstore knows under what heading to shelve the book." After giving it some thought, and with some uneasiness on my part, we decided to call them prose poems.[12]

Despite such ambiguities, it is unsatisfactory to define a significant literary form such as the prose poem primarily in terms of writers' or critics' uncertainties. As a significant part of contemporary literature in English, prose poetry deserves a clear, positive characterization of its features and qualities just as, for example, the lineated lyric poem or the novel does. This is especially important because the idea of poetic prose more generally is well established and has a history nearly as old as literature itself. The prose poem may be, in comparison, a new form, but its antecedents are venerable, and the idea that poetry may be written in prose is not anywhere near as radical as some writers suggest.

The Poetry Foundation states that "[t]he definition of a genre changes over time, and a text often interacts with multiple genres,"[13] which is certainly the case with prose poetry. The Foundation also contends, in the case of genres, and at the broadest level, that the primary candidates are poetry, drama, nonfiction, and fiction. This is a good, straightforward definition and, making use of it, one may understand prose poetry as a separate, identifiable, and distinctive literary form—part of the broad genre of poetry written in the mode of prose. Lewis Turco explores this point:

> [In] the Western *Judeo-Christian tradition* there is ample precedent for writing any of the *genres—song, narrative poetry,* and *dramatic poetry,* in either of the *modes—prose* or *verse*; therefore, genres do not depend on the modes in which they are written. "Verse," a mode, is not equivalent to "poetry," a genre. To ask the question "What is the difference between prose and poetry?" is to compare anchors with bullets.[14]

Santilli similarly points out that prose is a mode with certain general characteristics: "[W]hile prose poetry is a genre or form, poetic prose describes a prose *style*. It is precisely this style that cannot be contained inside the severe perimeters of the prose poem. Prose enacts a continuum, a process that moves the reader and itself inexorably onward (not necessarily forward). Poetic prose facilitates this movement by characteristically florid verbosity. The style of the prose poem, on the other hand, is constrained by a relatively unnatural brevity."[15]

Her discussion of poetic prose and its "florid verbosity" supports the importance of making a clear distinction between the prose poem (as a compressed and concise literary form) and the more general notion of poetic prose. While poetic prose often features an explicit use of elaborate literary figures and an expressively meandering way of moving—often across many pages—the prose poem is necessarily short, often less than one page. Prose poetry is a disciplined form that implicitly asserts and reveals some significant continuities between poetry and prose, making clear that poetry—as well as being written in verse or free verse—may be written in the mode of prose.

The opening of one of the well-known works from Simic's volume *The World Doesn't End* illustrates these distinctions nicely:

> We were so poor I had to take the place of the
> bait in the mousetrap. All alone in the cellar, I
> could hear them pacing upstairs, tossing and turn-
> ing in their beds.[16]

We discuss this work at greater length in the chapters that follow, but it is useful to note at this juncture that it is written in the mode of prose while inhabiting the genre of poetry, and it takes the form of a prose poem. This is to say that despite conveying a brief narrative, its main meanings derive from the weird, open, and poetic suggestiveness of its imagery. Works such as this one do not constitute a genre in their own right and are best understood as a form of poetry.

Prosaic Poetry and Poetic Prose

Before we discuss the features of prose poetry in more detail, it is worth remembering that the differences between lineated lyric poetry and poetic prose (other than in their use of lines and stanzas compared to sentences and paragraphs) have never been entirely clear-cut. This has especially been the case since the advent of so-called free verse in the nineteenth century, where many free verse poems tended to be prosaic in their rhythms, even as they exploited line breaks for poetic effect. The nineteenth-century American poet Walt Whitman, for instance, frequently constructed his poems as if they were an exotic species of prose:

> Trippers and askers surround me,
> People I meet, the effect upon me of my early life or the ward
>   and city I live in, or the nation,
> The latest dates, discoveries, inventions, societies, authors old and new,
> My dinner, dress, associates, looks, works, compliments, dues,
> The real or fancied indifference of some man or woman I love,
> The sickness of one of my folks or of myself, or ill-doing or loss or lack of
>   money, or depressions or exaltations,[17]

This example from "Song of Myself" exemplifies Whitman's fondness for catalogs or lists. It has a striking poetic effect that owes part of its power to literary techniques with broadly reiterative and repetitive tendencies that have been employed since antiquity. His poetic rhythms also draw on the demotic rhythms of speech and some of the rhythms of prose fiction—remembering that he started out as a novelist rather than a poet.

While in *Leaves of Grass* (1855) Whitman is indubitably a poet rather than a prose writer, it can be hard at times to pinpoint exactly what makes his work poetry, apart from his use of the reiterative and repetitive effects mentioned, rhythmic and figurative language (something also employed by prose writers), and his use of lineation (allowing each of his poetic lines a sense of standing apart from—while also interacting with—every other line). D. S. Mirsky writes that Whitman's "innovations in form are directly derived from his novelty of content . . . involving a liquidation of the dignity of the disparity between the conventional, stylized and retrospective idiom of elevated poetry and the language of the present."[18]

Whitman elevates his language, but he does so cunningly by accumulating and juxtaposing strings of words that are associated with both the commonplace and the abstract, while also suggesting, but failing to fulfill, possible narrative threads. For instance, when he evokes "My dinner, dress, associates, looks, compliments, dues, / The real or fancied indifference of some man or woman I love,"[19] we are privy only to glances at, and glimpses of, a much larger whole. In this way, his poetry often has a fragmentary air that emphasizes the evocative and the suggestive rather than the conclusive—despite the considerable length of some poems. He makes his free verse innovations into poetry partly through harnessing prose rhythms for poetic purposes and is one of the first writers in the English language to demonstrate how profoundly "prose" and "poetry" may be meshed in their various effects.

If poetry may make profitable use of "prosaic" effects, so a great deal of prose may be characterized as musical or rhythmical and thus, at least to some extent, "poetic"—and there are many examples throughout the history and development of prose writing traditions in English. Charles Dickens opens his long novel *Little Dorrit* (1855–57) with a rhythmic series of paragraphs. This work was begun in the same year that Whitman published his first version of "Song of Myself," and only a decade and a half prior to the publication of Charles Baudelaire's *Paris Spleen*, which we discuss as the book that inaugurated contemporary prose poetry. Dickens's language is hypnotic:

> Thirty years ago, Marseilles lay burning in the sun, one day.
>
> A blazing sun upon a fierce August day was no greater rarity in southern France then, than at any other time, before or since. Everything in Marseilles, and about Marseilles, had stared at the fervid sky, and been stared at in return, until a staring habit had become universal there. Strangers were stared out of countenance by staring white houses, staring white walls, staring white streets, staring tracts of arid road, staring hills from which verdure was burnt away. The only things to be seen not fixedly staring and glaring were the vines drooping under their load of grapes. These did occasionally wink a little, as the hot air barely moved their faint leaves.[20]

This is an example of discursive prose rather than of prose poetry, but it uses some of the devices often associated with poetry, most conspicuously, vivid image-making and insistent repetition, along with some noticeably iambic rhythms.

Although the passage is in one sense descriptive, as it develops over its first few pages it functions somewhat like a poem in becoming an extended metaphor for central preoccupations of the novel that it begins—foregrounding, for instance, tropes of confinement, the contrast between what is "outside" and what is "inside," dissipation of various kinds, and the idea of being watched. When considered next to the excerpt from Whitman's "Song of Myself," this passage demonstrates that prose and poetry often share features, and make use of similar or related techniques, even if they are not the same. Andy Brown—using the term "prose poetry" rather loosely—writes, "Prose poetry . . . occurs in the early sacred texts of other cultures" and "[a]ncient prose poetry also occurs in secular books."[21] He notes that long before Dickens, the tradition of poetic prose had myriad manifestations, and he cites the *Pillow Book* of Sei Shōnagon as an example of "a list-like book akin to many present-day variations on the prose poem."[22]

A Prosaic Age

We live in a prosaic age. Most of what we read in books, on the web, in emails, in text messages, on social media, and in the mass media is written in prose. The novel remains the most popular and salable literary form, and popular and genre prose fiction is published and sold in vast numbers across the world. And yet, readers continue to engage with poetry, especially when they want to express deep feelings or emotions connected to what they consider sacred. We all go to weddings and funerals where well-known poems, many of them written in verse, have a significant place in ceremonies, in much the same way that greeting cards use verse to mark an occasion or celebration.

However, the lineated lyric poem—usually a heightened form of writing—is now being written and read in different ways than it once was, and it does not serve all contemporary poetic needs. Jonathan Culler suggests that the reason for this is "the centrality of the novel to theoretical discourse as well as to literary experience and literary education."[23] People are schooled in, and increasingly tend to understand literature in terms of, the conventions of prose. This means that the traditional lyric poem's formalities may seem forced, puzzling, or out of place to many readers—and to some writers too. Even at weddings and funerals, their forms of utterance may seem to belong to another world, and to earlier conventions.

Prose poetry has the potential to cross the divide between the urge toward poetry—its capacity to articulate what is otherwise unsayable—and the more discursive and narrative-driven prose of novels, biographies, and the like. Prose poetry understands prose's conventions and its constituent parts—its sentences and paragraphs—while also being conspicuously a form of poetry, and sometimes even lyrical in its inflections. Prose poetry shares with traditional lyric poetry a resistance to conclusive theorization—that is, both forms engage with the mysterious and the ineffable—and, as mentioned above, it presents further challenges because it is poetry written in a mode more often associated with the fiction and nonfiction genres. Indeed, some theories about the lineated lyric poem may be applied directly to discussions of prose poetry, helping to confirm that the prose poem is a form of poetry. One example is Mutlu Konuk Blasing's statement: "Poetry is a cultural institution dedicated to remembering and displaying the emotionally and historically charged materiality of language,"[24] an assertion that both prose poems and lineated lyric poems are able to demonstrate.

Despite some broad similarities of this kind, lyric poetry and prose poetry do not operate in the same way, and scholars have been quick to discuss this. Mark Irwin highlights one of the points of divergence between the two kinds of writing when he argues that while prose poetry does not necessarily "tolerate distortion and disjunction more readily than the lyric poem," nevertheless "the prose poem does allow it to occur less dramatically. Its pedestrian, unadorned nature seems more open to sudden changes that might appear histrionic or cloying in verse."[25] Molly Peacock contends that "[p]oetry seeks to name; [conventional] prose seeks to explain."[26]

If "the prose poem reflects the crisis of lyric poetry in a prosaic age, where traditional notions of the lyric have become increasingly problematic,"[27] then prose poetry is not only a development of the way writers express the poetic impulse but is perhaps an index of how traditional lineated lyric poetry is increasingly being replaced—and, in the process, transformed—by prosaic modes. Adrian Wanner remarks on how, in the Russian nineteenth-century writer Ivan Turgenev's and in Baudelaire's prose poetry, one can "find individual prose poems . . . that feature a distinct rhythmic structure, an abundance of metaphors, or an emotional lyric content, [and] it is also possible to find other prose poems by the same authors that lack all of those features. Some texts . . . seem to be written in a deliberately plain, 'prosaic' fashion."[28]

Such points demonstrate that prose poems are not simply lineated lyric poems in another guise because, to a significant extent, they represent a transformation and reorientation of traditional lyric forms and conventions. Any suggestion to the contrary downplays the particular qualities that enable prose poems to create significantly different effects and meanings from the contemporary lineated lyric poem. These differences have to do with the way prose works on the page: its sentence and paragraph structures, its kinds of condensations, its refusal to break its sentences into lines in the manner of lineated poems, and its tendency—as Kathryn Oliver Mills states in discussing Baudelaire's prose poetry—to restore "the relationship between poetry and the world" and to register "everyday life."[29]

Furthermore, as Margueritte Murphy notes, prose poetry allows for the heterogeneous and heteroglossic much more than traditional lyric poetry, opening up the space of poetic utterance to greater variety than much of lyric poetry easily allows.[30] For example, in prose poems we often find the voice of an author mingled with the voices of characters; or other, sometimes intertextual or historical, voices; or contemporary references (bringing with them their own "voices"), in ways that create a sense of an unsettled whole; or a whole composed of disparate, disjunct, and sometimes fragmented parts. Such effects mimic some of the techniques of novels or short fiction but, in doing so, put them under the pressure of the prose poem's very limited space—and sometimes even force them into a kind of prose-poetical rupture.

For instance, in a work entitled "Oklahoma" (2017)—quoted at length in chapter 2—Hala Alyan includes, in a single paragraph, references to her childhood, the contemporary lives of the Cherokee in Oklahoma, and the history of European settlement of Oklahoma, as well as a voice that directly utters a phrase that encapsulates twenty-first-century racial prejudice: "For a place I hate," she begins, "I invoke you often. Stockholm's: I am eight years old and the telephone poles are down, the power plant at the edge of town spitting electricity."[31]

Such a poem combines and condenses the robust qualities of good prose with the figurative features of much lineated lyric poetry, and is an example of how the best prose poets pay the kind of attention to the resources and features of prose that good lyric poets pay to the resources of their poetic lines. Prose poets are particularly interested in how prose sentences and paragraphs may be poetically suggestive even when they may not have the kind of heightened tonality one would usually associate with the "poetic." Indeed, in some cases—and as Wanner has noted—prose poetry does not appear obviously "poetic" at all. That is one of its apparently contradictory or paradoxical features. It is able to find ways of identifying as poetry, even when employing "prosaic" techniques and effects.

Notwithstanding Simic's uncertainty about how to classify his small prose-poetical works, a writer cannot simply write a block of "poetic" text and then decide that it will work equally well as a lineated free verse poem or as a prose poem. Although the innovations of the French Romantic prose poets transformed French and international poetry, their prose poetry remained a form of poetry despite its construction in sentences and paragraphs. The tendency for this form of poetry to challenge or stretch our assumptions about what the poetic looks like is one of its strengths. Prose poetry implicitly states that the poetic penetrates further than perhaps any of us had previously imagined.

In successful prose poetry, the mode of prose is not used in the same way one finds in most conventional and discursive novels or nonfiction. Prose becomes a revitalized medium that focuses less on a narrative's progress through chronological time and more on creating what Jonathan Culler has referred to, when discussing the traditional lyric, as the "present time of discourse," with associated "ritualistic" and "hyperbolic" qualities.[32] Ali Smith even posits, "[t]he prose poem provides a home to the sentence that refuses to make sense and the paragraph that refuses to progress."[33] Because of its transformative elements, prose poetry is able to enliven the common prosaic language of our era, reminding us that many and diverse kinds of language use are, at least potentially, "poetic," and drawing attention to ways in which language itself, and its ways of making meaning, may be understood newly and differently. Now that meter and rhyme are not so often used in poetry, and now that free verse poetry may be very free indeed, poetry chiefly inheres in condensed and suggestive writing—some in lines and some in sentences—that is neither primarily aimed to accomplish a particular act in the world nor primarily directed toward narrative or explication.

This is why the term "prose poetry," while sometimes controversial, is an important one. Stephen Fredman prefers to use the term "poet's prose" instead of "prose poem" to refer to "[prose] works that are conceived of and read as extensions of poetry," believing "prose poem" to be "an oxymoron . . . redolent with the atmospheric sentiment of French Symbolism."[34] However, in the English-language tradition, to call prose poetry by a name such as "poet's prose" (or "poetic prose") radically changes the emphasis. The usual term, "prose poetry" rightly emphasizes that the form is poetry—as Terrance Hayes writes in his discussion of Lauren Russell's "Dream-Clung, Gone," "since 'poem' is the noun and 'prose' the adjective, the prose poem must essentially be a poem."[35] Therefore, prose poems have the features we have described while poet's prose often has other characteristics entirely.

Some Characterizations of the Prose Poem Form

In the twentieth and twenty-first centuries, the prose poem has evolved in numerous directions in various countries, and prose poets have done so many different things with the form that it is difficult to summarize all of its developments. Anthologists of prose poetry have frequently reiterated points similar to Delville's—that "there may be as many kinds of prose poems as there are practitioners of the prose poem."[36] Jeremy Noel-Tod says something similar in his editorial introduction to *The Penguin Book of the Prose Poem: From Baudelaire to Anne Carson* (2018), an anthology consisting of "two hundred prose poems from around the world."[37] He states, "After reading so many, I can only offer the simplest common denominator: a prose poem is a poem without line breaks. Beyond that, both its manner and its matter resist generalization."[38] In their introduction to *The Valley Press Anthology of Prose Poetry*, Anne Caldwell and Oz Hardwick comment that "many definitions have been proposed (or imposed), yet the prose poem always wriggles free through one of the cracks, dusts itself off, and stands proud as an outlaw challenging its own *Wanted* poster . . . [and] it is perhaps its mercurial resistance to definition which has led to a growth of interest in the prose poem in the second decade of the twentieth-first century."[39]

The poet Michael Benedikt is one of a number of writers who have attempted to define the main features of the prose poem more precisely, aiming in his introduction to *The Prose Poem: An International Anthology* (1976) to unify "different kinds of prose poems" by pointing to five properties that all prose poems have in common. He claims that they turn on "individual imagination" and, also, that they demonstrate an attention to the unconscious, an accelerated use of the colloquial, a visionary thrust, humor, and an element critical of oppressive realities.[40]

While Benedikt's summary is astute, it does not encompass many of the approaches, properties, and varieties evident in contemporary prose poetry being published internationally—something Holly Iglesias comments on when she writes that Benedikt's "selections in his anthology reflect this emphasis on the importance of the workings of the individual unconscious and on comic irony, but at the expense of works that are lyrical, unwitty, embodied or relational."[41]

In the second half of the twentieth century, Robert Bly's views on prose poetry were influential, partly because of his editorship of the literary magazines *The Fifties*, *The Sixties*, and *The Seventies*. He discussed prose poetry in various essays and interviews and, for instance, said to Peter Johnson in 1998, "the most wonderful thing about the prose poem is that no one has set up the standards yet." He also commented, "What is the proper subject for a prose poem? There is no answer for that, so you have to look at your own life."[42] Despite this, in his later essays, he outlined what he saw as the varieties of prose poetry. Iglesias summarizes these categories, pointing to their shortcomings:

> Bly's later essays delineated three distinct strains of prose poetry: fables (with David Ignatow, Charles Simic, and Russell Edson as modern masters), post-Romantic "fire prose" (perfected by Rimbaud), and the "object/thing poem" (as written by Bly, Francis Ponge, Tomas Tranströmer, and James Wright). Some of his commentary manifests the underpinnings of male prose poetry—anxiety, self-indulgence, distance from and yearning for the body, excess intellection.[43]

In making his distinctions, Bly did seem to neglect the work of significant women prose poets, and he also risked limiting rather than liberating the bounds of prose poetry and its possibilities. French scholar Suzanne Bernard takes a very different approach from Bly's in her outline of "four requirements" for the prose poem, but her list is broad and can perhaps be applied to other kinds of writing as well as the prose poem: "it had to embody the poet's intention, it had to have an organic unity, it had to be its own best excuse for being, and it had to be brief."[44]

The contemporary prose poem is so many things at once, and so protean and hybrid, that no summary will successfully delineate its borders or indicate the scope of its preoccupations and approaches. Indeed, prose poetry is undergoing a process not dissimilar to the emergence in the seventeenth and eighteenth centuries of the modern prose novel. The early novel included prose romances, sentimental works, realistic works, and a wide variety of other kinds of writing. Furthermore, the development of the novel involved a great deal of hybridization and experimentation. Patricia Meyer Spacks observes:

> By the 1760s, when [Laurence Sterne's] *Tristram Shandy* was being written, several distinct subgenres [of the novel] had been established . . . The playfulness of *Tristram Shandy*, then, not only foretells that of postmodernism . . .

[but] also testifies to how much had happened to the novel in the few years since its invention as a form distinct from the seventeenth-century romance.[45]

The prose poem is undergoing a similar evolution that sees many writers experimenting with the form and helping to make it a vigorous site of literary innovation.

Prose poetry's diversity does not challenge the integrity of its form. Rather, it attests to the form's resilience, along with its capacity to embrace great variety and to surprise in its expressiveness. This may make the contemporary prose poetry environment somewhat unstable, but variety and surprise are a characteristic of all truly significant literary forms and genres, as writers test what they can achieve within given boundaries and, in doing so, compel a form or genre to continue to evolve. Prose poetry's variousness is, for example, no greater than the diversity that continues to be a feature of the novel—*Tristram Shandy*'s (1759) experimentation with form has been extended by countless authors over the last three centuries and, as this has happened, definitions of the novel have continued to be modified. And, with respect to lineated lyric poetry, C. W. Truesdale has written, "though the prose poem has come down to us in many varieties, it is no more varied than its lineated counterpart for which that question of definition, seldom, if ever, arises."[46] While prose poetry possesses many different and sometimes incompatible-seeming characteristics, the form in general is able to be recognized by certain conspicuous features.

The Main Features of the Prose Poem

One of the popular definitions of prose poetry is by Benedikt, who suggests that prose poetry "is a genre of poetry, self-consciously written in prose, and characterized by the intense use of virtually all the devices of poetry."[47] This is true enough, but prose poems also have additional features. They are never entirely driven by narrative and are always trying to point to something about their language or their subject that sits outside of any narrative gestures they make (and frequently outside of the work itself). Consequently, prose poems may be understood as fragments—they never give the whole story and resist closure.

As a result of this compression and brevity, prose poets regularly make use of literary techniques that suggest additional meanings beyond the literal, emphasizing the evocative and even the ambiguous, and creating resonances that move expansively outward. In prose poems the "poetic" inhabits language and, as it were, colors sentences and paragraphs to the extent that their denotative qualities are overwhelmed by the connotative. Thus, prose poetry tends to work analogically, metaphorically, or metonymically (we discuss these features in subsequent chapters).

This emphasis on the connotative in prose poetry (i.e., the secondary or associative meanings of words and expressions) partly answers John Taylor's concern: "The greatest obstacle facing prose-poem investigators is comprehending how prose is given that extra 'something'—a wisp of charm, an aura of mystery, an electric shock—convincing us that we are dealing stylistically with a prose poem—that is, poetry—and not, say, a newspaper sketch, an oft-humorous literary form that took flight during the nineteenth century and sometimes approaches the prose poem in spirit."[48] Sometimes the abundance of connotation in prose poems creates a sense that its meanings are hard to pin down, or mysterious because so much suggestiveness is wrapped into its apparently simple form.

Prose poems frequently suggest that powerful unseen and unconscious forces are at work in human experience, as well as in language, and such forces are, for example, explored in the surrealistic and neo-surrealistic prose poetry traditions. These traditions emphasize the dreamlike, sometimes creating a sense that particular prose poems constitute instances of the Freudian *uncanny*: "everything that ought to have remained . . . secret and hidden but has come to light."[49] At other times, when prose poems work analogically, their compressed texts speak sideways, or point laterally to additional understandings, implicitly indicating issues and topics other than those they directly address. Alternatively, whole prose poems may become metaphorical to the extent that nothing in the work escapes the metaphorical tropes and structures. In such cases, there may be no "literal" reading of a prose poem available.

Prose poems also make use of various different typographical features that provide various signals to readers. For example, many prose poets emphasize that their works are prose poems by presenting them on the page as one, or a few, fully justified paragraphs. Each block of text is neatly rectangular and has a sense of being "made," much as many lineated poems do, because the form has the hallmarks of having been closely composed, with an outward appearance of regularity. These works are reminiscent of rooms viewed from above, suggesting the original meaning of the word "stanza" or "room."

Other prose poems are written in conventional paragraphs and appear at first glance to be ordinary prose. It is only upon reading them that surprises happen, and what appears to be a standard paragraph is outed as a prose poem—at which point poetry asserts itself over the idea of the prosaic. This unsettles the experience of reading because the familiar (the usual assumptions that attend on reading prose) is made strange. Gary Young is one of the major poet scholars focused on the orientation of the prose poem on the page. He has described the prose poem as "a poem that one might walk along rather than fall through."[50] In this way, Young points to the prose poem's "horizontal rather than vertical trajectory," which he says is evidence of its "democratic itinerary [and] engenders a resistance to hierarchy and to inflation."[51]

Reading prose poetry is often a fairly rapid experience, and some also tend to move quickly at the level of their sentences. In other respects, however, the experience can be drawn out, in the way that poetic tropes demand our attention and are able to slow our apprehension of time. Prose poems may also be just as rhythmic as lineated lyric poems, but their rhythms are those of prose rather than verse. Sometimes prose poems expand, balloon-like, as we read, and occasionally they seem much larger inside than on the outside, seeming to work a strange magic with our sense of time and space—not unlike a poetic version of the TARDIS. Many prose poems make significant use of visual (and other sensory) imagery, "showing" scenes and circumstances as vividly as a photograph and allowing the reader to enter works imaginatively—and, as it were, to "see" from inside them.

The Length of the Prose Poem

Prose poetry is almost always brief, as befits the fragmentary—most scholars agree on this—but determining the appropriate maximum length for the prose poem is a hotly debated topic. Murphy questions what "brief" really means. She asks, "While long prose poems are rarer than prose poems of a page, or two, or three, should they be excluded by definition?"[52] Jane Monson, on the other hand, is quite specific; prose poems should be "in length no more than a page, preferably half of one, focused, dense, justified, with an intuitive grasp of a good story and narrative, a keen eye for the unusual and surprising detail and images relative to that story, and a sharp ear for delivering elegant, witty, clear and subtly surreal pieces of conversation and brief occurrences, incidents or happenings."[53]

In her introduction to the *Prose Poem Issue* of the *Mississippi Review*, Julia Johnson embraces much longer examples of the form: "The prose poem's length is generally half a page to three or four pages . . . If it's longer than that, tension is weakened and it becomes more poetic prose than prose poetry."[54] J. S. Simon concurs with the importance of maintaining tension in prose poetry but does not specify what "observably 'short'" means: "not only are prose poems observably 'short' (and autonomous), but they must be so, for beyond a certain length, the tensions and impact are forfeited and [the prose poem] becomes—more or less—poetic prose."[55]

Because the prose poem turns on its appeal to compression and on establishing a tension generated by the close, and sometimes overlapping, contiguity between its parts—often connected to its refusal to be tied down to conclusive or single meanings—it is important that it does not begin to dilate. The brevity of the prose poem provides a necessary tension in the way that language intersects and unfolds within individual works, enabling the prose poem's "paradoxical way of combining suggestiveness and completeness."[56]

Works that do dilate quickly become a species of discursive or "poetic" prose rather than prose poems—and we will argue in the chapters that follow that this is true of some (often distinguished) works that have been called prose poems by their authors or by critics. These works tend to be insufficiently condensed or compressed to create the kinds of poetic effects we have outlined above as belonging to the prose poem. Perhaps for this reason, most of the prose poems collected in anthologies dedicated to the form are less than two pages in length, and an overwhelming number of them are less than half a page—although Jeremy Noel-Tod's 2018 anthology, *The Penguin Book of the Prose Poem*, includes more longer works than most anthologies.

Visually, the prose poem is easily identified if it is one page or less, as the reader is able to take in the entire work at a glance. In such cases, especially when the prose poem appears in a rectangular or justified form, there is considerable visual tension connected to the way in which it appears on the page—almost as if, to repurpose one of Steven Monte's observations, there is an invisible fence around the work.[57] It is true that prose poetry sequences may range across many pages—in some instances even taking up a whole volume—but their component parts are generally more or less discrete and relatively brief, once again, often no more than a page in length. Such works are different from a single book-length work, and Alan Wall acknowledges this when he writes that the prose poem "cannot be book-length, though enough of them put together can make up a book. The prose concerned should show the same fastidiousness in regard to lexis, and exhibit the same vigour and coherence of rhythm, as verse."[58]

Given these considerations, we will argue that the majority of prose poems—as opposed to examples of poetic prose of one kind or another—are no more than one standard-sized page in length. There are exceptions, including prose poems that incorporate extra space via "free-lines," which we discuss later in this volume, but certainly many of the most convincing prose poems—those that exemplify the possibilities of the form—make brevity and compression the rule.

A Brief History of the Prose Poem

Poetry has an ancient and venerable tradition (remembering—like the earliest extant version of the *Epic of Gilgamesh*—the Sumerian lyric "The Love Song of Shu-Sin" has been dated to approximately 2000 BCE[59]). Prose poetry may be a relatively new part of this tradition but, like the Sumerian lyric, it connects to a long-established human need to speak in ways that defy mundane and common-sense assumptions about the world, and that depart from the time-centered narratives and the discursive modes of most forms of storytelling. This is a need to speak of the unresolvable mysteries at the heart of both experience and language; to evoke, intuit, or summon the ineffable; and to celebrate what cannot be said through more prosaic or utilitarian uses of language.

Even in its contemporary manifestations, the prose poem has a complex history dating back to the eighteenth and nineteenth centuries—and earlier if one includes the late seventeenth-century Japanese development of the haibun, a form that combines haiku with tightly written, often imagistic prose poetry. Anthony Howell also connects the prose poem to the work of various "mystics and philosophers," contending that an "aphorism with its laconic precision is equivalent to a prose 'verse' and there are several fine exponents of this usage."[60] He gives an example from Baltasar Gracián's *The Oracle: A Manual of the Art of Discretion* (sometimes translated as *The Art of Worldly Wisdom*), first published in Spanish in 1647. He also mentions the *Maxims and Moral Reflections* of François VI, Duc de La Rochefoucauld, first published in 1665, commenting that "[o]ften the maxims are single sentences" and that "the sentence, polished, finely calibrated, becomes an object constructed with art—a European form of the Haiku."[61] He includes in his praise the prose of Jean Paul Friedrich Richter, observing that "[y]ou can tell it's poetry, surely, if you can open it anywhere and it takes your breath away."[62] Howell then identifies Thomas Traherne, in his seventeenth-century *Centuries of Meditations*, as "the pioneer of . . . [the prose poem] form" and characterizes the 1929 novel *Hebdomeros* by the Italian painter Giorgio de Chirico as "a novel-length poem in prose."[63]

Yet, however complex the prose poem's lineage may be, and however numerous and diverse its antecedents, the contemporary, vigorous form of the prose poem became established in the mid- and late nineteenth century when it was invented by a variety of groundbreaking French practitioners, including the poets Charles Baudelaire (in a work variously referred to as *Petits Poèmes en prose* or *Le Spleen de Paris* [*Paris Spleen*], 1869), Arthur Rimbaud (in *Une Saison en Enfer* [*A Season in Hell*], 1873; and *Illuminations*, 1886), and Stéphane Mallarmé (in *Divagations* [*Wanderings*], 1897). Also influential is the generally nostalgic works of Aloysius Bertrand in *Gaspard de la nuit: Fantaisies à la manière de Rembrandt et de Callot*, published in 1842, which powerfully impressed Baudelaire, and in which meditations, dreaming, and ideas about art take priority over any attempted narrative.

Such writers developed the prose poem as a new literary form in opposition to the conventional and rather inhibiting neoclassical rules of French prosody, which required poets to follow mandated metrical, rhythmic, and rhyming patterns. References to prose poetry's rebellious and subversive tendencies partly derive from the form's challenge to Alexandrine meter in nineteenth-century France and, in this context, prose poetry may be understood as a way of escaping from the confines of a conservative and stultifying literary traditionalism in that country. In his introduction to *Pastels in Prose* (1890), the first anthology of French prose poetry to be translated into English, W. D. Howells outlines the prose poem's "beautiful reticence . . . as if the very freedom which the poets had found in their emancipation from the artificial trammels of verse had put them on their honor, as it were, and bound them to brevity."[64]

Prose poetry was undoubtedly partly an escape of this kind—a kind of Romantic coup against the established literary order—but, in making it, Baudelaire,

Rimbaud, Mallarmé, and their contemporaries drew on and transformed the eighteenth-century tradition of the French *poème en prose*. Poèmes en prose were usually extended works of nostalgic poetic prose (and were themselves an attempt to break with neoclassical poetic forms). Nineteenth-century prose poets adapted this earlier poème en prose tradition by writing shorter, pithier, and more vernacular works than it had produced, as they frequently addressed aspects of city life.

Fabienne Moore, in his searching study of the eighteenth-century poème en prose, argues that the form enables the claim that "[p]rose poems are one of the least known 'inventions' of the French Enlightenment." He states, "the melancholy rising from modernity is tied to the rise of prose poems as a hybrid and unstable genre."[65] And, despite his caveat that "eighteenth-century prose poems defy terminology," he characterizes poèmes en prose in the following manner:

> As far as their poetic diction is concerned, parataxis (short, declarative sentences without coordination or clauses) remained a favorite choice, reminiscent of the Old Testament. "Poëmes en prose" were often divided into "cantos," like epic poems, and were usually long, from a few pages to several volumes. Titles, prefaces, and embedded meta-references invariably tried to establish the legitimacy of a poem *without* verse.[66]

In other words, like many apparently sudden literary innovations, the nineteenth-century prose poem grew out of an extended literary and cultural gestation in a society that had been trying for many decades to find new literary forms to express its sense of a changing zeitgeist. Although these changes began with the eighteenth-century Enlightenment—and notwithstanding the poème en prose's inventiveness—the Enlightenment poème en prose lacked the poetic energy and literary significance of the prose poetry produced by the Romantic French writers mentioned.

For example, when Moore writes of Jean-François Marmontel's 1767 novel, *Bélisaire*, he highlights how Enlightenment writers of poetic prose were working in a tradition that was yet to be fully realized: "[S]ymptomatic of the hybridity of Enlightenment 'poëms en prose,' it remains that Marmontel's experimental cadenced prose led to a dead-end: borrowing measure and rhetoric from a moribund neoclassical poetry failed to capture music and images congenial to prose."[67]

Indeed, the eighteenth-century poème en prose may be interpreted as part of the development of the novel rather than as a new poetic form, because the eighteenth-century novel and the idea of poetic prose initially evolved at the same time—to the extent that, as Steven Monte observes, "if the eighteenth-century *poème en prose* is itself a quasi-novel (a romance or epic written in prose), the success of the nineteenth-century novel exerts pressure on poets to remodel the traditional lyric."[68]

In this way, the French tradition of poème en prose may be understood as different from the modern prose poem but as laying the groundwork for it. The contemporary prose poem has a large taproot embedded in mid-nineteenth-century French literature, with smaller or lateral roots delving deeper into the eighteenth and seventeenth centuries. The prose poem should be considered a product of nineteenth-century Romanticism rather than of the eighteenth-century Enlightenment, but its debt to the eighteenth century is clear.

However, the French prose poem was not a typical manifestation—if there is such a thing—of French Romanticism. Baudelaire, Rimbaud, Mallarmé, and some of their peers grew sick of the more idealistic clichés of Romanticism and its more ego-centered poetic manifestations (notwithstanding their own capacity for self-absorption). They also became impatient with its veneration of classical culture and literature—one of Romanticism's most important features, which we discuss in chapter 2—believing that poetry needed to address contemporary issues and experience in blunt terms, including French society's failure to deliver what early Romantics had envisioned.

A pithy and brilliant formulation of these ideas occurs in a letter Arthur Rimbaud wrote to his friend Paul Demeny on May 15, 1871, in which he states that "Romanticism has never been carefully judged," that Romantics' songs are "seldom . . . *understood* by the singer," and that "reviving those antiquities" is for others.[69] Damian Catani observes that Baudelaire (and Balzac) scarified aspects of contemporary urban life, and were

> determined to replenish evil as a serious category of moral and intellectual thought . . . Their timely re-evaluation was based on the prescient realisation that a post-Romantic, post-theological reinvigoration of evil . . . would most fruitfully be realized through a direct engagement with the previously unexplored urban vice and criminality of the new, expanding capitalist metropolis.[70]

Catani also writes that Baudelaire's work focuses on "Paris of the 1850s and 1860s that was caught in the throes of . . . radical urban transformation" and that this "encounter with modernity [he] considered to be far more relevant . . . than the hackneyed theological metaphysical approach of late Romanticism."[71]

Baudelaire's preface to *Paris Spleen* celebrates the autonomy of prose fragments in defiance of conventional notions of organically unified works (we discuss this further in chapter 2) and claims that his prose poems arose out of his experience of the city. In saying this, he demonstrates that in its inaugural phase, prose poetry, as David Evans says, "must not be allowed to settle or become predictable," that "it is not simply in the static plan of a city that the inspiration for prose poetics is to be found" but that "a city [is] constantly in movement."[72] Nevertheless, Baudelaire, Rimbaud, and Mallarmé responded differently to the stimulus of the metropolis—for instance, Helen Abbott notes, "[t]he risks posed by opening up one's voice to the crowd through poetry are approached in different ways by Baudelaire and Mallarmé."[73] This is because Baudelaire grants intimate and public conversations "the same status,"[74] whereas Mallarmé does not, and Rimbaud very much went in his own, proto-surrealistic direction before he stopped writing lineated poetry and prose poetry altogether.

Following on from French examples, there were a few rather sporadic nineteenth-century examples of prose poetry written in English. One example is the English (and, for a time, Australian) Richard H. Horne's remarkably early "The Old Churchyard Tree: A Prose Poem" from 1850,[75] which Monte calls "a rarity" but notes that like most "English-language prose poems of this period," it is "as filled with awkward gestures toward the poetic as their French counterparts of the late eighteenth and early nineteeth centuries."[76] American author Emma Lazarus's "By the Waters of Babylon: Little Poems in Prose," from the late 1880s, begins memorably with the image of "The Spanish noon" as "a blaze of azure fire."[77] Such works remind one that, since the nineteenth century, poetic forms have generally become more prosaic—even as conventional verse forms continue in various guises. For example, despite continued use by some contemporary poets of meter and rhyme, in the twenty-first century most lineated lyric poetry is written in free verse, which is usually more prosaic in its rhythms than the traditional forms of verse it has replaced (at the end of the eighteenth century, almost all English-language poetry was written in verse).

Even elegies, traditionally written in poetic form, are flourishing in what John B. Vickery calls the "modern prose elegy."[78] Vickery identifies the prose elegy in the work of novelists as diverse as James Joyce, William Faulkner, Virginia Woolf, Ernest Hemingway, Malcolm Lowry, and Joan Didion. He writes:

> The intent is to trace the shift from the traditional elegy's concerns to the attitudes evinced in the modern elegiac temper. The older [poetic] pastoral elegy dwelt exclusively . . . with the death of an individual and how to cope with it. The twentieth century gradually transformed the elegy into a focus on the diversity of losses occurring in human life . . . To the death of the individual, the modern elegy added most of the forms of personal, intellectual, and cultural loss suffered by mankind.[79]

If the twentieth and twenty-first centuries may collectively be thought of as an age of prose, the growth of prose poetry is part of a broader development of prose modes, almost everywhere.

Prose Poetry as a Janus-faced Form

Our discussion earlier in this chapter about prose poetry's challenge to the notion that prose and poetry are, inherently, different kinds of writing not only takes up ideas considered by various contemporary critics, but it reflects debates about form and genre that were being contemplated even before the publication of Baudelaire's groundbreaking *Paris Spleen* in 1869. As we mention above, the idea of producing works written in poetic prose had begun to destabilize conventional notions about both poetry and prose well in advance of Baudelaire's work, primarily because of the hybrid nature of the eighteenth-century French poème en prose.

In the Romantic period, the more radical prose poetry of Baudelaire, Rimbaud, and others was immediately viewed in many quarters as a bastard form—Adrian Wanner remarks on the way in which Bertrand and Baudelaire created "a new, dynamic aesthetic of surprise, turning the unaesthetic and 'prosaic' into the object of poetic discourse, and replacing the traditional emotive voice of the lyric with that of an ironically detached *flâneur*."[80] Scott Carpenter explicitly identifies the perceived illegitimacy of this literary strategy in claiming, "Baudelaire's practice of prose poetry engages in the unsettling blurring of lines that we associate with counterfeits: it is a kind of poetry that 'masquerades' as everyday prose, while nevertheless leading to certain [poetic] effects."[81] Edward Kaplan calls prose poetry an "amalgam" and contends that "Baudelaire . . . tangles the web of dualistic categories as he formulates a confluence of opposites."[82]

In other words, prose poetry has long been characterized as a kind of genre-crossing ugly duckling, and such ideas are hard to shake. When, in a prose poem from his "Mercian Hymns" sequence, one of Geoffrey Hill's characters states "Not strangeness, but strange likeness,"[83] he might almost have been speaking about prose poetry itself. Prose poetry has "a strange likeness" to literary forms other than itself and yet it is different from all of them—or, to express this more accurately, it incorporates aspects of a variety of forms. It also tends to be characterized by various sorts of serious and not-so-serious playfulness. Ali Smith observes that it "retains its odour of paradox. Its facility for narrative play, and for play with language register, un-hierarchical patterns and unemphasised possibilities, its openness to 'unpoetic' language and language from a range of registers, are prospects that the form offers."[84]

Aware of such issues, and of the contrarian qualities associated with the form, a number of prose poets have resorted to writing explicitly and sometimes ironically about prose poetry, asserting in various works: "[a] prose poem should be as square as a Picasso pear"; "[p]rose-poetry is when a person behaves differently from what is considered normal"; "[w]e fill pre-existing forms and when we fill them we change them and are changed"; and "[t]he prose poem is not a real poem of course."[85] Campbell McGrath's "The Prose Poem" begins:

> On the map it is precise and rectilinear as a chessboard, though driving past you would hardly notice it, this boundary line or ragged margin, a shallow swale that cups a simple trickle of water, less rill than rivulet, more gully than dell, a tangled ditch grown up throughout with a fearsome assortment of wildflowers and bracken. There is no fence, though here and there a weathered post asserts a former claim.[86]

To a significant extent, the issues raised by these works, and by the critical views we have quoted, relate to how one understands genre—and, more particularly, whether genre classifications are ever really as fixed or clear as we tend to assume. John Frow claims that genre classifications are often problematic and questions whether "texts in fact 'belong' to a genre, in a simple type/token relation (general form/particular instance), or should we posit some more complex relation, in which texts would 'perform' a genre, or modify it in 'using' it?"[87]

Frow also asks, "What happens when genre frames change?" and "Do texts have a definite and fixed structure?"[88] If the broad classifications we apparently summon up by the terms "poetry" and "prose" may not denote clearly definable literary forms—although various forms, such as narrative poetry or the novel, are usually assumed to be a category of either poetry or prose fiction, but not both—and if the broad classifications we call "poetry" and "prose" are more elusive than we would often assume, then the prose poem may be a demonstration of how certain kinds of literary works appear unclassifiable primarily because of the shifting and sometimes ambiguous nature of the terms "poetry" and "prose."

In this way, in terms of genre and form, prose poetry emphasizes the instability of what may otherwise look fixed and known, also emphasizing what is fluid and coming into being. Jahan Ramazani observes that a "genre's others are often multiple,"[89] and the prose poem is the literary form that has frequently been characterized as "other" in this way. Frow has observed, "It seems to me important to stress the open-endedness of genres and the irreducibility of texts to a single interpretive framework . . . Texts work upon genres as much as they are shaped by them."[90] It may be true that prose poetry constitutes an unusually open literary form that is shifting our ideas of literary form and genre even as we write.

The prose poem form is Janus-faced, looking forward and backward, understanding transitions, providing passages and doorways. Space opens before and behind it, sometimes like closed rooms, sometimes like expanding fields. It understands both prose and poetry, and it comfortably inhabits the mutual space they offer. Prose poetry's challenge to conventional ideas about generic distinctions may be what makes it most modern (and postmodern) and which may see it become a defining twenty-first-century literary form. It may offer one way through the quagmire of generic classifications and, a little like a literary wormhole, take the reader into new and hitherto unexplored spaces.

Prose poetry may be conceived of as a new form of poetry to sit aside the forms of traditional lyric, narrative, and epic poetry. It may be viewed as a contemporary development of the possibilities of the poetic fragment, so beloved of the Romantic writers and so well suited to expressing meaning in a world where the grand narratives of the nineteenth century have long since been in disrepair. As the use of the prose mode in poetry challenges our understanding of literary forms and genres, it signals nothing less than that the main literary forms privileged in recent centuries—the novel, short fiction, lineated lyric poetry, and drama—may no longer confidently be said to constitute or describe the structures of contemporary "literature."

This is not a matter of agreeing with Maurice Blanchot that "[o]nly the book matters, such as it is, far from genres, outside of categories—prose, poetry, novel, testimony—under which it refuses to be classed."[91] Perhaps more crucially, an apparently undecidable literary form such as the prose poem opens up discussions about what the basis of poetry may be. If there are no firm zones of exclusion separating "poetry" and "prose," then the more important distinction is between what is poetic (whether it occurs in poetry or prose) and what is prosaic (whether it occurs in prose or poetry). Christopher Prendergast writes, "part of the lesson of Rimbaud's way with the prose poem or Laforgue's experiments with *verse libre* is the blurring of the poetic/prosaic distinction."[92] In the twenty-first century the blurring of poetic/prosaic boundaries has advanced to the extent that the flourishing of prose poetry seems inevitable. It is a distinctive form that is helping to change our very understanding of literary categories.

The Prose Poem and Subversion

The prose poems of Baudelaire, Rimbaud, and Mallarmé were questioned or repudiated in some quarters of nineteenth-century France for a variety of interconnected reasons—to do with their violations of what was understood to be correct poetic form, their sometimes lurid or unelevated subject matter, or because they were interpreted as critiquing the established French social and political orders. In these ways, early prose poetry was associated with the subversive, and understood to be a radical form associated with the French avant-garde.

We won't rehearse early critiques of the form in any detail—they have been well documented in other texts—but much that was radical in the nineteenth century has now become fairly commonplace. In the twentieth and twenty-first centuries all kinds of literature have been critical of social and political orders, and a sense of the fragmentation of culture has strongly shaped literary forms of all kinds. Thus, if prose poetry is still spoken of as a subversive form—and Margueritte Murphy says it is inherently subversive and even "hypersubversive"[93]—this is in the context of a great deal of subversive twenty-first-century literature. We might even suggest that subversive literary practice has now become more or less normalized.

One example is the development of the so-called lyric essay, which incorporates various kinds of autobiographical and quasi-autobiographical material into the essay form, while also frequently fragmenting and problematizing the essay's traditional forms. This problematization is sometimes squarely aimed at subverting the essay tradition, but more often it results from a lyric essayist's attempt to register the kinds of meanings and effects associated with broken, truncated, only partly known or fragmented experience. Deborah Tall and John D'Agata remark, "the lyric essay often accretes by fragments, taking shape mosaically . . . it may spiral in on itself, circling the core of a single image or idea,"[94] and Martha Aldrich adds:

> The lyric essay does not narrate a story so much as express a condition—often named, sometimes called human, but still to us unknown. It reverses foreground and background, cultivating leaps and juxtaposition, tensing between the presentational and the representational. Associative, meditative, it abhors journalistic reportage. Its incompleteness is Romantic, revealed in lyric fragmentation, the infusion of imagination into the debris of fact.[95]

Prose poets and lyric essayists are often, in their different ways, trying to get at the kinds of experiences they consider unable to be narrated by longer or more discursive literary forms, or fully evoked through traditional poetic forms—experiences that are hard to grasp or pin down, and are better gestured at than written out in full.

Many practitioners of both lyric essays and prose poetry try to find ways of speaking that have not been fully explored to date—combining fragments, elevated and ordinary diction, the quotidian, the ineffable, and almost anything else—from witty narratives like Benedikt's prose poem "The Moralist of Bananas," which begins, "A rustle from the vale—the Saint has gone out to the fields again, to the good, clear fields, there to preach a sermon to the bananas about the suggestiveness of their shapes,"[96] to sad metaphors such as "A poached egg without the pocket, embarrassed before the tongue's eye. Have you ever felt like that?"[97] in Peter Johnson's "Cannes." Some writers are also engaged in a deliberate process of sidestepping the expectations that long-established literary forms and genres bring with them because all established forms carry associations from other historical periods that can be inhibiting, or seem to be prescriptive, or that demand a kind of superficial polish and finish that they wish to eschew. This is evident from the discussions of many American neo-surrealist prose poets who are at pains to describe the ways in which their prose poetry does not draw on the French symbolists (discussed in chapter 3).

Some scholars, such as Monte and Murphy, focus on prose poetry's connection to American modernist poets, positing that previous scholarship has been French-centered.[98] Significant sections of Monte's and Murphy's books are devoted to discussions of John Ashbery. (We briefly discuss Ashbery's *Three Poems* in chapter 10.) The length of these influential works problematizes their categorization as prose poetry. It may be better to understand these sometimes-meandering works as a form of poetic prose. Similarly, the so-called language poets can be seen as interrogating the connections—or continuum—between prose poetry and poetic prose, given the length and approach of many of their works. Shifting emphasis away from categorization, Marjorie Perloff argues—in line with language poetry founding member, Charles Bernstein—"the important distinction to be made is not between 'story' and 'prose poem' or 'story' and 'essay' but . . . between different contexts of readings and different readerships."[99] Language poets' critique of conventional language use and its assumptions demands a new relationship between reader and text, and may be read as a form of subversion.

If, as we have indicated, prose poetry has frequently been defined as a form always and rather restlessly in opposition to, or undercutting other, more established literary forms and genres, this is a central reason why relatively few critics have been willing to fully recognize the prose poem for its own qualities. It has often been said to occupy a doubtful and in-between literary space, a kind of no-man's-land. But a great deal of prose poetry has been confidently written for a century and a half, and while the form may still be in the process of defining itself, and may sometimes still be subversive of conventional prose and lineated poetry, it is hardly nascent or unformed. It is much more than a form written in opposition to other forms and genres.

The Future of the Prose Poem

It is yet to be seen whether prose poetry will claim much of the territory occupied by the contemporary lineated lyric, but there is no question in the last few decades it has claimed *some* of this territory. It may well claim more as the twenty-first century progresses because (in most of its manifestations), it is a relatively user-friendly and versatile form. Prose poems often function like small, expansive packages of words that, while occasionally employing limited forms of narrative, ask the reader to engage with them immediately and as a whole. They are usually satisfying imaginatively because their emphasis is on connotation rather than denotation, and they also engage readers imaginatively by implicitly asking them to complete the information they supply. Many prose poems address familiar quotidian concerns, but their manner of doing so enables readers to gain new perspectives on situations that are both familiar in their outline and unfamiliar in the way in which they have been inflected poetically.

Prose poetry opens up the possibility that writers who would once have been poets, but who have not been schooled in ways of making lineated poems, may become poets by making use of prose as their chosen poetic medium. Certainly, as prose poetry mixes registers, moving fairly easily between elevated and demotic language, and as it offers the chance for writers to work impressionistically, metaphorically, and imagistically with prose paragraphs, so it enables prose writers who want to work in short forms an opportunity to expand their range into the poetic. Other very short forms, such as microfiction, are also available to prose writers, but where works of microfiction emphasize the movement of narrative through time—focusing on what happens, albeit in very few words—prose poetry tends to emphasize what *has happened* and *will always be happening*.

In the traditional lineated lyric, there is no real sense of chronological time, even if there is some narrative content, because the lyric exists to say what is and will be, rather than how one thing is contingent on another during a given time period—and many prose poems share this quality of seeming to exist outside of time. That is why Simic, who employs explicit narrative tropes in his prose poetry, remains a poet. His prose poetry is about certain qualities and inflections of existence, rather than about the *then and then* of narrative-driven storytelling. In the following prose poem, the shepherd's hour extends into the reader's time and space with its use of present tense, and its position as the final word. The hour is never fully realized and the person on the stove continues to be cooked:

> From inside the pot on the stove someone
> threatens the stars with a wooden spoon.
> Otherwise, cloudless calm. The shepherd's hour.[100]

What makes the prose poem form so flexible and appealing is its ability to place narrative in the service of poetry in a more naturalized way than in lineated lyric poems, because we are so used to narratives in prose—we often read various short and long prose narratives. Thus, a prose poem may play at creating a prose narrative without ever relinquishing its poetic purpose. And, more generally, prose poems may often seem to be what they are not, delighting or challenging the reader by the manner in which they manipulate readerly expectations.

Prose poetry has the great advantage of being, especially in its English-language manifestations, a relatively new form. It will, like all literary forms, age over time, but at the moment the boundaries of the prose poem are being expanded. In a prosaic age, poetry—which has always been at the center of human literary activity—may have found in prose poetry an important way forward. Prose poetry has the prospect of becoming as significant to the writing of poetry generally as free verse has been to the writing of lineated lyric poems. In offering new ways forward, it opens up numerous possibilities.

CHAPTER 2

The Prose Poem's Post-Romantic Inheritance

Prose Poetry's Connections to the Romantic Fragment

As we discussed in chapter 1, the contemporary English-language prose poem has its most obvious early roots in the nineteenth-century French Romantic prose poetry written by Charles Baudelaire, Arthur Rimbaud, and others. However, on a more general level, contemporary prose poetry's connection to Romanticism is even deeper than this would suggest because vestiges of Romanticism continue to cling to the prose poem form. If, as David Perkins suggested in the mid-twentieth century, "we are still living in the comet's tail of the early nineteenth century" or if, as Fiona J. Stafford remarks, Romantic poetry is perennially significant because it contains "urgent questions about the human condition and the surrounding world,"[1] this has implications for understanding contemporary prose poetry. Romanticism's "astonishing change of sensibility"[2] continues to inform twenty-first-century literary assumptions, and prose poetry's fragmentary nature may be seen to derive in significant part from Romanticism's example.

Although contemporary writers take the fragmentary nature of the prose poem for granted, it was once an important innovation to celebrate fragmentary literary forms—an innovation that took hold with the Romantic movement but that, as Andrew Allport observes, has been convincingly traced to the Italian Renaissance by Leonard Barkan and is "formally part of a mixed genre that goes back at least to Petrarch."[3] Literary fragments have been produced throughout human history and, even if one accepts the arguments by Elizabeth Wanning Harries that poetry fragments are frequently planned,[4] they are more often accidents of history than evidence of authors deciding or preferring to leave their works unfinished. Romanticism inaugurated the idea that fragmentary philosophical and literary works may have a special virtue *because* of their fragmentariness and, what is more, the fragment may be understood, somewhat paradoxically, as complete or finished.

A number of scholars, including Marvin Richards, Nikki Santilli, Jonathan Monroe, Stephen Fredman, and Michel Delville, have connected prose poetry to the Romantic fragment. They have done so by way of the German critical fragment—including the influential work of Friedrich Schlegel and Novalis—as well as the work of the English Romantic poets. They argue, for example, that prose poetry is "[a]t once whole and standing alone . . . [the fragment-ruin of prose poetry is] also incomplete and stand[s] for a greater whole," and "[t]he Romantic fragment provides the ideological basis for the prose poem form."[5] Santilli's *Such Rare Citings: The Prose Poem in English Literature* (2002) states "[t]he first substantial prose poetic forms emerge in the Romantic period with the appearance of the German critical fragment," while Jonathan Monroe's *A Poverty of Objects: The Prose Poem and the Politics of Genre* (1987) takes the position that "both Schlegel's fragments and the prose poetry of Baudelaire and his successors constitute privileged sites at the margins of literature where the necessarily dialogical, conflictual, and inescapably social nature of literary discourse comes into view."[6]

Given the relationship between prose poetry and the Romantic fragment, comprehending one offers the opportunity to better appreciate the other. Furthermore, if "the extended influence of Romantic fragments into Modernist and even Postmodernist poetry" is uncovered,[7] then this underscores the view that the contemporary prose poem is simultaneously a product of postmodernism, modernism, and Romanticism. While contemporary prose poetry is sometimes self-consciously fractured and fragmentary, destabilizing and interrupting notions of TimeSpace in ways Romantic writers rarely attempted (see chapter 6 for our discussion of TimeSpace), the prose poem's Romantic inheritance remains.

As already discussed, the contemporary form of the prose poem is perhaps best dated from 1869 when Baudelaire's *Paris Spleen* was posthumously published. While Baudelaire follows Bertrand's general example in *Gaspard de la nuit* (1842), Baudelaire's prose poetry is modern, urban, and engaged with the quotidian in a way never attempted by Bertrand. He produces a series of works proclaiming their fragmentary nature not only as an aesthetic virtue but to register the fragment's autonomy. For example, "A Joker" opens with images in a "metropolis" and is both fragmentary and fluent:

> Explosive New Year's Day: chaos of mud and snow, criss-crossed by a thousand carriages, sparkling with toys and toffee, crawling with greed and despair, standard delirium of a metropolis, made to disturb the brain of the sturdiest solitary.[8]

It ends with the narrator's anger at an upper-class Frenchman's buffoonery, but the scene and narrative remain largely unresolved. In his brief preface to *Paris Spleen*, Baudelaire explicitly celebrates such fragmentariness, asserting his fragments do not need to be part of any greater and unifying narrative: "I will not hold [the reader] to the unbroken thread of some superfluous plot. . . . Chop it into many fragments and you will see how each is able to exist apart."[9]

This preface may appear casual enough and, given the shifting literary contexts in which it appeared (it was first published in *La Presse* on August 26, 1862, as an introduction to twenty of Baudelaire's prose poems), it may be interpreted as, to some extent, cynical or opportunist—or even, as Kaplan suggests, as "a disguised parody of the genre."[10] Raymond Mackenzie believes it "raises as many questions as it resolves."[11] However, its significance cannot easily be overstated. In it, Baudelaire declares that prose may be written without the conventional superstructures of plot and traditional narrative and may align itself to the incomplete and the disconnected.

The statement gathers together a great deal that the Romantics had been preoccupied with for decades. They had been finding ways to disrupt superfluity of all kinds in making their literary works—trying to break with conventional (and, they believed, outdated) narrative structures and techniques, and also to break with the strictures of traditional poetic methods and assumptions. As the nineteenth century progressed, they turned their gaze more and more toward their own day-to-day experiences, and their own feelings, trying to escape the sentimentalizing tendencies of much of that century's heroic, formalist, narrative-driven, or conventionally sanctioned poetry and prose.

In effect, many writers had lost faith with the established literary order, just as many had lost faith with the established political, social, and ideological orders. This loss of faith was complicated by what Andrew M. Stauffer suggests was the Romantics' emphasis on "emotional affect and transmission: sensibility and the sublime" at a time when they were "newly pressurized by the discourse of the Revolution and the Terror," following the American Revolution (1765–83), the French Revolution (1789), and the European revolutions of 1848. He claims this resulted in a dilemma or series of paradoxes that included being "filled with fury, yet pleasingly terrified."[12]

After *Paris Spleen* the prose poem became a symbol of a new way of writing—a form of literary plain-speaking, however ornate and elaborate some prose poems were in practice. It was a form not dressed in literature's conventional fineries and, instead, brought street life, autobiographical memories, personal feelings, and subjective impressions into its sphere, sometimes all at once. Its narratives did not necessarily cohere and were not always completed. In the hands of Arthur Rimbaud, especially in his last work, the *Illuminations*, prose poetry may also be said to have inaugurated the movement toward what became known as surrealism in the 1920s—an idea of literature, and art more generally, as antirationalist and connected to dream-life and the unconscious.

Central to all of these developments was the idea that literature was fragmentary and its forms were to some extent arbitrary. For instance, in the case of *Illuminations* (written from 1873–75; published 1886), the manuscript passed through various hands prior to publication in such a way that no one knows what order the poems should be published in—and many would claim it doesn't matter. This reminds one of Baudelaire's assertion that the narratives in *Paris Spleen* could be read in any order.

Prose Poetry as New and Old

As prose poetry enacted part of the Romantics' project to break with established and conventional literary forms, it became a new idea continuously associated with the subversion of an old idea (literary forms as they had been). This is a central reason why the prose poem form has since then been so resistant to conclusive definition. It still has the air of an unformed child about it. No matter how grown up and how well formed it is, the old and graceful forms it left behind still look to some people like "poetry" or "prose."

Yet, the prose poem is one of the new norms and, indeed, it is a form that helped shift international literature toward the innovations of modernism. It also still carries some of the tendencies of the relatively brief Romantic period with an admirable facility—so often encapsulating a small and fragmented evocation of experience. And it is well adapted to the postmodern twenty-first century, offering expressive possibilities well suited to the cacophony of contemporary broken encounters and fractured narratives, new technologies, and profoundly uncertain and sometimes opaque subjectivities. Ira Sadoff, in his analysis of "Diane Williams's jarringly difficult postmodern prose poetry or poetic prose," makes a similar point to Baudelaire and Rimbaud when he states, "A reader may move in and out of making connections while at the same time certain passages read as if overhearing someone's private conversation."[13]

Many of prose poetry's writerly, aesthetic, and philosophical imperatives grew out of the Romantic cast of mind. Romantic writers and thinkers everywhere referenced a classical past that was literally in ruins—most famously the ancient built legacies of Egypt, Greece, and Rome, along with the relatively few classical literary and philosophical texts that still existed. Very little of this glorious inheritance from the ancient world was complete, whether literary works, buildings, paintings, or sculptures. Most works had simply perished, and those that survived were often mere shreds of papyrus, or occasional quotations in the (also fragmentary) works of other ancient writers—or bits of mosaics, bronze fragments, or marble torsos without arms or heads.

Yet enough remained that was influential and awe-inspiring. In reference to the Elgin Marbles, David Lowenthal comments, "The emotional power of a mutilated marble was held to more than compensate for its lost formal perfection . . . Repair was no longer required for antiquities to be appreciated; fragmentation was becoming a positive virtue."[14] Romantics doubted that structures as profound, monumental, and mysterious as the pyramids of Giza or Khafre (or the Parthenon, or many other Egyptian, Greek, and Roman ruins) could ever again be made, so they celebrated these achievements. They wondered, too, at how so much knowledge about almost every significant field of human activity had been produced by the ancients in a relatively short period of time. These civilizations were simultaneously remote and admirable; their legacy was damaged, and most of what they had created was irretrievable.

In this sense, much of Romanticism is informed by the idea that we live in the aftermath of greatness, some of which approaches the divine, and that writing, and making art more generally, is a way of recollecting—partially and unsatisfactorily—what we cannot possess. Sophie Thomas makes the connection between the "ruin" and the "fragment":

> Essentially, ruins are highly evocative forms of the fragment, and they operate according to its logic: they suggest an absent whole, and indeed occupy an ambivalent space between the part and the past whole, whose presence they affirm and negate (affirm, paradoxically, by negation) . . . to the extent that they are themselves preserved . . . Notions of hope, memorialization and restoration all thus adhere to the ruin as an object of contemplation.[15]

The Romantic fragment, in recognizing the incomplete and broken nature of the world, was created out of idealism and nostalgia. It was partly driven by a regret that things were no longer as they once were—that the heroic age had irretrievably passed—and there is something almost excruciating about this aspect of Romanticism. Writers turned toward self-expression and, in many cases, the evocation of a deeply personal subjectivity, partly as a way of finding in personal apprehension, and in evocations of the quotidian, an expression of their sense of belonging amid acknowledged imperfection. If bigger ideas, and history itself, were compromised, various forms of self-narrative opened the prospect of being able to freshen perception through individual acts of imagination and, in doing so, construe a tarnished and worn reality in ways that would enable a new apprehension of the world.

For instance, it was a Romantic idea to understand the self as more or less separate from the social world, and this idea sits at the heart of a literary form—the fragment—that so often focuses on individual experience. J. M. Fitzgerald identifies an extended poem—"The Prelude"—by the Romantic poet William Wordsworth as "the first work of Western literature that took the perspective that by telling one's story one revealed truths about the self."[16] Fitzgerald states that the poem led to the contemporary notions "that each individual constructs themselves . . . and that each individual's story is his or her own unique[ly]."[17]

In attempting to make things new, and to register their individual sensibilities and apprehensions, the Romantic writers' particular attraction to the fragmentary was crucial to their recognition that they could often only gesture at completeness because the "whole" was not available. They became interested in the ineffable and the sublime, looking for what was grand even when it was only able to be intuited through limited individual experience and was unable to be fully comprehended or expressed. They were preoccupied by trying to articulate their awareness of the self's problematic relationship with external reality.

This was true in different centers of Romanticism, including the United Kingdom, Germany, and France, despite there being major differences in how Romanticism manifested itself in different countries. Indeed, various European Romanticisms profoundly influenced one another, to the extent that Dennis F. Mahony identifies the late eighteenth-century "outburst of intellectual, literary, and artistic creativity within German-speaking lands" as "signal[ing] the start of the Age of Romanticism throughout Europe and even the Americas."[18] French Romanticism, for instance, was cognizant of German and English models but was troubled by particular, far-reaching political and social upheavals—including, as Fabienne Moore writes, "the collapse of the monarchy . . . the capsizing of the Revolution [of 1789] into the Terror, and the downfall of Napoleon after a 20-year reign."[19] Moore also observes in France that the "poetry of this tumultuous historical period, from the last decade of Louis XVI's reign [1774–92] to the Empire, is a kaleidoscope of themes and styles, a mixture of old and new, with no equivalent figureheads to the central six poets of English Romanticism."[20]

By the time Baudelaire was writing, in the mid-nineteenth century, the works of German and English Romantic writers were well known in France—including the influential Novalis and the main English Romantic poets. Eric Partridge comments, "[a]s a force of impulsion . . . English literature very vitally affected French Romanticism," and he also identifies some of the English-language writers who directly influenced Baudelaire, such as Poe (whom he emulated and whose works he translated) and De Quincey.[21] Baudelaire was also aware of German models, and Jonathan Monroe writes that the "formal struggle that Bertrand, Baudelaire, and Rimbaud each in his turn would decide in favor of prose, the printed medium of the modern age, is anticipated by Novalis, briefly, brilliantly."[22]

In highlighting some of these links Paul Davies emphasizes that English Romanticism was more literary and less philosophical than German Romanticism, which "developed a program for literature and culture that aimed at all fields of art, science, and society."[23] The extent of such differences is important but, as Christoph Bode notes, it should not obscure the connections, and notable similarities, between various Romantic enterprises in different places. All of these Romanticisms grew out of, accompanied, and helped to propel a transformation of the established social and political order at a time when social cohesion was strained. Bode suggests, "we reconceptualize European Romanticism as a *set of responses* . . . to a historically specific challenge: the *challenge* of the ever-accelerating modernization of European society."[24]

While there is no one pan-European Romantic movement, there are broad tendencies that apply to Romanticism in general—and, significantly, nineteenth-century Romantic writers in Germany and the United Kingdom produced literary and philosophical fragments that were not only an important influence on Baudelaire's writing but that bear a continuing relationship to the fragmentary form of the prose poem. These writers include Samuel Taylor Coleridge in England and

Friedrich Schlegel in Germany, both of whom were influenced by—as well as critical of—Immanuel Kant's ideas, and who "experimented with the form of philosophy, composing fragments usually conceived as 'Bruchstücke,' or parts broken off from a projected whole."[25] In one sense, for many writers the fragmentary in one form or another became almost all there was. In their fragmentary work, the part or fragment may be said to stand in for an implied whole—at which it gestures. The whole was either inconceivable, or inexpressible in words, or risked being deformed by any attempt at full expression. This responds to the idea that while completion "is a feature of a state long past" a fragment "might well be still awaiting its completion in the future."[26] Furthermore, there were aesthetic preferences at work in these matters. Michael Bradshaw writes that "Many Romantic writers . . . [saw] some sort of cachet in stopping short of an ending, almost as if a proper determined ending were in some sense vulgar."[27]

As many Romantic writers and artists concluded that no totality could be fully articulated in a world where ancient grandeur was compromised and broken, so they idealized what was ruined, and emulated what could not be reconstituted. In doing so, they joined antiquarian interests to larger aesthetic, literary, and philosophical concerns—Stephen Bann argues that "the antiquarian has a vital part to play in heralding the full-blooded historical-mindedness of the Romantic epoch."[28] Kelly Eileen Battles observes that "the antiquarian impulse involves the expansion of the concept of fragmentation to include not only materiality (ruins, artifacts, etc.), but also fragmented narrative forms and the privileging of the historical anecdote to the exclusion of linear grand narratives."[29] Along with Coleridge in England and Schlegel in Germany, the concept of fragmentation influenced English poets as diverse as Wordsworth, Keats, Shelley, Blake, and Byron—not to mention the brilliant and influential proto-Romantic poet and hoaxer Thomas Chatterton—and in Germany fragmentation was especially important to Novalis's questing work.

William Vaughan, simultaneously referring to the work of the English painter William Turner, the German philosopher Friedrich Schlegel, and the English poet and philosopher Samuel Taylor Coleridge, comments that "[t]o some extent in self-conscious opposition to Classicism, Romanticism represented itself as the art of incompleteness made necessary by the ineffable and eternally evolving processes of the universe,"[30] suggesting how keenly aware the Romantics were of what was unsayable, and of how the incomplete gesture or articulation was a way of acknowledging the inexpressibility attendant on a great deal of experience. Memorably, Isaiah Berlin characterizes these Romantic apprehensions and preoccupations as

> a new and restless spirit, seeking violently to burst through old and cramping forms, a nervous preoccupation with perpetually changing inner states of consciousness, a longing for the unbounded and the indefinable, for per-

petual movement and change, an effort to return to the forgotten sources of life, a passionate effort at self-assertion both individual and collective, a search after means of expressing an unappeasable yearning for unattainable goals.[31]

Such ideas remain crucially important because they have been carried forward into the twenty-first century even as they have suffered the sea changes of a sometimes disillusioned or world-weary modernism and postmodernism. Fragmented forms, condensed and incomplete yet gesturing at large and sometimes ineffable ideas, have influenced almost all modern forms of literary production. Even many contemporary literary novels—an extended form suited to "whole" stories—do not aim to complete their narratives, and many contemporary poems are impressionistic and open.

The "Open" and the Inconclusive

A well-known passage from Coleridge's letter to John Thelwall of October 16, 1797, sums up many currents of the late eighteenth- and early nineteenth-century zeitgeist, including the connection between the small and the grand:

> I can *at times* feel strongly the beauties, you describe, in themselves & for themselves—but more frequently *all things* appear little—all the knowledge, that can be acquired, child's play—the universe itself—what but an immense heap of *little* things?—I can contemplate nothing but parts, & parts are all *little*—!—My mind feels as if it ached to behold & know something *great*—something *one & indivisible* and it is only in the faith of this that rocks or waterfalls, mountains or caverns give me the sense of sublimity or majesty!—But in this faith *all things* counterfeit infinity![32]

Thomas McFarland, following Fritz Strich, argues that Romantic writers and thinkers found themselves confronting "the attendant paradox whereby the perception of parts and fragments implies the hypothetical wholeness of infinity, but the impossibility of grasping that entity."[33] Where infinity is concerned, fragments make finite and incomplete gestures at an unencompassable totality. D. F. Rauber observes:

> The great formal problem of the romantic poet can be stated briefly as the devising of means to embody the infinite in a finite, discrete, and sequential medium . . . the fragment constitutes a perfect formal solution to the problem . . . it matches romantic ideals and tone as fully and completely as the closed couplet matches the ideals of eighteenth-century neoclassicism.[34]

The German poet and philosopher Novalis (1772–1801) also addresses these issues in his *Logological Fragments*, written at the end of the eighteenth century—texts that are simultaneously philosophical and prose-poetical in being highly suggestive and allusive. They are dependent as much upon the presentation and combination of sometimes disparate ideas as on the development of a discursive argument or extended narrative structure:

> Only what is incomplete can be comprehended—can take us further. What is complete is only enjoyed. If we want to comprehend nature we must postulate it as incomplete, to reach an unknown variable in this way. All determination is relative.[35]

Novalis also states:

> As one progresses so much becomes dispensable—much appears in a different light . . . That which is imperfect appears most tolerably as a fragment—and thus this form of communication is to be recommended above that which as a whole is not yet finished.[36]

Therefore, while the incomplete is comprehensible, the complete or the perfected resists understanding, and the imperfect and fragmentary (in its gesture at an unachievable perfectibility) is preferable to an unattainable or unsettled whole. In one of his *Critical Fragments* Schlegel goes so far as to suggest that "many a work of art whose coherence is never questioned is . . . not a complete work but a fragment, or one or more fragments."[37]

This last point draws attention to the Romantics' awareness of the brokenness of the things of the world, and the idea that coherence is unachievable. This awareness may have been expressed differently by different writers—one need only think of the powerfully divergent preoccupations of Blake, Wordsworth, and Byron—but tropes of fragmentation haunt almost all of the major works of the Romantic period. Michael O'Brien states that this is because "[t]heory and reality became dissonant, young men could no longer read Gibbon or Condorcet without a sense of disjuncture . . . Romanticism . . . appealed to a generation who felt the immediate past unnourishing, the present unreliable, the future unpredictable."[38]

The Romantic fragment embodies this sense of disjuncture, and Coleridge famously left a variety of important poems as fragments, including "Kubla Khan" (completed 1797; published 1816)—in which case he disingenuously blamed the intervention of "a person on business from Porlock"[39]—for the intractability of his poetic material. His gesture was characteristic of the period in general, and there was an impetus to more closely connect poetry to prose. Jeffrey C. Robinson notes that Wordsworth's "Preface to Lyrical Ballads" (1800) "argues for the near identity of poetry and prose [in] driving to recover and stimulate through poetry an essential human spirit available to all persons."[40] Wordsworth never entirely conflates poetry and prose in this famous preface, but he writes:

> [N]ot only the language of a large portion of every good poem, even of the most elevated character, must necessarily, except with reference to the metre,

in no respect differ from that of good prose, but likewise that some of the most interesting parts of the best poems will be found to be strictly the language of prose when prose is well written.[41]

The democratization of literature had begun, accompanied by an urge to relate poetry more directly to prose and to the quotidian.

Keats, with his strong interest in writers such as Spenser and Shakespeare, was less immediately concerned than Wordsworth with "all persons" but he, too, was aware the old edifices were no longer easily adaptable to contemporary literature, and fragmentation was one result. His poems "Hyperion" (1820) and "The Fall of Hyperion" (1856) have been read as works whose incompleteness helps to define them and their poetic character.[42] Categorized as a "dependent" fragment by Marjorie Levinson, and as an "exercise in the poet's career,"[43] such works emphasize absence as powerfully as they register presence. Or, to put this differently, in registering a presence that also incorporates significant absence and indeterminacy, they appear to assert that complete edifices are unachievable. Far from expressing narrative failure, Keats's choice to leave "Hyperion" as a fragment has been interpreted as demonstrating maturity and an understanding of "an absence of meaning at the heart of things."[44]

In Shelley's case, McFarland remarks, "one can simply open the Oxford edition of Shelley's poetical works (one could do the same with the new Penguin edition of Wordsworth's poems), and in the table of contents observe such titles as 'Prince Athanase: A Fragment'; 'Fragment: Home'; 'Fragment of a Ghost Story'; 'Fragment: To One Singing'; 'A Fragment: To Music'; 'Another Fragment to Music.' "[45] He also writes that "Shelley's fragmentariness is only one illustration of the intensified occurrence of disparactive forms in the Romantic era," understanding the disparactive "triad" as "[i]ncompletion, fragmentation, and ruin."[46] He further comments that "the Elgin marbles—those supreme testimonies to significance within ruin—serve as a kind of objective correlative for the culture and history of the epoch" and, in doing so, endorses and expands upon Schlegel's twenty-fourth *Athenaeum Fragment* from 1798: "Many of the works of the ancients have become fragments. Many modern works are fragments as soon as they are written."[47]

Notwithstanding Barkan's observation, "the non finito is not a mere romantic anachronism,"[48] the idea of a fragment as self-sufficient contradicted an assumption that had been prevalent until the Romantic period across all main literary genres, including poetry. The assumption was that works of literature, and other works of art, should be formally completed. In the English Renaissance, for example, this urge toward completion saw Christopher Marlowe's *Hero and Leander* "finished" by George Chapman—and finished again, rather less impressively, by Henry Petowe. Although many literary works from the period, and from earlier periods, remained incomplete—because of their authors' deaths, or because they grew sick of their work, or because their work was too ambitious for their capacities (Chaucer's *The Canterbury Tales* [1387] and Spenser's *The Faerie Queene* [1590] are famous examples)—this was not usually a deliberate or avowed literary strategy. For example, Spenser's "Amoretti 33" may be as much a literary performance of mea culpa as a sincere expression of a sense of wrongdoing, but it indicates how Spenser publicly rued his inability to complete his masterpiece. The sonnet begins:

> Great wrong I do, I can it not deny,
> To that most sacred Empress, my dear dread,
> Not finishing her *Queen of Faery*,[49]

The Augustans, too, famously celebrated a neoclassical idea of harmony and resolution, perhaps most tellingly expressed in Alexander Pope's invocation of the great chain of being—a chain that has aesthetic as well as religious, social, and political implications: "And if each system in gradation roll / Alike essential to th' amazing whole."[50]

Many Romantics remained cognizant of the "amazing whole" referred to by Pope, but unlike Pope they had little confidence their works might in any way fully encompass such a thing. Coleridge's lament in the letter to Thelwall quoted above, he "can contemplate nothing but parts,"[51] reflects a general sense that this "whole" was not only out of reach but that literary works might only gesture at it. In this context, the fragment symbolizes the limitations of human apprehension and the relative inaccessibility of the sublime and infinite. In addition to this—in the spirit of Novalis's fragments—the imperfect was elevated above the perfect, and the broken and incomplete was paradoxically elevated to the status of a whole.

Schlegel and the Fragment as a Closed Form Resisting Closure

The Romantic fragment's refusal to be pinned down, its resistance to closure and its "inherent multiplicity" in the way it is always itself and yet suggestive of more than itself,[52] reinforces the sense of expansiveness it so often conveys. Schlegel celebrates such expansiveness, and Romantic poetry's diversity more generally, in his late eighteenth-century manifesto of Romantic poetics:

> Romantic poetry is a progressive, universal poetry. Its aim isn't merely to reunite all the separate species of poetry and put poetry in touch with philosophy and rhetoric. It tries to and should mix and fuse poetry and prose, inspiration and criticism, the poetry of art and the poetry of nature; and make poetry lively and sociable, and life and society poetical. . . . Other kinds of poetry are finished and are now capable of being fully analyzed. The romantic kind of poetry is still in the state of becoming; that, in fact, is its real essence: that it

should forever be becoming and never be perfected. It can be exhausted by no theory and only a divinatory criticism would dare try to characterize its ideal.[53]

In this celebrated paragraph, Schlegel reintegrates poetry and prose as a fusing of disciplines—and, significantly, he attempts to unite philosophy and poetry. Monroe claims that "Schlegel's theory recommends itself as a point of departure for exploring the larger horizon within which the poetry/prose problematic is inscribed."[54] Schlegel asserts that while poetry is about life, it simultaneously extends beyond knowledge to embrace infinite progression and the unknowable. He posits that Romantic poetry is inexhaustible, heterogeneous, and, importantly, imperfect.

Schlegel's celebrated definition of the Romantic fragment is much terser. A well-known translation reads, "A fragment, like a miniature work of art, has to be entirely isolated from the surrounding world and be complete in itself like a porcupine."[55] Although the image of a porcupine makes reference to writing because of its quills, this fragment has been the subject of animated debate. On a first reading, Schlegel's point about isolation appears to contradict his argument that Romantic poetry should be "lively and sociable." Yet "Igel" may be translated as "hedgehog," and Randy Norman Innes writes, "a hedgehog's spines . . . cannot be discharged. A hedgehog rolls itself into a ball but does not attack; its spines are . . . used to collect berries . . . and thus [it] attaches itself to its environment."[56]

Similarly, Michael Bradshaw praises the "hedgehog analogy" for the way in which it promotes the fragment as both connected to the word and yet simultaneously isolated: "[It] is brilliantly chosen, capturing a mixture of independence, obstinacy and comedy in the fragment's much-prized rejection of attempts to contain or absorb it: the fragment is a creature which possesses agency and mobility."[57] Fragments may not present wholes, but in suggesting them, they metonymically stand in for the absent and (at least notionally) completed work, asserting the sufficiency of knowing less rather than more. As fragments affirm the possibility of addressing "more," they simultaneously characterize this "more" as neither fully available nor fully knowable.

It is useful at this point to quote the opening of Schlegel's *Athenaeum Fragment 77* where he states, "A dialogue is a chain or garland of fragments."[58] In this light, the Romantic fragment may even be imagined as a garlanded hedgehog, a paradoxical metaphor suggesting how individual fragments turn in on themselves, garland-like, and are simultaneously in dialogue with larger, "universal" issues. The fragment as hedgehog connects with the world even as it defends itself against it. Charles Rosen elaborates upon this circular structure in his observation:

> The Romantic Fragment is . . . a closed structure, but its closure is a formality: it may be separated from the rest of the universe, but it implies the existence of what is outside itself not by reference but by its instability. The form is not

fixed but is torn apart or exploded by paradox, by ambiguity, just as the opening song of [Robert Schumann's song cycle] *Dichterliebe* is a closed, circular form in which beginning and end are unstable—implying a past before the song begins and a future after its final chord.[59]

Even Marjorie Levinson's probing taxonomy and phenomenology of Romantic fragment poems, which offer a "reading protocol," do not fully secure the fragment's shifting form. Her focus on different kinds of fragments emphasizes the numerous interpretative strategies used by readers of fragments to "fill in the blanks."[60] However, an issue with such a taxonomy is that one may, from time to time, be tempted to dispute the categorization of one or another particular fragment. For example, "Kubla Khan" may be a complete fragment that "makes its readers connect its separate antithetical movements and fuse its imagery,"[61] but that is not necessarily how all readers understand it. Even Levinson's insightful and suggestive work does not necessarily tighten the boundaries around each of the fragments she mentions or rein in the ambiguity and indeterminacy of the form. The literary fragment continues to open out, to challenge and test its readers' subjective acts of understanding and interpretation.

Ossian's Prose-Poetical Fragments

As writers from the Romantic period self-consciously and concertedly produced a great many fragments, they had a highly influential literary model that for a considerable period was almost all-pervasive in literary communities throughout Europe. This model was written in English and subsequently widely translated. These were works by the influential proto-Romantic writer James Macpherson (1736–96), collected under the title *The Poems of Ossian*, which significantly influenced Goethe, Byron, Blake, Coleridge, Wordsworth, and numerous others, including European painters. Editions of *Ossian* are readily available in print and online so we won't quote from the works, which benefit from being read at length. However, these works are notable for being the first sustained group of English poetical works composed in prose.

They are a hybrid set of works, partly derived from original Scots Gaelic (and possibly also Irish Gaelic) that Macpherson "Englished"—and, for the most part, they are Macpherson's own invention. This was a new kind of work that united the epic tradition with a deep subjectivity, making out of loss and lament—and a kind of literary keening—an attempt to shore up the ruins of an ancient Gaelic culture. Macpherson's work evoked a heroic past many people wished to believe in at a time when the brutal Highland Clearances were gathering momentum and Scottish Gaelic societies and cultural and literary traditions were being overrun, eroded, and, to a considerable extent, obliterated by the English. Robert Crawford suggests, in this sense, that Macpherson's literary mission was akin to those of the later modernists, T. S. Eliot and Ezra Pound, in that each writer responded to "the danger of cultural fragmentation lead[ing] to the self-conscious use of the fragment (not least the ancient fragment) . . . as a way of speaking out of this position of break-up."[62]

Macpherson's first 1760 edition of groundbreaking poetic prose was tantalizingly entitled *Fragments of Ancient Poetry, Collected in the Highlands of Scotland, and Translated from the Gaelic or Erse Language*. Shortly afterward, Macpherson expanded *Ossian* to include, among other works, his epic about Fingal. Macpherson represented all of these works as fragments of a largely lost literary culture. He writes:

> [A]fter a peregrination of six months, the translator collected from tradition, and some manuscripts, all the poems in the following collection, and some more still in his hands, though rendered less complete by the ravages of time . . . excepting the present poem, those pieces are in a great measure lost, and there only remain a few fragments of them in the hands of the translator.[63]

Because Macpherson concocted his "translations" of *Ossian* from putative fragments of Scots Gaelic poetry, he has been variously labeled a hoaxer or fraudster. As a result, and because *Ossian* is now seen as a period piece and is no longer fashionable, it has not been accorded a great deal of recent critical attention. For example, in 2009 Thomas M. Curley stated that "Macpherson went to his grave perpetrating literary fraud by helping to make public a false Gaelic 'original' to validate his mainly counterfeit English *Ossian*."[64] While Curley's point was true enough, it did not give Macpherson the credit he deserved for creating a significant work of literature that influenced Romanticism worldwide.

Thomas Chatterton also perpetrated a significant literary hoax within a few years of the publication of *Ossian*, in which he invented an author, the fifteenth-century monk-poet Thomas Rowley, along with Rowley's fragmentary works. Through doing so—and not unlike Macpherson—he created a model for a new way of writing. It was as if Romanticism needed a refurbished idea of the past in order to create its fresh and present reality, and Macpherson and Chatterton provided the kinds of "past" literatures that Romanticism craved—even though such literatures were actually contemporary expressions of an emerging Romantic sensibility. Both writers provided Romanticism with influential models for combining antiquarian interests with a new fragmentary poetics; both were significant feats of creative brilliance while also being complex literary hoaxes.

Dafydd Moore has written of "the regularity of Ossian's prose-poetry . . . and [its] lyrical/dramatic nature,"[65] which is unlike contemporary prose poetry as we have come to understand it from the examples of Baudelaire and Rimbaud. *Ossian* is sensuous and, strangely, creates a sense of external drama emerging from deeply subjective and often dreamlike sequences of poetic prose. Nevertheless, it was the first significant signal in English that strict boundaries between poetry and prose were breaking down. It also indicated that fragmented literary works offered an opportunity to place (in Macpherson's case, a rather indeterminate) suggestiveness and an explicit emotiveness at the forefront of literary works. John J. Dunn observes:

> That Macpherson chose to call his poems "fragments" is indicative of another quality that made them unusual in their day. The poems have a spontaneity that is suggested by the fact that the poets seem to be creating their songs as the direct reflection of an emotional experience. In contrast to the image of the poet as the orderer, the craftsman, the poets of the *Fragments* have a kind of artlessness (to us a very studied one, to be sure) that gave them an aura of sincerity and honesty.[66]

Macpherson's "translations" constitute a radical experiment in the prosody and subject matter of English-language poetry that helped to change the course of English literature, no matter how artificial and contrived much of *Ossian* seems today. In 1847 Asa Humphrey provides a short quotation from *Ossian*—"The music of Carryl, was, like the memory of joys that are past, pleasant and mournful to the soul"—and writes, "[T]his is a species of verse, unlike to all others: it being without form, like other poems, without metre, and without order in the arrangement of its feet, or its numbers; and may, perhaps, not properly be ranked, as one of the orders of English verse."[67] E.H.W. Meyerstein adds, "Macpherson can, without extravagance, be regarded as the main originator (after the translators of the Authorized Version) of what's known as 'free verse.' "[68]

It is possible to go further and understand the example of *Ossian* as highly influential in the development of the prose poem. A few critics, including Michael Benedikt and Robert Crawford, have recognized this.[69] Crawford writes that *Ossian* "is vital to the growth of the prose poem," while Rachel Barenblat contends through this work, "the seeds of the English-language prose poem were sown."[70] While English-language poets mainly continued to compose in meter until the end of the nineteenth century—when Oscar Wilde, partly influenced by French models, briefly attempted to stimulate the writing of prose poetry in English—the early example of *Ossian* opened up the possibility that English poetry might eschew meter and find ways of speaking "unlike to all others."

Contemporary Prose Poetry's Romantic Inheritance

Contemporary prose poetry speaks in ways that many of the Romantics would not recognize. While the Romantic fragment was a precursor to, and provided an important model for, prose poets, contemporary prose poets have taken the idea of fragmentation in numerous directions. We would like to illustrate this by focusing on a few examples of contemporary prose poetry that reveal affiliations with

Romanticism but that simultaneously offer a critique or subversion of Romantic ideas and assumptions. These are fairly characteristic responses by twenty-first-century prose poets to Romantic tropes, given that many larger Romantic ideals have long since seemed unrealizable, and also given that Romanticism has been criticized for its complex and sometimes ambiguous associations with rapacious eighteenth- and nineteenth-century European colonial ventures.

An important general issue for contemporary prose poets—to an even greater extent than their Romantic predecessors—is that fragmentation does not necessarily imply something that is lost or belonging to the past. What fragments do almost inevitably suggest is a connection to something that has a further existence, or is completed, outside of the fragment. Prize-winning author Lydia Davis observes, "[w]e can't think of fragment without thinking of whole. The word fragment implies the word whole. A fragment would seem to be part of a whole, a broken-off part of a whole."[71] Davis identifies the fragment as metonymic, as standing in for something outside of the work the fragment signals, even as it is unable to fully represent it.

In the Romantic period, this quality—the fragment's ability to house or implicate what is greater than itself—was fundamental to the form's boundlessness of suggestion and evocation. For contemporary prose poets, the fragmentary nature of their work is able to open up similar possibilities and suggestiveness but is also often associated with a sense of doubt, hesitancy, constraint, or anxiety. Contemporary prose poetry gestures toward a world fraught with political, social, environmental, and ideological complexity. Just as many postmodern concerns can be traced back to Romantic preoccupations, contemporary prose poets—like their Romantic counterparts—are not always sure how these issues might be encompassed in their works.

Edward Larissy notes that there is a "genetic thesis about the persistence of Romanticism in the present, both in thematic and stylistic tendencies."[72] The idea that "[m]odernism is essentially a remoulding of Romanticism" has led to the "proposition that Postmodernism is also yet another mutation of the original stock."[73] There have been challenges to this lineage from some scholars, and the ache "to behold & know something *great*,"[74] as Coleridge mentions in his letter to Thelwall, is viewed skeptically by most twenty-first-century prose poets. However, even this attitude is not so different from that of many Romantics, who increasingly found their ideals unrealizable. This may be a reason why some of the more wide-ranging and ambitious contemporary prose poems are broadly surrealist in tendency—it is in the evocation of dreamlike or surreal situations that they are able to find the ground on which to motion the large, the unconstrained, and the untrammeled.

As a result of this modern zeitgeist—which has inherited Romanticism's focus on the self and on individual apprehension, but which has largely parted company with Romanticism's high idealism—contemporary prose poetry often has a quizzical, playful, experimental, or exploratory quality (sometimes all of these characteristics), as if it is an incursion into uncertain territory. While the focus on subjectivity remains, the contemporary prose poet's sense of a larger reality outside of a prose poem is likely to be informed more by science, technology, or quotidian reality than by ideas of beauty or the Romantic sublime. Even when some of the larger abstractions loved by the Romantics are invoked by contemporary prose poets, there is usually a cautionary or questioning note.

For example, Jane Satterfield addresses nature—a subject dear to Romantic poets—and alludes to Wordsworth's famous remark, "Poetry is the spontaneous overflow of powerful feelings: it takes its origin from emotion recollected in tranquillity."[75] However, her prose poem does not celebrate nature as a subject for poetry; it debunks its Romantic connotations and repeatedly interposes a contemporary version of the "real" between nature, Romantic contemplation, and the writer/reader. The poem, entitled "Why I Don't Write Nature Poems," begins:

> Because I'm always wearing the wrong shoes, I rarely stray from the path. There's *recollect*, there's *tranquility* and the way the trains punctuate each hour, shrill the shaken fields. Let's bide a bit here, thinking why we love them—the tracks, the transit, *a train's a metaphor for so many things in life*. Like me, too busy eyeing up the buffet from the back of the line to consider a phalanx of phlox, the tabby stray cavorting in the hedge. I don't see a cow meadow as any kind of invocation.[76]

Satterfield's attitude is wry, ironic, and acutely aware of, but unwilling to be taken in by, received Romantic tropes. Many twenty-first-century prose poems make use of fragmented quotations or allusions in this way, indicating how their received literary and cultural heritage is fractured. This is even more evident in the original publication of this prose poem in the *Beltway Poetry Quarterly*,[77] where the omission of apostrophes gives the prose poem an even greater sense of incompleteness. For example, in the line "I'm always wearing the wrong shoes," Satterfield plays with the idea of punctuation, writing of "the way the trains punctuate each hour." The lack of apostrophes gives a sense of the casual or quotidian to the work by eliminating formalities. In both versions, the work's more erudite appeals to tranquillity and metaphor are placed in italics to separate them from images of the "buffet" and the "stray tabby."[78]

John Kinsella's "Graphology 300: Against 'Nature Writing'" is a free-line prose poem (a mode we discuss in chapter 4) that uses a list form in its strident assertions that Nature writers are "hypocrites":

> Nature writing equals the new racketeering.
> Nature writers make good use of plane travel and restaurants serving up nature.
> Nature writing equals recognition as gratification.

> Nature writers wear tough boots and mark their trail out hiking. They need to get back. They drive cars.[79]

The repetitive use of "Nature Writer" in the list form, along with the placement of "Nature Writing" in the title in quotation marks, aims to expose the hypocrisy of those who say they are invested in the environment but are, sometimes sanctimoniously, destroying it.

Many contemporary works also address the reader directly, implicating them, as it were, in understanding that their engagement with a prose poem remains an act of readerly decision-making. In "Warning to the Reader," for example, Robert Bly invokes ideas of beauty that would be familiar to the Romantics, but as soon as he establishes this trope he undercuts it, insisting that his poem addresses darker concerns:

> Sometimes farm granaries become especially beautiful when all the oats or wheat are gone, and wind has swept the rough floor clean. Standing inside, we see around us, coming in through the cracks between shrunken wall boards, bands or strips of sunlight. So in a poem about imprisonment, one sees a little light. . . .
>
> I say to the reader, beware. Readers who love poems of light may sit hunched in the corner with nothing in their gizzards for four days, light failing, the eyes glazed . . .
>
> They may end as a mound of feathers and a skull on the open boardwood floor . . .[80]

This prose poem ends as a kind of cautionary tale for the reader, suggesting those infatuated with light—a favorite trope in many Romantic poems, most famously expressed in Shelley's image of "a dome of many-colored glass"[81]—may end up imprisoned. Metaphorically, this is a plea for readers to look beyond beautiful imagery in poetry toward bigger and more troubling issues; toward, one might say, the contemporary "real." It is a way of simultaneously invoking postmodernity's Romantic inheritance and claiming we need to look beyond this inheritance. It is revealing that the last two sentences of Bly's work end in ellipses as he emphasizes his work's fragmented and indeterminate condition, leaving the reader to resolve the issues that the work has raised.

Hala Alyan's "Oklahoma" also deals with troubling issues, and the problematized language insists that the reader engage with colonialism's cultural and racial violence—and consider their own postcolonial situation. The work begins by invoking the extensive US state of Oklahoma and its history, which saw the indigenous Cherokee (and other American Indian tribes) harried, assaulted, and murdered:

> For a place I hate, I invoke you often. Stockholm's: I am eight years old and the telephone poles are down, the power plant at the edge of town spitting

electricity. Before the pickup trucks, the strip malls, dirt beaten by Cherokee feet. *Osiyo, tsilugi.* Rope swung from mule to tent to man, tornadoes came, the wind rearranged the face of the land like a chessboard. This was before the gold rush, the greed of engines, before white men pressing against brown women, nailing crosses by the river, before the slow songs of cotton plantations, the hymns toward God, the murdered dangling like earrings.[82]

Alyan's use of Cherokee words for "hello" and "welcome" in this prose poem is bitterly ironic and, in mentioning these words out of their linguistic and cultural contexts, she makes a gesture toward the kinds of social and cultural fragmentation that the Cherokee suffered at the hands of European settlers. Later in the poem her statement that "a boy whispers *sand monkey*" indicates that racial prejudice still exists,[83] given that this is a derogatory term for people from the Middle East, and Hala Alyan is of Palestinian heritage.

Much of the depredation this poem alludes to occurred during the Romantic period, and it is salutary to consider that as the Romantics idealized the "noble savage," representatives of their civilizations were destroying indigenous cultures in many parts of the world. This poem bluntly critiques such activity, and at its conclusion even the concept of "Heaven" is problematized, domesticated, and fragmented: "Heaven is pressed in a pleather booth at the Olive Garden, sipping Pepsi between my gapped teeth, listening to my father mispronounce his meal."[84]

Cecilia Woloch's "Postcard to Ilya Kaminsky from a Dream at the Edge of the Sea" invokes the kind of dream imagery that so entranced the Romantics—the most famous examples of which are Coleridge's "Kubla Khan: or, A Vision in a Dream; A Fragment," and John Keats's fragment "The Fall of Hyperion," in which he writes, "Poesy alone can tell her dreams, / With the fine spell of words."[85] Woloch's poem presents a postmodern view of the capacity of dreams to translate the poet from a place of disappointment to the realization of a visionary possibility:

I was leaving a country of rain for a country of apples. I hadn't much time. I told my beloved to wear his bathrobe, his cowboy boots, a black patch like a pirate might wear over his sharpest eye. . . . A feathery breeze. Then a white tree blossomed over the bed, all white blossoms, a painted tree. "*Oh*," I said, or my love said to me. We want to be human, always, again, so we knelt like children at prayer while our lost mothers hushed us. A halo of bees. I was dreaming as hard as I could dream. It was fast—how the apples fattened and fell. The country that rose up to meet me was steep as a mirror; the gold hook gleamed.[86]

In Woloch's prose poem, while there are Romantic tropes ("a country of apples," "a white tree blossom[ing]," and "a halo of bees"),[87] the work ends by suggesting that its vision is either solipsistic (a view in a mirror) or fraught with danger—the image of the gold hook is at once appealing and threatening. Like the Romantics, Woloch exploits the suggestive possibilities of the fragment, leaving her dream narrative incomplete and refusing to provide it with a resolution. We may wake, but only by exiting her poem.

Many contemporary prose poems provide such insights into the "self," its subjectivity and its perceptions. Anne Carson's brief prose poem "On Hedonism" does something similar but with a sense of ironic disjuncture in its image-making. The speaker of the poem may not be the poet, but the first-person pronoun functions for the reader as a notional self-projection, and the poem's speaker claims to have something interesting to say about herself as well as the poem's ostensible subject:

> Beauty makes me hopeless. I don't care why anymore I just want to get away. When I look at the city of Paris I long to wrap my legs around it. When I watch you dancing there is a heartless immensity like a sailor in a dead-calm sea. Desires as round as peaches bloom in me all night, I no longer gather what falls.[88]

This prose poem's strategy is reminiscent of much Romantic poetry in the way it suggests much more than it explicitly says, and in the way it avoids discursively explicating the issues it opens up. Carson's interest in the idea of "beauty" and "immensity" also connects it to the widespread Romantic interest in abstractions that relate to aesthetic appreciation and value. Keats's famous conclusion to "Ode on a Grecian Urn" (1820), "Beauty is truth, truth beauty,"[89] is a fine example of this, and Carson's invocation of such ideas also derives from the ancient Greek preoccupation with aesthetics—connecting, in turn, back to the Romantic interest in antiquity.

Similarly, Anne Caldwell's "Wild Garlic and Detours" appears to offer a Romantic picture of the wild landscape in its images of a "deep ravine," "banks of wild garlic," the "gather[ing] of bluebells," and "meadowsweet." However, the prose poem undercuts this with its elegiac tone and appeal to the uncanny in the "dead . . . walking backwards." Alice, the Carrollian figure of innocence, exhibits clairvoyance in this prose poem. Her sensory contact with the dead enables a kind of environmental elegy:

> Alice can sense them all, pulling away from shadows of their loved ones, late in the evening when everything cools and lengthens and light catches the beech leaves.
>
> The dead are walking backwards, skirting through the woods towards the Calder River and Crimsworth's deep ravine, murmuring to each other. Some are lingering near the water; some are climbing up through the banks of wild garlic, some gather bluebells to remind themselves of the living, to remind

themselves that summer's nearly here and soon the meadowsweet will drown them all in scent.[90]

The works quoted above are fragments of prose poems emphasizing gaps and spaces, and these poets give priority to what Rosmarie Waldrop calls "Gap Gardening." She says that a "great challenge of the [prose poetry] form is to compensate for its absence of turning, or margin. I try to place the vacancy *inside* the text. I cultivate cuts, discontinuity, leaps, shifts of reference."[91] These works leave the reader to do considerable interpretive work in reading them. They are not full-fledged Romantic works, but their fragmentation and use of Romantic tropes gestures at their Romantic inheritance. The friction they generate between an occasionally wild imagination and vestigial moments of reasoned analysis is similar to the tension in so many Romantic works between the imaginary and dreamlike, and the urge toward rational understanding.

Emma Francis might have been speaking of such works when contending that "the deconstruction of the grand narratives of Romanticism which Postmodernism would seek to enact is already implicit or explicit in Romanticism itself."[92] This is a point that also connects to Margueritte Murphy's argument that, "[t]he prose poem is potentially or formally 'postmodern' according to Lyotard's definition: 'the unpresentable in presentation itself.'"[93]

Exclusion and Restriction in Prose Poetry

Romanticism laid much of the groundwork for the literary forms that emerged during the modernist and postmodernist periods and, as it longed for what it could not have—the large, the infinite, and the past—so it implicitly recognized (as do almost all twenty-first-century writers) that coherence and monolithic wholes are frequently neither available nor necessarily desirable. To emphasize this point, Nikki Santilli's characterization of prose poetry might apply equally well to many Romantic fragments:

> [A] high level of intelligibility within a minimal number of sentences is, I believe, made possible by the absences it accommodates. As a fragment, the individual prose piece is an inevitably elliptical text and always stands in relation to a larger absent whole that represents the sum of its unselected contexts. I give the term "implied context" to this active space of signification.[94]

Prose poems, like the Romantic fragment, frequently make the implicit claim that understanding is often arrived at through the *exclusion* of information. The reader is asked to complete the work through an active process of reading, enabling them to add their own supplement to the texts they encounter. As Molly Abel Travis argues,

[A]gency in reading [is] compulsive, reiterative role-playing in which individuals attempt to find themselves by going outside the self, engaging in literary performance in the hope of fully and finally identifying the self through self-differentiation. Such finality is never achieved, for the self is perpetually in process. Furthermore, readers never escape a social context; they are both constructed and constructing in that they read as part of interpretive communities and are involved in collective cultural imagining and reimagining.[95]

The fragmentary prose poem implicitly suggests that many experiences are themselves inherently fragmented or incoherent. Many studies into the nature of autobiographical memory over recent decades support such a conclusion, and Martin Conway even says that "there are no such things as autobiographical memories at least in the sense of discrete, holistic, units in long-term memory."[96] In other words, we all tend to know the world through moments of fragmented and sometimes disjunctive apprehension. We all tend to "read" and remember the world through incomplete parcels of experience. As the Romantics delved into subjectivity and the nature of memory, so they were confronted by the mind's inability to know the "whole" of anything.

The contemporary prose poem's indebtedness to the Romantic fragment reminds us that it may be understood as transgressive of the more claustrophobic boundaries of traditional forms because it evolved in opposition to such forms. It remains illustrative of Schlegel's hedgehog and garland metaphors—self-sufficient yet engaged with a wider world, turned in on itself yet acknowledging often unstated beginnings and endings, autonomous yet part of a continuing dialogue about the relationship of the fragment to the finite and the infinite. As John Taylor argues, prose poems have a "predilection for the most puzzling kinds of associative thinking . . . short prose poems give an impression of wandering or leaping quite far, to unexpected endings that are often, in fact, not really endings."[97]

In this sense, prose poetry's contemporary rejuvenation of Romantic fragmentation heralds an *apophrades*, or return of the dead. In discussing Schlegel and the Romantic fragment, Otabe Tanehisa writes, "The fragment can be termed 'ripe . . . and . . . complete' because of its functions of intimation and suggestion,"[98] and this description applies equally well to a great deal of prose poetry.

Of Friedrich Hölderlin's (1770–1843) late poetry and fragments, Richard Sieburth states they are "above all works in progress, neither beginnings nor endings but becomings,"[99] linking the fragment and ruin:

[T]he modern imagination invents itself (and thereby reinvents antiquity) out of the evidence of wreckage; it has only fragments to shore against its ruins. The eloquent debris of Palmyra or Herculaneum finds its philological equivalent in the miscellaneous scraps of Pindar that Hölderlin translated . . . to scrutinize a fragment is to move from the presence of a part to the absence of the whole, to seize upon the sign as witness of something that is forever elsewhere.[100]

This is reminiscent of Schlegel's assertion that "[t]he romantic kind of poetry is still in the state of becoming; that, in fact, is its real essence: that it should forever be becoming and never be perfected."[101]

It may be that the prose poem is the current state of "becoming" of the kind of poetry instigated by the Romantic fragment. Prose poems are, on the face of it, well suited to postmodernism's assumptions that multiple views and texts have replaced totalizing visions, and that difference and diversity are hallmarks of a healthy, questioning art that addresses both future and past. If Romantic and postmodern views are in significant respects divergent, many Romantics and contemporary writers would nevertheless agree about that.

CHAPTER 3

Prose Poetry, Rhythm, and the City

Cadence and Musicality in Prose Poetry

The rhythms of prose poetry are different from those found in metered verse, and vary, too, from the rhythms of free verse. The main differences relate to what has sometimes been understood as a deficiency in prose poetry—namely, that prose poets do not have meter or the poetic line when they try to achieve effects of cadence or musicality. However, as Charles Harper Webb writes, "Sound, rhythm, and internal rhyme can be mobilized as easily [in prose poetry] as in lined verse."[1] This is because prose poets have the movement of the sentence and the various resources of the paragraph at their disposal.

Because of the English language's grammatical flexibility, these resources allow for an almost infinite rhythmic variety in prose poems. Such variety is a crucial part of the prose poetry tradition, notwithstanding the deliberately fractured rhythms or flat tonality of some works. As David Caddy states, the prose poem "has the potential to build pace, rhythm, music and produce meaning as much as free verse, only it has to generate tension, drama and crises through sentence structure, relationship and language use alone."[2]

Similarly, Derek Attridge makes the following distinction between prose poetry and the rhythmic life of verse: "If it is to be something other than prose, prose-poetry must make the fullest use of the inherent rhythmic properties of the language. It cannot rely, as free verse can, on externally imposed interruptions [such as line breaks] to heighten the reader's consciousness of movement and duration."[3] He praises Geoffrey Hill's prose poem sequence *Mercian Hymns* for "its scrupulous control of rhythmic form," after commenting that certain rhythms occur as a matter of course in the English language and that, generally speaking, "it is all too easy to take a piece of nonmetrical language and find rhythmic ingenuities in it."[4] His astute analysis of Hill's work relies on finding disguised metrical effects in his prose poetry—what he calls "the consistent separation of beats by single or double offbeats" and "the steady sequence of alternations."[5]

This analytical approach allows Attridge to do justice to Hill's writing, but it is less useful in explicating the rhythms of a great deal of contemporary prose poetry. While there is no doubt that meter (along with other devices of conventional poetic rhythm) is often a ghost in the machine of prose poetry, many prose poets eschew such effects. Russell Edson is an example, focusing as he does in many of his prose poems on creating a detached, neutral, and often alienated narrative voice. This voice contains various subtleties, but it is deliberately unmetrical. His prose poetry is interested in the irregular, sometimes monotonous or colloquial rhythms of contemporary prose—rhythms that in many cases have their origins in urban or suburban contexts and settings.

Robert Alexander and Jorie Graham both argue for the importance of the rhythm of everyday speech in the prose poem. Alexander makes a case for the prose poem form as best capturing American speech patterns: "What we have in the prose poem is a piece of writing grounded in the real world, whose rhythms and intonations embody not a traditional English prosody, but rather the speech patterns of everyday America. And therefore, in my opinion, the prose poem is a form particularly suited to American poetry."[6]

Similarly, Graham—whose own poetry sometimes uses long, almost prose-poetical lines—makes a related observation when discussing the prose poems included in *The Best American Poetry, 1990*: "One important formal development is the recent popularity of prose poems . . . they are certainly—in many cases—the most extreme in their attempt to use the strategies of 'normal' articulate speech to reach the reader. Their number, variety and sheer quality . . . caused me to think of this volume as, in part, a subterranean exploration of the form."[7]

This has, perhaps, led Jeremy Noel-Tod to refer to the "plainer style" of prose poetry, "imitative of speech," as "employ[ing] the formulas and rhythms of storytelling, with all their alluring familiarity and suspense."[8] This variety of prose poetry appeals to quotidian cadences and, as we discuss in chapter 5, it sometimes conjures the neo-surreal (at times introducing the mischievous lilt associated with a joke).

However, Attridge is right to draw attention to the way in which prose poetry belongs to the English language's extraordinarily rich and diverse poetic heritage. This is a heritage that is familiar to most prose poets—who are also cognizant of the way in which ideas of the "poetic" have changed. Most importantly, around the beginning of the nineteenth century, the very idea of the poetic began to shift. At this time, the influential English Romantic poet William Wordsworth articulated a new approach to poetry, writing in his famous *Preface to Lyrical Ballads* (1800; rev. 1802) that "[t]here will also be found in these volumes little of what is usually called poetic diction."[9] Wordsworth commented that his poems contained language that "though naturally arranged and according to the strict laws of metre, does not differ from that of prose."[10]

Wordsworth wrote lineated poetry, but in expressing a view that prose and poetry ought to be written in the same kind of language, and in repudiating what he understood to be "poetic diction," Wordsworth opened the way for English-language poets to explicitly recognize the connections between poetry and prose. In other words—and although he may not have known it—he helped to lay the ground not only for English-language free verse but for English-language prose poetry, too.

Furthermore, in the mid-nineteenth century in America, Henry David Thoreau published the influential *Walden* (1854). This is partly a personal memoir, partly an extended essay, and partly a quasi-philosophical transcendentalist text, written in prose that is often dense and figurative. It has been compared to Wordsworth's poetry and to prose poetry—Lance Newman argues that "the book recapitulates the structure of a Wordsworthian lyric poem," and David Faflick writes, "The conventional critical view on *Walden* . . . has judged Thoreau's work a coherent prose poem."[11] In the second half of the nineteenth century, Walt Whitman created a new, sometimes "prosaic" free verse poetry in his collection *Leaves of Grass*—various editions of which were published between 1855 and 1892. In 1869 in France, Charles Baudelaire produced *Paris Spleen*, which, as we have said, is the first book of modern prose poetry.

Nevertheless, free verse poetry and prose poetry did not immediately become the general poetic practice in the English language. Neither Victorian-era poets (1837–1901) nor the early twentieth-century Georgian poets in England had much of a taste for it. This was despite the innovations of various writers, such as Matthew Arnold's publication in 1867 of the famous "free verse" poem "Dover Beach" (which is actually written in a mixture of free verse and iambic meter), Christina Rossetti's explorations of a loosely metered rhymed poetry, and Oscar Wilde's six rather overwritten conversational pieces he called *Poems in Prose*—first published in 1894 in the *Fortnightly Review*.[12]

In the early twentieth century the rise of the short-lived but highly influential imagist movement—inaugurated by T. E. Hulme's poetry in 1909 and more formally "announced" by Ezra Pound in 1912 in Harriet Monroe's *Poetry* magazine—helped to usher modernism into the English-speaking literary world. It also introduced a new idea of free verse, partly based on French, Chinese, and Japanese models (we discuss the effects of this movement at greater length in chapter 7). Such free verse opened up poetry in general to the rhythmic effects of prose, and these rhythms are demonstrable in the most famous of Hulme's early imagist poems, entitled "Autumn":

A touch of cold in the Autumn night—
I walked abroad,
And saw the ruddy moon lean over a hedge
Like a red-faced farmer.
I did not stop to speak, but nodded,
And round about were the wistful stars
With white faces like town children.[13]

Although the third line of this poem, "And saw the ruddy moon lean over a hedge," is not far removed from a line of iambic pentameter, overall the rhythms of the poem are prose rhythms. Thus, while this is a carefully constructed and modulated poem, it is made of sentences as much as of poetic lines. This may be demonstrated by formatting it as a prose poem:

> A touch of cold in the Autumn night—I walked abroad, and saw the ruddy moon lean over a hedge like a red-faced farmer. I did not stop to speak, but nodded, and round about were the wistful stars with white faces like town children.

This prose version of the poem is considerably less successful than the original version, chiefly because the lineation in the original poem opens up its images for the reader and also opens up the language of the poem to the night that surrounds it and the moon that watches it. Indeed, the rhythms of the original poem are modulated so they sit within, and are controlled by, the line breaks. However, the poem does function reasonably well, if somewhat clumsily, as a prose poem simply because its tautly constructed sentences are not unlike the sentences of any prose poem, at least to the extent that the use of language—in Wordsworth's phrase—"does not differ from that of prose."[14]

This is an example of how the language and rhythms of contemporary lineated poetry often bear a close resemblance to the language and rhythms of prose poetry, even if (as we discuss in chapter 4) lineated poetry's use of the poetic line and its tendency to invoke expectations of formal closure make it a very different literary form to prose poetry. However, as Clements and Dunham argue, "The prose poem is no less equipped than verse, then, to build rhythm and music, to produce meaning, or to affect a reader."[15]

Another way of understanding the intersections between the language of lineated poetry and prose poetry is to extend our observation (given in chapter 1) that prose has always contained rhetorical and rhythmic effects related to those one finds in both verse and free verse poetry. This includes some of the effects usually associated with meter—except when they occur in prose, they do not establish any regular rhythmical pattern even while they may introduce some of the musical effects, or effects of cadence, associated with meter.

Examples abound, including from orators such as Edmund Burke (1730–97). Here is an excerpt from Burke's observations about Marie Antoinette:

> It is now sixteen or seventeen years since I saw the queen of France, then the dauphiness, at Versailles; and surely never lighted on this orb, which she hardly seemed to touch, a more delightful vision. I saw her just above the horizon, decorating and cheering the elevated sphere she just began to move in,—glittering like the morning-star, full of life, and splendor, and joy. Oh! what a revolution! and what an heart must I have, to contemplate without emotion that elevation and that fall![16]

It is easy to see how Burke makes use of various devices and techniques to give his passage a sense of music and flow. For example, his relatively long, modulated sentences help to create a rhythmical sense of forward momentum, while the phrase "And surely never lighted on this orb" is a line of fairly regular iambic pentameter, helping to establish the passage's rhythmic patterns. There is a main figure of speech—the earth or "orb" or "elevated sphere"—that Burke elaborates and develops, including through his play on the word "revolution." There are also related tropes conveying a sense of immediate authorial involvement in the passage—expressions such as "I saw" and "what an heart must I have."

Contemporary prose poets have similar resources at their disposal, enabling them to create persuasive rhythmical effects. These effects give a musicality to the works that contain them—even as some works also undercut aspects of such "musicality" due to their failure to generate meter and rhyme's sustained repetitive effects, or by deliberately creating broken rhythms. Clive Scott comments on this phenomenon in discussing his approach to translating Rimbaud's prose poetry in *Illuminations*. He observes that "rhythm in the prose poem . . . constantly questions itself, improvises itself, interrupts its own continuities."[17]

Scott states that while the pattern of meter and rhyme in regular verse "promises the recurrences of cyclical time," prose poetry "launches us into the unprotected presentness of linear time, where no recurrence is predicted."[18] He adds that "the prose poem, by virtue of its very rhythmic inchoateness, is both non-metrical and potentially metrical. Accordingly, the clinging memory of cyclical time . . . the memory of a kind of regular verse which haunts, and which one tries to undo, creates sharply conflicting tugs in the verbal texture."[19]

It is debatable how often, or how completely, prose poetry "launches . . . into linear time."[20] We commented in chapter 1 that prose poetry is not necessarily a discursive or narrative-centered form and that it frequently creates what Jonathan Culler (when discussing lineated lyric poetry) refers to as the "present time of discourse."[21] However, many prose poems undoubtedly mimic the movement of linear time rather than using verse's recurrent poetic rhythms and structures, even as they also present their content as an image or idea belonging to poetry's present moment. In chapter 6 we discuss this in reference to TimeSpace and the prose poem's expression of the ever-present moment in compressed images that trigger recollection.

Certainly, many prose poems include the kind of verbal "tugs" that Scott mentions. Here, for instance, is part of C. K. Williams's "Silence":

The heron methodically pacing like an old-time librarian down the stream through the patch of woods at the end of the field, those great wings tucked in as neatly as clean sheets, is so intent on keeping her silence, extracting one leg, bending it like a paper clip, placing it back, then bending the other, the first again, that her concentration radiates out into the listening world, and everything obediently hushes, the ragged grasses that rise from the water, the light-sliced vault of sparkling aspens.[22]

The rhythm of this work is fairly regular and beautifully modulated, and the whole paragraph (the first of two in this work) is made up of a single sentence in which phrases flow easily as the poem marks the progress of a "pacing" heron. Part of the rhythmic skill of this work is its activation of disguised or suppressed metrical effects (but without clear regularity or recurrence), so the phrase "bending it like a paper clip" is mostly iambic tetrameter, as is the phrase "the light-sliced vault of sparkling aspens." Tugs in the language of this work occur when these metrical effects are pressured by the unmetrical phrases that hem them in—such as the blunt and prosaic phrase "extracting one leg."

This prose poem is ghosted by meter even as it insists on its prosaic nature, and its mixed rhythms create the kinds of prose-poetical effects that lift the writing away from the narrative-driven features of conventional prose. The evocation of the pacing heron is valuable not because of its story (the sense of the heron moving through time) but because of the prose poem's fine observations and superb image-making. The work employs a conspicuously lyrical use of language (notwithstanding its verbal "tugs") because Williams successfully combines the language of prose with various judiciously inserted poetic tropes and phrases. The accumulating rhythms of the phrases—"is so intent on keeping her silence, extracting one leg, bending it like a paper clip, placing it back, then bending the other"—constitute a fine demonstration of this lyrical tendency, while also alluding to the contemporary, postindustrial world.

In other words, for every neo-surrealist fable by a prose poet, such as Russell Edson conveyed in a relatively uninflected prose (which simultaneously mimics and subverts a great deal of short prose fiction), there are works that exploit the musical resources of prose in myriad ways. The manipulation of the English language's stress patterns not only results in the traces of meter already mentioned, but they enable the exploration of highly complex language patterns in general.

To give another example, Charles Rafferty's "The Pond" opens with a brief, almost blunt, declarative statement that ends softly with the "y" of the word "supply," a word that has a partial equivalence in length with "goldenrod" in the prose poem's second sentence:

> The world is in short supply. This field of goldenrod will never be enough, and the ocean feels suddenly crossable. In every apple an orchard waits, but who has twenty years to cultivate it? Above our house, the contrails of the jets have turned into actual clouds. The rain they promise is another lie. Meanwhile, the taste of my blood implies that I am rusting, that a broken machine lies half-submerged in the pond I carry with me.[23]

One need only imagine the first sentence of this work rewritten as "The world is in short store" to gauge how the "y" of "supply" softens and lengthens the opening of the poem in a musical way.

The word "supply" also helps to establish a kind of template for the remainder of the prose poem, where a series of fairly blunt assertions are qualified, extended, or softened by suggestive imagery tied to the natural world ("field of goldenrod," "an orchard waits," "actual clouds"); by the repeated contrast of large, evocative concepts ("the world," "the ocean," "an orchard," "the rain") with tropes of limitation ("never be enough," "suddenly crossable," "who has twenty years," "another lie"); through the poem's repetition of shifting "o" sounds ("short," "goldenrod," "ocean," "crossable," "orchard," "contrails," "clouds," "blood," "pond"); and through the cadences of the middle part of the work, where the second, third, and fourth sentences are constructed as more or less balanced pairs of statements.

In each of these balanced statements, the second part significantly extends, complicates, or qualifies the first part. For example: (1) "This field of goldenrod will never be enough" (2) "and the ocean feels suddenly crossable"; and (1) "Above our house, the contrails of the jets" (2) "have turned into actual clouds." Thus, the rhythmic life of this poem and its musicality—and we have only mentioned a few salient features of a rhythmically complex work—makes a significant contribution to the way its meanings are structured and understood.

Harmony Holiday's "Crisis Actor" displays a different kind of musicality, drawing on contemporary music and dance rhythms, as well as the vernacular. The poem's opening sentence speaks in the first person, but the poem destabilizes this voice, introducing the third person in its second and third sentences, before returning to the first person in "Just tryna make it real baby, like it is":

> Ruby, please. A night shift nurse fell asleep at the wheel. The whole earth had a fever and the heated pulse beats faster 'til everything picturesque has her reeling. Just tryna make it real baby, like it is. He condescends. Twitching a trio of flax seeds between the thumb and forefinger in a dirty spiral, these are full of phytoestrogens that turn the gender . . . generic . . . generous. Hey, girl! Crease in her *hey* the size of turning.[24]

This is only the beginning of the prose poem, but already the contrast between short, staccato phrases ("Ruby, please," "He condescends," "Hey girl!") and extended sentences (such as "The whole earth had a fever and the heated pulse beats faster 'til everything picturesque has her reeling")—along with the playful use of ellipses to further vary the work's rhythm in the punning triad "gender . . . generic . . . generous"—all contribute to the work's creation of a sense of congestion, activity, and crisis. Various meanings may be sifted from the divergent statements as they press each other in sudden-seeming juxtapositions—without always clearly cohering—but these meanings are often elusive, or take time to understand. In this way, the prose poem creates a sense that the sometimes coiled, sometimes released rhythms of its sentences constitute a great deal of its purpose.

Emily Berry's "Some Fears" makes conspicuous use of repetition in the one long sentence that constitutes the majority of the work. The fears invoked are divided by semicolons and presented as an extended list, creating a fast beat that mimics how fear can accelerate one's breathing and heart rate:

> Fear of breezes; fear of quarrels at night-time; fear of wreckage; fear of one's reflection in spoons; fear of children's footprints; fear of the theory behind architecture; fear of boldness; fear of catching anxiousness from dogs; fear of ragged-right margins.[25]

The reference to "ragged-right margins" is a clever, self-reflexive moment that also points to a fear of breaking the boundaries of the prose poem box. While Berry's fears may seem overwhelming as the list grows, the prose poem contains these fears in a justified block—the opposite of the "ragged right margin." The first long sentence ends with "fear of fear; fear of help." In the second, shorter sentence that concludes the work, the commas in place of semicolons accelerate the pace and provide a final, poignant moment when the furious speed slows: "Fear of asking for, receiving, refusing, giving, or being denied help."

Each of the four contemporary prose poems quoted above engage with contemporary issues. "Silence" asks for scrupulous attention to be given to the things and activities of the world, drawing attention to their simultaneous closeness and otherness. It implies significant issues related to history, and ethics attach to an appreciation of what is "other" in this way. "The Pond" links the idea of a failing humanity, conjured by the speaker's image of himself as a "rusting . . . broken machine," to climate change and the depletion of the world's resources. "Crisis Actor" generates a picture of a restlessly urban and unsatisfactory modernity, conjuring near its conclusion a vision of "a double suicide, American, pie and guns and obscene convenience." "Some Fears" presents postmodern alienation set to the beat of anxieties finding refuge in the fully justified paragraph of prose poetry.

These prose poems belong to the postmodern zeitgeist in which poetry in general—and prose poetry in particular—takes for granted the postindustrial, posttechnological, and urbanized age in which it is written. Daniel Kozak suggests that "within postmodernism the starting point is recognition and celebration of a 'fragmentary living' in contemporary metropolises,"[26] and each of these works in its own way understands contemporary urban realities and their fracturing of experience. Two of these works address this phenomenon obliquely, while "Crisis Actor" and "Some Fears" do so overtly.

Perhaps, then, it is no surprise that musicians Patti Smith and Art Garfunkel are both attracted to the prose poem form and its ability to evoke the rhythms of lived experience. Smith's works of poetic prose are often rhythmically rambling, and sometimes discordant. Even in her most somber, elegiac moments, she is freewheeling: "a ribbon of life snapping—pitched and tossed, wrapping round a wrist, gasping upon a wave or trampled on below."[27] Garfunkel has written eighty-two poems entitled *Still Water Prose Poems* (1989). They are more constrained but similarly focused on rhythm. Discussing his creative process, he states: "You're completely wrapped up with how to express [a theme] with sentences that have a rhythm; with inflections and accents on the words so that there's a dance, with a rhyme that's subtle and internal."[28]

For example, prose poem 81 was composed in New York in June 1985, and there is a quotidian musicality in Garfunkel's evocation of city life. He begins with a sentence that may be referring to Bob Dylan's song "Lay Lady Lay": "There she'd be beside me in our big brass bed" and ends with the first notes of a musical scale: "nee, nee, nee, nee."[29] The city of New York is prominent in this work—Garfunkel even brands the prose poem with the place and date of composition. Like its subject matter, this prose poem's rhythms are indubitably contemporary.

Many prose poets address the urban environment directly and even insouciantly. For example, in the anthology *Cities: Ten Poets, Ten Cities*, poets chose to write prose poems about cities in which they have been intimately involved. These included Pooja Nansi on Mumbai, Subhash Jaireth on Moscow, and Niloofar Fanaiyan on Haifa. Alvin Pang writes playfully about Singapore:

1.290270,103.851959 (2017)

"We had to make it look a bit more like Singapore—given it was Singapore"

not sporting lah, make people go extra drawsnakeaddleg mile to make the place look more like its own self. you see lah, all those years of speakgoodenglish until now people cannot tell this from manchester. got tall building, got peoplemountainpeoplesea shopping centre crowd, got rain, got grumpy taxi driver, got rush hour traffic, got scottish bridge, even got big grey building with fake greek columns, just like theirs![30]

In this work the compression of compound words like "speakgoodenglish" and "peoplemountainpeoplesea," coupled with exclamations like "lah" are parodic, especially when connected to the work's epigraph. Pang makes his prose poem "like Singapore" by parodying stereotypical views of the city—and, in doing this, he draws attention to its uniqueness. The prose poem form offers a fragment of the city that stands in for its complexities. Pang states, "Singapore is still often glossed in reductive terms, but I wanted to make poems that sound out its diverse and often complex landscapes, textures, contours, memories and resonances."[31]

Poetry and the City

If postmodern twenty-first-century fragmentation is often symbolized by the city, this is because the proliferation and growth of major cities is one of the defining characteristics of the twentieth and twenty-first centuries. Approximately half of the world's population now lives in cities—a relatively recent phenomenon that means vast numbers of people, and many writers, have experiences of city life more or less in common. We say "more or less" because city living both connects city dwellers and separates them. As has frequently been observed, modern cities are so big and unmanageable that their inhabitants are often pushed apart—and even isolated—by a sense of their dislocation from the broader community.

Because so many people live in cities, a great deal of contemporary literature, including the prose poem, directly evokes city or suburban living—or raises issues connected to globalization or to the social and political dimensions of urban living. While cities have featured in poetry of all kinds since ancient times—Burton Pike writes that "we cannot imagine *Gilgamesh*, the Bible, the *Iliad*, or the *Aeneid*, without their cities"[32]—such issues have been most central to poetry since the rise of industrialization in the mid-eighteenth and nineteenth centuries.

The English Romantic poets featured cities in important works—William Blake's "London" (1794) and William Wordsworth's "The Prelude" (1805 and 1850) are examples of famous poems excoriating the rise of cities—and the nineteenth-century English Victorian poets also wrote about cities.[33] Perhaps the most impressive of these works is Elizabeth Barrett Browning's verse novel, *Aurora Leigh*. This features the cities of Florence, London, and Paris, and represents city slums and their streets as "graves, where men alive / Packed close with earthworms, burr unconsciously."[34]

Also writing in the mid-nineteenth century, Whitman was fascinated by and documented the rise of the urban centers of Brooklyn and Manhattan. In his "Crossing Brooklyn Ferry" (first published in 1856 under the title "Sun-Down Poem"), he addresses these "cities," asking them to

> . . . bring your freight, bring your shows, ample and
>   sufficient rivers,
> Expand, being than which none else is perhaps more spiritual,
> Keep your places, objects than which none else is more lasting.[35]

Yet, even when Brooklyn and Manhattan were still relatively uncluttered—in 1856 the population was less than a million in the two urban centers combined—Whitman's articulation of a vision of city life characterized by a "spiritual" "well-join'd scheme" faltered.[36]

Whitman was born in a fairly sparsely populated Long Island in 1819, and he witnessed—along with numerous other nineteenth-century writers, including Baudelaire in a rapidly developing Paris—the environment of his childhood being irrevocably changed. He watched the expanding metropolises of Manhattan and Brooklyn with an ambivalent and conflicted gaze. Laure Katsaros comments that "the seemingly endless flow of energy in Whitman's utopian New York is shadowed by the uncanny realization that memories of the past and harrowing premonitions of the future contaminate the present."[37]

A few decades after "Crossing Brooklyn Ferry" was published, the Boston poet Louise Imogen Guiney (1861–1920) wrote a sonnet entitled "The Lights of London" (1898) that evoked another of the world's growing metropolises in doubtful terms:

> Her booths begin to flare; and gases bright
> Prick door and window; all her streets obscure
> Sparkle and swarm with nothing true nor sure,
> Full as a marsh of mist and winking light;[38]

Later still, in 1912 Amy Lowell published a poem, "New York at Night," in which "sharp jags / Cut brutally into a sky / Of leaden heaviness," and by the time the modernist poet T. S. Eliot published "Preludes" in 1915, the city—in this case Boston—was envisioned as a place of stretched souls and "broken blinds and chimney-pots."[39] Eliot's "The Waste Land" (1922) further transformed his vision of London into an "Unreal city, / Under the brown fog of a winter dawn."[40]

In the 1930s Stephen Spender wrote a well-known poem beginning "After they have tired of the brilliance of cities,"[41] a lyrical, idealistic, and left-wing critique of a civilization that would soon be plunged into the carnage of the Second World War. In the mid-twentieth century New Yorker Frank O'Hara wrote poems that, in the words of Hazel Smith, "vary in the degree to which they dislocate the city."[42] Many of these poems attest to O'Hara's perambulation though urban spaces, which was a kind of urban mapping. Smith quotes the opening of O'Hara's poem "The Day Lady Died," first published in 1964, memorializing the singer Billie Holiday:

> It is 12:20 in New York a Friday
> three days after Bastille day, yes
> it is 1959 and I go get a shoeshine
> because I will get off the 4:19 in Easthampton
> at 7:15 and then go straight to dinner
> and I don't know the people who will feed me[43]

In the twentieth century, and with the rise of modernism, cities and poetry became so closely identified, it became impossible to think of twentieth-century poetry without thinking of urban experience. The subsequent advent of the postmodern in the mid-twentieth century was inextricably linked to pluralism and eclecticism in the understanding and planning of cities, in the reconstruction of their histories, and in the writing that depicts or evokes them.

This is explored by Donna Stonecipher in her book of prose poetry *Model City* (2015), with its repetition of the words "it was like" and the accompanying trope of nostalgia:

It was like noticing hotel after hotel going up all over the city with unstoppable force and imagining a city consisting only of hotels, a city composed solely of expensive emptinesses. . . .

*

It was like thinking about the nights you walked through the city feeling threatened by the rampantly multiplying hotel rooms, as if vacancy were a disease invading the city's—and therefore your—interior.[44]

Similarly, Rob Fitterman, in his book of poetic prose *This Window Makes Me Feel* (2018), refers to New York and 9/11 in its epigraph, "New York City - 8:35 AM, September 11, 2001."[45] Its focus on the window—a key trope in writing about 9/11—is "solely composed with repurposed web language,"[46] and every sentence begins with the title phrase:

> This window makes me feel like I'm protected. This window makes me feel like people don't know much about recent history, at least as far as trivia goes. This window makes me feel whole and emotionally satisfied. This window makes me feel like I'm flying all over the place, gliding and swirling down suddenly.[47]

The long, fully justified block of text becomes both window and twin towers on each double-page spread.

Prose Poetry and Early Modernism

The urban-focused nineteenth-century French prose poem represents one of the indisputable beginnings of international modernism, even if one defines modernism's main period as belonging to the twentieth century. Marshall Berman contends that "Baudelaire's Modernism . . . may turn out to be even more relevant in our time than it was in his own . . . [to] the urban men and women of today."[48] Contemporary prose poetry was created by Baudelaire, Rimbaud, and their French contemporaries out of the experience of the city, and since Baudelaire, prose poetry has continued to attach itself to the city. Cole Swensen captures the origins of this in her essay "Poetry City" (2004) when she argues that in modernism,

> [p]rose poetry was the most radical new poetic form, and the one most tied to the urban . . . its block structure . . . echoes the delimitation of space by city streets. Even cities without a grid structure, such as Paris, where the prose

poem originated, still divide space relatively uniformly. The city occurs in chunks just large enough to hold in the mind, just as a prose poem is usually a single gesture, whether image, thought, or impression. The second collection of prose poems ever written was Baudelaire's *Paris Spleen*, and many of them directly address Paris.[49]

Baudelaire's *Paris Spleen* is centered on his responses to nineteenth-century Paris, and he famously states in his preface to this work: "Above all, it's from being in crowded towns, from the criss-cross of their innumerable ways, that this obsessive ideal [the miracle of a poetic prose] is born."[50] What's more, Baudelaire's approach to writing about Paris was as modern as the city itself, emphasizing evocation over clear descriptive detail. Walter Benjamin notices this in his remark, "Baudelaire describes neither the Parisians nor their city. Avoiding such descriptions enables him to invoke the former in the figure of the latter."[51] In "Good Dogs," for example, Baudelaire provides the reader with a powerful and emblematic set of images:

> I sing the dog of calamities, whether wandering alone in the circuitous ravines of immense cities, or having declared, batting clever eyes, to some abandoned man, "Take me with you, and perhaps our two miseries will add up to a kind of happiness."[52]

Since the nineteenth century, prose poetry has always maintained this connection with urban living, no matter how far from cities some individual prose poets have ranged. Arnold Weinstein identifies prose poetry as part of "the foundational nineteenth-century works that are [the] substratum" of "the modernist city in literature," and that "convey the very rhythms and creatures of urban existence: spasmodic, lurching, awash in stimuli."[53] Santilli explores these associations in *Such Rare Citings*, focusing on the prose poem as a vehicle for "a new vocabulary to deal with the changing cosmography that was emerging with the industrial age: the growth of the city."[54]

Nineteenth-century prose poetry in Paris—like Whitman's nineteenth-century free verse experiments in America in *Leaves of Grass*—found ways of turning language to new ends and adapting it to a new urban milieu. In the twenty-first century it is easy to forget that urban sprawl was only just beginning—in 1850 the largest city in the world, London, only had a population of about 2.3 million people. The rapidity of mid-nineteenth-century urban expansion was unprecedented, and writers and artists everywhere were trying to find ways of registering the shock occasioned by this expansion, as well as the loss of the places urbanization swallowed up. This last phenomenon led to what Arnold Weinstein calls modernism's preoccupation with the "conjunction of personal and urban past . . . Over and over we find that the modernist city text has a memorializing function."[55]

As cities grew, social relations within them became so complex and opaque they resisted full understanding. Christophe Den Tandt identifies the metropolis as "the visible token of the resistances to representation caused by complex social interconnections."[56] This was such a significant development that by the second half of the twentieth century, images of cities, both past and present, began to stand metonymically for, and bleed into, the very idea of postmodernity. In a poem entitled "Waiting for the Light" (2017), Alice Ostriker comments, "we have become an urban species."[57]

Bearing these developments in mind, some critics have argued that prose poetry is more suited to writing about urban experience than lineated poetry. Donna Stonecipher has written extensively on this issue in the aptly entitled *Prose Poetry and the City* (2017), arguing for "prose poetry as ontologically urban, as uniquely expressive of urban experience."[58] She contends:

> On a purely formal level, the caryatid of the lineated poem does not allow for the rich, productive tension and confusion between self and other, self and society, emotion and rationalization that . . . the mode of "poems in prose" does.[59]

Whether or not this is true—as we have mentioned, there have been many fine lineated poems about the city—there is no doubt that the contemporary prose poem remains connected to its origins in the city and is made of language tending to be simultaneously poetic and—through its fragmentation—capable of registering the intensity and fractures of urban living. However, this is not always obvious, and as Stonecipher says, "the urbanism of prose poetry" may be "expressed as an unspoken undercurrent, a context that is understood but not necessarily directly addressed."[60]

The Flaneur and the City

In Baudelaire's conception of the artist as flaneur, the modern poet and prose poet were understood as standing apart from, while also being immersed in, the hubbub of Parisian life—as a simultaneously involved-and-uninvolved spectator and artist. For Baudelaire, traditional French lyric utterance and sensibility was at once too formal, orderly, and elevated to deal with the down-at-heel, the tawdry, and the unruly so central to the daily experiences of city-dwellers. In 1857 he disrupted French poetic and moral conventions with his volume of poetry *The Flowers of Evil* (*Les Fleurs du mal*), for which he was prosecuted and fined for insulting public decency.

When he subsequently wrote his volume of prose poetry, *Paris Spleen*, he found this form could, as it were, travel with him to all parts of the city. *The Flowers of Evil* repurposes and radicalizes old poetic forms—what Peter Broome calls "its predilection for the disciplines of the sonnet, its classic Alexandrines, its stout stanza-forms and fully fashioned rhyming patterns"[61]—in order to adapt these forms to contemporary urban realities. *Paris Spleen* invents an innovative prose poetry intimately attuned to chaotic urban experiences and their disruptive encounters.

In this way, Baudelaire had a great deal in common with Walt Whitman, notwithstanding their different personalities and predilections, the different poetries they wrote and the different countries they inhabited. Many scholars have commented on these writers' shared preoccupations, the most important of which revolved around their related (if separate) experiences of the burgeoning nineteenth-century city. Laure Katsaros notices both poets' preoccupation with death:

> In Baudelaire's "Parisian Scenes" [in *The Flowers of Evil*], elderly beggars, decrepit hags, and blind men teetering on the edge of the abyss haunt the streets and boulevards of the city. . . . "Crossing Brooklyn Ferry" displays no such monstrosities . . . and yet Whitman's New York is as much of a necropolis as Baudelaire's Paris.[62]

Bojana Aćamović agrees that Whitman's poetic impulse connects him to Baudelaire—particularly to the concept of the flaneur as Baudelaire elaborated it in his book of essays *The Painter of Modern Life* (1863). Aćamović states, "Among the numerous facets of Whitman's complex poetic 'I' are features related to both the flâneur and the bohemian."[63]

Baudelaire did not invent the idea of the flaneur but took considerable pains to articulate a view of the flaneur as a type of the modern artist. However, he reserved his idea of the flaneur for men, characterizing women as little more than objects for the male artist's gaze. Elizabeth Wilson comments, "in feminist debate" the flaneur "represents men's visual and voyeuristic mastery over women."[64] Janet Wolff observes:

> In Baudelaire's essays and poems, women appear very often. Modernity breeds, or makes visible, a number of categories of female city-dwellers. Among those most prominent in these texts are: the prostitute, the widow, the old lady, the lesbian, the murder victim, and the passing unknown woman . . . none of these women meet the poet as his equal.[65]

The flaneur, as imagined by Baudelaire, is an observer and perambulator in the midst of, but also keeping somewhat apart from, the urban throng—and he is not to be confused with a "mere" flaneur.[66] He is able to appreciate "the ephemeral, the fugitive, the contingent."[67] In depicting such an artist, Baudelaire is especially interested in how he finds the immutable and "eternal" in the transitory: "Sometimes he is a poet . . . he is the painter of the passing moment and of all the suggestions of eternity that it contains."[68]

Baudelaire's interest in the bohemian life—closely connected to his idea of the flaneur—has also been widely discussed, perhaps most notably by Walter Benjamin, who comments that Baudelaire's bohemianism was related to his historical period, when "[e]ach person [in Paris] was in a more or less blunted state of revolt against society and faced a more or less precarious future."[69] Jerrold Seigel understands Parisian mid-nineteenth-century Bohemia as bordered by "poverty and hope, art and illusion, love and shame, work, gaiety, courage, slander, necessity, and the hospital."[70] He claims Baudelaire was a reluctant bohemian but that, with a characteristic ambivalence, he "shared its friendships, frequented its circles and cafés, partook of the messy, *débraillé* style he despised."[71] Mallarmé's *Divagations* (1897) is an important related text—not only for its symbolist aesthetics but for its connection to flaneurism. The critical reflections and prose poems in *Divagations* are wanderings or reveries, and there is a suggestion that the title of the work was based on the poet Jules Laforgue's "aphorism, 'Mallarmé est un sage qui divague' (Mallarmé is a wandering sage),"[72] which casts Mallarmé in a role akin to that of the flaneur.

Prose poetry arose when Paris was not only being remodeled by Georges-Eugène Haussmann—the implications of which we discuss at greater length in chapter 7—but when it was becoming too big to be fully "mapped." Arthur Rimbaud's *Illuminations* (published 1886; composed 1873–75), which were partly written in response to his experiences of nineteenth-century Paris and London, addresses this idea of the incomprehensibility of the city directly: "At several points on the copper footbridges, the platforms, the stairways that wind around covered markets and pillars, I thought I could judge the depth of the city! It's the wonder of it that I was unable to seize."[73] As Aimée Israel-Pelletier expresses it, Rimbaud gives voice to the idea that "the tourist (poet, reader, blind man)" may perceive "something of the structure of the city" and may have a "general sense . . . of its 'colossal' and 'barbaric' dimensions," but, nevertheless, "still the city escapes him. It is not legible. . . . The city is not coherent. It cannot be mapped."[74]

This observation is reminiscent of Michel de Certeau's famous characterization of the blindness of city inhabitants in his meditation "Walking in the City," first published in France in 1980. This focuses on Manhattan as an exemplar of the modern urban center. The city's inhabitants do not have access to a "celestial eye" and are thus unable to see and comprehend the entire city:

> The ordinary practitioners of the city live "down below," below the thresholds at which visibility begins. They walk—an elementary form of this experience of the city; . . . The paths that correspond in this intertwining, unrecognized poems in which each body is an element signed by many others, elude legibility. It is as though the practices organizing a bustling city were characterized by their blindness.[75]

In de Certeau's conception, the city is like a text that city walkers may inscribe with their "unrecognized" poems.

Other writers have argued that literature and the arts, including poems, may function to create an alternative city. For instance, C. Bruna Mancini writes that "the image of the city—created by literature and painting, and perfected by the cinematographic language—precedes the city itself; even better, it is through it that the traveller seems to be attracted into its texture/web of streets, buildings, monuments."[76] She also says:

> The urban *image*, portrayed by the artists in their works, becomes an icon with a vigorous expressive meaning. It makes the city legible, memorable, *imaginable*. Close to every single *real* city, standing out in all its concreteness, there is an *imaginary, remembered, narrated/narrative* city; or better, there are many different *imagined* cities ... Thus the urban text(ure) gives birth to powerful and inseparable "doubles" of itself: imagined, unreal, or even hyperreal cities whose magic and seductive images make them more real than "the" real.[77]

Mancini's perspective is particularly relevant to an appreciation of prose poetry, precisely because so many prose poems represent a partial, often idiosyncratic mapping of city life—not in its totality but in its fragmented, dreamlike, sometimes hyperreal parts. Murphy reflects on this characteristic of the prose poem, emphasizing its suitability for exploring the flaneur's perspectives:

> The prose poem affords a particular lens on the city: typically it is not the broad perspective ... but detailed meditations on its corners and passages, narratives of fleeting and random experience on its sidewalks and streets, descriptions of activities peculiar to urban life (for instance, the deep flânerie celebrated in Baudelaire's "The Crowds").[78]

From the nineteenth century onward, cities increasingly began to be imagined as incomprehensible or invisible, except in parts. In 1972 Italian writer Italo Calvino took up this idea in his novel—or book of poetic prose—entitled *Invisible Cities*, evoking fifty-five "imagined, unreal, or even hyperreal cities" in a conspicuously neo-surreal and postmodern manner.[79]

City Rhythms

If prose poetry may be understood as a form of the imaginative mapping of the city, such mapping takes place partly through their rhythmical life—and urban rhythms tend to be more various than the rhythms of rural environments. And, as we discussed earlier in this chapter, the rhythms of prose poetry tend to have more variety and unpredictability than the rhythms of the metered and lineated verse that preceded them. Of course, this is not always because of prose poetry's origins in the city, but there is no doubt that some of the rhythms in prose poems come from the prose poet's sense of actually or imaginatively perambulating through urban spaces.

Indeed, poetry in general has often been connected to perambulation of one kind or another—and, in particular, metered verse has been compared to the rhythms associated with walking. Many poets have also attested to the usefulness of walking when composing verse or poetry. Famous examples from the Romantic period in England are William Wordsworth and Thomas De Quincey. De Quincey comments, "I have always found it easier to think over a matter of perplexity whilst walking in wide open spaces,"[80] and Françoise Dupeyron-Lafay credits him, flaneur-like, with "relocat[ing] the 'peripatetic' in a new spatial and social environment."[81]

De Quincey gives an entertaining firsthand account of Wordsworth's enjoyment of walking: "[H]is legs were pointedly condemned by all the female connoisseurs in legs that ever I heard lecture upon that topic . . . and undoubtedly they had been serviceable legs . . . [because] I calculate . . . Wordsworth must have traversed a distance of 175[,000] to 180,000 English miles—a mode of exertion which, to him, stood in the stead of wine, spirits, and all other stimulants whatsoever."[82]

Through walking, Wordsworth met many of the people whom he later used as subjects for his poetry. He also composed by a process of "bumming." One of Wordsworth's former gardeners was reported by Canon Hardwicke Drummond Rawnsley as saying, "[h]e would set his head a bit forrad, and put his hands behint his back. And then he would start a bumming, and it was bum, bum, bum, Stop; then bum, bum, bum, reet down till t'other end, and then he'd set down and git a bit o'paper out and write a bit."[83]

In other words, Wordsworth often composed poetry by walking back and forth and, as William Hazlitt recounts, he "always wrote (if he could) walking up and down a straight gravel-walk, or in some spot where the continuity of his verse met with no collateral interruption."[84] He wrote most often in iambic rhythms that are composed of two-syllable poetic "feet," each of which consists of an unstressed followed by a stressed syllable (although all poets vary the regularity of their stresses to add variety to their poetry). Of course, the word "feet" connects meter in poetry with walking and Marc Shell suggests, "It is as if poetry and prose had a cadence—in much the way that a walker's footfall or musician's foot-beat or foot-tap does."[85]

It is impossible to conclusively demonstrate that iambic rhythms in poetry ever correspond to the rhythms of a poet's walking, except to give an example so that readers may make up their own minds. Here are four lines of iambic pentameter from Wordsworth's famous poem "Lines Composed a Few Miles above Tintern Abbey":

> A motion and a spirit, that impels
> All thinking things, all objects of all thought,
> And rolls through all things. Therefore am I still
> A lover of the meadows and the woods[86]

This poetry is characteristic of Wordsworth's blank verse in that it mixes the rhythms of speech with the regular pulse or footfall of the iambic pentameter line. Wordsworth's poetic rhythms are certainly akin to the rhythms of a country rambler, even if the progress of language is never identical to the movement of a body in space and time.

In the nineteenth-century city new urban spaces created opportunities for new sorts of perambulation by poets and prose poets alike. Françoise Dupeyron-Lafay says of De Quincey's prose, "although he was a Romantic, the modalities of walking in his texts sowed the seeds of many modern urban *topoi*" and identifies "his pioneering (dis)figuration of the modern city as an enigmatic and alien mindscape."[87] An example from De Quincey's *Suspiria de Profundis* is his rhythmically beguiling evocation of the city, which "like a mighty galleon with all her apparel mounted, streamers flying, and tackling perfect, seems floating along the noiseless depths of ocean."[88]

City walking had more broken rhythms and many more disruptions than "walking up and down a straight gravel-walk."[89] Although it is impossible to analyze the rhythms of Baudelaire's prose poetry, or that of his French contemporaries, without recourse to the French language—something we will not attempt given that our focus is on the English-language prose poem—one may note that David Evans identifies Baudelaire's "poetic" technique as residing partly in its symbolic content, including its focus on the urban:

> Just as Baudelaire's later verse problematizes metrical rhythm, *Le Spleen de Paris* presents a revolutionary notion of form as a process rather than a product. This is articulated through two recurrent symbols of the prose poetic endeavour: the urban model and the clouds.[90]

Evans also states that "[i]f rhythm articulates the necessary aesthetic hierarchy by which the people who believe in Poetry . . . find certain structures more beautiful than others, it is imperative . . . [to] advance beyond the reductive verse/prose dichotomy."[91] This is to suggest that the rhythms of prose poetry are not necessarily deficient because they lack the recurrence of effects so often associated with lineated poetry, and they should be judged according to their own lights.

Santilli even compares Baudelaire's inspiration for the prose poetry in *Paris Spleen* to the kinds of influences that saw jazz invented:

> Baudelaire [in his preface to *Paris Spleen*] suggests that the innovation he seeks will be found inside music itself; a new prose that flows and convulses with

the new rhythms and disruptions of modern life. Such connection with the spontaneous expression of an individual will later be found in jazz music [including syncopation and swing in general and the jazz solo].[92]

Charles Fort's volume of prose poems, *Mrs. Belladonna's Supper Club Waltz* (2013), refers to such musical influences. The opening of his prose poem "Darvil and Black Eyed Peas on New Year's Eve" demonstrates how his prose poetic rhythms often flow and convulse:

> What kind of man, a wing-tipped drinker of Guinness stout and Laphroaig straight up, leapfrogged into his junkyard throne wearing a widower's cape, held a wooden staff with a serpent's head, its tongue dipped in blue salt?[93]

The appeal to jazz in a range of syncopations and improvisations is evident in the loose, free style. Its rhythm is somewhat reminiscent of Jean Toomer's hybrid book *Cane* (1923), evident in "Seventh Street." This is the first piece of the second section and, as Farah Jasmine Griffin notes, is "framed on either side by verse [and] . . . marked by an immediate change in rhythm, pace, and content. In this respect, it is like the urban blues."[94]

> Seventh Street is a bastard of Prohibition and the War. A crude-boned, soft-skinned wedge of nigger life breathing its loafer air, jazz songs and love, thrusting unconscious rhythms, black reddish blood into the white and whitewashed wood of Washington. Stale soggy wood of Washington. Wedges rust in soggy wood . . . Split it! In two! Again! Shred it! . . . the sun. Wedges are brilliant in the sun; ribbons of wet wood dry and blow away.[95]

Seventh Street was the main street in the African American neighborhood in Washington, and Toomer believed its "novelty was due to the unprecedented rhythms and aesthetics of the urban landscape determined by new technologies."[96] In a letter to Lola Ridge he stated, "I think my own contribution will curiously blend the rhythm of peasanty [sic] with the rhythm of machines. A syncopation, a slow jazz, a sharp intense motion, subtilized, fused to a terse lyricism."[97] Toomer's rhythms include the motion and sound of automobiles as an important part of the spontaneous rhythms of urban life. The prose poem form creates faster and more compressed repetitions, and encourages improvisation in a more quotidian form, than lineated poetry. As jazz "was largely the creation of black musicians working in New Orleans before the turn of the century,"[98] African American writers often appeal to jazz rhythms in an effort to give priority to improvisation and liberation. If prose poetry arose in nineteenth-century France as a form of resistance, it is also appropriate for exploring African American spiritual and social emancipation through jazz rhythms.

Like Toomer's prose poems, C. S. Giscombe's works are in "restless transit and constant motion, especially across lines of nation, race, and ethnicity."[99] He emphasizes intimacies of place and voice in his prose poems, writing in "Palaver": "Neighborhood? Proximities change on you sooner or later."[100] However, it is the opening line of "Far" that clearly demonstrates his use of syncopation and extended alliteration: "Inland suffers its foxes: full-moon fox, far-flung fox—flung him yonder! went the story—or some fox worn like a weasel round the neck."[101] The complex rhythm is reminiscent of jazz music and ragged time in spiritual music. These priorities of place, voice, and motion are combined in Giscombe's "Afro-Prairie" with its oft-quoted line "Tempting for the voice to locate its noise, to speak of or from."[102]

Benjamin R. Lempert suggests that "jazz has provided many African American poems the means for exploring and/or foregrounding their African Americanness," and Harryette Mullen, Harmony Holiday (both discussed at other junctures), Terrance Hayes, and Yusef Komunyakaa are contemporary African American poets who make use of music and rhythm in their prose poems as a way of expressing identity. One of Hayes's prose poems begins "I commit to vote in 2018 because a land governed by unkindness reaps no kindness."[103] It proceeds to use a series of repetitions of the phrases "I commit to vote" and "A land governed by" to create rhythm. Hayes also repeats a line from the Jimi Hendrix song "Machine Gun": "I pick up my axe & fight like a farmer" to foreground the importance of music in protest and, ultimately, resistance. Komunyakaa's poetry is steeped in a love of jazz and blues that resonates with a dual purpose: "to express racial iniquity and as a catharsis to heal the wounds which resulted from hatred and bigotry."[104] His sequence of prose poems entitled "Debriefing Ghosts"—about returning to Vietnam—uses syncopated rhythms. For example, in "The Deck" there is the movement of "this old, silly, wrong-footed dance," and "Ghost Video" presents "Two defeated soldiers—three arms and three legs—dressed in jungle fatigues."[105] These prose poems are haunted by absence, the specter of war, and, in their connection to jazz, can be read as expressing the blues through a series of narrative and imagist fragments.

An interest in the rhythms of prose may also be seen in considerably earlier English-language examples of prose poetry, particularly those from the early modernist period. Murphy states, "[t]he power of this fragmentary writing is tied to new sensations in the city and consequent anxieties, and even informs prose poems set elsewhere."[106] She quotes various examples from the prose poetry of Jessie Dismorr, who was also a visual artist. Dismorr's "June Night" includes the following sentences: "Towards the red glare of the illuminated city we race through interminable suburbs. These are the bare wings and corridors that give on to the stage. Swiftness at least is exquisite."[107]

One may immediately see that Dismorr's rhythms and imagery are influenced by the city, but they nevertheless remain the fairly conventional rhythms of a great deal of prose and are not closely connected to actual perambulation. "June Night" inhabits the uncomfortable ground between the short story and prose poem forms, and its conventionality is highlighted by the appearance of T. S. Eliot's thoroughly modernist free verse poems "Preludes" and "Rhapsody of a Windy Night" in the same issue of *BLAST* magazine that features Dismorr's work.[108] Her aesthetic preferences have barely been touched by the sensibilities of French symbolists such as Baudelaire or Rimbaud.

In general terms, early twentieth-century English-language prose poetry did not become rhythmically adventurous until considerably later in the twentieth century. However, there were some fine exceptions, such as in the experimental prose poetry of Gertrude Stein in *Tender Buttons* and some of Amy Lowell's sensuous prose poetry. Stein's famous "A Carafe, that is a Blind Glass" exploits what Christopher J. Knight refers to as "paratactic" techniques, which is to say she "places one thing next to another without forging a hierarchy of value."[109] She also makes good use of disruptive rhythms, signaling to the reader hers is no ordinary species of prose:

> A kind in glass and a cousin, a spectacle and nothing strange a single hurt color and an arrangement in a system to pointing. All this and not ordinary, not unordered in not resembling. The difference is spreading.[110]

Amy Lowell's prose poetry is conscious of the diverse rhythmic resources of prose, nicely exemplified in her sequence "Spring Day" (1916).[111] This consists of five separate works entitled "Bath," "Breakfast Table," "Walk," "Midday and Afternoon," and "Night and Sleep." Here one finds dancing sunshine ("Little spots of sunshine lie on the surface of the water and dance, dance, and their reflections wobble deliciously over the ceiling; a stir of my finger sets them whirring, reeling"); shouting butter-pats ("A stack of butter-pats, pyramidal, shout orange through the white, scream, flutter, call: 'Yellow! Yellow! Yellow!'"); the urban ("Swirl of crowded streets. Shock and recoil of traffic" and "Electric signs gleam out along the shop fronts"); and walkers ("a girl with a gay Spring hat and blowing skirts . . . Tap, tap, the little heels pat the pavement" and "I am a piece of the town, a bit of blown dust, thrust along with the crowd. Proud to feel the pavement under me, reeling with feet").[112]

Such writing—perambulating, cadenced, sometimes staccato, occasionally hypnotic, and frequently dramatic—reminds us of Dorothy Richardson Jones's remark that the critic George Saintsbury "more than once refers to prosody as akin to dancing and also says he did much of his thinking about prosody while walking."[113] Lowell's walking is very different from Wordsworth's, as it moves with a modernist urban sensibility—a sensibility not unlike that of some of the postimpressionist painters. In such work prose poetry begins to come into its own as a poetic form.

A mid-twentieth-century prose poem, "The Unremitting Stain" by Holly Beye, also uses prose for conspicuously poetic purposes, albeit with mixed success. It begins:

> Does your blood run cold at this thought: that you, standing knee-deep in that eighteen years' October night, with your kisses on the stranger's mouth teaching fire to the stars, now O destroyed dear curled-leaf girl, like wintered grasses hilltop the barren winds . . .[114]

Late twentieth and twenty-first-century prose poets employ rhythm in all sorts of ways, uninhibited by the conventions of lineated poetry, whether in meter or free verse. In such works, prose poetry has a rhythmic life that belongs, inimitably, only to the prose poetry form. Here is the beginning of Roo Borson's "City," which registers rushes and shocks in its mixed rhythms, as well as through its diverse images of the city's overall illegibility ("mirrors trying to come clear") and its remnant "clues" of unreadable incidents:

> Rushes of silver light. A little wind plays by itself in the corner of the plaza with whatever it can find: a lost leaf, a bit of wrapper. Tall shocks of light from the buildings which are only mirrors trying to come clear. A gull, squawking, dips around the Royal Bank tower. Here and there the bombed-out look of bare structure: steel waiting for glass. Only the clues. A pair of trousers stuffed into a hedge, no explanations. A single shoe overturned on Yonge Street, passed back and forth all night by the wheels of opposing cars, now left alone in the morning light, pointing north.[115]

Keith Ekiss's "Into the City" is cognizant of prose poetry's appeal to the fragment and the Romantic ruin, both in its use of vocabulary such as "fracture," "vestiges," and "ruins," and in its use of punctuation, which produces halted and broken rhythms:

> A history written in brick and fracture. All around you were vestiges: ornate colonnades, statues of soldiers, streets minted with the names of robber barons, a dome rusted to the color of the dollar. Once the city shook and burned. Now it seemed the citizens were in ruins: pink facade of the hospital through mist, the sick with views of the ocean and bridge.[116]

Many other twenty-first-century prose poems do not explicitly refer to walking or the city but are important for their appeal to a kind of rhythmic wandering. For example, in Yasmin Belkhyr's "Interlude with Drug of Choice," the rhythmic jerkiness functions to interrupt the poem's continuities and convey a sense of opacity in the face of trauma:

> Angie thinks river. Thinks swollen rock. Thinks Tom, mouth sore. Thinks light, spilled and leaking. Angie thinks pills, spark, click. Huck and his foxhole. Huck and all his shred. Angie doesn't think dead boy. Live boy. Angie thinks mountain, clouds of heavy paint. Fist of slow. Angie thinks fish, frozen. Eyes sliced and craving. Winter of burnt tongue. Winter of weave.[117]

Louise Wallace's "Ahakoa he iti he pounamu | Although it is small it is greenstone" (2017) is also quintessentially prose poetic in its rhythmic life, simultaneously staccato and lyrical in evoking the difficulties of loss and memory:

> I choose pounamu / it is a river stone / she was of the earth / she was orchids in the hothouse / less difficult than her husband / fruit trees / their hard graft / plums / nectarines / a child we never spoke of / another a castaway / I choose to plant my legs / to ground them / I am the child of which we won't speak / I am the castaway / I am orchids / fruit trees / I can bear more than you think / I am a river stone / and I choose a ring made of pounamu / to remind me[118]

Erika Meitner's "A Brief Ontological Investigation" (2018) is also about flowing phrases and sentences, and a kind of rhythmic recurrence (very different from the recurrent patterns of verse), which even a short excerpt reveals:

> ... I mean, we all overflow; we all feel an abundance of something but sometimes it's just emptiness: vacant page, busy signal, radio static, implacable repeat rut where the tone arm reaches across a spinning vinyl record to play it again, rest its delicate needle in a groove and caress forever the same sound from the same body.[119]

These last few examples do not all demonstrate a rhythm that is allied to walking, but each work shows how the prose poetry sentence has become a form of perambulation in itself, as poets follow the form and shape of their works, with greater or lesser fluency, and with purpose, taking the reader on imaginative journeys.

As we mentioned above, C. Bruna Mancini writes, "the urban text(ure) gives birth to powerful and inseparable 'doubles' of itself,"[120] and we would add that by the twenty-first century, the urban language of the prose poem had given birth to powerful and inseparable doubles of contemporary experience in general. Andrew Estes contends:

> Postmodern walking returns the act to the city. The luminous connection with place [of the Romantics] however is lost. What one has instead is an ever-shifting landscape of signs without referents. This is not a uniquely negative experience, because, although one cannot find oneself in Romantic nature, one is free to construct identities out of a myriad of texts.[121]

The identities in the texts of contemporary prose poetry move in many directions, and with all sorts of rhythms. The prose poem now often consists of the urban voice speaking of every kind of experience it can imagine as it takes the reader to the strange places the city dweller knows or imagines. Sometimes these are journeys to the fantastical and the "hyperreal" (the hyperreal, the surreal, and the urban often go hand in hand), and sometimes these are recollections of what the city has obliterated. Baudelaire and Whitman, in making poetry that exploited the rhythms of contemporary prose, were also making a new poetry of urban spaces. The effects of their separate experiments in radicalizing the poetic are still coming into being, most conspicuously through the contemporary prose poem in all of its intrinsically peripatetic and perambulatory rhythmic life.

PART 2

෮

AGAINST CONVENTION

CHAPTER 4

Ideas of Open Form and Closure in Prose Poetry

Poetry: Open and Closed

Traditional lyric poetry tends to emphasize resolution, however momentary the emotion or circumstance it conjures. A Shakespearean sonnet, for example, follows its formalities toward closure:

> Shall I compare thee to a summer's day?
> Thou art more lovely and more temperate:
> Rough winds do shake the darling buds of May,
> And summer's lease hath all too short a date:
> Sometime too hot the eye of heaven shines,
> And often is his gold complexion dimmed;
> And every fair from fair sometime declines,
> By chance, or nature's changing course, untrimmed:
> But thy eternal summer shall not fade,
> Nor lose possession of that fair thou ow'st,
> Nor shall death brag thou wander'st in his shade
> When in eternal lines to time thou grow'st:
>   So long as men can breathe or eyes can see,
>   So long lives this, and this gives life to thee.[1]

The form of this famous poem is partly its point. To a considerable extent, Shakespeare's skill is demonstrated in the way in which he is able to give his poem a sense of being finished. Many lineated lyric poems are, to a significant extent, formally completed or closed, and the reading experience is partly a matter of becoming acquainted with what a poem says is the case or claims to have happened. We would note with Barbara Herrnstein Smith (1968) that where lineated lyric poems are concerned, "it may be that we acknowledge a poem as whole or complete when . . . we experience at its conclusion the sense of closure."[2]

However, despite the powerful sense of closure conveyed by many poems, in another sense, poetry tends to be an open form. This is because of the high level of suggestiveness of numerous verse or free verse poems, whose meanings are more expansive than any single interpretation of them may provide. They often seem protean, too, in that they frequently acquire new meanings with new generations of readers. We do not, for example, read Shakespeare's sonnets in exactly the way that Shakespeare's contemporaries read them. We bring new assumptions about humanity and society to our readings of these works and, in any case, some of the language Shakespeare used has altered in meaning—often in fundamental ways. When he writes "gentle" in the line "Gentle thou art" in Sonnet 41,[3] we have largely lost one of the word's primary meanings. It used to signify possession of "the qualities appropriate to a gentleman . . . align[ed] . . . with a particular status and rank in society."[4]

Yet, notwithstanding their shifting meanings and protean suggestiveness, Smith observes that formally constructed poems that make use of meter and other formal poetic devices tend to be "framed," much like a painting, and thus are separated "from a 'ground' of less highly structured speech and sound."[5] As a result, while lineated lyric poetry is typically highly suggestive and *open* to various interpretations, it simultaneously tends toward conveying the sense of formal resolution and the *closure* we have mentioned.

The attention to formal elements in lineated lyric poetry, including the beginnings and endings of lines and the opening and closing of works, is very different from other kinds of less formalized writing—including prose poetry, where sentences are drawn together in paragraphs rather than separated. Prose poetry refuses lineated poetry's rhythmic closure even as it visually preempts its conclusion in the capacious white space that follows the last sentence of the paragraph. Mary Ann Caws argues that "in the prose poem, the final framing edge is of especial importance, acting retrospectively to construct or deconstruct what has been built."[6]

Smith also makes a distinction between the "integrity" of a poetic utterance, involving "the sense of internal coherence and distinct identity," and the sense of "*completeness*."[7] She points out, "Even a poetic fragment has coherence and a distinct identity . . . [but] [i]t will not, however, have closure."[8] For Smith, this is a highly significant issue, because, she suggests, "closure is often strengthened by convention: the reader's sense of finality will be reinforced by the appearance, at the conclusion of a poem, of certain formal and thematic elements."[9]

In other words, openness and closure are likely to be manifested very differently in lineated poems compared to prose poems. The sense of openness that is a feature of most prose poems is connected to the fragmentary nature of the prose poetry form. Prose poems have their own integrity as works, but their sense of completeness turns on their appeal to incompleteness in the same way as the literary fragment. Structurally, prose poetry's use of the sentence rather than the line as its unit of composition allows the poet to engage in "narrative digression," which Stephen Fredman identifies as "a natural counterpart to the generative sentence, where . . . grammar leads the writing through a succession of ideas, resisting the gravitational pull of the 'complete thought.'"[10] In this way, the prose poem progresses in ways that are not always linear, often giving priority to divergence over denouement.

In *The Party Train: A Collection of North American Prose Poetry* (1996), Alexander points out that Ginsberg published "The Bricklayer's Lunch Hour" as both a lineated poem and a prose poem. In the book *Empty Mirror: Early Poems* (1961), it is published as a free verse work ending with the lines:

> . . . A small cat walks to him
> along the top of the wall. He picks
> it up, takes off his cap, and puts it
> over the kitten's body for a moment.
> Meanwhile it is darkening as if to rain
> and the wind on top of the trees in the
> street comes through almost harshly.[11]

In Charles Henri Ford's "A Little Anthology of the Poem in Prose" (1953), it is published as a prose poem:

> . . . A small cat walks to him along the top of the wall. He picks it up, takes off his cap, and puts it over the kitten's body for a moment to try it out. Meanwhile it is darkening as if to rain.[12]

Significantly, when Ginsberg rewrote the lineated poem as a prose poem, he "left it largely unchanged, except for deleting the final clause,"[13] opening the poem up to greater suggestiveness. This intervention on Ginsberg's part may support the idea that prose poetry often functions by eschewing closure and opening possibilities for writer and reader alike. It also makes the point that some free verse functions as a kind of proto-prose poetry, making use of prosaic rhythms largely driven by the structure and rhythms of sentences.

Lyn Hejinian discusses the idea of "open text" in her essay "The Rejection of Closure," emphasizing how expectations connected to language and power structures relate to the act of writing:

> The writer relinquishes total control and challenges authority as a principle and control as a motive. The "open text" often emphasizes or foregrounds process, either the process of the original composition or of subsequent compositions by readers, and thus resists the cultural tendencies that seek to identify and fix material and turn it into a product; that is, it resists reduction and commodification.[14]

In this way, Hejinian prefers texts that are open to multiple meanings, discussing the way the reader moves into the gaps and spaces of interpretation. Later, she revised and extended some of her ideas in "Continuing Against Closure," where she advocates for writing on the margin:

> [S]till arguing my case against closure, I can speak in favor of the border, which I would characterize not as a circumscribing margin but as the middle—the intermediary, even interstitial zone that lies between any one country or culture and another, and between any one thing and another.[15]

A language poet, Hejinian favors using a disjunctive and fragmented approach to disrupt meaning. Her major work, *My Life and My Life in the Nineties* (2013), which we discuss in chapter 9, was revised three times over a twenty-year period. The appeal to the "border" is perhaps best achieved in a form like prose poetry, which is so often defined by its rectangularity. However, Hejinian experiments with form, extending the prose poem into experimental poetic prose. *My Life and My Life in the Nineties* also demonstrates that just because a text has been published doesn't mean it is "closed"; it can be revised and changed over time. Marvin Richards similarly critiques the idea of closure by focusing on the importance of play:

> Closure is achieved only when the multiple possibilities of meaning are reduced to fit into a critic's grid of interpretation by which all "play"—the opposite of closure—is eliminated, or at least mastered in a dialectical synthesis that gives the "true" meaning of the poem.[16]

Linda Black's illustrated prose poetry sequence, *The Son of a Shoemaker* (2012), embodies this idea of play, comprised as it is of eighteen found prose poems collaged from Constance Buel Burnett's 1943 semifictional biography of Hans Christian Andersen. Based on a form like biography, which tends to be linear and make a direct appeal to closure, Black's sequence avoids linearity and instead prioritizes play, juxtaposition, and inversions. An example is "The Most Exciting Beliefs Could Be Written in Verse," which begins:

> A long blue reflection moved almost unnoticed. Impecunious and with tails. Mumbled incredulously into a piece of cake. More perplexing than any riddle of state he had never had to solve. Burning tapers cracked their whips. On trays in an upstairs room.[17]

Black supports the idea that the prose poetry form "allows for an ending that isn't an ending . . . as in etching I'd want an image, fine detail, but also degrees of dark or shade with less definition, something implied, unseen, reverberating in the shadows."[18] Her writing opens up numerous possibilities and is an excellent example of how the prose poem is closed (often boxlike) while simultaneously resisting closure, opening itself to the space of suggestion and indeterminacy. As Akane Kawakami states, "the prose poem is more interested in processes than conclusions—in open-ended [and] possible readings."[19]

The Prose Poetry "Box" and Visual Containment

Prose poetry is often identifiable by its rectangular or boxlike shape. Whether one or both margins are justified, it is visually contained in a way that lineated poetry is not. This is because prose poems are composed of sentences rather than lines, which usually extend to—and wrap at—the right margin. It is difficult to find a discussion of prose poetry without some reference to its visual appearance: Alexander Long refers to Kathleen McGookey's prose poems as "compact boxes of words," and Jane Monson identifies prose poetry as a "peculiar paragraphed discipline."[20]

Using its shape as a springboard, scholars have likened prose poems to objects such as the postcard, envelope, room on a floor plan, and frame. Louis Jenkins even characterizes the prose poem as a minimalist suitcase that allows the reader to take flight: "Think of the prose poem as a box . . . the box is made for travel, quick and light. Think of the prose poem as a small suitcase. One must pack carefully, only the essentials, too much and the reader won't get off the ground."[21] It is this flexibility of form that has inspired Gerry LaFemina to comment on its expansiveness and its ability to morph into a variety of different rectangular things: "[T]he prose poem for all its boxiness, can be anything. Think of the rectangles in your life: The midway booth where you shoot water into clown mouths, the bed you dream in, the gift-wrapped box."[22]

Significantly, the prose poetry "box" is often imagined as something quotidian, identifying the prose poem as utilitarian and accessible. Charles Simic's use of this boxlike shape in his book of prose poetry *Dime-Story Alchemy: The Art of Joseph Cornell* (1992) connects to Cornell's construction of rectangular shadow boxes containing "disparate bits and bobs, such as clay tobacco pipes, corks, marbles and postage stamps."[23] Simic writes that he was prompted to "do something like that myself as a poet," and the accumulation and placement of found objects in his work "result[s] in fantastic poetic dioramas."[24] In this way, the prose poetry box is as much about what is inside the box as it is about the box itself and what is external to it.

Luke Kennard also plays with this concept in "Book II, Anagrams" in *Cain: Poems*, where a box of black text is framed by a box of red text. In combination, these forms help to reimagine Genesis 4:9–12 and the figure of Cain. Alison Strub uses two parallel boxes on each page in *Lillian, Fred* (2016) to juxtapose the dialogue of the two eponymous characters. The prose poems voiced by Lillian privilege Fred's narrative as they all begin with the line "Fred says my dream," while those voiced by Fred begin with a question to Lillian. Strub uses these techniques to claim a space for Lillian and yet simultaneously undermine it, making a powerful statement about women being silenced even when they are given room to speak. In her book *Flèche* (2019), Mary Jean Chan uses the prose poem form in a variety of rich and textured ways to explore identity and lived experience. Two poems, "Safe Space (I)" and "Safe Space (II)," are perfect squares of text on the page that both conceal and expose. Presented as important interstitial spaces, the first prose poem is set in a closet and the second in the bathroom. Both are retreats for the narrator, who is comforted by the protection they offer from external forces.

The prose poem has been identified as both confining and liberating in the way it presses text into its frame, while simultaneously bursting from its margins to reach outside itself. Holly Iglesias's *Boxing Inside the Box: Women's Prose Poetry* (2004) politicizes this aspect of prose poetry by arguing that "women articulat[e] the constraints of gender in prose poems, battling against confinement, boxing inside the box."[25] Iglesias puts the box under pressure by linking it to a "pressure cooker," and also reclaims the derogatory slang term "box," used for women's genitalia:

> It speaks from inside a box of text of the confinement of gender construction. It uses the box as a pressure cooker, sand box, sanctuary, laboratory, dungeon, treasure chest, fleshing out a sensibility of grief and mischief, terror and outrage, menace and joy, sabotage and restoration.[26]

In Iglesias's quotation, the prose poem's complexity comes from its concurrent identification as "dungeon" and "sanctuary," demonstrating the prose poem's ability to house varying and sometimes tautologous or seemingly contradictory impulses. It has the ability to encompass big and small, or—if we concentrate on the visual—big within small.

Abigail Beckel and Kathleen Rooney also make this point when they argue, "Prose poems are little boxes that contain big things. Or small things that mean big things. Or small things that mean small things."[27] If prose poems are seen visually as one (or sometimes more than one) relatively small paragraph, then it is through their implications, figurative suggestiveness, and gaps and spaces that they are able to extend outward. When Beckel and Rooney liken prose poems to "Blocks, patches, scraps, chunks, fragments,"[28] they extend this idea, acknowledging the prose poem's connection to the fragmentary in many of its forms.

Prose poems can be simultaneously small and large. Nikki Santilli writes in the preface to *This Line Is Not For Turning: An Anthology of Contemporary British Prose Poetry* (2011) that the "prose poem form oscillates constantly between what it expresses (presses out) from its miniature physical form and the wider worlds to which it gestures, beyond its own edges."[29] While this is not to suggest all prose poems may be construed as boxes, such a comparison highlights the compressed form of the prose poem, composed of relatively few sentences. This is very different indeed from lineated poetry, the writing of which requires the poet to decide where to stop each line. Carrie Etter argues, "[t]his means that instead of looking at a poem's line and stanza lengths' contribution to structure, [in prose poetry] we consider sentence and paragraph lengths as well as sentence types."[30] The prose poem may be a condensed form, but its sentences sometimes stretch in ways that are rare in lines of lineated poetry.

To shift the metaphor for a moment, although the prose poem's main unit is most often identified as a paragraph rather than a stanza, Robert Miltner combines both terms. In discussing his book *Hotel Utopia* (2011), he likens his prose poems to a hotel in which "each prose poem box is a different room" and calls the prose poem paragraph a stanzagraph, "a break in the box negotiated between what a paragraph does in prose and a stanza does in poetry."[31] While "stanzagraph" is a term that has yet to catch on, it makes the point that the prose poetry paragraph and the poetic stanza are similar in being—metaphorically speaking—somewhat like rooms. This is not a new discovery, and most recently, this comparison of prose poetry with houses, blueprints, dwellings, or rooms has been explored by Nikki Wallschlaeger in *Houses* (2015), where colored houses—notably the iconic "White House"—expose the nature of race relations in America. Amelia Martens's *Purgatory* (2012) is a tour through a sequence of rooms containing uncanny reflections of suffering, and Ian Seed's *New York Hotel* (2018) references a kind of neo-surrealist Chelsea Hotel, turning on an appeal to dreamy outsiders and those characters trapped by their encounters with others, or by their isolation.

This comparison between prose poems and houses draws attention to the similarity between the prose poem's rectangular shape on the page and the act of looking from above at a room's plan. In this way, prose poems may be viewed as contained and restrictive "rooms" that "contain," and are able to release, significant effects related to condensed language, poetic imagery, "open" linguistic spaces, and a ramifying suggestiveness. Just as one enters a particular room within a house, prose poems inhabit spaces that begin where there is no obvious beginning, and they conclude without necessarily representing an end.

Prose poems often open questions and scenarios, creating tropes of indeterminacy and ambiguity, where the structure and patterning of the kind employed by many lineated lyric poems is absent, where narrative gestures are partial and fragmentary, and where the condensations of poetry are able to flow naturally within paragraphs rather than being constrained by the truncations of poetic lineation. Imaginative tropes, allusions, and suggestive possibilities are coaxed into unusual, sometimes reactive proximities and, as a result, prose poems frequently open up, TARDIS-like, to reveal much more than their size on the page would appear to allow. A successful prose poem's combined suggestive power may far exceed the individual suggestiveness of any of its parts.

Prose Poetry, Seduction, and the Right Margin

Scholars and poets are quick to point out the importance of prose poetry's visual cues. For instance, Margueritte Murphy, Jonathan Monroe, and Robert Alexander point to prose poetry's subversion in the way it destabilizes readers' expectations by preparing them to accept a story or nonfiction paragraph rather than a poem. As Murphy states, "each prose poem must suggest a traditional prose genre to some extent in order to subvert it. The prose poem, then, may be seen as a battlefield where conventional prose of some sort appears and is defeated by the text's drive to innovate and to differentiate itself, to construct a self-defining 'poeticity' (a term in itself problematized by the prose poem)."[32] Similarly, Edson argues: "Superficially a prose poem should look somewhat like a page from a child's primer, indented paragraph beginnings, justified margins. In other words, the prose poem should not announce that it is a special prose; if it is, the reader will know it. The idea is to get away from obvious ornament, and the obligations implied therein. Let those who play tennis play their tennis."[33]

When a reader approaches a prose poem, the right- and left-justified form prepares them for the paragraph rather than the stanza. Alexander discusses the relationship of the sentence and paragraph to the quotidian:

> When we open a book, we approach the piece of writing in the context of our knowledge of literature. This knowledge serves as the frame within which we see the particular book we're reading . . . The impulse of prose, it seems to me, is to tell a story—a story grounded in the real world—and this is true whether we are reading a newspaper, a letter, a biography, or a novel. Prose can therefore speak of everyday experience in ways difficult if not impossible for free verse.[34]

In other words, the prose poem's containment within one or more paragraphs—something readers immediately register as a visual cue—promises a contained, reasonably complete, and narrative-driven rendering of experience, yet delivers, instead, a fragmented narrative replete with metaphorical gaps and spaces. A. E. Stallings's sequence "Battle of Plataea: Aftermath," in her book of poetry *Like* (2018), plays on these visual cues. Composed of five fully justified paragraphs with subheadings such as "Lampon the Aegeinite," the poem could initially be mistaken for history or entries in an encyclopedia. However, the poetic circling and use of metaphor and imagery clearly expose it as a sequence of prose poems.

Additionally, the prose poem's usual brevity is at odds with conventional expectations attached to the reading of prose and, as a result, the reader is left wondering: "What happens next?," "Where is the rest of this narrative?," and "What comes after the final line?" Thomas Shapcott argues that the form of the prose poem undermines a wide range of expectations:

> Very often the "poetic" part of the prose poem is expressed through an appeal to illogic: to states of receptivity which deny what we have come to expect prose to offer—that is, rational discourse, descriptive clarity, even rhetoric in its conventional sense of persuasion, of using language to set certain cogs in

motion. The prose poem creates its lyrical frisson by pointing the reader's anticipatory glands in that direction, and then somehow working a change.[35]

It is for these reasons the prose poem may be said to be both complete and endlessly searching for completeness or resolution. As a form, it is always in the state of becoming.

In James Tate's terms, the prose poem's apparent approachability becomes a "means of seduction": "For one thing, the deceptively simple packaging: the paragraph. People generally do not run for cover when they are confronted with a paragraph or two. The paragraph says to them: I won't take much of your time, and, if you don't mind me saying so, I am not known to be arcane, obtuse, precious or high-fallutin'. Come on in."[36]

If poetry is "high-fallutin'" and prose is unassuming, many prose poets have discussed the ways in which this can work in their favor, garnering a readership that may be suspicious of lineated poetry. Kathleen McGookey is one such writer, claiming that a "reader could pick up one of my prose poems and not realize she should be on guard. By the time she realizes it isn't an interview with Princess Fergie in *The Ladies' Home Journal*, I hope she's hooked."[37] Similarly, Iglesias writes: "That uncanny, boxy shape invites compression and difficulty and mayhem because it is a tight container and because it defies the reader's expectations of what a poem is. Instead of the lovely curvature of lineated verse, a prose poem asserts the value of the mundane—of objects and people and language itself under pressure. In addition, they are evocative objects themselves, recalling postcards, snapshots, to-do lists, diary entries."[38]

However, there are poets and scholars who find prose poetry's visual connection to prose charmless, and who are not seduced by the form. Thomas Larson believes that the prose poem's visual attributes are deceptive:

[T]he prose poem is blocky, spatially inelegant, print-dependent, unmetered, and unsyllabic. The prose poem is an inland sea, bordering continents; it is a poem become a paragraph, the apotheosis of free verse, the incantation of poetic diction flattened by sentences. Why does the poet need prose? What's wrong with verse? . . . What happens when a poem's vestigial calling is abandoned or disenjambed?[39]

Larson argues that prose poetry ruptures poetry's lineation in ineffective ways, and whether they are invested in prose poetry or not, this emphasis on the line (as opposed to the sentence) is what many poets and scholars use to distinguish traditional lyric poetry from prose poetry. However, such a distinction is not as straightforward as it may appear. While "disenjambment" and a lack of line breaks is certainly one of the features of prose poetry, Hadara Bar-Nadav's "Who Is Flying This Plane? The Prose Poem and the Life of the Line" (2011) refers to the box shape of the prose poem as "cagey" and comments that its "inherent tension" stems from "the mission of its line to continue on forever (despite the margin) and to be turned (because of the margin)."[40]

In this context it is worth mentioning Richard Price's prose poem "Hedge Sparrows" (2005), which is composed of a single continuous sentence and formatted as a fully justified block of text, beginning: "You don't see many hedges these days, and the hedges you do see they're not that thorny, it's a shame."[41] While the publication of this prose poem online would technically allow it to be reproduced as one long, continuous line—something that would be impossible in traditional publishing on the page—the paragraph allows for a series of juxtapositions that would be lost in a single, unbroken line. For example, the repetition of the word "hedges" is more noticeable and powerful when visually reinforced within the text block—and even the use of the word "hedgerow" suggests the poet was experimenting with borders, which would become irrelevant if the line went "on forever" and ignored the right margin.

This indicates that the parallel sentences that comprise most prose poems are an important feature of their composition, not just in the way they form a box or rectangle but because of the effects of juxtaposition and parallelism in sentences—or what one may broadly call contiguity. In this way, the margin matters to the prose poet, even as "they write both through and against the margin, even as it is arbitrarily assigned."[42] The right margin creates friction between the visual containment of the sentence and its desire for liberation. It pushes a reader's eye back across a prose poem and draws attention to what the prose poem paragraph holds as a whole.

The question then becomes whether the prose poem is indeed "disenjambed," or if it simply has a different relationship to the line and margin compared to the lineated poem. Bar-Nadav understands that prose poems have an important relationship with the right margin, but one that is often discretionary because it is driven by a publication's style: "Rather than consider the prose poem a poetic form or genre without line-breaks, I would argue that the prose poem indeed contains line-breaks that are given over to chance operations and the margins established by a particular writer, journal, or publisher, or those set by or on a computer, typewriter, or printing press."[43]

This is of particular interest, as the majority of lineated poems, and even experimental poems, are often faithfully reproduced in print and online publications. When the line finishes prior to the right margin, or words are scattered across the page in the original composition, print and online publications aim to replicate this. However, across a wide range of publications, the prose poem is rarely reproduced in exactly the same way. As a result, it may seem that where a prose poem's sentences turn at the right margin is unimportant. In prose poems, there is usually no mandated end of line to protect and reproduce (we discuss this further in chapter 10).

Of course, in some cases prose poems are crafted specifically to reduce the left and/or right margin. This may be seen in the tapered prose poems in Claudia Rankine's *Citizen: An American Lyric* (which function as a metaphor for what she sees as the narrow-mindedness of some Americans). It is also evident in Cassandra Atherton's "Rapunzel," which aims to replicate Rapunzel's long hair in a prose poem produced as a slender column; Charlotte Eichler's "The Coffin Calendars," shaped like a casket; Lily Hoang's *Changing* (2008), with its calligraphic use of hexagrams to write a new translation of the "I Ching"; Theo Hummer's "Moravia: Postcards,"[44] where two squares of prose poetry sit side by side and form rectangles reminiscent of postcards; and Gavin Selerie's "Casement," which leaves a white rectangle in the middle of the prose poem to approximate framed window glass.[45]

These prose poems could be considered hybrid concrete prose poems. Indeed, as the prose poem form often appears as a box shape on the page or screen due to its manipulation of white space and text, there is a visual connection to the concrete or shape poem that has a long history dating back to antiquity, including to Greek Alexandria in the third century BC, where poems took the shape of objects they were written on. The term "concrete poetry" was used in 1908 by Ernest Fenollosa and revived by, among others, Max Bill and Öyvind Fahlström in the 1950s, and was taken up and elaborated in the writings and activities of the Noigandres group. Guillaume Apollinaire's *Calligrammes: Poems of Peace and War (1913–1916)* (1918) is an important early example of this form of writing.[46]

The shape poem became more ideogrammatic in the hands of poets such as E. E. Cummings and Ezra Pound, but it is John Hollander who is perhaps most famous for his patterned poems. His book *Types of Shape* (1969; expanded edition 1991) includes a range of shape verse, including the famous "Swan and Shadow" where the outline of the swan and its reflection on water demonstrate how the concrete poem becomes visual art. While the prose poem, when it appears as a relatively neat box on the page, could be seen to connect to the tradition of the concrete poem, it is only when the margins have been reduced or increased to create a specific box or rectangular shape, or when the poet plays typographically with a specific box shape to create a synergy between it and the subject matter, that the prose poem can be considered concrete. In such cases, as with the prose poems listed above, Bar-Nadav's arguments about the poet's relative loss of control over the published prose poem's final appearance is especially pertinent. If a publication has even slightly wider or thinner margins than the original prose poem, the place where the sentence wraps at the right margin may shift, sometimes significantly altering the effect of the work.

The anthology *Great American Prose Poems: From Poe to the Present* (2003), edited by David Lehman, fully justifies all the prose poems to the same margins—even where prose poems were originally published with a ragged right margin—and in many cases the sentences have shifted. For example, all of Simic's prose poems in *The World Doesn't End* (1989) have an unjustified right margin, but his prose poems from that volume in Lehman's anthology are fully justified. His well-known prose poem "We Were So Poor" also has very different breaks at the right margin. When originally published, the prose poem opened as follows:

> We were so poor I had to take the place of the
> bait in the mousetrap. All alone in the cellar, I
> could hear them pacing upstairs, tossing and turn-
> ing in their beds.[47]

In Lehman's anthology, it appears in the following form:

> We were so poor I had to take the place of the bait in the mouse-
> trap. All alone in the cellar, I could hear them pacing upstairs, tossing
> and turning in their beds.[48]

Interestingly, in Simic's *New and Selected Poems, 1962–2012* (2013), the work is again formatted differently:

> We were so poor I had to take the place of the bait in the
> mousetrap. All alone in the cellar, I could hear them pacing
> upstairs, tossing and turning in their beds.[49]

This prose poem can also be found in different forms on the internet.

Whether such variations in the formatting of prose poetry matters depends on the attitudes of authors and readers. Some authors will care, and some readers will prefer one version over others. For instance, we prefer the first iteration of Simic's work above because of the way it pushes the syntactical units of this very short poem down the page, making it appear denser and more urgent.

The growing sophistication of online publishing already allows most websites to reproduce prose poems as originally published—although sometimes it requires additional work to do so—but it remains to be seen whether prose poets will become more involved in this issue (some are already involved; the majority do not seem to mind very much how their prose poems are reproduced). If they do begin to care more, then the right margin in prose poems will become even more important than it already is.

Contemporary Reinventions of the Haibun and Other Prose Poetry Varieties

In discussing issues of camouflage and the right margin, it is also important to examine whether prose poems may take a form similar to lineated poems. In other words, can prose poetry—usually expressed in sentences—be structured in a way that incorporates line breaks? Lineated prose poems are certainly not a common occurrence, but John Kinsella has identified W. G. Sebald's *After Nature* (2011) as a "lineated 'prose poem,'"[50] and some of Rimbaud's poetry has also been labeled in the same way, provoking Clive Scott to ask of Vincent O'Sullivan's "Nights of Dreaming," "Is this a lineated prose poem *à la* Rimbaud?"[51] To further complicate this discussion, René Char's "Companions in the Garden" (1959) might also be considered a lineated prose poem because of the way Char deliberately chooses to place sentences on different lines rather than running the sentences one after another within a more traditional prose poetry block of text.

If contemporary prose poetry began, in part, as a liberation from the strict French Alexandrine in the nineteenth century, in the twenty-first century a lot of contemporary prose poetry is exploring ways of challenging prose poetry's fairly ubiquitous box shape. This is occurring in two main ways. First, it is evident in prose poems that blur the boundaries between, or combine, prose poetry and lineated poetry. Second, it may be seen in works that challenge the traditional length of the prose poem (usually considered to be no more than about a page). Such works either connect prose poems in a long narrative or are labeled book-length prose poems—or prose poetry novels (we explore these approaches in chapter 10).

Such challenges to the prose poem "box" are not new; as we have pointed out, prose poetry is not always formatted as a rectangular box, in any case, and the option of pairing it with other forms goes back to the haibun tradition in Japan. Indeed, prose poetry has enduring links with Japanese poetry. Dennis Keene points out that "it is arguable that the poem in prose in some form has a much longer history in Japanese than it has in French."[52] The haibun has been defined as "a prose poem that contains one or more haiku" (an early and influential very short Japanese poetic form).[53]

Prose poets Robert Bly and Luke Kennard have helped define and theorize the haiku and haibun forms for English-language readers—and Bly is known for his work of translating haiku, which has had a significant influence on his own poetry. For example, he expanded the number of prose poems originally published in two chapbooks—*The Morning Glory* (1970) and *Point Reyes Poems* (1974)—for his 1975 collection, also called *The Morning Glory*. He uses one of Bashō's haikus in translation as an introduction to this book:

The morning glory—
another thing
that will never be my friend.[54]

Some contemporary prose poets reflect on traditional Japanese forms of poetry and reimagine postmodern versions of them. Kennard identifies this in John Ash's poetry, "in particular his technique of inverting his standard poetic voice within his travelogue prose poems. This is traced back to Bashō's 16th century travelogues, as self-conscious and self-referential as anything which is today classed as postmodern."[55]

Also, Anne Waldman's book *Marriage: A Sentence* (2000) is based on the haibun, as is Steve Myers's "Haibun for Smoke and Fog" (2007) and Ocean Vuong's "Immigrant Haibun" in *Night Sky with Exit Wounds* (2016), demonstrating the different but complementary approaches to the sentence, and the right margin, that may be employed by the haibun and the prose poem.

Aimee Nezhukumatathil's "Summer Haibun" is a good example of the way the haibun form juxtaposes prose poetry and haiku, providing two perspectives of the one event or idea. It opens with:

> To everything, there is a season of parrots. Instead of feathers, we searched the sky for meteors on our last night. Salamanders use the stars to find their way home. Who knew they could see that far, fix the tiny beads of their eyes on distant arrangements of lights so as to return to wet and wild nests?

And ends with the haiku:

> the cool night before
> star showers: so sticky so
> warm so full of light[56]

Contemporary haibun often retain their connection to travel, referencing the "Eastern tradition of poetic pilgrimage . . . in the poetry and travel journals of the Japanese poets Saigyō (1118–90) and Sōgi (1421–1502), who influenced Bashō's own travel journals."[57] Furthermore, Kennard points out, "What immediately strikes the reader is not only how self-conscious Bashō's work is, but how self-consciously aware it is of the poetic tradition."[58] This tradition makes the haibun especially pertinent for poets, like Jenny Xie, as they search for ways to express multiple perspectives on discovery in travel.

However, there are also contemporary haibun that ignore or renounce these connections. For example, torrin a. greathouse's "Burning Haibun" begins, "once, my mother accused me of throwing alcohol & gasoline on my emotions. once my father's breath was a guilty verdict,"[59] eschewing capital letters to emphasize the narrator's problematized sense of self-worth. The haiku sections use erasure to underline this point.

Sei Shōnagon's *The Pillow Book* (completed 1002), and the work of Matsuo Bashō, continue to inspire prose poets. For instance, Suzanne Buffam in *A Pillow Book* riffs on Shōnagon's original, in a series of linked prose poems and fragments that could be identified as zuihitsu. The zuihitsu form has recently been defined in the following way:

> Originating in 8th[-]century Japan and flourishing during the Edo period (around the 17th century) the zuihitsu is [a] hybrid prose-poem form that collects, in a list-like way, the personal musings and observations of the poet

as she brings her attention to her inner and outer landscapes. It splices these subjective offerings together in a fragmented way, leaping from one association to the next. The word *zuihitsu* in Japanese means something close to "following the brush."[60]

Buffam's book is a hybrid work that contains prose poems and ruminates on dreaming, insomnia, and the intimate spaces of night:

> Last night I had a dream so vivid I didn't bother to record it on my pillow. I was sipping a large stein of sangria at some sort of nightmarish gala, leaning on the arm of a once-powerful older man I'd met in college, upon whom I was now, in the dream, in the awkward position of passing literary judgment. He was wearing a white guayabera shirt with pink stitching, and what hair of his remained was slicked across a forehead speckled with age. I woke angry and aroused and could not get back to sleep. Was this a Prophetic Dream? A Psychological Healing Dream? A Belief Dream? The only option I could rule out for certain was a Dream of Daily Life.[61]

She also refers to Shōnagon as a way of understanding the enduring relevance of *The Pillow Book* and of the writing process, with a focus on women:

> I now had a vast quantity of paper at my disposal, reports the nonchalant Shōnagon, and I set about filling the notebooks with odd facts, stories from the past, and all sorts of other things, often including the most trivial material.[62]

Kimiko Hahn is the most prominent contemporary proponent of the zuihitsu form, evident in her books, including *The Unbearable Heart* (1995), *The Narrow Road to the Interior* (2006), and *A Field Guide to the Intractable* (2009). The following excerpt from Hahn's "Cutting" demonstrates its postmodern "fragmented and multiple subjectivity,"[63] and the way in which the zuihitsu's reinvention situates it as a variety of the prose poem form:

> Why is pain deeper than pleasure, though it is a pleasure to cry so loud the arthritic dog hobbles off the sunny carpet, so loud I do not hear the phone ring, so loud I feel a passion for mother I thought I reserved for lovers. I insert a CD and sing about a love abandoned, because there are no other lyrics for this.
>
> Pulling off a crewneck sweater I bend my glasses and for the next few days wear the frames off-center not realizing the dizzy view is in fact physical.
>
> Theresa, David, Liz, Mark, Sharon, Denise, Carmen, Sonia, Susan, Lee, Cheryl, Susan, Jo, John, Jerry, Doug, Earlene, Marie, Robbin, Jessica, Kiana, Patricia, Bob, Donna, Orinne, Shigemi—

Suddenly the tasks we put off need to get done: defrost the freezer, pay the preschool bill, order more checks.

For 49 days after her own mother's death she did not eat meat. I didn't know, mother. I'm sorry, I didn't know.

The sudden scent of her spills from her handbag—leather, lotion, mints, coins. I cannot stand.[64]

The initial experience of randomness and splintered subjectivity in the grouped sentences is undercut by the reader who follows the poet's trail and, in doing so, pieces together the juxtaposed fragments and miscellany. In this way, lists and thoughts—like mental flotsam and jetsam—become part of the poem's interiority, creating a kind of haphazard journal, fractured lyric essay, and postfeminist elegy, all expressed in the prose poem form. Iglesias discusses Hahn's use of the zuihitsu as "a hybrid form where grief is released and solace comes from continuity."[65] Furthermore, Iglesias makes the point Hahn's—and we would add, Buffam's—books, in referring to Shōnagon's *The Pillow Book*, "demonstrate . . . the evolving vitality of an ancient woman's form."[66]

Similarly, Jenny Xie uses both contemporary haibun and zuihitsu in her book *Eye Level* (2018), which is based on her experience of living in Cambodia as a foreigner and explores interiority and outsiderness. "Visual Orders" is a fourteen-part poem that can be identified as postmodern zuihitsu. The first three parts are:

[1]

Harvest the eyes from the ocular cavities.
Complete in themselves:
a pair of globes with their own meridians.

[2]

What atrophies without the ending of a gaze? The visible object is constituted by sight. But where to spend one's sight, a soft currency? To be profligate in taking in the outer world is to shortchange the interior one.

Though this assumes a clean separation, a zero-sum game.

[3]

To draw in-lines across the lids.
To dip into small pots of pigment
To brush two dozen times
To flush with water and tame with oil
To restrain and to spill in appropriate measure
To drink from the soft and silvery pane
To extract the root of the solitary so as to appear[67]

IDEAS OF OPEN FORM AND CLOSURE IN PROSE POETRY   95

What these Japanese forms and their postmodern reimaginings prioritize and problematize is the use of lines and sentences, of poetry, poetic prose, and prose poetry in combination.

Following Sally Ashton—quoted in Brian Clements and Jamey Dunham's anthology, *An Introduction to the Prose Poem* (2009)—these works might also be classified as containing "free-line" prose poems:

> With free-line form, the construction varies from poet to poet but generally consists of stand-alone sentences running margin to margin and separated by a skipped line. It's as if stanzas compromised [*sic*] of one sentence made up the poem. The skipped line's empty space achieves a momentary stillness, like an exhaled breath, between sentences.[68]

It is worth noting that Ron Silliman labels these as "single sentence paragraphs,"[69] but this term has largely become associated with grammar and prose rather than the analysis of poetry. Also, the notion of the single sentence paragraph risks constituting each sentence as a more or less autonomous entity. By contrast, the idea of the free-line prose poem allows for connections between sentences, identifying them as part of a single work and giving them room to breathe in the spaces at the right margin—and breathe between sentences, too.

Ashton's "Origins of Sublime" is an example of this form. Each line begins with an em dash, while the poem ends with the idea of breath, which Ashton gives priority to as part of the form:

> —Out there great gray bodies twist in the sea.
> —He leans and watches the children play soccer while shadows lengthen.
> —All undiscovered the place where it rains, or where great bodies dive and moan.
> —Quiet as the casks where grapes dream.
> —You open your eyes to the same room and sun drifts simple shafts across the bed.
> —Everything going fast like a ripe tomato with a split in its side.
> —Rain in the alley, on the air conditioner. Clean streets, wet garbage.
> —That kind.
> —Our lot narrow and deep.
> —Each night the stars burn like whiskey, blurred like a headache.
> —I've found what seems a silence holds traffic hum, voices calling, the smell of supper cooking, someone scuffing their feet.
> —And the slapping sound of sex.
> —The scrape of insect wings, the exhalation of breath.[70]

In this poem, sentences still wrap at the right margin if they are long enough, however, each sentence begins on a new line rather than continuing on from the previous sentence. While the prose poem box shape is still more or less preserved, it is spaced and airy. And, while the em dashes connect the sentences, they also help to demonstrate their independence.

Works such as this look quite a lot like free verse, but lineated poetry has a different rhythmic structure to the prose poem as its organizing principle—even free verse poetry, as Dana Gioia states, "seeks the same neural effect [as the poem in meter] by different means."[71] Additionally, it is important to remember that prose poetry and lineated poetry (in meter or free verse) are different from each other in their approaches to closure. The use of the free-line in prose poetry opens up the work by harnessing white space and, in taking up more room, loses the tight compression of the more usual box-shaped prose poem paragraph.

For this reason, we use Ashton's free-line in our discussion of prose poetry but extend the definition to include a range of approaches where sentences are separated from the body of the prose poem. The free-line varies from poet to poet, with some utilizing one skipped line and others skipping many lines, so the sentence is surrounded by space. In some cases these gaps or spaces can be read as the site of what Silliman identifies in "The New Sentence" as "torquing," which "enhance[s] ambiguity and polysemy."[72] The free-line prose poem incorporates this tension into its sentences and the gaps between them.

Ocean Vuong's long prose poem "Trevor" (2016) uses the free-line in juxtaposition with the clusters of continuous sentences commonly associated with prose poetry, along with short sentences that eschew the skipped line—but fail to meet the right margin. The skipped lines in "Trevor" act as absent lines ghosting the sentences above and below them. This puts the free-line text under scrutiny, lending the language an air of vulnerability. Such writing is as close to free verse as we are likely to find in a prose poem. Poet and scholar Marvin Bell states, "I think of prose poetry as a form of free verse,"[73] and Vuong's poem illustrates that the two kinds of work are sometimes closely related in their poetic techniques.

In "Trevor" the use of different numbers of spaces between and around lines enacts the prose poem's sense of confusion and ambivalence. The sentences are both compressed into tight blocks and exposed in space, creating a simultaneous sense of the open and hidden:

Trevor rusted pick-up & no license.

Trevor 15; blue jeans streaked with deer blood.

Trevor too fast & not enough.

Trevor waving his John Deere hat from the driveway as you ride by on your squeaky Schwinn.

Trevor who fingered a freshman girl then tossed her panties in the lake *for fun.*

For summer. For your hands

were wet & Trevor's a name like a truck revving up in the night. Who snuck out to meet a boy like you. Yellow & nearly nothing. Trevor going 60 through

IDEAS OF OPEN FORM AND CLOSURE IN PROSE POETRY 97

his daddy's wheat field. Who jams all his fries into whopper & chews with two feet on the gas. Your eyes closed in the passenger, the wheat a yellow confetti.

Three freckles on his nose.

Three periods to a boy-sentence.

. . . .

//

Trevor pointing at the one-winged starling spinning in dirt & takes it for something new. Something smoldering like a word. Like a Trevor

who knocked on your window at three in the morning, who you thought was smiling until you saw the blade held over his mouth. *I made this, I made this for you,* he said, the knife suddenly in your hand. Trevor later[74]

"Trevor" also uses the double forward slash. In critical discourse, a forward slash is often used to demonstrate a line break in a poem when part of the poem is quoted in a sentence, while a double forward slash often denotes a stanza break, or indicates that a whole line of poetry has been elided. In "Trevor," Vuong repurposes the double forward slash to indicate the simultaneous continuation and division of sections, and to suggest that hidden or missing parts are crucial to the understanding and interpretation of the poem. Furthermore, Vuong uses the single forward slash in prose poems such as "Partly True Poem Reflected in a Mirror." If this prose poem were to be lineated where the single forward slashes are inserted, it would not become a successful lineated poem—demonstrating that prose poems and lineated poems are, indeed, fundamentally different poetic forms:

> i want to find a gun / and change myself / he said / in the dream only a week before his mother called / no hello only / her breath a windmill crashing slowly into my head / this face already changed since heavy rain left november too bloody / to read in a boy finds a bridge and becomes / everywhere and i decide[75]

The use of the free-line is becoming a focus for many other poets too. Significantly, the joining of free verse with free-line prose poetry does not suggest that they are interchangeable, merely that there are varying modes of prose poetry, some of which are hybrid or mixed modes. Ocean Vuong is a poet who experiments with hybridity. His poem "On Earth We Are Briefly Gorgeous," published in *Poetry* in 2014, is an excellent example because it contains, among other things, lineated poetry, prose poetry, poetry with different uses of the indented line, poetry with em dashes, and poetry that activates the page's white space.

Another example of a free-line prose poem is Tania Hershman's "Powers of Ten" (2018), which uses the free-line in combination with the prose poem box and single sentences, or words with no skipped line. In this excerpt, the repetitive fragments play with ideas of scale: the brief, compressed sentences in the paragraph appear smaller than those below them that fail to run all the way to the right margin, partly because the paragraph form allows its sentences no significant space to breathe:

> Even the background stars. Even the background. Stars will appear. Background stars will appear. To converge. Stars back and ground appears. To ground appears. Appear, star! To will, even back to stars. Converge, will and stars, appear ground.
>
> We pause to start back home.
> Home.
> Back we start.
> Pause.
>
> This emptiness is normal.[76]

Barbara Tran's *In the Mynah Bird's Own Words* has been called "an assemblage of lined poems and prose poems."[77] Her long sequence "Rosary" demonstrates these hallmarks where a prose poem is followed by a lineated poem. Here are excerpts from the last two poems in this sequence:

> *measure*
>
> . . . She knew also that there was a child growing inside some other woman's womb, and that it would be born first, and that her husband would be there. Still, she had four children in tow, all of whom would cry out "Ba!' on cue. They had had enough rice with *canh* for dinner. Now that they were in the United States of America, with all its Independence and escalators, its planes, trains, and fast ways of getting away, they weren't letting go.
>
> *epilogue*
>
> . . . At seventeen,
> my mother counted her Hail Mary's
> on the little white beads
> of her rosary. Now she counts them off
> on the heads of her seven children,
> counting herself as eight,
> and her husband,
> as one and ten.[78]

Similarly, Laura Kasischke's book *Space, in Chains* (2011) has poems "laid out in a hybrid prose poem manner [and] . . . several that make conventional use of

IDEAS OF OPEN FORM AND CLOSURE IN PROSE POETRY ⁐ 99

white space."[79] The poem "Memory of Grief" blurs the line between lineated and prose poetry because there is very little difference in tone, cadence, and compression among the three parts of the poem, other than the disposition of sentences and the lineation:

> I remember a four-legged animal strolling through a fire. Poverty in a prom dress. A girl in a bed trying to tune the AM radio to the voices of the dead. A temple constructed out of cobwebs into which the responsibilities of my daily life were swept. Driving through a Stop sign waving to the woman on the corner, who looked on, horrified.
>
> But I remember, too, the way,
> loving everyone equally because each of us would die,
> I walked among the crowds of them, wearing
> my disguise.
> And how, when it was over, I found myself
> here again
> with a small plastic bag on my arm, just
>
> another impatient immortal
> sighing and fidgeting in an unmoving line.[80]

Lauren Russell's "Dream-Clung, Gone" juxtaposes prose poetry with more formal-looking quatrains that bracket the prose poem. Terrance Hayes argues that Russell "stitches poem (identified by the frame of quatrains) to prose (identified by the four lines inhabited by Absence)."[81] Her juxtaposition of the two quatrains with the prose poem paragraph in the middle play with brokenness. The alignment of the quatrains suggests visually they could be two halves of a paragraph and emphasize the central prose poem's fragmentation and connectedness:

> Undertow of dive bar juke unboxed
> Driving past a rust-red door unjambed
> Coin-operated groove side-shimmies, unflung
> A seamlessly upholstered stool's unwound
>
> Once I fell in love with an Absence. It outgrew the apartment and wouldn't take off its clothes. After we moved it turned taut and slinky, hid in shadows or slid provocatively beneath my coat. Three winters now and the Absence is restless. It's blown across the river, arrives late when it meets me for beer. The Absence is singing:
>
>   This is the song of a dawned dance
>   This is the dance of a dusk-drawn song
>   This is the fall of a moaned trance
>   This is the clang of a dream-clung gong[82]

More on Prose Poetry and Lineation

Short literary works employing lines/sentences that stop before the right margin may only be considered prose poems if they also appeal to a sentence-driven rather than line-driven rhythmic structure and resist closure. This is even true of the relatively underexplored form of the so-called prose poem sonnet. Indeed, the comparison of sonnets and prose poems is pertinent given that both are often box-shaped and, in contemporary poetry, both are protean forms. Terrance Hayes notes that a sonnet is "a centuries old box always waiting to be reshaped, adapted, filled with new words,"[83] and prose poetry can equally be identified as a box that adapts to change. Notable examples of the prose poem sonnet date back to works such as Emerson's "Woods: A Prose Sonnet" (1839) and include more recent examples: some of the works in Emmanuel Hocquard's *A Test of Solitude* (translated by Rosmarie Waldrop, 2007), some of Paul Munden's *Chromatic* (2017), and Janet Kaplan's *Dreamlife of a Philanthropist: Prose Poems and Sonnets* (2011); also Katharine Coles's "Sonnet in Prose" (2019), and the prose poem sonnet sequence "Early Poem" in Lucy Ives's *Orange Roses* (2013). This last work draws attention to the sonnet form by counting sentences (rather than lines) and defies convention by counting one hundred of them across a group of prose poem "sonnets":

> The first sentence is a sentence about writing. The second sentence tells you it's alright to lose interest. You might be one of those people who sits back in his or her chair without interest, and this would have been the third sentence you would have read. The fourth sentence, what does that say, that says something about how I genuinely feel, even if it no longer matters how I genuinely feel, that has not even become the topic of another book.[84]

Patience Agbabi has written some of the most interesting hybrid prose poems, which incorporate the agony aunt Q and A column form. "Problem Pages" is a series of epistolary prose poem sonnets addressed "Dear Patience." Agbabi writes these letters from famous poets, such as Milton, Shakespeare, and Edna St. Vincent Millay, and responds by offering advice. "Patience" is an amusing play on the poet's name and the attribute often needed in solving problems. In "FROM AFRICA SINGING," Agbabi writes a letter from "June Jordan" likening the sonnet to "a clenched fist in a European cage."[85] To "Gwendolyn Brooks," in "KNEW WHITE SPEECH," she writes, "Some say poetry+politics=propaganda. That blackpoet+sonnet=sellout."[86]

As Carole Birkan Berz argues, Agbabi "replicates the proportion of the sonnet with a prose 'octave' and 'sestet' set as two blocks of justified bold and regular typeface. In . . . 'TWO LOVES I HAVE,' Agbabi uses a parodic-satirical mode of self-representation to subvert traditional expectations of the sonnet in terms of race and gender in the public artistic sphere, while expressing doubt that these can ever be overturned. In 'FROM AFRICA SINGING,' she combines parody with the 'sonnet on the sonnet' genre."[87] In this artful and hybrid play with form, Agbabi defamiliarizes and self-reflexively critiques the sonnet tradition's preoccupation with love.

It is also worth noting that in Joel Brouwer's book *Centuries* (2003), the prose poems consist of exactly one hundred words. These are reminiscent of Ives's one hundred sentences in their playful approach to formal structure, while in Janet Kaplan's book, the "sonnets" are comprised of fourteen numbered paragraphs using fragments, mini-observations, and quotations. In the same spirit of defiance, the International Prose Poetry Institute's series of five prose poetry chapbooks, collectively entitled *Prosody* (2018), creatively explore features typically associated with lineated poetry. The twenty-one prose poems in each of the chapbooks—*Stanza*, *Line*, *Metre*, *Rhyme*, and *Enjambment*—actively and playfully engage with metrical patterns and intonation, and even with rhyme.

Finally, the formalist poet and translator A. E. Stallings's villanelle "Austerity Measures" was republished in prose poem form as a kind of epigraph in *Austerity Measures: The New Greek Poetry*. The poem "repurpos[es] a news headline . . . using that headline's last word as one of the two repeating rhymes of a villanelle embedded in a prose poem."[88] It begins self-reflexively: "If you believe the headlines, then we're sunk. The dateline oracle, giddy with dread: Greece downgraded deeper into junk. Stash cash beneath the mattress, pack the trunk."[89] While this poem, because of the rhyme and meter embedded within it, works better in its lineated form,[90] as a prose poem it has the advantage of mirroring the form of a newspaper article, on which it was based.

Of course, distinctions between the sentence and the line depend on an interpretation of where on the continuum poetry becomes prose and the line becomes a sentence—something that is not always easy to determine and is further complicated by some of the terms critics use, such as Fredman's preference for "poet's prose" instead of "prose poetry." In the examples above, we see that a significant number of contemporary prose poems are focused on the relationship between the sentence and the line. In combining prose poetry with lineated poems, or in aiming to create a free-line prose poem, poets are exploring some of the multiple perspectives, techniques, and subjectivities that are available to all prose poets, if they choose to make use of them, and that are strikingly characteristic of postmodernist literary modes and forms.

If one is sometimes left wondering whether the authors of hybrid forms of prose poetry—or of poetry more generally—know whether their works are, or should be called, "poetry" or "prose," this serves to emphasize how contemporary poetry may simultaneously be both prose and poetry. Sometimes such works manifest as prose poetry, and sometimes they manifest as hybrid works that combine lineated poetry and prose poetry in inventive and challenging ways.

CHAPTER 5

Neo-Surrealism within the Prose Poetry Tradition

The "American" Prose Poem

Prose poetry in its various manifestations travels across international boundaries to such an extent that it is hard to generalize about the national character of contemporary prose poetry being written in English. However, the proliferation of prose poetry has led to the widely debated idea that American prose poetry is in some respects different from other prose poetry. David Lehman is keen to point to the way the American prose poem keeps "a respectful distance" from prose poetry's "modern French tradition"[1]—most notably the French *poème en prose*—and Russell Edson remarks: "[T]he prose poem comes to us [Americans] not so much from the idea of the *poème en prose*, but out of modern poetry itself . . . I don't think a line of European virtuosos is necessary to find the availability of the prose poem in America."[2]

Michel Delville, in *The American Prose Poem: Poetic Form and the Boundaries of Genre* (1998), discusses the limitations of identifying quintessentially "American" features in prose poems: "Now that a number of general trends have established themselves as characteristic of 'the' American prose poem, the genre is likely to be further institutionalized into the canon of American poetry under various restrictive labels, such as the Deep Image prose poem, the neo-Surrealist fable, or the language-oriented New Prose Poem."[3] In a 2002 essay he also points to "the neo-surrealist, absurdist fable" as being "the most popular subgenre of the American prose poem,"[4] identifying this form as being inaugurated by Russell Edson's *The Very Thing that Happens* (1964).

The term "neo-surrealism" does not have to be restrictive but may be used as a way of opening up an understanding of certain key features of prose poetry internationally. And while American prose poets are certainly not the first to experiment with surrealism—for example, what is sometimes considered the first book of prose poetry, Aloysius Bertrand's *Gaspard de la nuit* has been described as "not-clearly lit . . . dreamlike . . . surreal"[5]—many contemporary American prose poets demonstrate a particular interest in absurdism and neo-surrealism. As a result, neo-surrealism is arguably best exemplified by American prose poets—in terms of the number of writers employing such techniques and the quality of neo-surrealistic works being written. In America, neo-surrealistic prose poetry is primarily, but by no means exclusively, identified with Nin Andrews, Michael Benedikt, Joel Brouwer, Maxine Chernoff, Harry Crosby, Russell Edson, David Ignatow, Louis Jenkins, Christopher Kennedy, Peter Johnson, Morton Marcus, Charles Simic, Mark Strand, Jessica Treat, James Tate, and James Wright.

Steven Monte, in his *Invisible Fences: Prose Poetry as a Genre in French and American Literature* (2000), comments on the "propaganda value of this idea" of an American prose poem,[6] and, unlike Lehman, doubts whether the American prose poem may be thought of as independent from its French forerunners. He speculates, "[i]t may be that American poets and critics, especially those who are noticeably defensive, have based their claims on a single type of French poem or a straw-man symbolist poem." Nevertheless, he also writes that "[r]egardless of its taxonomic value, [the term] 'American' is potentially an important interpretive frame for some works,"[7] and emphasizes that contemporary prose poetry does not simply emulate its nineteenth-century French models. Rather, the prose poetry form has found a multiplicity of different voices and approaches over the last century and a half, and has developed in ways reflecting twentieth- and twenty-first-century issues and preoccupations.

Notwithstanding its contemporaneity, the neo-surrealistic strand of prose poetry maintains a clear—if sometimes lateral—connection to the strange and often dreamlike works produced by nineteenth-century French prose poets such as Charles Baudelaire and Arthur Rimbaud. Baudelaire and Rimbaud were interested in the way in which dreamlike imagery and the evocation of reverie may make prose works into poetic forms of utterance. An example is Baudelaire's "To Each His Chimæra" in *Paris Spleen*, beginning:

> Under a wide gray sky, in a great dusty plain, pathless, grassless, without so much as a thistle or a nettle, I came across some men walking, their shoulders bent.
> Each carried on his back an enormous Chimæra, heavy as a sack of flour or charcoal, or a Roman foot-soldier's pack.[8]

This is a vision out of a nightmare, and its dreamlike and surrealistic elements are to the fore. It is reminiscent of some of Francisco Goya's grotesque imagery in his series of prints *Los desastres de la Guerra* (*Disasters of War*) (1810–20), especially in its focus on the unrelieved and unremitting nature of the human condition.

Arthur Rimbaud is even more of a protosurrealist than Baudelaire. In a famous letter to Georges Izambard of May 13, 1871, Rimbaud states he is trying to reach "the unknown by the derangement of *all the senses*."[9] Surrealism arose as a movement in the 1920s, and Henri Peyre writes, "The Surrealists admired Rimbaud's vision of poetry as a magical means for discovering the unknown; his reliance on reverie; his violent images; his desire to liberate his ego and his art from all restrictions."[10] In other words, Rimbaud anticipated many surrealist preoccupations. His interest in dreamlike imagery is apparent in his poetry even before he turned to prose poetry, but it is most evident in his major and groundbreaking prose-poetical works *A Season in Hell* (1873) and *Illuminations* (1886).

More generally, many late nineteenth-century French prose poems are symbolist in the way they express, name, and reinflect elusive inner states of mind and being connected to the imagination, the spiritual, and sometimes to varieties of mysticism. Symbolism values dream imagery and often addresses aspects of external reality through giving emphasis to more or less abstract symbols over "realistic" description. Symbolism was a widespread and highly influential movement, sometimes said to be inaugurated by Baudelaire's volume of poetry *The Flowers of Evil*, and also linked to the poets Paul Verlaine and Stéphane Mallarmé, among others. It even has its own manifesto, *Le Symbolisme* (*Symbolism*), written by Jean Moréas and published in the newspaper *Le Figaro* in 1886.

Symbolist ideas were expressed somewhat differently in the visual arts and in writing. One of the best definitions of the aims of symbolism as it applies to literature was formulated by the poet and art critic Émile Verhaeren in 1887:

> We start with the thing seen, heard, smelled, touched, tasted, in order to bring out the evocation and the sum through its idea. A poet looks at Paris crawling with nighttime lights, scattered into an infinity of fires and colossal with shadow and depth. If we give a direct view of it, as [the novelist, Émile] Zola might do, by describing its streets, squares, monuments, gas lamps, nocturnal seas of ink . . . nothing would be less Symbolist. If conversely he presents the mind with an indirect, evocative vision, if he says: "an immense algebra whose key has been lost," this phrase alone will conjure up . . . the luminous, shadowy and extraordinary Paris.[11]

Symbolism helped create or influenced various avant-garde movements in the twentieth century, to the extent that Patrick McGuinness writes, "From Apollinaire to Francis Jammes, from Valéry Larbaud to Jean Cocteau, from Paul-Jean Toulet and Léon-Paul Fargue to Breton and the surrealists, the influence of Symbolism is as pervasive as it is formative."[12]

Symbolist techniques have also infiltrated the work of writers in all parts of the world. For instance, Luke Kennard has recently said that Anne Carson's essayistic prose poetry sequence, "Irony Is Not Enough: Essay on My Life as Catherine Deneuve" (2000), contains "a simple narrative of passing infatuation" that "is elliptical and serves . . . as a frame for the poem's moments of startling sensory clarity which are very much in the symbolist mode."[13]

Symbolism influenced many of the ideas that André Breton articulated in his 1924 *Le Manifeste du Surréalism* (*Manifesto of Surrealism*), when he conceived of surrealism as expressing the way thought functioned without regard to reason, making unconscious connections, exploiting dream imagery, and juxtaposing apparently distant realities. Since then surrealism has had a profound influence on poetry and art, insisting art should bring unconscious material and irrational relationships to light.

The Neo-surreal

The neo-surreal is a postmodern outgrowth of such preoccupations. It has reaffirmed the exploration of the irrational and strange as central to artistic practice. However, many contemporary neo-surrealistic works tend to emphasize disruptive effects and narrative disjuncture without turning inward to locate and articulate unconscious experiences and impulses. The neo-surreal is a useful "interpretive frame" for late twentieth- and twenty-first-century American prose poetry because of the tonality and attitude of numerous neo-surreal prose poems.

Even more than many nineteenth-century French examples—and not discounting the weirdness of some of Rimbaud's brilliant and influential prose poetry—numerous contemporary neo-surreal American prose poems not only problematize but depart almost entirely from commonsense notions about the world. These prose poems gather force through exploring their internal worlds and developing strange, associative logic as they do so. They rely on various kinds of absurdity, urban fantasy, magical realist techniques, and a sometimes fairly flat tonality that de-emphasizes *affect*, to create a sense of the uncanny and unreal, defamiliarizing the known. Many of them make serious poetic statements through creating strange depictions that function as analogies for the contemporary world or contemporary issues, questioning and troubling assumptions about how we live.

Thus, to some extent, the differences in the appeal to surrealism in French versus American prose poetry hinge on varying interpretations of the word "surreal" and the accompanying styles used to explore it. Scholars such as Paul Breslin and Robert Pinsky have argued that what has been identified as the American surreal is actually not surreal at all. They contend that while contemporary American prose poets may distort their imagery, making it strange and sometimes disturbing, this does not, in itself, constitute a genuine surrealism.

Indeed, there have been many criticisms aimed at American neo-surrealist prose poetry. Pinsky emphasizes its "mock-naïve teen-age sort of detachment," while Paul Breslin dismisses it as composed of "trivial mystifications."[14] Similarly, while Dana Gioia points out the importance of the prose poem form in America, he laments its narrow use: "Indeed, the most influential form in American poetry over this quarter century has been the prose poem ... In theory, the prose poem is the most protean form of free verse in which all line breaks disappear as a highly charged lyric poem achieves the ultimate organic form. In recent American practice, however, it has mostly become a kind of absurdist parable."

Despite this, as Peter Henry notes, American neo-surrealist poets (not always writing prose poetry) have been the recipients of many awards, which he says demonstrates their place in the "poetry establishment": "They were showered with

106   CHAPTER 5

American Academy of Arts and Letters Awards (James Tate in 1974, Mark Strand in 1975, Charles Simic in 1976, and Charles Wright in 1977) and Guggenheim Fellowships (Mark Strand in 1974, Charles Wright in 1975, James Tate in 1976, and Greg Orr in 1977)."[15]

In order to illustrate the surrealistic strain of prose poetry, it is worth examining an example from the work of one of the leading figures in the surrealist movement, Paul Éluard (1895–1952). In Éluard's "Elle est" (She Exists)—a powerful prose poem—the quotidian becomes an intoxicating dreamscape expressed in dense adjectival sentences. Éluard uses automatic writing, free association, and wordplay to transform the ordinary into the surreal:

> She exists, but only at midnight, when the wings of the white birds have folded on the ignorance of darkness, when their sister, whose pearls cannot be counted, has hidden her hands in her lifeless hair, when the victor delights in his own tears, weary of worshipping the not-yet-known, the virile and gleaming armor of sensuality. So kind is she that my heart has been transformed.[16]

This does not sound like the contemporary strain of American neo-surrealism. American prose poems often prioritize the absurd and oneiric as features of daily life in a pared-back and prosaic style. In many such American prose poems, the surreal is not transformative but a necessary part of life. At its most overtly political, American neo-surrealist poetry has even been identified as "a poetic mode of Cold War dissent."[17]

Dana Gioia's comment about James Tate's neo-surrealist poetry could equally be applied to the majority of American poets working in this genre: "he had domesticated surrealism. He had taken this foreign style which had almost always seemed slightly alien in English . . . and made it sound not just native but utterly down-home."[18] In this way, American prose poems locate the surreal in the most banal or even "kitchen sink" moments. In Tate's prose poem "The Cowboy" (2008), for example, the narrator finds that he is unknowingly in possession of an extraterrestrial, which he discovers while holding a bag of groceries. Part of this poem reads:

> I nearly dropped the groceries. There was a nearly transparent
> fellow with large pink eyes standing about three feet tall. "Why
> did you tell them I was dead? That was a lie," he said. "You
> speak English," I said. "I listen to the radio. It wasn't very
> hard to learn. Also we have television. We get all your channels.
> I like cowboys, especially John Ford movies. They're the best,"
> he said. "What am I going to do with you?" I said. "Take me
> to meet a real cowboy. That would make me happy," he said.[19]

Similarly, Tate's book *The Government Lake*, published posthumously in 2019, contains the last prose poem he wrote, which describes the narrator's accomplishments from "read[ing] a book by a dove" to eating "a cheeseburger every day for a year,"[20] pairing the fantastic with the quotidian.

Another way of considering the differences between the two traditions is through what John Taylor has identified as a contrast of approaches to fact and idea: "American poets tend to begin with a fact and work toward an idea, while their French counterparts begin with an idea and work toward a fact."[21] Applied to surrealist poetry, this observation rightly identifies the French tradition as focusing more on conjuring a sense of the dreamlike and what is hidden in the mind, while the Americans frequently start with something more concrete—both seemingly working from different directions but toward a similar end.

For example, Éluard's "She Exists" begins with a sense of the uncanny, and with abstractions about life and death, while Tate's "The Cowboy" begins with a plain and yet discomfiting narrative gesture: "Someone had spread an elaborate rumor about me, that I was in possession of an extraterrestrial being."[22] While the narrator is sad when the extraterrestrial says he is going to die, there is no philosophically transformative moment, other than the poignantly comic suggestion that the narrator might become a "cowboy," in fulfillment of the extraterrestrial's dying wish. Robert Alexander notes the prevalence of humor in such works, writing, "What's particularly interesting is that humor . . . has become an important aspect, almost a convention, of American prose poetry."[23] Indeed, readings of the humor in neo-surrealist prose poems have threatened to undercut their importance.

Luke Kennard, who has written extensively on prose poetry and surrealism, praises the neo-surrealist prose poem for its contemporary relevance,

> humour and elements of the absurd function, via self-consciousness, as thoroughly serious within the prose poem. Manifestations of such should not be dismissed as a light-hearted and anachronistic tribute to Surrealism as a historical movement. Rather such work should be appreciated and analysed for its latent content: its capacity for examining the illogicality of the systems by which we live through the combination of prose (argument, narrative) and poetry (imagery, tangent, rhythm).[24]

It is also worth noting that there are some American prose poems that have been dubbed examples of "late surrealism" because they focus less on narrative and fact. They intersect with the language poets for their reliance on postmodern writing techniques,[25] and for their move away from what they identified as modernist egocentrism. Consistent with the label "late surrealism," many of these prose poems continue to borrow techniques, such as unexpected juxtapositions, repetition, and word association, from French surrealist prose poems and acknowledge the general importance of surrealism in the arts. Ron Silliman has identified and theorized on the "New Prose Poem" as a language-centered, primarily scriptural medium distinct from surrealism because of its use of "The New Sentence," which "focus[es] attention at the level of the language in front of the reader."[26] However, as John Bradley suggests, Silliman's nod to the French symbolists means that many "New Prose Poems" have an implicit element of homage to French surrealist prose poems despite Silliman's disclaimer.[27]

For example, parts of Silliman's prose poem "You" (2008) from *The Alphabet* bear similarities to early French surrealist prose poems. "New Prose Poems" often turn more on abstraction than fact and aim for the transformative; in the section below, this is focused through the repetitious referencing of hands and gloves as ambiguous symbols:

XXXVII

> As the pop foul descends from the heavens into the crowd, hands and gloves shoot skyward, bodies thrusting themselves up, straining, grasping, parody of a scene on Iwo Jima, while below others cringe & cower, popcorn, beers, sodas spilling in all directions, the sculptural effect complete (at least half of the participants appear to have their eyes shut), a phenomenon that repeats in smaller and less hysterical numbers again and again as the loose ball bounces untouched from section to section until a boy with an oversized blue glove smothers it against his chest.[28]

The "New Prose Poem" focuses on foregrounding and defamiliarizing language while incorporating many of the features of the surreal and neo-surreal. Perhaps Silliman's most significant contribution to discussions of prose poetry and the surreal is his argument that due to prose poetry's disruption of a conventional sense of closure, it is "perfect for hallucinated, fantastic and dreamlike contents, for pieces with multiple locales and times squeezed into few words."[29] This is something Kennard also acknowledges when he states: "Prose poetry is more spacious; it tends to contain complete sentences; it allows for more incongruity and complex yet visible patterns; already at odds with the supposed purpose of prose (to convey information clearly) it is, in fact, the ideal Surrealist form."[30] As Kennard explicitly connects aspects of the surreal with the prose poem, he appears to confirm that some prose poets see themselves as reworking the surreal in new contexts and with new emphases.

Harryette Mullen's *Sleeping with the Dictionary* (2002), which uses Breton's quotation "Dark words / more radiant / than onyx" as an epigraph, has a neo-surrealist emphasis and links intimacy with the unconscious and dreaming.[31] Mullen reinterprets surrealism for a culturally diverse readership, shifting the surreal into a postmodern and postcolonial context:

> To go through all these motions and procedures, groping in the dark for an alluring word, is the poet's nocturnal mission. Aroused by myriad possibilities, we try out the most perverse positions in the practice of our nightly act, the

penetration of the denotative body of the work. Any exit from the logic of language might be an entry in a symptomatic dictionary. The alphabetical order of this ample block of knowledge might render a dense lexicon of lucid hallucinations. Beside the bed, a pad lies open to record the meandering of migratory words.[32]

Mullen also incorporates Oulipian—or constrained writing—techniques in her employment of dictionary games.

The Quotidian and the Extraordinary in American Prose Poetry

With its emphasis on "psychic automatism" involving "the actual functioning of thought,"[33] Breton's 1924 *Manifesto of Surrealism* is still the most cited source in discussions of surrealism. More recently, Andrew Joron has defined how he understands surrealism in postmodernity: "Surrealism is the practice of conjuring Otherness, of realizing the infinite negativity of desire in order to address, and to redress, the poverty of the positive fact." He states that "in surrealism th[e] identification [of reality and desire] leads, not to reconciliation, but to *antagonistic embrace*."[34] This "embrace" is frequently strange and sometimes uncanny, and while neither of these terms is synonymous with the surreal, they do speak to some of the effects of the surreal. As Joron remarks, Philip Lamantia asked in one of his poems, in postmodern society, "What is not strange?"[35] Joron suggests that the surreal needs redefining for poets and artists who are so immersed in "strangeness" that it has become commonplace.

Gioia states that an American new surrealism took hold in the 1960s, involving writers who "had grown up on cartoons and movies . . . [and] who did not necessarily see high culture and popular culture in opposition."[36] Similarly, Simic argues: "Surrealism means nothing in a country like ours where supposedly millions of Americans took joyrides in UFOs. Our cities are full of homeless and mad people going around talking to themselves. Not many people seem to notice them. I watch them and eavesdrop on them."[37]

Many scholars—such as Joron and Henry—divide American neo-surrealist poets into two waves. The first wave begins in the 1950s and includes Robert Bly and James Wright—so-called Deep Image poets (Bly disliked the term) who identified strongly with the Latin American and Spanish surrealist traditions. These writers were committed to accessing the unconscious for their poetic purposes, believing that one of the important routes there was via visual imagery. Bly, in his influential essay "Leaping Poetry: An Idea with Poems and Translations," originally published in 1972, states, "In many ancient works of art we notice a long floating leap . . . from the conscious to the unconscious and back again, a leap from the known part of the mind to the unknown part and back to the known."[38]

However, Deep Image poets are different from the surrealists. As Christopher Beach points out, "they did not go as far as the Surrealists in their attempt to overturn social and artistic convention or to challenge the rationality of poetic language and syntax. While we may find dreamlike or nightmarish scenes in the work of Deep Image poets, we do not find the type of free association or the kind of bizarre and shocking images found in Surrealist writing."[39]

The second wave of neo-surreal poets are said to have been influenced by Bly and Wright and include "Mark Strand, Charles Simic, James Tate, Diane Wakoski, Bill Knott, Russell Edson, Greg Orr, and Frank Stanford, as well as Charles Wright and Larry Levis."[40] As we have indicated, the identification of the neo-surreal is an attempt to update the surreal, and Paul Zweig suggests that by the 1970s, American surrealists were distinguishable by their "[c]arefully composed dream poems, incoherent torrents of language, obscure humor, jiving anti-rhetoric, nonsense, fantasy landscapes, images, obscure abstraction."[41]

Prose poetry is suited to such neo-surrealistic maneuvers because it is a relatively short form that, while making use of some narrative techniques, tends to move impressionistically, analogically, and more or less immediately. It is a form that has a license to be more lateral than, and even estranged from, what is typically the chronology-driven sequencing of conventional narrative prose, as well as from the formalities of lyric poetry, including its line breaks. This license includes the quarrying of the unconscious, and the poet and scholar Michael Benedikt has claimed this to be an important feature of the form: "The attention to the unconscious, and to its particular logic, unfettered by the relatively formalistic interruptions of the line break, remains the most immediately apparent property of the prose poem."[42]

Although Stephen Fredman is skeptical of Benedikt's claims for prose poetry's connections to the unconscious, many contemporary prose poems certainly possess the kind of quirkiness or humorousness—and sometimes even an appeal to the abject—that arises from the dislocation of everyday expectations. They tend to make deliberate and self-conscious use of disjunctive effects, and many of them aim at generating dreamlike or surrealistic disjunctions. This is partly because in postmodern life the real and the dreamlike often intersect, even in waking life.

Scholars have also commented on the rectangular or box shape of the prose poem as the perfect vehicle to contain the unconscious and to confront the surreal and neo-surreal. Danielle Mitchell states that the surreal narrative is "especially amiable when caged in the prose poem . . . instead of being restrictive, the prose poem is permissive,"[43] giving Zachary Schomburg's "The Fire Cycle" (2009) as an example:

There are trees and they are on fire. There are hummingbirds and they are on fire. There are graves and they are on fire and the things coming out of the graves are on fire. The house you grew up in is on fire. There is a gigantic trebuchet on fire on the edge of a crater and the crater is on fire. There is a complex system of tunnels deep underneath the surface with only one entrance and one exit and the entire system is filled with fire. There is a wooden cage we're trapped in, too large to see, and it is on fire. There are jaguars on fire. Wolves. Spiders. Wolf-spiders on fire. If there were people. If our fathers were alive. If we had a daughter. Fire to the edges. Fire in the river beds. Fire between the mattresses of the bed you were born in. Fire in your mother's belly. There is a little boy wearing a fire shirt holding a baby lamb. There is a little girl in a fire skirt asking if she can ride the baby lamb like a horse. There is you on top of me with thighs of fire while a hot red fog hovers in your hair. There is me on top of you wearing a fire shirt and then pulling the fire shirt over my head and tossing it like a fireball through the fog at a new kind of dinosaur. There are meteorites disintegrating in the atmosphere just a few thousand feet above us and tiny fireballs are falling down around us, pooling around us, forming a kind of fire lake which then forms a kind of fire cloud. There is this feeling I get when I am with you. There is our future house burning like a star on the hill. There is our dark flickering shadow. There is my hand on fire in your hand on fire, my body on fire above your body on fire, our tongues made of ash. We are rocks on a distant and uninhabitable planet. We have our whole life ahead of us.[44]

The self-reflexive "cage" referred to in Schomburg's prose poem provides a visual image that limits the fire cycle. At the same time, the justification of both margins promotes a sense that the poem fully encompasses its unruly subject. Even as everything starts to burn, the visual cues of the prose poem suggest that the fire is contained and the revelation that the narrator is trapped in a burning cage turns out to be a conceit where his desire for his lover threatens to incinerate them both.

Arielle Goldberg has identified prose poetry as "solid blocks of text—dependable, accessible-looking little bricks—in which [she is] set free to be as fanciful as [she] like[s]."[45] Experimentation with the neo-surreal can easily be undertaken in the prose poem form because its block of text looks reassuringly familiar—like sentences in any fragment of prose—and prose poems tend not to direct the reader in the same way that lineated poems do (line breaks constitute a kind of instruction to the reader, and, as we discussed in chapter 4, lineated poems possess a sense of formality and closure less evident in prose poetry). It is only once the reader is "inside" the prose poem that its poetic qualities begin to take effect, as the apparently familiar prose sentences become figurative and inflected as poetry.

The majority of American neo-surrealistic prose poems are not as obviously highly "poetic" as some of their French surrealist counterparts. Nevertheless, their analogical tendencies are often coupled with overt metaphors and metaphorical language, however plainly this is expressed. This strand of writing runs counter to the prevalent confessional strand in American lineated lyric poetry, undercutting any expectation on the reader's part that poetry may be directly connected to the poet's autobiography. Instead, many neo-surrealistic prose poems create clearly fictional settings and worlds and, in doing so, take the prose poem into directions that express some of the form's narrative potential, as well as its potential to speak strangely and sometimes opaquely back to the society that produces it.

For example, in Jack Anderson's "Thimbleism" (1998), the narrator sees a woman on the Staten Island Ferry who is able to make the stars twinkle by wiggling her fingers. Copying her, he finds he also has the same ability. The prose poem ends:

> When I reached home and told my neighbor what had happened, he said, "It's too bad you don't live in the backwoods South. Because there you could gather all the superstitious people in the county and set yourself up as the leader of a new sect . . . But here in New York no one will believe you. You'll never get famous and you'll never get rich."[46]

This prose poem contains echoes of magical realism, and while the action is set in New York, the extraordinary ability to control the heavens works to distract the reader from the implicit criticisms of idolatry in contemporary American society. The amusing reference to "Thimbleism" and people's blind faith in a "religion" built on worshipping a golden thimble, is cleverly satirical. Also, when the eye on the greenback (representing providence) is replaced by a golden thimble, a fusing of the ordinary and the remarkable occurs. Even the "gold thimble" is oxymoronic in the way in which something quotidian is made valuable. Anderson makes the point that New Yorkers are unlikely to be taken in by Thimbleism, with the suggestion that worshipping "false gods" has been commonplace in the city, with people getting rich and famous from ridiculous schemes; New Yorkers have become jaded.

The neo-surrealist appeal to magical realism—or, as has been more recently identified, urban fantasy—displaces contemporary problems in order to comment on them more fully or obliquely. Many neo-surrealist prose poems manage to incorporate such elements, grounding the reader in the everyday but also making their poetic worlds and assumptions strange. Magical realist elements have been identified by Nin Andrews in the prose poetry of Claire Bateman, Amelia Martens, Shivani Mehta, Tom Whalen, and Jeff Friedman,[47] and many of the prose poems in these poets' oeuvres also contain moments of urban fantasy.

In Claire Bateman's prose poem "Distinction" (2003), the reader is addressed in second person with the news that they have won a magical comb that will, among other things, comb out sadness and "existential misgivings":

> CONGRATULATIONS!
> You, (*insert name here*), have just won A UNIQUE &
> FABULOUS PRIZE.
> Within the next 24 hours, you are GUARANTEED to receive the
> *one & only* COMB OF THE WORLD— . . .
>
> THE COMB OF THE WORLD works wonders with phobias
>   & existential misgivings—YOU, yes, YOU will now be able
>   to separate wave from particle, fact from inference, truth
>   from prevarication.
> No more shadowy rustlings in the soul's undergrowth. No more
>   tough little colonies of unregenerate sadnesses, or ragged
>   ambiguities scuttling just out of reach. . . .[48]

The unreal or magical element of the magical comb is applied to real-world sorrows, and the ordinary begins to appear as miraculous as the miracle comb.

One way in which urban fantasy differs from magical realism is its evocation of fantasy creatures within urban cityscapes that interact with the general population but only reveal themselves to a protagonist or narrator.[49] In Jeff Friedman's prose poem "Catching the Monster," the narrator encounters a monster:

> On Main Street, I spot the monster in the crowd. He's clean shaven, but there are red nicks on his cheeks and chin. He's got long claws that can rip a chest apart in seconds. No one in the crowd appears to notice that the monster is among them. I follow closely weaving in and out until I'm almost stepping on his heels. Suddenly he turns to face me. "You're a monster," I say. He licks the stain of blood from his lips. "Is that so bad?" he asks.[50]

In this way, while elements of urban fantasy and magical realism within the contemporary prose poem are often discussed as offshoots of the surreal, they are more immediately features of, or echoes within, the American neo-surreal, and they heighten and often transform the reader's sense of the strangeness of quotidian experience.

Creative definitions of the neo-surreal and of prose poetry both insist on the importance of the quotidian. This is emphasized by the way in which, as Lehman has argued, prose poetry "disguises its true nature. The prose poet can appropriate . . . the newspaper article, the memo, the list, the parable, the speech, the dialogue. It is a form that sets store by its use of the demotic."[51] Certainly, the quotidian and demotic in prose poetry are significant features of its composition. Wallace

Stevens described in his poetry "the malady of the quotidian," but Siobhan Phillips notices that Stevens also called the quotidian "a 'health,' a rejuvenating 'over and over' of renewed mornings"[52]—and such a remark might apply equally to a great many prose poems.

This turn from viewing the mundane as tedious, to contemplating the everyday as rich and memorable, represents an important perceptual shift and emphasizes the way in which contemporary writers of all kinds explore connections between the mundane and significant existential truths. Jennifer Anna Gosetti-Ferencei believes that the ordinary can only be understood via the phenomenon of the extraordinary, and vice versa, that "modern poetry seems in part devoted to defending the margins of unknowability that surround the horizons of the known."[53] Prose poetry may be the poetic form that does this best, anchored as it is in the ubiquitous structure of the prose paragraph even as it disrupts the kinds of expectations usually associated with reading prose.

Furthermore, humor often dwells in the juxtaposition of the real and the neo-surreal. American poets frequently invoke the quotidian by turning to comedy in grappling with a sense of prose poetry's appeal—including using metaphors about food. Charles Simic, for example, states in "A Long Course in Miracles":

> Prose poems are the culinary equivalent of peasant dishes, like paella and gumbo, which bring together a great variety of ingredients and flavors, and which in the end, thanks to the art of the cook, somehow blend. Except, the parallel is not exact. Prose poetry does not follow a recipe. The dishes it concocts are unpredictable and often vary from poem to poem.[54]

The focus on "peasant dishes" suggests that prose poems are not exclusive or elitist and, following Simic, we would agree that prose poetry often returns poetry to the realm of colloquial utterance even more decidedly than contemporary free verse poetry. Simic's analogy also understands prose poems as an inventive and unpredictable concoction. American prose poet Louis Jenkins highlights this unpredictability in his definition of the form, which appears to refer to Peter Johnson's statement connecting prose poetry and banana peels:

> Think of the prose poem as a box, perhaps the lunch box dad brought home from work at night. What's inside? Some waxed paper, a banana peel, half a peanut butter-jelly sandwich. Not so much a hint of how the day has gone perhaps, but the magic for having made a mysterious journey and returned. The dried out pb&j tastier than anything made flesh.[55]

The connection between black humor and prose poetry is emphasized when Johnson quotes Bruce Jay Friedman's observation that defining black humor is like trying to define "an elbow or a corned-beef sandwich," after which he adds that "much the same can be said about prose poetry."[56] The banana peel, pb&j, corned beef, and elbow connect the prose poem with what David Lehman calls "the allegorical formula that would align the prose poem with 'working-class discourse' undermining the lyric structures of the upper bourgeoisie."[57] It is worth noting that this is also reminiscent of Breton's extrapolation of the tenets of surrealism in *Le Manifeste du Surréalism*, where he invokes Comte de Lautréamont's juxtaposition of two objects representing suburban banality in *Les Chants de Maldoror*: "as beautiful as the chance encounter of a sewing machine and an umbrella on an operating table."[58]

Francis Ponge, who was a friend of surrealist poets, including André Breton and Paul Éluard, created a sense of the extraordinary in his prose poems by focusing them on objects and their interior lives. His collection *Soap* details many different facets of the imagined life of this object and is both witty and poignant:

> There is so much to say about soap. Precisely everything that it tells about itself until the complete disappearance, the exhaustion of the subject. This is just the object suited to me.
>
> *
>
> Soap has so much to say. May it say it with volubility, enthusiasm. When it has finished saying it, it no longer is.[59]

There is something remarkable and unexpected in these juxtapositions, consistent with José Rodríguez Feo's comment on the "mysterious relation between the quotidian and the marvelous."[60] Prose poetry is a form well adapted to the exploration of such preoccupations because "[t]he poem uses a prose style to play up an extraordinary situation, or on an apparently mundane story that becomes wildly stylised."[61] Neo-surreal prose poems—especially those featuring elements of magical realism or urban fantasy—embrace this notion of the extraordinary happening in an ordinary setting, often with enchorial dialogue or other demotic features. The juxtaposition of the ordinary and extraordinary—or even internalization of one within the other—heightens the demotic mode by including apparently incongruous elements.

This connects to the question of whether American neo-surrealist prose poetry is more prosaic than poetic. Some American neo-surreal prose poets work with fairly prosaic sentences and rhythms, and many do not fully right-justify their block of prose poetical text. Sometimes, in the use of dialogue, their prose poems fall short of the right margin and sometimes they are divided into paragraphs or single sentences (or the one-sentence paragraph that Silliman identified).[62] Occasionally these works have a visual resemblance to very brief short stories.

In Tom Whalen's prose poem "The Doll's Alienation," for example, the action is divided into short paragraphs ending with the following:

> The doll's roach-infested dress. Her smudged make-up. Last night she did not dream. Or the night before.

On the top shelf, in the dark, she listens to the child making love to someone else.[63]

The fairly prosaic layout of this prose poem, and its use of relatively simple language, looks like a great deal of contemporary prose. However, the reader's expectations are altered once they begin reading the work, and the demotic style serves to heighten the sense of strangeness it conveys. The matter-of-fact language and unremarkable setting encases the extraordinary firmly within the quotidian.

Simic, Edson, and the Neo-Surreal

In the 1960s and 1970s in America, a group of poets influenced by European surrealism began experimenting with it in new contexts. Of these poets, Simic and Edson are two of the most eminent and helped define neo-surrealist prose poetry in the United States. Simic was born in Yugoslavia and immigrated at sixteen years old; Edson was born in America. This helps explain some of the differences between their prose poems, which Gioia has identified as Simic's "atavistic" attitude to surrealism and Edson's more straightforward regard for it, mostly based on his work's ability to stage "everyman scenarios."[64]

Simic's connection to neo-surrealistic techniques may be illustrated by a well-known prose poem in which the narrator's mother is a "braid of black smoke" and the narrator is floating over "burning cities." This work turns on surreal images of mother and child in the universe presented in a dreamlike narrative. Part of its appeal derives from imagery of the kind often associated with the operations of the unconscious mind, in which the qualities of animate and inanimate things readily merge:

> My mother was a braid of black smoke.
>   She bore me swaddled over the burning cities.
>   The sky was a vast and windy place for a child to play.
>   We met many others who were just like us. They were trying
> to put on their overcoats with arms made of smoke.
>   The high heavens were full of little shrunken deaf ears
> instead of stars.[65]

Such a prose poem may not be read literally. It is, instead, a work that asserts another kind of reality—and, in doing so, it implicitly asks the reader to reconsider their assumptions about the world, giving priority to the imagination and disturbing usual hierarchies of knowledge and understanding.

Furthermore, Simic's regard for the French surrealist prose poets is evident in his referencing of Baudelaire and Breton, alongside the American prose poet Mark Strand, in his "Seven Prose Poems" from 2005. We quote the opening of two of these works:

> I ran into the poet Mark Strand on the street. He immediately challenged me by drinking a glass of wine while standing on his head. I was astonished. He didn't even spill a drop. It was one of the bottles Baudelaire stole from his stepfather the Ambassador in 1848.[66]
>
> My father loved the strange books of André Breton. He'd raise the wine glass and toast those far-off evenings "when butterflies formed a single uncut ribbon."[67]

This writing recasts surrealism and represents a significant development of the neo-surreal in American prose poetry. Simic pays homage to the French surrealists but flags that he is doing something new.

However, Simic's contemporary Russell Edson has quipped: "Why should we have to be surrealists? Breton didn't invent our imaginations."[68] Edson's rejection of automatic writing and his investment in the "logic of composition" drives this statement,[69] and despite his disclaimer, he frequently employs surrealistic techniques in his prose poetry, moving surrealism toward a neo-surrealist grotesque and the abject. One of his prose poems begins:

> You haven't finished your ape, said mother to father, who had monkey hair and blood on his whiskers.
> I've had enough monkey, cried father.
> You didn't eat the hands, and I went to all the trouble to make onion rings for its fingers, said mother.
> I'll just nibble on its forehead, and then I've had enough, said father.[70]

The rather flat and matter-of-fact tonality of this dinner table conversation, coupled with clichéd phrases, heightens the simultaneous sense of strangeness and abjection this prose poem conveys as it encapsulates the extraordinary in the ordinary and conjures the bizarre in the image of "onion rings for its fingers." The choice of "ape" for dinner not only foregrounds the way in which we eat various animals while giving little or no thought to their separate creaturely life but is particularly confronting if we consider a Darwinian reading in which the family may be construed as cannibals.

Mark Tursi writes that Edson's prose poetry follows "a 'logic-of-the-absurd'[;] these poems do not uncover or reveal a Jungian collective unconscious or Bretonian sense of a 'real functioning of thought,' but, rather, they present a disjointed phantasmagoric and anecdotal impulse. This gesture of absurdity draws on the unconscious mind in order to poke fun at, as well as to unsettle, what it is that makes us most human: our blunders, our paranoia, our fears, our joys, our loves, our (false) certainties, and our confusions."[71] Edson's prose poems can be identified as neo-surreal fables that often employ elements of magical realism to heighten their absurdity, even as this is expressed in strangely commonplace terms.

Michel Delville discusses the similarity of some of Edson's prose poems to the French surrealist Max Jacob's poetry for "an ability to tell a strange, snowballing tall tale for its own sake and to twist it into a self-contained poem."[72]

> One of the typical "recipes" for this particular kind of prose poem involves a modern everyman who suddenly tumbles into an alternative reality in which he loses control over himself, sometimes to the point of being irremediably absorbed—both figuratively and literally—by his immediate and, most often, domestic everyday environment. Often, the turning point at which something goes wrong or just does not seem right propels the protagonist into a logic-of-the-absurd sequence, the stages of which are depicted, one after the other, with painstaking, almost hallucinatory precision. Constantly fusing and confusing the banal and the bizarre, Edson delights in having a seemingly innocuous situation undergo the most unlikely and uncanny metamorphoses.[73]

In Simic's and Edson's prose poetry, not only is the extraordinary often made ordinary, but the ordinary is made extraordinary. The two-way process is crucial to understanding how their poems destabilize conventional expectations, and then continue to destabilize them. In the nonchalant delivery of the astonishing, the extraordinary becomes a "given" that the reader is obliged to accept if they are to stay with a poem.

David Lehman has provided a persuasive analysis of this poetic strategy in his explications of two of Simic's best-known prose poems. The first is the analysis of the opening lines of "I was stolen":

> I was stolen by the gypsies. My parents stole
> me right back. Then the gypsies stole me again.
> This went on for some time.[74]

Lehman focuses specifically on the speed of these sentences, arguing that "[t]he succession of sentences, not lines, moves at a speed faster than verse. Then comes the formulaic last sentence to slow down the action. The effect is to make the extraordinary seem somehow routine and it has everything to do with the rhythms of narrative prose."[75]

With reference to the prose poem "We Were So Poor," Lehman rightly draws attention to Simic's "understated prose style" and the way in which it is "at the service of the fantastic and the surreal."[76] However, it is Simic's appeal to the demotic in this prose poem that makes its extraordinary features so unexpected, heightening the absurdism:

> We were so poor I had to take the place of the
> bait in the mousetrap. All alone in the cellar, I
> could hear them pacing upstairs, tossing and turn-

ing in their beds. "These are dark and evil days,"
the mouse told me as he nibbled my ear. Years
passed. My mother wore a cat-fur collar which
she stroked until its sparks lit up the cellar.[77]

The unadorned sentences are mostly composed of single-syllable words, creating a short, swift narrative progression. The opening line, "We were so poor," can even be read as a reference to the pared-back, spare sentences that work to expose the absurdism of the narrator "taking the place of bait." At the end of this first line, the reader can then be said to take "the bait," continuing to read in order to try to understand the bizarre circumstances that the prose poem unfolds. The use of clichés, such as "tossing and turning" and "dark and evil days," appeals to the demotic even as it is embedded within the work's bizarre and fable-like narrative.

Both of these prose poems employ the strategy of condensing significant passages of time into very few words—"this went on for some time" and "Years passed." Such remarks are humorous and they also (briefly) slow the narrative's speed. Additionally, in the second poem, the concept that the narrator has been nibbled on as bait for "years" is bracketed by two examples of anthropomorphism—the mouse speaking to the narrator and the mother who is in a "cat-fur collar." Such irreducible moments may be considered as neo-surrealist echoes of magical realism. They work to bring the quotidian and the fantastic together with a nonchalance that encourages the reader to consider the possibility that "magic happens"—even if such "magic" is neither transformative nor affords the narrator consolation.

The conclusion of the prose poem is electric with the static created by the action of the mother stroking her collar. Michel Delville describes Simic's voice in this prose poem as "alternately poignant and detached, deeply tragic and ruthlessly ironic."[78] This appeal to binaries exposes the kinds of tensions often at work in the prose poetry form while affirming that oppositions can "spark" off one another in the neo-surreal reading experience. When Silliman speaks of prose poetry's appropriateness for housing encounters with the magnificent,[79] he may not have had Simic's poems in mind, but there is certainly something magnificent about Simic's marriage of matter-of-factness with large flights of fancy, a sense that word and meaning in such works are always haunted by dreamy and baffling improbabilities. Almost paradoxically, the matter-of-fact, somewhat fatalistic voice Simic employs in so many of these works functions in tandem with the demotic to heighten his utterance while also connecting it to the day-to-day.

Russell Edson has been dubbed the "Godfather of the Prose Poem in America" by *Booklist*'s Ray Olson and has referred to himself as "Little Mister Prose Poem."[80] Accepting the term "neo-surrealist" as a description of his prose poetry, Edson says his "ideal" prose poem "takes the commonplace, makes it strange and then leaves it there."[81] Edson's prose poems often feature an ordinary family or domestic setting that is ruptured by a conspicuous uneasiness, often in the form of the uncanny or absurd. Such works frequently contain a dreamlike or visionary quality, but Edson's work turns more on creating a persistent sense of an alternative reality than on evoking discrete extraordinary moments. For example, in "Erasing Amyloo" (1994), one of Edson's characters erases his daughter and all her possessions:

> A father with a huge eraser erases his daughter. When he finishes there's only a red smudge on the wall.
> His wife says, where is Amyloo?
> She's a mistake, I erased her.[82]

Lee Upton argues, in the erasure of the female child, Edson is exploring the way "[w]omen are, in one way or another, expunged—by political will, by the patriarchal family, and by metaphorical construction."[83] Additionally, while Edson may expose the vulnerabilities of being a woman in a patriarchal society, the male narrator's further act (as the work continues) of erasing himself from his wife's memory can also be read as a disturbing male fantasy of liberation from the responsibilities of matrimony and fatherhood.

The eraser in this prose poem is a precursor to Bateman's "magic comb of the world." The employment of this everyday image heightens the work's disturbing and implicit questioning of what we value and why, and quizzes the reader as to whether the prose poem's apparent absurdity is as disconnected from real-world human behavior as it may initially appear to be. The demotic is crucial to the work's success and inheres in its dialogue. As husband and wife engage in question and answer, their simplicity of communication seems strangely inadequate to, and pointedly contrasts with, the extraordinary events the prose poem recounts.

"Erasing Amyloo" is as much about what is not there—or what has been erased—as what remains. This is a theme Edson often uses in order to create a sense of poignancy and to heighten the sardonic moment. Edson also uses ellipses to gesture toward the unknown or hidden. For instance, "The Rat's Legs" (2004) ends with an ellipsis:

> I met a rat under a bridge. And we sat there in the mud discussing the rat's loveliness.
> I asked, what is it about you that has caused men to write odes?
> My legs, said the rat, for it has always been that men have liked to run their hands up my legs to my secret parts; it's nature . . .[84]

The anthropomorphism of the rat is reminiscent of Simic's mouse in "We Were So Poor." However, in Edson's prose poem there is an abject moment where the reader is positioned by the work to imagine the rat's "secret parts." While this is another reference to the "unseen," it turns on an uncomfortable humorousness. Readers' responses to the work vary, but along with the mention of "odes," part of its function is to critique the male objectification of women, displacing this issue into a situation involving a genderless rodent. And there is a double irony at work—not only does this invoke ideas of the grotesque but, even as the speaker asks the rat, "what is it about you that has caused men to write odes?," he is writing his own prose poem about the rat.

The construction and rhythms of Simic's and Edson's prose poems depend on their use of often terse and highly controlled sequences of sentences. Flagging the importance of the sentence in prose poetry—and, in doing so, making an important point about what constitutes prose poetry—Lehman writes that Simic's prose poems could be treated as "prose fiction except for their extreme brevity, the ambiguous ways they achieve resolution, and their author's unmistakably poetic intent."[85] In both Edson's and Simic's works there is an emphasis on small syntactical units that are often about the same size as a line in a lyric poem but do not function in the quasi-autonomous way of so many poetic lines.

Instead, these prose poems carry the reader swiftly forward and through their one or more paragraphs, often invoking a narrative frame only to divert their ostensible narrative structure into poetic byways. It is also worth noting that Simic, typically, does not fully right-justify his prose poems, unlike many contemporary prose poets. This helps him to achieve a characteristically droll or wry tonality.

Such a tonality appeals to some readers more than others. Holly Iglesias points out the way in which late twentieth-century prose poetry in America developed a male-centered tradition, quoting Peter Johnson's phrase, "The Wise-Guy School of Poetry" in her analysis, along with Pinsky's coinage, "one-of-the-guys surrealism."[86] She comments that the popularity of American neo-surreal prose poems created an expectation that the prose poem would include humor, which worked to exclude women prose poets from writing "angry, un-funny prose poems" about "the pain and silence of containment."[87]

Interestingly, some women have employed neo-surrealistic techniques in their prose poetry. Delville says, "Among the younger generation of American fabulists, the name of Maxine Chernoff stands out."[88] In Chernoff's prose poem "Kill Yourself with an *Objet D'art*," first published in 1978, she mentions the unconscious, Sigmund Freud, and the surrealist painter Max Ernst, among a variety of other references. In this way, and in its ironic and rather absurdist mode of address, the work pays homage to (and begins to rewrite) so much that informs the neo-surrealistic strand of American prose poetry:

> Choose a heavy one shaped like (a) your first ride in a car or (b) the Hitchcock leg-of-lamb, served at dinner to the unsuspecting detective. Or a light *objet d'art*, (c) an ice cube in whose reflection is suggested the history of the subconscious.[89]

The Neo-surreal in Australia and Britain

While it is not always helpful to discuss prose poems by nationality, given prose poetry is a highly diverse international form, there is no question that the neo-surreal in prose poetry is differently nuanced in different countries. For instance, the prose poem is gaining popularity in Australia, and neo-surrealist Australian prose poets are an important part of this growing culture—perhaps because, like America, it is a relatively "new" country with a colonial past.

However, the Australian neo-surreal rarely sounds quite like the Americans. Australian writers tend to produce a more emphatic form of neo-surrealism that often incorporates black humor or a blunter kind of seriousness than the majority of neo-surreal American works, and is rarely as droll or amusing. Such effects are frequently enhanced, rather than softened, by being joined with a laconic style. Where Simic and Edson make considerable use of unadorned sentences to complicate the extraordinary, many Australian prose poets use a loose, casual style to discuss heightened moments of anguish.

Here are three brief examples. The first is from Gary Catalano. In "Incident from a War," he transforms a potentially devastating moment:

> When the enemy planes flew over our city they disgorged
> not bombs but loaves of bread. Can you imagine our
> surprise? We ventured outside after those planes had
> disappeared from the sky, and what did we find there but
> heaps of broken bread at which the pigeons were already
> feeding?[90]

Rather than extinguishing life, the enemy has dropped food. This is a strangely poignant and absurdist moment that casts the mind toward the repeated destruction of war and also toward the grotesque more generally. In making his poetic gesture, perhaps Catalano is making reference to the Christian idea of breaking bread and, if understood as black humor, the work might even be read as a kind of Last Supper. The strangeness of loaves being dropped from the sky may also obscurely refer to the pumpkins the American military dropped as practice prior to dropping the atomic bomb on Hiroshima in 1945.

Even if such references are not explicit, the poem powerfully conjures the threat of the bomb precisely because it refuses to comment directly on it. What is absent in this poem is therefore most present—a maneuver that characterizes many prose poems—and the anticlimactic, ordinary image of the feeding pigeons recognizes the immense loss and suffering that warfare brings with it. The upbeat language, including the question "Can you imagine our surprise?," is a clever device that works to heighten the horror of the city's potential annihilation—even if, in this particular work, such annihilation has been postponed.

In Polish-born Alex Skovron's work, "Supplication" may not be neo-surrealist in any strict sense, but it discomposes the reality we know in a poem that, by its end, is increasingly dreamlike. It begins:

> LET THE FILM turn before it touches the Moment. Let the motorcade stop, drift backward down the plaza. Let the jetliner freeze, metres short of the tower, flow back out of the frame like a toy wing at the sling's limit. Let the black plumes billowing from the edifice be reinhaled to unmask the blue. Let the bullet thread with a thud back in the barrel crouching in the gateway, the victim clinch his scarf and vanish within.[91]

The work refers to some of the greatest horrors in world history—beginning with the assassination of John F. Kennedy—and is presented as if in a film being wound backward (perhaps referencing the disturbing Zapruder film that captures Kennedy's assassination). Skovron reverses many significant "Moment[s]"—to ask, for example, what if 9/11 hadn't occurred or Hitler had not come to power? In the phrase "Let the ovens clang open,"[92] the onomatopoeia even dares to confront the Nazi genocide.

Skovron does not suggest that these events may be erased. Rather, he reminds the reader that moments and occasions like these are so momentous that they may appear forever poised in the historical view, and may also presage similar future events. In this way, while there are familiar historical events and phrases in this prose poem, the sense of disjuncture that the poem imposes on them becomes a form of the neo-surreal's "antagonistic embrace."

Ania Walwicz writes frenetically and often without punctuation. Also born in Poland and having migrated to Australia at twelve years old, she "draws on the tradition of the European surrealist practice" to elucidate the migrant experience in many of her prose poems.[93] This work is often neo-surrealistic in its emphasis on the postcolonial uncanny and elements of urban fantasy. For example, in "Neons" (1996) Walwicz points to postfeminist constructions of female sexuality and performance:

> . . . dress to top fashion strut get them wiggle pink face daze me amaze shine me neons on sweet buzz meter front room seat skip dance non stop favourite flower colour allans sweets on river shine thrill me thrill me rise in a loop get up early do lots the more better fast faster lit light on me in such show glow me ania it's now don't wait hurry up top tip they clap they whistle stomp yell out aloud more on high want more and more fresh new dare do do new do now very it just here spot lit wear shiny glisteny get tight tonight darling neon electric[94]

The humor in these Australian prose poems is somewhat different from that of the Americans. Catalano and Skovron transform the horrors of war into something darkly comic and strangely ominous—and Skovron's poem is more ominous than humorous—while Walwicz presents a jarring and staccato series of absurdisms to draw attention to postfeminist objectification, fetishization, and empowerment. If these prose poems can be read as a form of Australian neo-surrealism, they are more direct overall than the American work and less preoccupied with overt narrative tropes. While Australian and American prose poetry comes in many varieties, these examples highlight significant differences between prose poetry in these two countries.

Until recently, prose poetry has not been particularly popular in the United Kingdom, and Bill Manhire links this to a wariness about surrealism: "The prose poem has a very doubtful life in England—perhaps because surrealism (to which the form has links) never caught on there, perhaps because poetry in English was never as inflexible as poetry in other languages."[95] While David Miller and Rupert Loydell's 1996 anthology, *A Curious Architecture: A Selection of Contemporary Prose Poems*, is primarily comprised of prose poets from the United Kingdom and offers important commentary on the form, *This Line Is Not For Turning: An Anthology of Contemporary British Prose Poetry*, published in 2011, is the first contemporary anthology of prose poetry that exclusively features writers from Britain. In her introduction to the anthology, Jane Monson states that prose poetry is a neglected form in Britain, and Beverly Ellis, in reviewing the book, suggests that in some quarters in Britain, "the prose poem has been regarded as an upstart form—or no form at all."[96]

While prose poems in these publications are fairly varied, those aiming to critique society or conventional mores (as many neo-surrealist works do) tend to be satirical, or they challenge or ridicule authority fairly directly. For example, Sylvia Fairclough's "Unavailable" (2011) is a wry parody of those who are in positions of power:

> Someone had folded her clothes and put them on the bed, stripped now to a thick plastic sheet. On top of her nightie was a menu card; under 'special requests' she had scratched: *rarsbries*.
>
> In smudged red ink, someone had stamped: UNAVAILABLE.[97]

The publication of *The Valley Press Anthology of Prose Poetry* in 2019 marks the first British anthology with a strong selection of neo-surreal prose poems. Editors Anne Caldwell and Oz Hardwick "aim[ed] to showcase the variety of work being produced by contemporary writers born in—or working in—Great Britain and Northern Ireland."[98] Poems such as Luke Kennard's "A.I.," Linda Black's "My Mother is Locked in a Jar of Ginger," George Szirtes's "Twelve Dark Passages No. 6," Winston Plowes's "The Rooms Behind the Eyes," Ian Seed's "The House that Jack Built," and Jane Burn's "Picture of the Dead Woman as a Bride" demonstrate a range of prose poets working confidently with neo-surrealist ideas.

George Szirtes, Pascale Petit, Simon Armitage, Linda Black, Ian Seed, Luke Kennard (who drew attention to the prose poetry form in Britain by being the youngest poet shortlisted for the Forward Prize for his book of prose poetry *The Harbour Beyond the Movie*), and Anthony Caleshu, an American expatriate in Britain, are conspicuous UK practitioners of the neo-surreal. One may note that currently there are more men than women working consistently with the neo-surreal in their prose poems—or perhaps, like the Americans, men are having more success in getting their collections of neo-surreal prose poetry published. As the form continues to proliferate in the United Kingdom, it remains to be seen whether similar collections written by women are published in the same numbers.

As major proponents of the neo-surreal prose poem in Britain, Ian Seed and Oz Hardwick could loosely be described as British counterparts to Simic and Edson in their commitment to idiosyncratic neo-surreal parables. Many of Seed's prose poems are set in the United Kingdom, and European countries, such as Italy and Poland, also feature heavily in his work. His prose poems, like Simic's, appeal to the extraordinary in the everyday but convey a different sense of humor and a greater degree of whimsy. The endings of his poems frequently invoke the unexpected, as with his poem "A Life," set in a "cartoon world," which concludes:

> I came to the sea, but since it was a cartoon sea, would I get wet if I stepped into it? I was afraid to try, but here was a mermaid inviting me in. If I held her hand, would I feel it in mine? If she wanted to make love, what would I do?[99]

Like Edson, Hardwick never completely dissolves the world in his neo-surreal prose poems and seeks out a space for the fantastic—and at times, the absurd—in his evocations of the quotidian. For example, in "Graduation," the protagonist opens his "never even emptied schoolbag" after decades of having left it in the cupboard:

> Then once, when he was visiting his now-aged parents, he had an urge to look, and there it was, still. With pre-emptive tears prickling his eyes, he opened it and saw that the books had grown back into trees, with damp grass all around, and there were birds like notes on telegraph wires, singing a song he'd written in an abandoned bandstand: it was about cheap sparkling cider, the smell of fireworks, subtle indentations in a sloping lawn.[100]

Kennard's and Caleshu's use of the neo-surreal is more darkly comic, and sometimes more directly political, than many American neo-surreal prose poems. In "No Stars" Kennard comments on contemporary horror films and, in doing so, deconstructs ideas of mortality and intimacy:

> At that time it was customary to wear a complete adult human skeleton around one's neck, which made moving house harder than ever and embrac-

ing almost impossible. There was a wild panic to the blue sky. The clack of our skeletons as we leant in to embrace, until we came to associate affection with clacking. But still we dated.[101]

Caleshu's "With Your Permission, Allow Me To Perform Exemplary Surgery On Your Brain," is both abject and darkly philosophical in its commentary on the unthinkable and unknowable:

> Elbow-deep in your head, the surgeon of your dreams may not be me, prodding your temporal lobe with a virtual pen, but both of us can see there's much to be gained in terms of scintillation and smell. Though we aim to find and reflect all the mystery in the world, it's as hard to possess as it is to predict.[102]

Simon Armitage has written a number of prose poems that have elements of the neo-surreal, including "The Christening" (2011), which begins:

> I am a sperm whale. I carry up to 2.5 tonnes of an oil-like
> balm in my huge, coffin-shaped head. I have a brain the
> size of a basketball, and on that basis alone am entitled
> to my opinions. I am a sperm whale. When I breathe in the
> fluid in my head cools to a dense wax and I nosedive into
> the depths.[103]

Such a work relies on developing and extending an absurd notion and, in doing so, introducing more and more humorous elements that estrange the reader from any sense of the "real." There are serious themes at work in this prose poem—relating to the natural world, the preservation of wild animals, and ideas about belief—but a poem like this never becomes surreal in the sense that Breton would have recognized, no matter how accomplished it is.

Marc Atkins writes works that are surreal in the original sense of the term, but even Atkins's works tend to play metapoetically with their neo-surrealisms, as his book *The Logic of the Stairwell and Other Images* (2011) illustrates. This takes the reader into the world of sleep, dreams, and an alternative reality, but it does not discompose its world entirely. In reading it, we still feel reasonably well anchored to our usual apprehensions. In the following excerpt from the first section of "Afterwords," Atkins's hallucinatory moments are almost contemplative:

> Sip the day. Entering a long room long lost images slip by before me. We rode on at a loss and promise keeping a pace in step for a bed was at every mile. Should you pull me gently into your loving corner set adrift those careless enough to be walled in. I am the dawn and the dusk pity that when caressing my deadly lungs. Watch for the famous patients who hide an array of tortured calotypes in their flower baskets . . .[104]

Pascale Petit is a French-born British prose poet and one of the few women in the United Kingdom who regularly makes use of the neo-surreal, often via explorations of myth. Her long two-part prose poem, "My Larzac Childhood," focuses on transformation and begins by evoking supernatural moments that alleviate the mundanity of daily chores. It ends with an exchange between the volcanic child and the mother she has resurrected from the earth:

> I call her and she rises, trailing a rain of roots and stalactites, like the stormcloud at the end of childhood's summer.
>
> She sits with me at the table, a hulk of electric air; a river's catch. Raised and suspended . . .
>
> My plate spins and I start eating Catherine wheels. I drink the wine of newborn stars; sip cognac old as Centaurus.[105]

In general, then, there is no doubt that English-language prose poets everywhere are making their own versions of the neo-surreal—especially the Americans with their diverse and well-developed neo-surreal tradition. Recent and contemporary pratitioners of the neo-surreal undoubtedly adopt different manners and methods than those of their European surrealist forerunners, but their sense of purpose is clear—and the quality of the best twentieth- and early twenty-first-century neo-surreal prose poetry stands up well against the prose poems of nineteenth-century French luminaries such as Baudelaire and Rimbaud. In exploring the stuff of dreams and nightmares, and through exploiting prose poetry's capacity to unite the demotic, the quotidian, and the apparently fantastical in potent and disturbing combinations, English-language neo-surreal prose poetry constitutes a great deal of varied and fascinating work.

CHAPTER 6

Prose Poetry and TimeSpace

Time and Space

It is now generally accepted for observers of an event that time and space are unified. There are many different ways of naming the connection between time and space, including space-time, timespace, or—our preferred term—TimeSpace, which Immanuel Wallerstein coined in 1991.[1] His removal of the hyphen from between the words and his retention of their capital letters attempts to abolish any prioritization of one concept over the other. Wallerstein argues that the term TimeSpace highlights the interdependency or indissolubility of time and space in human experience. The concept is a useful tool for analyzing prose poetry because time and space function differently in prose poetry compared to lineated poetry or prose fiction.

As we have discussed, a prose poem's characteristic form is a condensed and highly suggestive paragraph, or a brief series of paragraphs, and typically contains no line breaks of the kind one finds in lineated poetry. The sense of TimeSpace within such works tends to be compressed and intensified. This is unlike lineated poetry because although lineated lyric poems, in particular, often create a sense of considerable compression and intensity, the relative abundance of white space in such works creates a countervailing sense that there is room to think and breathe. Prose poetry is also unlike prose fiction, in which the emphasis on narrative progression gives priority to a sense of directed forward movement through TimeSpace—an emphasis that is very different from the effects created by most prose poems.

Furthermore, what has been called the "friction of distance" is lessened by prose poetry's tightly packed, often fully justified blocks of text on the page or screen. Everything in a typical prose poem is more or less contiguous with everything else. Thus, the prose poem has the capacity to change, and even distort, the reader's sense of time and space. While a prose poem may create an impression of forward momentum as the grammar and sequencing of the prose poem's tightly packed sentences carry the reader forward, its poetic tropes simultaneously complicate or problematize any sense of one-way progression. As a result, prose poems usually yield for the reader a complex textual engagement in which ideas and motifs frequently fold back on themselves, or present unresolved issues for consideration.

When analyzing TimeSpace in literature, various scholars turn to Russian philosopher and literary critic Mikhail Bakhtin's theory of the literary chronotope (usually translated as time-space), which denotes the "intrinsic connectedness of temporal and space relationships."[2] In addition to being influenced by Einstein's theory of relativity, Bakhtin's ideas about chronotopes build on Immanuel Kant's view that human beings structure and understand the universe as a fusing of space and time. While Kant and Einstein maintain a central focus on human experience and perception in the real world and on the laws of physics governing the universe, Bakhtin is primarily interested in literary texts and their historical manifestations, and the organizational processes of literature.

He posits that every narrative text has at its base a definable fictional universe akin to the physical world and, therefore, considerations that apply to the real world are relevant to literary works. The chronotope is one way of differentiating literary genres or categories based on their different features and worldviews.[3] Examples of chronotopes Bakhtin mentions—and he states that different chronotopes may coexist and even contradict one another in a single work—include "the idyll," the "road," "parlours and salons," the "provincial town," the "threshold," and "biographical time."[4] In applying such concepts Bakhtin notes, for instance, that a key to the novels of Russian author Leo Tolstoy is understanding how "biographical time . . . flows smoothly in the spaces—the interior spaces—of townhouses and estates of the nobility."[5] He contends, "Tolstoy loves duration, the stretching out of time."[6]

Although Bakhtin is acutely aware of the irreducibility of the TimeSpace connection, he is generally most interested in time and narrative, writing that the significance of chronotopes

> is their meaning for *narrative*. They are the organising centers for the fundamental narrative events of the novel. The chronotope is the place where the knots of narrative are tied and untied. It can be said without qualification that to them belongs the meaning that shapes narrative . . . [and that they provide] the ground essential for the showing-forth . . . of events. And this is so thanks precisely to the special increase in density and concreteness of time markers—the time of human life, and historical time—that occurs within well-delineated spatial areas.[7]

Because Bakhtin was mainly concerned with the novel, some scholars have questioned the relevance of chronotopes to poetry—particularly nonnarrative or lyric poetry. Peter Barry writes, "The real problem is . . . that a great deal of contemporary poetry is really without any identifiable chronotope at all."[8] Lineated lyric poetry is often considered to have limited plots, characters, and scenes, and its line breaks often disrupt the usual flow of syntax along with the unfolding of time, space, and meaning that we are familiar with in most discursive prose.

In prose poetry, too, chronotopes do not operate in ways that are consistent with Bakhtin's characterization of their operation in the novel, nor do they usually conform to the ways we usually understand quotidian time and space. Chronotopes in prose poetry are often part of a narrative structure, but because the narratives of prose poems are so frequently severely compressed and fragmented, their chronotopes do not develop in the manner that a novelist would develop them. For example, if the chronotope of the "road" occurs in a prose poem, it is highly unlikely to suggest the significant and extended unfolding narrative familiar to us from so many road novels.

Thus, the form of the prose poem is visually and spatially compressed, and prose poems tend to move quickly (and not always evenly), disrupting any apprehension of the smooth flow of time or of a fully realized spatial dimension. Prose poems contain what one may call "informational gaps or spaces"—what is not fully told by or represented in the text—that cause the narrative flow (the reader's sense of such works' movement through time) to be problematized, even as the form itself tends to push a reader along at speed. As a result, the chronotopes within prose poems are mostly incompletely expressed or realized and tend to have a suggestive, truncated, fragmentary, or elusive quality. Because prose poems do not develop their chronotopes fully, they leave the reader to bring their own inflections to them.

If the compression of prose poetry is one of the major features of the form, discussions of TimeSpace theory have linked compression to speed and dynamism. The idea of compression also has a broader relevance. Anthropologist and geographer David Harvey argues that globalism and technology have caused a sense of the "compression" of space and time.[9] We discuss this idea at greater length at this juncture and also in chapter 10. However, as we introduce the concepts of TimeSpace and the chronotope, it is worth noting that experiences of living with a "sense of compression" and at speed is one of the most significant features of postmodernity finding expression in contemporary literature—with the prose poem being a prime site for such expression.

It is also true that while prose poetry tends to move quickly, there is a counterbalancing tendency in many prose poems connected to the nature of lyric utterance (many, but not all, prose poems have lyric features). As Katharine Coles remarks:

> The prose poem . . . navigates time and retards its own syntax through lyric rather than narrative motion, through sonic and figurative recursion and retard rather than propulsion . . . Inside it, as in an image, everything happens at once, though syntax, proceeding one word at a time, wants it not to.[10]

We mention this because even as many prose poems move quickly, compelling the reader onward, they also demand the kind of attention at the level of words, phrases, and sentences that many conventional prose works do not. Prose poetry is often quick to encounter and slow to fully apprehend.

TimeSpace and Poetry

Even before Einstein's theory of special relativity, poets demonstrated a natural inclination to couple space with time. Marvell's "To His Coy Mistress" begins with the famous line, "Had we but world enough, and time," and Whitman's "Song of Myself" states, "I know I have the best of time and space, and was never measured and never will be measured."[11] Shakespeare's sonnets and plays also often explore the intimate relationship between space, time, and motion, perhaps most famously in Macbeth's soliloquy including the line "Tomorrow, and tomorrow, and tomorrow,"[12] with its emphasis on the repetition and monotony of life.

This soliloquy provides a good example of how poetry's lineation (and its meter, enjambment, and particular rhythmic effects—all techniques associated with the poetic line) may be put to brilliant use. Even if we only look at the opening lines of this speech, we find a great deal:

She should have died hereafter;
There would have been a time for such a word—
Tomorrow, and tomorrow, and tomorrow,
Creeps in this petty pace from day to day,
To the last syllable of recorded time;
And all our yesterdays have lighted fools
The way to dusty death.[13]

This passage has an authoritative and stately air—appropriate to the character of a king—that partly derives from the measured progress of its lines of iambic pentameter. The poetry's phrasing and diction compel attention because it mixes direct statements with tropes that demand that the reader pause and consider their import. While it is possible to read this passage quickly, to do so would be to resist its various strategies that aim to slow the reader.

For instance, while the assertion "There would have been time for such a word" is, in one sense, simply a comment on the untimeliness of Lady Macbeth's death, it also poses implicit questions: When would such a time be appropriate, and how does one conceive of such a time? (One of the reasons this poetic line resonates so effectively—like a quivering string on a musical instrument—is that there is white space before and after it, and it sounds loudly in such space.) As if to answer these questions, the next line's repetition suggests that such a time is an indefinite series of tomorrows away—positing the notion that Macbeth is hopelessly and irretrievably lost from his own right time and identity.

The metaphors that follow diminish him—and humanity in general—through their references to pettiness and foolishness, and, as they do, the plosive "p" and "d" alliterations in the fourth line are hard to utter at speed. For the duration of this line, the "petty pace" is ours as readers, emphasizing how Macbeth's particular crisis, at a more general level, may be an enduring crisis for us all. Lineated poetry such as this differs from prose poetry in its vertical rather than horizontal trajectory and results in a different kind of momentum. Encounters with white space on the page (or computer screen) may slow a poem, as in this example from *Macbeth*—not only because of the poetic effects and techniques already identified, but because, as Jen Crawford notes, "the breaking of the line for the space of the page can offer an encounter with 'surrounding silence.'"[14] In other words, the spaces in and around lineated poetry act as a significant form of punctuation, and even of dilation.

In the majority of lineated poems, white space is normally most noticeable between stanzas and at the end of each line, where the text ends before the right margin. These are the places where the reader typically pauses or hesitates (even if unaware of doing so) before moving to the next line—and this process occurs in poems of all kinds. For instance, such effects are evident even in a relatively formal, rhymed, musical, and flowing nineteenth-century poem that unfolds a coherent and connected set of thoughts and feelings—Elizabeth Barrett Browning's "How Do I Love Thee?" (Sonnet 43).

Browning's poem capitalizes on the presence of white space at the poem's right margin through its use of end-stopped and enjambed metrical lines. Additionally, other punctuation in the work emphasizes the caesuras in the poem, creating the effect of a twinned pause (or breath) in various lines. These techniques contribute to the sonnet's unhurried pace and flexible rhythms, its impression of composure, and the sense that a kind of stillness inhabits the work:

> How do I love thee? Let me count the ways.
> I love thee to the depth and breadth and height
> My soul can reach, when feeling out of sight
> For the ends of Being and ideal Grace.
> I love thee to the level of every day's
> Most quiet need, by sun and candlelight.
> I love thee freely, as men strive for Right;
> I love thee purely, as they turn from Praise.
> I love thee with the passion put to use
> In my old griefs, and with my childhood's faith.
> I love thee with a love I seemed to lose
> With my lost saints—I love thee with the breath,
> Smiles, tears, of all my life!—and, if God choose,
> I shall but love thee better after death.[15]

The use in this poem of five—occasionally inverted—iambic feet per line, cadenced rhythms, and an overarching metrical structure reminds one of the ancient connection between lyric poetry and song. The poem's form and rhythm, and even the way it constructs a significant part of its meaning through insistent, rather rhetorical repetition, along with its employment of the large abstractions "Right" and "Praise," implicitly asks the reader to take their time.

Seven of the poem's lines come nearly to a halt. This, the metrical regularity, and the chiming of rhymes combines with the white space around the poem to create a sense for the reader not unlike the verbal equivalent of the tolling of bells. The white space resonates and opens out as the poem proceeds, and a sympathetic reader will begin to inhabit the poem viscerally, hearing it much as they might hear a tune. This sonnet also introduces various pauses of differing lengths as it progresses, making use of mid- and end-of-line commas and periods until it builds to an exclamation mark coupled with an em dash in its penultimate line. Such effects add variety to Browning's marshaling of her iambic pentameter, assisting her to create a sense of escalating intensity and emotion.

The nineteenth century's most radical innovator in his use of white space in poetry was the French symbolist Stéphane Mallarmé (1842–98), whose early writing owed a debt to Charles Baudelaire. In his preface to his radical and groundbreaking late work, *A Roll of the Dice* (*Un Coup de Dés*)—first published in the late nineteenth century just prior to Mallarmé's death and fairly frequently republished and translated since—Mallarmé discusses the importance of white space and the syncopation between space and text. He writes that "The 'white spaces' . . . assume importance, are the first that strike our eyes; versification has always required them, usually as an encompassing silence."[16] Mallarmé also discusses how the effect of reading lines of a poem across "this copied distance" of the double page "seems to sometimes accelerate and slow the movement, articulating it, even intimating it through a simultaneous vision of the Page."[17]

Stonecipher states, "*Un Coup de Dés* was the most radical poetic use of space ever published up to that point,"[18] and an example of Mallarmé's use of white space is evident in the brief excerpt on the next page.* Many critics have discussed the use of white space in Mallarmé's poetry, perhaps most notably Jacques Derrida, who comments on how "Mallarmé *describes* the suspensive value of the title [of a poem], or more precisely of the empty space it marks out at the top of the page."[20] Derrida also states, "What ruins the '*pious capital letter*' of the title and works towards the decapitation or ungluing of the text is the regular intervention of the blanks, the ordered return of the white spaces."[21] Pamela Marie Hoffer adds, "Mallarmé uses the disposition of words on the page to create gaps in meaning, silences . . . *Absence*, in the form of blank spaces, is hyperbolically *present* in his writing."[22] Jean-Paul Sartre notices that in Mallarmé's poetry, "Meaning is a second

---

*It should be noted that we cannot quote this as it occurs in the source text because there the poem runs across the wide space of a double-page text and thus contains even more white space than we are able to show.

NOTHING

of the memorable crisis
or if it were
the event

fulfilled in light of all voided outcomes
human

WILL HAVE TAKEN PLACE
an ordinary elevation pours absence[19]

silence deep within silence ... What is involved here is not the mere absence of a particular being, but a 'quivering disappearance.'"[23]

To some extent, these philosophers and critics take their cue from Mallarmé's own statements. In his essay "Crisis of Verse," he claims that in "the book of verse ... [e]verything is suspended, an arrangement of fragments with alternations and confrontations, adding up to a total rhythm, which would be the poem stilled, in the blanks."[24] Because of these "blanks," in addressing poems such as *A Roll of the Dice*, the reader must create bridges or rafts between lines in the search to suture the poem's almost freely floating phrases into a set of coherent meanings. A slow pace of reading results because readers are confronted with significant and, to some extent, unresolvable gaps in meaning.

The spaces in this poem create pauses of differing lengths—and a sense of intensification too—that contribute to opening out its suggestiveness. The reader is compelled to pay a great deal of attention to the relatively few, almost freely floating words and phrases, while the gaps in the poem also underline the importance of the capitalized words, opening the poem into a consideration of emptiness and timelessness. The meshing of time and space is strongly emphasized in such writing—to the extent that, in general terms, *A Roll of the Dice* may be said to present a detached chronotope of both timeless absence and articulate emptiness in its structure and content (words such as "NOTHING," "voided," and "absence" in the quoted excerpt emphasize such a reading).

An encounter with this poem is not only slowed by the conspicuous extravagance of space, but it is further slowed by the reader's tendency to revisit lines, or even to reread the whole text. The reader searches the poem's spaces to make connections between its words and to unlock the poem's aggregate set of meanings. The white space partly functions as an aporia or undecidability, emphasizing that the poem is unable to complete itself and implying that it is the reader's responsibility to try to do so. (We discuss aspects of this process in more detail in chapter 8 in our discussion of metaphor and metonymy in prose poetry.)

Thus, white space functions as a breathing space, or space of recollection or reflection for the reader—and, in some cases it may even encourage extended contemplation. Even enjambed lines in a lineated poem function differently from sentences in prose poems, because they also float in a greater expanse of space than one will find in the crowded and sometimes cramped quarters of a prose poem. In her focus on the city, Stonecipher reminds us that space is "luxurious" and invokes "silence" in the "open space, space to breathe."[25] White space has the potential to elongate the time of reading and to stretch out the reader's sense of a work.

In Fiona Benson's lyric "Demeter," the lines—many of them enjambed—are spread down the page in a vertical trajectory, never meeting the right margin. These lines generate the prosaic rhythms one finds in many "free verse" poems, yet because of its lineation, it is quite unlike a prose poem—especially in the way the poem's text interacts with white space. Here is a section of the poem:

> I head down the path hoping she'll come
> but when I look back she's gone and my own voice
> snags at her name like barbed wire on skin.
> When I see her again she's halfway down the field
> emerging from behind another bale
> as if they were portals or wormholes to pass her
> through this sun-bleached meadow—impossible—
> her mouth is bruised with blackberry juice
> and she keeps disappearing, the way a cormorant
> will dive, then reappear a mile upriver,
> disappearing, as if into hell through the shadow
> of a hay bale—Demeter will be screaming soon,
> cutting her wrists with broken glass,[26]

While this poem has something of a headlong quality, its judicious use of enjambment, allied with occasional commas and an end-of-line em dash, encourages the reader to pause at the end of lines as they meet the irregular raft of white space that stretches from each line's end to the page's right margin.

Indeed, even the effects of enjambment are heightened as the reader makes this momentary pause. Although each line in the poem is part of a longer sentence, it may also be read and understood independently (even as such a reading to some extent fractures the grammar). For example, the passage "When I see her again / she's halfway down the field / emerging from behind another bale / as if they were portals or wormholes to pass her" consists of clauses and phrases that build sequentially on one another—and the end-of-line pauses heighten the passage's descriptive and dramatic power, allowing the reader to digest and assimilate the import of the poem's imagery and associated narrative as it unfolds. Significantly, the use of the em dashes around the word "—impossible—" extends that word into the long white space on the right of the line. White space matters to such a work in important ways, even if, as we read, we may barely notice it.

Some more prosaic works spread sentences out on the page, making use of repetitious effects (and sometimes the free-line, which we discussed in chapter 4). For instance, Joe Brainard's long hybrid work, "I Remember"—characterized by Judith A. Hoffberg as using a "declarative prose-poem mode"[27]—employs free verse techniques that owe something to those of Walt Whitman. Here is a brief excerpt from early in the work:

> I remember when I thought that if you did anything bad, policemen would put you in jail
> I remember one very cold and black night on the beach alone with Frank O'Hara. He ran into the ocean naked and it scared me to death.
> I remember lightning.
> I remember wild red poppies in Italy.

I remember selling blood every three months on Second Avenue.

I remember a boy I once made love with and after it was all over he asked me if I believed in God.

I remember when I thought that anything old was very valuable.[28]

The insistently repetitious use of "I remember" is not unlike an exaggerated version of Browning's "I love thee" in its poetic effect, except that Brainard pushes his repetition much further. Overall, such techniques prolong the reading experience because readers are encouraged to breathe between and around the sentences and to register the spaces between them—not unlike the way they are encouraged to pause at the end of many of the lines of Browning's sonnet. Brainard's work is structured like a very extended and loose free verse lyric, but its prosy lines and insistent engagement with the quotidian make it more a work of poetic prose than (an elongated) lyric poem.

In discussing William Wordsworth's poetry, Christopher Ricks quotes from his "Home at Grasmere": "Dreamlike the blending also of the whole / Harmonious Landscape, all along the shore / The boundary lost—the line invisible / That parts the image from reality."[29] He comments:

> The boundary is also that which we cross when we pass from one "line" to another; "the line invisible" (following the dash—) is . . . "invisible" because it is emblematised on the page by the white space . . . Invisible, but not non-existent; there is no thing solidly there, no formal punctuation, but there is nevertheless the parting—by means of a significant space, a significant vacancy—of one thing from another.[30]

This nicely summarizes the way in which lineated poetry so often makes use of its line breaks, not only to slow the progress of a poem, however imperceptibly, but to create a sense that a poem is buttressed by empty and often highly suggestive space, and crowded, as it were, by absence and the ineffable.

Thus, in general terms, the connections between time and space in poetry are deep and inextricable. When one speaks of the movement of time and the function of space in a poem, one is partly speaking of the content of a work, and partly speaking of the disposition of white space—either at the level of line breaks and stanza breaks or in terms of the entire layout of a contemporary work such as Mallarmé's *A Roll of the Dice*. In every case, white space interacts with the words of a poem, so one is always faced with understanding the relationships between the various poetic elements one encounters, including a work's absences and gaps.

Analyses of TimeSpace in poetry need to consider the interaction between a poem's language and the language's situation within—and construal of—space. The way in which this situation and construal affects a reader's apprehension of time also needs consideration. These are complex issues because, for example, if Mallarmé's work expands the reader's awareness of space—and construes it as absence and emptiness—it also simultaneously occupies that space, filling it with an active and heightened verbal suggestiveness. The poem simultaneously moves the reader through time and slows the reader's apprehension of time by enriching space in a highly suggestive way. It creates the paradox that the reader's awareness of emptiness is heightened by the poem's insistence on its own suggestive and engaging presence, and by use of tropes related to the passage of time, such as "the event / fulfilled" and the idea of what "WILL HAVE TAKEN PLACE."

Prose Poetry in TimeSpace

Prose poetry does not possess the kinds of spaces found in Mallarmé's poetry, nor does it make use of poetic lines amid "encompassing silence" in the manner of the examples from Shakespeare and Browning. Instead, it encourages a horizontal sliding across the page on the part of the reader. James Harms expresses this poetically when he discusses the way prose poems "feel horizontal in their rhetorical designs, like waves rushing up the beach, slowly flattening out into foam and a thin sheet of water, then receding back to the depths."[31] This immediately creates a reading velocity different from almost all lineated poetry. The tallying moment for many prose poems occurs only at their conclusion where, finally encountering white space, and freed from the work's dense construction of TimeSpace, the reader starts to breathe more freely, piece the work together imaginatively, and reflect on the language, tropes, and meanings they have encountered.

As John Sibley Williams says, "All forms of poetry manipulate the page's white space for certain effects. Oddly structured, experimental poems often provide vast gaps between words or lines, which separates [sic] key ideas or images from each other and fosters a sense of distance. The prose poem does the opposite. Readers will react differently to this spatial oddity, as the compact, close-knit images provide no breathing room or safe, eye-friendly white space."[32]

Because prose poetry utilizes the sentence rather than the line as its main unit of composition, it does not invite and parry a set of relationships between truncated lines and white space on a ragged right margin. Prose poetry tends to fill its internal space and simultaneously create a border that encloses its language somewhat like a perimeter fence. (However, this border is to some extent porous, because of the tendency of white space to leak into verbal constructs, no matter how tightly they are made.) Overall, prose poetry's relationship to the right margin is fairly consistent with Mary Oliver's comment that "prose is printed (or written) within the confines of margins, while poetry is written in lines that do not necessarily pay any attention to the margins, especially the right margin."[33] Morton Marcus takes this a step further to argue that prose poetry liberates poets from "the tyranny of the line."[34]

Prose poetry takes some of its cues from prose fiction—not only in the way it establishes its relationship to the right margin but also in its composition of sentences. Yet, while neither prose fiction nor prose poetry usually makes active use of an expanse of white space at the right margin, there are exceptions. For instance, when dialogue occurs in prose fiction—and this is also true of some prose poems—every new utterance by a speaker begins a new line. Short lines of dialogue, in particular, often sit in large amounts of space. However, the effect of encountering such dialogue in prose poetry is different from the effect of encountering it in prose fiction.

In prose fiction, an abundance of white space usually encourages readers to follow a vertical trajectory, skipping quickly down the page. Because prose fiction does not have the same focus as poetry on allying a poetic suggestiveness to its economy of language, the white space that abuts the dialogue of prose fiction does not reverberate with the kinds of secondary or connotative meanings that are activated by most lineated poems or prose poems. Thus, the white space tends not to slow the experience of reading (lines of prose fiction dialogue do not usually encourage reflection or a pause for breath at the right margin) and, as a result, "white space" has much less of a role to play in prose fiction than in prose poetry.

An example may be found in Raymond Carver's well-known short story "Will You Please Be Quiet, Please?" (from his book by the same title). Here the narrative gestures and dialogue are spare and quickly moving, and the reader's eyes move quickly, too:

> Carl passed the tube.
> Jack stood up and stretched.
> "Where are you going, honey?" Mary asked.
> "No place," Jack said. He sat down and shook his head and grinned.
>   "Jesus."
> Helen laughed.
> "What's funny?" Jack said after a long time.
> "God, I don't know," Helen said. She wiped her eyes and laughed again,
>   and Mary and Carl laughed.[35]

It is easy to see that the role played by white space in such a work is fairly minimal—although there are a few places in the story where a particularly suggestive phrase reverberates a little in the space that abuts it. Prose poems that use dialogue in a similar way encourage much more of that kind of reverberation, mainly through their introduction of poetic tropes that move outward, as it were, to populate the surrounding space.

An example is "The Dummies" by Russell Edson. This prose poem is not obviously "poetic," yet its dialogue is of a very different order from that of the Carver story. There is no real narrative development but rather the presentation of an absurd situation that comments ironically on understanding human identity and motive. The work opens in the following manner:

A contortionist had twisted himself in such a way as to be suddenly sitting on his own knee.

His wife asked, What's that on your knee?

Embarrassed, the twisted contortionist said, It's my dummy.

Why is it sitting on your knee?

I'm making it talk.[36]

In a prose poem such as this one, white space begins to crowd the work, picking up its resonances, not unlike the example we gave from Brainard's "I Remember." Unlike the sense of forward progression in the Carver excerpt, Edson does not allow us to follow his narrative in a single direction through a relatively uncluttered evocation of TimeSpace. Instead, the TimeSpace of his work is unlocatable—it is a TimeSpace in which markedly strange things occur and readers are never sure where they are.

TimeSpace and Velocity in Prose Poetry

If time and space are entwined, then the popular view that time is somehow more active than space requires revision. Geographers John May and Nigel Thrift argue, in a dualistic conception of the relationship of time and space, that "Time is understood as the domain of dynamism and Progress and the spatial is relegated to the realm of stasis and excavated of any meaningful politics."[37] The reasons for joining TimeSpace into a single concept include the effort to read time and space not only as one entity but as of equal significance in terms of our understanding of speed and velocity. Perhaps most importantly, in terms of its relevance to prose poetry—and as mentioned earlier in this chapter—David Harvey argues that globalism and new technologies have caused a profound compression of time-space:

> As space appears to shrink to a "global village" of telecommunications and a "spaceship earth" of economic and ecological interdependencies . . . and as time horizons shorten to the point where the present is all there is (the world of the schizophrenic), so we have to learn how to cope with an overwhelming sense of *compression* of our spatial and temporal worlds.[38]

The world appears smaller because of our ability to contact people almost anywhere and at great speed via new communication technologies, the online experience has a beguiling sense of immediacy, and we may also travel across continents with relative ease. We live in separate nations but, for example, space is compressed by globalized production, and a major rise or decline in the value of stocks in one country has the capacity to influence stock prices everywhere.

Issues connected to speed, compression, and internationalism find voice in the contemporary prose poem, partly because the prose poetry form is (usually) both spatially compressed and well suited to encapsulating postmodernity's diverse and sometimes clashing voices. Kim Knowles and her colleagues have argued that "[s]paces in texts demarcate the boundaries of words, headers and sub-headers, paragraphs and sections. They visually reinforce the conceptual organization of a given text, and at the same time facilitate the process of perception by guiding the eye and the mind of the reader."[39] The compressed paragraphs and sentences of prose poems draw material together into a kind of cocoon of utterance, a tight space that in limiting and restricting its material also builds up and holds in (and sometimes then releases) a powerful verbal energy.

Some lineated poems work in a similar way but, as we have discussed, such works are in dialogue with an abundance of white space and may release their verbal energy at almost any point, or continuously. In prose poetry, the pervasive sense of constriction and compression holds energy in until the work's conclusion. Anthony Howell attributes this to the "throughness" of prose, arguing that "[w]ith it, we travel on through one sentence to the next, and we are building something by going towards it."[40]

The prose poem's appearance as a paragraph or paragraphs means that readers approach its text in a different way from their approach to a lineated poem. Their initial expectation is usually that the prose poem will conform to the rules of the conventional prose paragraph; their subsequent engagement with confined poetic tropes often occasions a disturbing sense of the known being radically defamiliarized.

Robert Lowes plays humorously with this sort of disruption in "The Unity of the Paragraph." In the following excerpt, he simultaneously alludes to and subverts the notion that the paragraph may function conventionally, unify its material, and cohere. The work is also self-referential in discussing the importance of paragraphs in the prose poem form:

> This paragraph is willing to die for unity. If a paragraph is divided, how can husband and wife cohere? How can atomic nuclei continue to hug themselves? If a paragraph doesn't develop its topic sentence with supporting details, can anyone believe in God?[41]

The droll and abstract imagery of "atomic nuclei . . . hug[ging] themselves" coupled with the equally strange imagery of the "husband and wife coher[ing]" creates a parodic sense of an energized intimacy. And Lowes's comment that the paragraph must "develop its topic sentence" as a way to "God"—while ludicrous in any literal sense—refers to the importance of discursive structure and momentum in works of conventional prose, a momentum taking the reader predictably through TimeSpace.

On one level, the absurdity of Lowes's work may cause readers not to take it seriously; on another level, this prose poem emphasizes that prose poetry in general is likely to break, subvert, destabilize, or question the unities of space and time. And, in addition, Lowes's work moves quickly and follows a series of weird associations. The writing takes us rapidly from idea to idea.

Abigail Beckel, in her introduction to the *Prose Poem Issue* of the *Beltway Poetry Quarterly*, emphasizes the importance of the lack of lineation in prose poetry:

> The signature element of prose poetry is that it has no line breaks . . . A prose poem looks like a block of text on the page, running from left to right margins without care where the lines break. It's a chunk of prose that reads like poetry. In a prose poem, the unit of rhythm is the sentence rather than the enjambed line, but those sentences must be imbued with the lyricism and sonic play of a lined poem. A prose poem is not a lined poem smooshed together with the line breaks removed. It's usually obvious when a poet has tried this approach, as the tension still resides in the old lines and you can hear them begging for enjambment.[42]

Beckel also comments, "The ability to create a breathless gallop of words is one of the gifts of the prose poem form,"[43] summarizing the quality of onrushing momentum that accompanies so many prose poems—of images and events colliding or rushing forward.

This idea of the limited "breath" in a prose poem is a significant feature of the form, taken up by a range of critics and practitioners in their discussions of the prose poem and velocity.[44] Poet Morton Marcus chooses the prose poem for its long series of phrases: "My choice to abandon the line has allowed me to pursue an unshackled phrase as my basic unit of rhythm, which at times extends phrases to thirteen and even fifteen beats before a caesura—'a sweep of words.'"[45]

This point is reiterated by Diane Wakoski, who turns to prosody to argue, "if a poem is written in lines then a prose poem is one very long line, one very long breath."[46] These expressions of limited air are further developed by Donna Stonecipher in her focus on prose poetry and the city when she asks if the prose poem "is breathless in the sense that it is claustrophobic, that one can't get any air in it."[47]

In their own ways, Beckel, Marcus, Wakoski, and Stonecipher all identify signature parts of the prose poem's evocation of TimeSpace. A truncation of time and a reduction of space work together, often breathlessly within prose poetry's energized and intimate confines. When Beckel states that there is little room to breathe in prose poems,[48] not only does she refer to this compression of the form but she indicates the way in which prose poetry's lines and sentences so often push inward as well as forward, in what Carol Dorf calls "rapid shocks; [where] the frame [of the prose poem] compresses the embedded stories into the present."[49] If a prose poem takes the form of a fully justified block of text, then its four "walls" encourage a ricocheting of ideas that continue to bounce around the poem's structure even after the reader has completed the work.

While, as we have mentioned, there are some prose poems that do not fit this rectangular or "box" structure—such as those prose poems consisting of dialogue falling down a page or prose poems using broken fragments or the free-line—even in most of these cases the reader is asked to engage with a small chunk or chunks of text, or sentences drawn together, rather than a series of lines that break artificially before an open right margin. Prose poetry's paragraphs tend to be squeezed and contained even when, from time to time, they meet a field of white space:

> The snow spits into the porch and onto my wrists. I clutch at your remote voice and whisper surfacing thoughts into the thick espresso view. We are not on the phone, we are downstairs awake, staying up late for the third night in a row, like mothers on the cusp of delivery. The house creaks as I inhale.
>
> Okay?
>
> Okay?
>
> Next door's Tom tiptoes past a refracting beam, a grumbling door or, a saddened window anticipating its use as a hollow moon dips into the frame, lowers her lids but doesn't let them shut.
>
> Through the cracks private words string by then pop as though balloons. Down shrivels the casing onto the ledge and up flies helium.[50]

In this prose poem, "The Snow Spits," Kate North's repetition of the question "Okay?" not only works to question whether everything is actually "Okay," conveying apprehension and anxiety, but it also contrasts with, and thus underscores, the density of the paragraphs above and below these words.

As well as often being identified as boxlike, prose poetry has been likened to frames, postcards, windows, and cages. In this poem, the white space around the longer paragraphs' justified sentences emphasizes the compressed, oblong shape of the text, which almost has an appearance of being etched around the words. In this respect, it is useful to return to the analogy between prose poetry and rooms—something Robert Alexander and Dennis Maloney may have had in mind when they entitled their anthology of prose poetry *The House of Your Dream*.[51] The room-like shapes of "The Snow Spits" contain imaginative tropes, allusions, and suggestive possibilities, all of which are housed together in unusual and reactive proximities.

This prose poem invokes, activates, and personifies the chronotope of the house, both in its form of the prose poem—in looking at the work, one can imagine a view of three rooms and a connecting passageway—and through coupling the house's creaking with the narrator's inhaling. It is as if breathing within the house permits it a kind of creaturely life. Yet such prose poetry paragraphs present rooms that are not very "roomy" and, hence, without an open right margin, and with little space in which to breathe with freedom, the prose poem operates in, and accentuates its sense of, a claustrophobic TimeSpace.

Clements and Dunham point to the way in which prose poetry's TimeSpace is dependent on the way sentences interact. When sentences are tightly juxtaposed and pursuing poetic aims, this has a significant impact on how we read them: "In verse or free verse, the tension between line structure and sentence structure is an important machine for the generation of pace, rhythm, and sometimes, meaning. In the prose poem, pace and rhythm must be built entirely within the sentence itself and in the play among sentences."[52]

An example of the way a prose poem compresses space and manipulates rhythmic effects may be found in Gian Lombardo's untitled prose poem from his collection *Machines We Have Built*. This is composed of a tight three-sentence paragraph, focused on movement:

> MAKE YOURSELF SMART. NOT IN AN OBVIOUS WAY. On tip-toes, chin resting on the top rail following the path of what drops to the street, rolls along, caroms against a curb, spins and whirls as it nearly comes to rest in the onslaught of traffic.[53]

This is a brief and, verbally, dense work. Yet the reading experience is relatively fast-paced, particularly as the prose poem gathers momentum and follows "what drops to the street" through its various "caroms," "spins," and "whirls." The long final sentence careens through the work's compressed TimeSpace, ensuring that the reader and the prose poem only come to rest at the end of the text. However, even here movement continues through the final oxymoronic image of "rest[ing] in the onslaught of traffic." As the reader enters the white space beyond this final line, they have the opportunity to take stock and consider the import of their encounter with a work that foregrounds the movement of language as much as it focuses on activity in a city street.

In a prose poem by Gary Young, the evocation of the plight of parents and patients in a hospital is heightened by the use of commas and the lack of white space at the right margin (or anywhere else in the work). The cadence is rhythmic and steady, and like the entries in the journal mentioned, the number of people affected by cancer, and their experiences of trauma and pain, accumulate like items on a list:

> I discovered a journal in the children's ward, and read, I'm a mother, my little boy has cancer. Further on, a girl has written, this is my nineteenth operation. She says, sometimes it's easier to write than to talk, and I'm so afraid. She's offered me a page in the book. My son is sleeping in the room next door. This afternoon, I held my whole weight to his body while a doctor drove needles deep into his leg. My son screamed, Daddy, they're hurting me, don't let them hurt me, make them stop. I want to write, how brave you are, but I need a little courage of my own, so I write, forgive me, I know I let them hurt you, please don't worry. If I have to, I can do it again.[54]

The disturbing subject matter of a sick child undergoing complex and overwhelming treatment is mirrored by the packed paragraph of text with continuous, pressing sentences. With no lines meeting open white space at the right margin, and no associated opportunities to pause for breath or reflection—and with commas and full stops that barely indicate a real pause before the next phrase or sentence arrives—the prose poem is almost enclosed.

Young achieves this effect partly because he chooses not to put his dialogue in quotation marks, or to use a new line for a new speaker, thus avoiding any kind of vertical trajectory in his work. He ensures that his prose poem remains contained within its own rectangle. The reader is, as it were, hemmed in. The reader is also encouraged to keep forging ahead, following the sentences and their grammar, just as the father must continue making decisions for his son. This focus on limited time and space—both within the situation the poem evokes and within the work itself—reinforces the way in which many people in crisis situations have little available time and a sense of closing space. Young's frequent repetition of the first-person pronoun in his prose poem's cramped space further emphasizes the sense of personal entrapment it conveys.

Prose Poetry's Extended TimeSpaces

Notwithstanding prose poetry's compression, brevity, verbal dexterity, and an associated sense of rapid movement, prose poems often suggest or imply large worlds. Additionally, Paul Munden identifies what he calls "an elastic treatment of time as a frequent trope" in the prose poems he has anthologized.[55] He remarks:

> [I]f a lineated poem can handle a vast yet instant time-shift with . . . aplomb . . . [w]hy suggest that the prose poem is better equipped? The answer, I believe, has something to do with the prose poem's casual poise, its appropriation of prose for its poetic purpose, where swift and brief fluidity of syntactical movement blurs the radical time shifts.[56]

Certainly, prose poetry's succinct, sometimes fractured narratives move rapidly through and around significant periods of TimeSpace, and prose-poetical sentences often announce moments of transition and disjuncture within the TimeSpace field. Munden created a list of lines from prose poems that collapse large periods of time—including phrases such as "That was thirty-three years ago," "for a hundred years the heat rises," and "for fifty years no-one saw her open it." He posits that a loose equivalent of the sonnet's *volta* (the "turn" in the sonnet between lines 8 and 9, or sometimes before the final couplet) is the prose poem's time shift.[57]

Ian Seed's prose poem "All Kinds of Dust" is a good example of prose poetry's appeal to complex TimeSpaces:

Music was our first love, but there was little time for that. For years we assembled our ideas cautiously as we travelled from land to land, compiling our survey. One day we were drawn to a tavern by the sound of singing. A fatal error. The tune of the gipsy fiddle gave us glimpses of a reality we had long buried deep beneath the surface. All kinds of dead people came to life, an old skull, lain long in the snow, abandoned in search of something more exotic and otherworldly, whatever could be lifted and turned slowly to reflect the light coming from the next room. . . .[58]

Seed's prose poem contains numerous references to TimeSpace relations—employing phrases such as "little time," "One day," "For years," "long buried," and "lain long," combined with references to "travel[ing] from land to land," "old skulls," "cautiously," and "slowly"—that all join to conjure a long and deep TimeSpace perspective. The effect is intensified when these references are packed into a single paragraph, demonstrating the elasticity of the prose poem form in compressing TimeSpace. The work is rapidly delivered to the reader, both foreshortening its perspectives and—in doing so—giving emphasis to the extended sense of time that the poem conveys.

The "moment" of a prose poem is often a merging of TimeSpaces. The prose-poetic present that is evoked in many prose poems is actually an amalgamation of past and present, or of past, present, and future. Seed's work is an example, presenting a potent combination of past-present relationships that directly implicate an uncertain future. Such effects result, in part, from the cramming and pressing of an incompletely rendered time-and-space-shifting narrative, and its associated figurative language, into sentences of mixed length, creating a rapid-fire effect. There is, so to speak, a ricocheting of ideas between the four sides of this prose poem, resulting in everything mentioned within the work being almost simultaneously present in the reader's imagination.

Linda Black has written that the prose poem form "encourages thoughts to be continuous, to twist and turn, hold themselves up short, or open out into a broader perspective, sometimes travelling at great speed."[59] Because prose poetry often cramps its evocations of TimeSpace through a series of breathless compressions—even as it opens outward to embrace broader perspectives—it tends to retain a residual and fruitful tension between the compact bounds of the work and larger frames of reference.

Compared to the writer of conventional prose, the author of a prose poem must be highly selective about what to include and what to reject. For the same reason, the action in a prose poem paragraph is often accentuated or extended further than a reader might expect of a short work. Matthea Harvey's "The Backyard Mermaid" combines action, intensity, and speed. In the following excerpt, by placing a mythical sea creature in a contemporary setting, she collapses large TimeSpaces and conflates the historical and mythological with the contemporary and local "backyard," evoking the mysterious and the quotidian at once:

She didn't even know she had a name until one day she heard the human explaining to another one, "Oh that's just the backyard mermaid." Backyard Mermaid she murmured, as if in prayer. On days when there's no sprinkler to comb through her curls, no rain pouring in glorious torrents from the gutters, no dew in the grass for her to nuzzle with her nose, not even a mud puddle in the kiddie pool, she wonders how much longer she can bear this life. The front yard thud of the newspaper every morning. Singing songs to the unresponsive push mower in the garage. Wriggling under fence after fence to reach the house four down which has an aquarium in the back window. She wants to get lost in that sad glowing square of blue. Don't you?[60]

The use of commas in this excerpt demonstrates how prose poetry is able to make judicious use of punctuation and tight phrasing to squeeze a plethora of imagery into a small space—in this case, images of a "sprinkler," a "comb," "curls," "rain," "torrents," "gutters," "dew," "grass," "nose," a "mud puddle," and a "kiddie pool." The end of the sentence that includes this imagery—which asks "how much longer she can bear this life"—acknowledges the work's conjuring of tropes of absence along with a profound and pervasive sense of deficiency.

In creating this sense of deficiency, the work conveys to the reader a feeling of being surrounded, and even hemmed in, a feeling that is exacerbated by the lack of any room to breathe at each phrase's or sentence's end. The absence of the lineated poem's space at the right margin is telling. The forward pressure of this work, and its tightly packed content, adds significant emphasis to the intimacy of its final moment, when it is revealed that the Backyard Mermaid wants to replace her patch of backyard grass with a neighbor's aquarium—exchanging one cramped space for another. If the prose poetry form may be characterized as a compressed form where large, sometimes immeasurable issues are contained by a small block (or blocks) of text, then Harvey may be exploring this quality self-reflexively. And the "glowing square of blue" may be an analogy for the prose poem's rectangular shape, with its compressed, evocative TimeSpace.

The momentum and breathlessness of "The Backyard Mermaid" mirrors the urgency of desire enacted at the conclusion of the prose poem, in an address to the second person (or reader): "Don't you?" The long vowel sound in "you" and the question mark extend the prose poem into white space in its one significant tallying moment: its conclusion. As this occurs, the reader is left to consider the metaphorical implications of the poem, and the way in which the "sad glowing square of blue" may stand in for any number of dreams, failures, or idealizations.

Kevin Brophy's prose poem "The Night's Insomnia" employs one long sentence to explore an enduring night. The cadence of the repetition of the words "if the" acts as a lullaby and mimics the monotony of sleeplessness:

> If the night is long, and there can be no sleep, if the lullaby is nowhere in your heart, if morning comes to its new days exhausted, if all your novels strike wrong tones, if your waking dream is always of oblivion, if those cold

coins of regret buy nothing now, and some high court sits in sleepless confusion, if the night is the one who won't leave you, close your eyes and put your head just here where my own poor heart has learned that the night, poor night, wide-eyed and blind, must cling to you its only companion.[61]

Brophy is both a practitioner and a scholar of prose poetry, and his works are known for their play with language and form. Here, cause and effect are separated, and fulfillment delayed, so that the prose poem dwells on what is absent and missing.

James Longenbach argues that "the effect of our more typical notion of a prose poem depends on the deletion of lineation from the formal decorum of poetry, and the absence of the line would not be interesting if we did not feel the possibility of its presence."[62] Mary Jean Chan in *Flèche* (2019), Heather Christle in *The Trees The Trees* (2011), and Kaveh Akbar's "Calling a Wolf a Wolf (Inpatient)" experiment with the effects of this absence, or foreground it through various techniques, making it visually apparent. Some of Christle's and Chan's prose poems are composed of a series of broken phrases in a fully justified box of text. The spaces between phrases enforce breaks, not unlike the ends of each line in lineated poetry. While the phrases work together, the gaps create stress fractures in the prose poetry box and can be read as ghostings of lineation. Furthermore, the striking use of gaps and spaces with fully justified text in Chan's poems works to blur the boundaries between lineated poetry and prose poetry.

The use of white space in Akbar's "Calling a Wolf a Wolf (Inpatient)" is also almost a ghosting of lineation in the way it breaks sentences into sometimes discordant, component parts:

like the sky I've been too quiet   everyone's forgotten I'm here   I've tried all the usual tricks   pretending I've just been made terrifying   like a suddenly carnivorous horse   like a rabid hissing sapphire   the medical response has been clear   *sit patiently until invited to leave*   outside the lake is evaporating   dry blue like a galley proof   a month ago they dragged up a drowned tourist. . . .[63]

Through his use of white space, Akbar emphasizes the fragmentary nature of the prose poem and the fractured nature of the experiences it evokes. The juxtaposition of segmented phrases and clauses, with their single-breath-sized insertions of white space, opens up the work a little without yielding the expansive resources of white space available to lineated poems. Instead, the prose poem form encourages the reader to leap over these gaps or spaces in order to piece the poem together, with an emphasis on overall speed and propulsion. Yet the white spaces do function to allow some air into the prose poem. It is as if a closed room has its vents open.

Similarly, Chekwube O. Danladi's "Tomorrow, Chaka Demus Will Play" (2017) pays homage to lineation in her use of the forward slash (which is one of the commonly used symbols for a line ending). However, in this prose poem the forward slash creates the sense of a pause or hesitation without significantly disrupting the prose poem's forward flow:

> while I braid my hair long / thump coconut oil between the sections / crack palm nut with my teeth / rub the meat on my belly / I'll want to go dancing / might go to the Shake and Bake / I'll bless Ma with a salah / tuck a miniskirt in my purse for later / might wear lip-stick too / there'll still black henna on my hands from Zaynab's wedding / . . .[64]

Danladi's use of slashes creates a tight rhythm that builds as the prose poem progresses. The rhythmic beat in this work is also emphasized by the use of verbs such as "thump," "crack," "rub," and "Shake and Bake." Such a use of forward slashes draws words and phrases together, even as it appears to gesture at separation. The work takes the form of a long, fractured sentence, with the forward slashes suggesting that everything mentioned may be read as a cascading series of alternatives. As in Akbar's prose poem, the reader is presented with a series of fragmented but connected tropes.

TimeSpace and the Prose Poem

Understanding TimeSpace in prose poetry is a complicated matter. Perhaps the most important overriding issue is that prose poetry's constituent sentences, while progressing at the level of grammar, are almost always also held in a kind of suspension—and thus their movement through TimeSpace is never aimed at the kind of narrative completion found in so much prose fiction. Instead, the prose poem tends to turn back on itself, like a snake biting its tail. Additionally, it may have a (sometimes disguised) lyric dimension, inhabiting, as Jonathan Culler states, the "present time"—and we would add space—"of [poetic] discourse."[65] In most prose poems, tropes of TimeSpace are invoked not to carry the reader through a narrative arc but to position her or him as the witness of, or readerly participant in, an unending episode always occurring in the prose poem's contained, condensed, and resonant space.

Especially in their boxlike manifestations, prose poems tend to evoke the ideas of rooms, and of compressed TimeSpaces, only opening out at their conclusion, and then—in a kind of miracle of expansiveness—tending to move outward into a larger sense of the world that the explicit themes and tropes in the prose poem have only hinted at. Readers move fairly quickly through such works, following their sentences like a trail, and as they do so, they are taken toward new, sometimes unfamiliar forms of apprehension and understanding. The narrative tropes in prose poems frequently lead back to where they began—which is to say, back to the point where the prose poet implicitly asks the reader, "Have you considered this?"

We understand TimeSpace differently in different kinds of works, because literature is always, one way or the other, about how we situate ourselves imaginatively in time and space. In the case of Mallarmé's *A Roll of the Dice*, we are taken to a place of undecidability where time and space are slowed, and white space presses on and frames the text—becoming its own (implicit) chronotope connoting various kinds of silence and absence. In prose poems, we are so often compelled to encounter a pressing, suggestive amalgam of contiguous words and meanings where our sense of TimeSpace is simultaneously small and large, compressed and (eventually) extraordinarily expansive.

At the end of a prose poem, as we move from the work's close and sometimes claustrophobic boundaries into a larger space of contemplation and consideration, we have the experience of completing the work imaginatively. In this sense, Harvey's "glowing square of blue" may be understood as referring to the imaginative processes of mind that allow the two-dimensional box of the prose poem to become an evocative and shimmering multidimensional container of meanings. We follow the prose poem's sentences to their end and know that what we have read provides a poetic sense of TimeSpace outside of our conventional assumptions and understandings. Prose poetry is a vehicle that allows us to travel through the small and large at once, through strange reaches and quirky occasions of simultaneously experienced time and space.

PART 3

METHODS AND CONTEXTS

CHAPTER 7

The Image and Memory in Reading Prose Poetry

Prose Poetry, Photography, and the Nineteenth Century

The prose poem—so frequently presented as a rectangular box on a page—is the literary form that most often resembles a still photograph. While the prose poetry "box" and metaphors concerning its shape have been discussed in previous chapters, in this chapter we explore the visual similarity of the prose poem to the photograph—and, later in the chapter, we will examine the way prose poems may resemble a still frame capture from a film. Now often viewed on digital devices, the prose poem form mimics both the photograph (often in landscape mode) and the rectangular screen on which it is viewed. Furthermore, as we discussed in chapter 2, many prose poems rely on providing a mere fragment or momentary evocation of a scene or set of circumstances and rarely attempt to represent the passing of time discursively (instead, yielding only a glimpse into a larger, implied narrative).

We don't wish to push the comparison between prose poems and photographs too far—some prose poems are less like images than others. However, the comparison is a useful way of highlighting the conspicuously imagistic features of many prose poems and the extent to which the reader is required to respond to them in much the same way as many images are "read." Prose poems often provide no more than a "snapshot" of experience yet, like numerous successful photographs, are characterized by significant connotative meanings and an allied suggestiveness—and they frequently rely on rich and evocative visual imagery to create such effects.

Susan Sontag writes, "A photograph is only a fragment, and with the passage of time its moorings come unstuck. It drifts away into a soft abstract pastness, open to any kind of reading . . . A photograph could also be described as a quotation."[1] She observes that "[b]oth [poetry and photography] imply discontinuity, disarticulated forms and compensatory unity: wrenching things from their context (to see them in a fresh way), bringing things together elliptically, according to the imperious but often arbitrary demands of subjectivity."[2] Such statements may be repurposed to refer to prose poetry. Prose poems, too, often give the impression of being like quotations—pieces of text excerpted from a whole that is not otherwise immediately available (we have discussed in previous chapters how prose poetry often stands in metonymically for an implied whole and invokes the indeterminate).

Importantly, the connection between prose poetry and photography is also historical. Baudelaire's prose poems in *Paris Spleen*, which inaugurated the contemporary prose poem form, were written between 1855 and 1867 at a time when the city of Paris was being utterly transformed. As Shelley Rice observes, "Georges-Eugène Haussmann . . . was systematically demolishing the medieval Paris of Baudelaire's youth and building in its place the city of today."[3] This was also the period when photography was first developed—the earliest surviving photograph, *View from the Window at le Gras* by Nicéphore Niépce, is from 1826 or 1827, the daguerreotype technique was publicly announced in 1839, and the improved wet collodion process was invented by Frederick Scott Archer in 1851. Photographic technology helped to shape the public view of the rapidly changing city, as "various photographers worked to come to terms with the transformation of Paris."[4]

The combination of nostalgia, modernity, and fragmentation found in Baudelaire's prose poems is not unlike the qualities evident in many photographs from the period. For example, Charles Marville produced a series of mid-nineteenth-century photographs documenting the city of Paris before, during, and after Haussmann's renovations. These images are poignant, especially because the relatively long exposure times they required mean they are largely devoid of people—although figures are occasionally present, like representatives of a passing age. In many of these images the buildings stand in a kind of ghostliness. An example is the image, readily available online, entitled *Rue Fresnel from the Dead End of Versailles*, in which the old street recedes into a spectral transparency.

Margueritte Murphy discusses the interrelation of photography and prose poetry with reference to Andreas Huyssen's identification of the "metropolitan miniature" as "a paradigmatic modernist form that sought to capture the fleeting and fragmentary experiences of metropolitan life, emphasizing both their transitory variety and their simultaneous ossification."[5] She draws attention to the prose poem's relationship with the visual arts and its "claim to pictorial representation" as part of its "self-definition."[6]

While Huyssen observes that photographs, including "snapshots," may be connected to miniature literary forms (such as the prose poem), he emphasizes "the temporal rather than the spatial dimension" (we would argue that the spatial is also important in this respect), contending that "[s]napshots can be fundamentally opaque and resist rendering a mystery they harbor."[7] He quotes one of Roland Barthes's most telling insights in observing that "any snapshot may have its *punctum*, the dimension of the photograph that eludes transparence, 'that accident which pricks me (but also bruises me, is poignant to me)' . . . Similarly, the modern [literary] miniature seems easily legible at first sight, but more often than not it resists facile understanding."[8]

Margaret Moores also discusses the importance of the *punctum* in her composition of ekphrastic poems based on family photographs. She searches for ways to replicate the *punctum* in her poetry and has argued she is only able to achieve this by incorporating fragments of memory and a sense of mortality or transience into her collection. The last few sentences of her prose poem "Obituary" demonstrate the link between the visual (photographs and painting), *punctum* (in this case, memory and mortality), and prose poetry:

> We sit down later with a box of photographs to look for pictures she could paint. If we enlarge the print she can see details. She magnifies a shot where a figure in a red jacket stands on a river bank. "I could put a figure in," she says. "I hope I can. I have to train my brain to see around the hole." Sometimes I forget that she can't see or hear well. I forget to speak loudly. I'm impatient. "You know," she says. "My father died when I was 24. He never spoke about my mother and I didn't know how to ask."[9]

Similarly, Zarah Butcher-McGunnigle's *Autobiography of a Marguerite* (2014) contains a series of ekphrastic prose poems based on family photographs. Beginning with a colored image of a baby in a cot (presumably Butcher-McGunnigle) and a prose poem reproduced beneath, the photograph and prose poem serve, in combination, as an epigraph. In this format, the similarities between the prose poem and photograph are evident; they both hang in the space, much as on a gallery wall. Similarly, the book ends with a sequence of twelve ekphrastic prose poems and photographs. Beneath a photograph of what appears to be the author and her mother, a prose poem encourages the reader's/viewer's gaze with the opening line, "Everything is a painting if you look long enough."[10]

These prose poems are consistent with Huyssen's views of the way in which photography and miniature literary forms may be read together. Huyssen contends, in discussing the work of early twentieth-century German writer, theorist, and cultural critic Siegfried Kracauer, that both literary miniatures and photographs may present

> this unexpected eruption onto the scene of vision that . . . Merleau-Ponty described in its temporal dimension as the "holding open" of the moment in space toward its present, its past, and its future. . . . Deciphering the *punctum* in Barthes perhaps corresponds to what Kracauer had in mind when he spoke of "deciphering the dreamlike spoken images of cities." . . . This job of deciphering cannot be done by urban photography alone; it needs the literary articulation in the miniature . . .[11]

Photographic images undoubtedly influenced Baudelaire's groundbreaking prose poetry, even though he famously dismissed photographic portraits as "trivial images on a scrap of metal," and said of photography more generally that if it "is allowed to supplement art in some of its functions, it will soon have supplanted or corrupted it altogether."[12] Notwithstanding his reactionary public attitude to photography, he had photographic portraits taken by Étienne Carjat in 1863 and by Nadar (Gaspard-Félix Tournachon) in 1865, and also wrote to his mother in 1865, "I'd love to have a photograph of you."[13]

In other words, photographs had become an irresistible part of Baudelaire's milieu by the time he began composing prose poetry, and Lauren Weingarden "interprets Baudelaire's *Fleurs du Mal* . . . and *Le Spleen de Paris* . . . as the verbal counterparts of the photographs [documenting Paris's modernization], representing 'living' records of Baudelaire's melancholy and disaffection" with the city.[14] Photography represented a way of seeing the world that was new, disturbing, and fashionable, giving attention to the momentary and the fragmentary in a way painters had rarely attempted. Impressionism was invented in France in the 1860s, in the same decade that Baudelaire's *Paris Spleen* was published, as painters also responded to the advent of photography—not only its usurpation of much of the demand for "realistic" images but also its emphasis on transient effects of light. The advent of impressionism, like the advent of an innovative and contemporary prose poetry, indicated how much the arts were in flux and attuned to new expressive modes and possibilities.

As well as being a response to visual stimuli, Huyssen claims Baudelaire's prose poetry may be understood as "a strategy to appropriate and to transform the genres of *la petite presse*," which were publishing "narrative short prose, miniature portraits, celebrity anecdotes, brief dialogues, fictive letters, reflections, society gossip," and the like.[15] Additionally, Simon Morley summarizes the way in which the use of words also changed profoundly during this time, ramifying into diverse areas of public life. Not only were there rapidly expanding markets for books and other forms of literature, such as journals and newspapers, but words were "on walls, shopfronts, billboards, advertising pillars, street signs, passing vehicles."[16] In these places they were often joined to, or juxtaposed with, imagery, and the result was a "visual cacophony."[17] The tendency for both words and images to be seen as complex signs rather than as windows depicting more or less transparent views of reality became increasingly prevalent during this period.

Furthermore, many visual artists began to move away from "realistic" representation even as they gave their viewers subjective "impressions" of what they had seen just the previous day, or in the weeks or months before. Well in advance of the publication in France in 1886 of Jean Moreas's *Symbolist Manifesto*, the artistic and literary die was cast, with Baudelaire as one of the most important writers to signal the way forward. His lineated lyric poetry in *The Flowers of Evil* (1857) and his prose poetry in *Paris Spleen* (1869) are highly subjective and impressionistic—so much so that Jean-Paul Sartre characterizes Baudelaire as "bending over his own reflection like Narcissus."[18]

Baudelaire's poetic enterprise put the city, modernity, and the subjective and imagistic fragmentation of experience at the heart of a new poetics:

Explosive New Year's Day: chaos of mud and snow, criss-crossed by a thousand carriages, sparkling with toys and toffee, crawling with greed and despair, standard delirium of a metropolis, made to disturb the brain of the sturdiest solitary.[19]

Arthur Rimbaud was another poet who understood the power of the image and connected his writing to the practice of visual artists. In 1886, some of his groundbreaking *Illuminations* were published by *La Vogue* in Paris, and Paul Verlaine asserts that the title of this work refers to the colored plates of engravers.[20] Graham Robb nicely summarizes Rimbaud's attempt in *Illuminations* to strip his writing of traditional poetic trappings, and to allow the image to function cleanly: "Despite the variety of forms—visions, parables, riddles, isolated phrases, a prose 'sonnet' and the first free-verse poems in French literature—the *Illuminations* have a recognizable stylistic fingerprint: the almost total absence of comparisons and analogies. Every image exists in its own right. Nothing defers to a higher authority."[21]

Such an approach to writing bears comparison to photographic images, and Clive Scott makes the connection: "Photography belongs to the linear time of the irretrievable and that is why its referentiality is always slipping away from it, even while its indexicality clings on. What does something that you see now refer to, if it is a 'this was'? . . . The Rimbaldian word/image, like the photograph, is caught between the desire to be a contact with reality and the inescapability of representation."[22]

John Ashbery adds, "the crystalline jumble of Rimbaud's *Illuminations*, like a disordered collection of magic lantern slides, each an 'intense and rapid dream,' in his words, is still emitting pulses."[23] Imagery in Rimbaud's prose poems sits alertly like condensed and beaconing units of sometimes indeterminate meaning. In one sense, the early twentieth-century imagists did not need to invent imagism because Rimbaud had done it before them—even if rather more idiosyncratically than the model they adopted more than two decades later. Aimée Israel-Pelletier claims that Rimbaud's prose poems—such as "After the Flood," "Flowers," "Barbarian," and "Historic Evening"—have "strikingness because they provide in excess and with intensity details that will not be assimilated or . . . that resist absorption. As [Michael Fried] has shown . . . strikingness is the dominant trait of Impressionism and the quality for which the Impressionist painters, starting with Manet, most deliberately aimed."[24]

As an example, the first prose poem of *Illuminations* confirms this emphasis on "strikingness," and also serves as an illustration of William Berg's contention that "[t]he intrusion of the visual into the verbal medium creates shocks, gaps, frozen moments in the reading process that highlight essential themes, properties, and problems of the medium":[25]

> After the Flood
>
> No sooner had the notion of the Flood regained its composure,
> Than a hare paused amid the gorse and trembling bellflowers and said its prayer to the rainbow through the spider's web.
> Oh the precious stones that were hiding,—the flowers that were already peeking out.
> Stalls were erected in the dirty main street, and boats were towed toward the sea, which rose in layers above as in old engravings.
> Blood flowed in Bluebeard's house,—in the slaughterhouses,—in the amphitheatres, where God's seal turned the windows livid. Blood and milk flowed.[26]

Ever since Baudelaire and Rimbaud, many prose poems have been dependent on striking visual imagery, enabling us to "see" what they are invoking—and this remains true into the twenty-first century. Indeed, some contemporary prose poets connect photography and prose poetry in descriptions of their creative practice, or in references to photographs in their works.

Anne Caldwell discusses the creation of a prose poem as a process akin to developing a photograph, stating, "Like a photograph being processed in the traditional way, in a dark room, the writing of a prose poem could mirror a chemical process that relies on containment within a frame."[27] She also suggests that "[t]he prose poem, like a photograph—particularly a landscape photograph—can capture a moment in time but also gesture to the bigger space beyond the frame and the time just before and just after visual composition or writing. There is a tension here but it is a thoroughly creative one."[28]

An earlier and subversive example of foregrounding the photographic process in prose poetry is Harry Crosby's "Photoheliograph" from *Chariot of the Sun* (1928). In this calligrammatic prose poem, Crosby playfully invokes the photographic exposure of the sun blackening a plate. The prose poem box is comprised solely from the word "black" repeated in columns and the word "SUN" in capital letters at its center.

Maxine Chernoff's prose poem "Lost and Found" uses a form of mise en abyme in her consideration of both the shape and content of photographs. It begins:

> I am looking for the photo that would make all the difference in my life. It's very small and subject to fits of amnesia, turning up in poker hands, grocery carts, under the unturned stone. The photo shows me at the lost and found looking for an earlier photo, the one that would have made all the difference then. My past evades me like a politician.[29]

In this prose poem, the photograph is anthropomorphically elusive and its image is recursive, emphasizing what is lost even as it is found.

Kristin Sanders's chapbook, *This Is a Map of Their Watching Me* (2015), charts a relationship between a writer and an artist that is momentarily compared in the opening pages to the problematic relationship between nineteenth-century French neurologist Jean-Martin Charcot and Louise Augustine Gleizes, his much-photographed patient who made him famous. The book is composed of prose poems described as "Notes to Accompany the Images," and the images are a series of figures (not in sequence) listed in the table of contents, for example, "Fig. 8: Don't look. Look." All but one of the figures are frames with nothing inside of them—blank spaces. The conspicuous lack of images is gestured at ironically in the book's final section, "Images to accompany the Notes" with its comment: "We will have to ask the artist for his permission."[30] Prior to this, one frame contains text quizzing the nature of the male gaze, and the acts of seeing and being seen, invoking the "shape" of watching and being watched, and ending (pointedly) with "Your eye. Your eye."[31] Through such techniques Sanders makes powerful statements about the objectification of women and troubling aspects of playing the role of muse.

Seeing and Reading Art in Words

Prose poems about photographs or works of visual art are, broadly speaking, ekphrastic in nature, and Elizabeth Bergmann Loizeaux observes that twentieth-century poets wrote ekphrastic poems in such numbers that "[i]f the record of ekphrastic production can be a measure, images are more urgent [for poets] in the twentieth century than ever before."[32] W.J.T. Mitchell identifies a cultural "pictorial turn" in "the second half of the twentieth century," arguing that "[m]ost important, it is the realization that while the problem of pictorial representation has always been with us, it presses inescapably now, and with unprecedented force, on every level of culture."[33]

Extending this idea by relating it to the way in which readers encounter poetry, Cole Swensen begins her essay, "To Writewithize," by claiming,

> For most people in the western world today, poetry is primarily a visual experience. Even the most avid reading-goers probably encounter much more poetry through the eye than they do through the ear. And perhaps a growing recognition of this shift from aural to visual apprehension and its importance explains an increased emphasis on the visual aspects of language in general in recent years.[34]

Contemporary ekphrastic works are thus part of a pressing contemporary interest in connections between language and other forms of art, especially the visual arts. A recent ekphrastic prose poem by Elizabeth Paul, for example, pays homage to the miniature, and demonstrates how prose poetry may make seeing—or "an attention to what's nearest"—its primary subject:

Pianist and Still-Life, 1924, Henri Matisse

> It doesn't take much—just an attention to what's nearest—to notice how precious this place is, like a dollhouse anticipating our humanity. The black staves of sheet music, the grain of a piano's wood, the brass studs along the base of an armchair. We are living in miniature. The whole inner world of the woman fits in a straight back chair and pours into the piano and out with the music, across the wall in triple octaves, arching like a celebrated entrance to the room in which she sits. There is nowhere else to go. Our biggest dreams can't contain the sheen of pink satin or exceed the fullness of a single whole note.[35]

In this prose poem, listening and seeing are coupled together in the idea of "attention," but it is the visual cues and their specificity that allow the reader into the poem—examples are "black staves of sheet music," "grain of a piano's wood," and "brass studs." The prose poem depends on such details to convey its scene in miniature—rather like the dollhouse it mentions or even somewhat like looking at a photograph—and to set up the idea that what is outside the pianist may connect to her "inner" life. This, too, is evoked in visual imagery as what is "inner . . . pours . . . out with the music," so that triple octaves arch "like a celebrated entrance to the room," and the experience of seeing and hearing is likened to a "sheen of pink satin." In this way, Paul makes reference to the form of the prose poem, its inner life inside the margins and its reaching beyond them.

Robert Miltner's ekphrastic "Quebec Express," written in response to the oil painting *Le Rapide* by Jean-Paul Lemieux, powerfully expresses how the "canvas" of a painting (and one might also read here: the words of a prose poem or the boundaries of a photograph) may have "limitless" implications:

> Terrifying space trapped in a limitless canvas. Dazzling snow etching the horizon & disappearing into the periphery, a nearly impervious border. The immense white scene is disrupted by stands of conifers forming obsidian humps along a liminal division. A smoke-colored sky clouds into a coal-dust stratosphere. The arrival of graphite & steel lines divides the vanishing point from its widening panorama, its curve slight as a migratory bird's trajectory like beak or eye or pincer or maw. The tremor like a rapid mammal constructed of iron & rust. Like the past bearing down to erase the future.[36]

In this prose poem, the usual boundaries of a work of art are problematized by the way snow "disappears into the periphery" despite "a nearly impervious border," and by the work's opening statement that the canvas is "limitless." We "see" "dazzling snow," "conifers forming obsidian humps," and a "smoke-colored sky," and yet the poem, even more than the painting it refers to, eludes our grasp, as if its visual details are indexes of what is unsayable (and perhaps unseeable). When the poem ends with the idea of "the past bearing down to erase the future," it moves decisively toward the ineffable, suggesting that what we see signals nothing less than a form of approaching oblivion.

Patrick Wright's "Black Square" responds to Kazimir Malevich's famous painting *Black Square* (of which there are four versions). Wright is drawn to abstract and monochromatic artwork, and in this prose poem, he attempts to "mimic the shape of the square."[37] The work begins:

> In this light the surface is a black mirror. I don't want to see
> myself seeing back, not seeing black. Behind cut glass a black
> cat in a coal bunker, fur curled in a corner. Learn to see flat,
> see flatly in the way Freud listened. Does matt pain glisten—
> a sea creature raised from lightlessness; or is this vantablack,
> sense-deprivation, an anechoic chamber? The only sound is
> the nervous system, heart hurtling inside my cranium.[38]

Wright has a strong focus on the margins of his work. He states, "the borders of Malevich's square determine the line breaks of the poem. The result is a sort of calligram or concrete poem, with considered use of lineation and white space."[39] His precise attention to lineation is very different from most prose poets who accept that sentences of prose poetry wrap arbitrarily at the right margin. For this reason, and as he identifies, his prose poem has much in common with the concrete poem, making it a hybrid as well as ekphrastic work.

The ekphrastic mode also encompasses complete volumes of prose poetry, such as Mary Jo Bang's *A Doll for Throwing: Poems* (2017), which draws its title from German designer Alma Siedhoff-Buscher's *Wurfpuppe*, produced at the Bauhaus. The *Wurfpuppe* is a flexible woven doll that lands gracefully when thrown. These prose poems incorporate numerous cultural references and are voiced by a speaker who inhabits various periods of time, sometimes adopting the character of the photographer, Lucia Moholy. "Mask Photo" begins:

> 1.
>
> Life as a dressed doll. A graveled path no
> wider than a balance beam. You come to
> yourself in a dream where a woman's face
> is imported from the ancient era. Myth
> always works like this: all goddesses get
> dressed out in qualities and roped into
> whatever arena you choose to believe in.[40]

Bang's prose poems demonstrate the flexibility of a poetic form that has its own, sometimes unruly, grace. They reveal the way in which—as well as exploring artistic creation and visual art—prose poetry may embrace memory material, an issue we have already flagged and that we return to later in this chapter.

John Berger remarks, "Every image embodies a way of seeing," highlighting the subjective nature of photographs and paintings, which represent "the specific vision of the image-maker."[41] Many prose poems, such as those by Elizabeth Paul, Patrick Wright, Robert Miltner, and Mary Jo Bang, also embody a way of perceiving or "seeing" the world. They do so largely through arranging and inflecting their visual imagery in particular ways. While many lineated lyric poems may have a related preoccupation with imagery—after all, the early twentieth-century imagists such as T. E. Hulme, Ezra Pound, and Hilda Doolittle were lyric poets—a conspicuous feature of prose poetry is its simultaneous emphasis on the visual, the fleeting, and the suggestive, often in a single, rectangular block of text. Prose poetry tends to favor discontinuities and the evocative. Even more than contemporary lineated lyric poetry, it celebrates the momentary and articulates the nature of quotidian experience that is snatched from its time and its "moorings."[42]

Recognizing such connections, numerous visual artists, photographers, and prose poets have made an explicit connection between prose poetry and the visual arts. To single out just a few of many possible examples, the title of *Pastels in Prose* (1890) refers to the visual arts. And, as we discussed in chapter 3, Margueritte Murphy highlights how Jessie Dismorr "contributed both prints . . . and prose poems" to the second issue of the magazine *BLAST* (1915).[43] Seventy-five years later, in 1990, Carrie Mae Weems exhibited a series of photographs interspersed with texts entitled *Kitchen Table Series*.

While these texts may not be prose poems in any strict sense—they are in the form of personal meditations (one begins: "She felt monogamy had a place but invested it with little value"[44])—they indicate how easily short prose works may sit alongside photographs in a complementary relationship, often functioning as a form of extended captioning. Weems comments that when brought together, text and photographs "form yet a third thing, something that is dynamic and complex and allows you to read something else about the photographs. I don't think of them as being necessarily dependent on one another. Rather, they exist side by side, in tandem."[45]

One of Daniel Spoerri's *tableaux-pièges* (picture-traps) entitled "Prose Poems" (readily available online) derives, according to a 2004 gallery label, "from the book by the Swiss poet Robert Walser (*Dichtungen in Prosa*, or 'Poems in Prose')."[46] The image shows the remains of a meal, appearing to obliquely emphasize the quotidian preoccupations of many prose poems, as well as showing the book from which the work draws its title.

Photographer Heidi Mae Niska and poet Julie Gard collaborated on a 2018 exhibition entitled *Threads: A Photography and Prose Poetry Collaboration*. Gard's prose poem "White Approach," which is paired in the exhibition with a subtle, almost abstract image showing what looks like a sheen of water with fishlike forms, begins:

> A patch of birch bark is the surface of a lake, its lenticels silver fish, siscowet, paperbelly, moving just beneath the surface, that or elegant canoes.[47]

Such a work—and the collaboration more generally—emphasizes not only the act of seeing but its attendant ambiguities, where an image may be bark or water, and may contain lenticels, fish, or canoes. As it develops the prose poem makes further mileage from such ambiguities by connecting them to "the heart I lost, the heart I look for," suggesting that the uncertain territory of the emotions is as unstable as issues attending to imagery and perception.

In 2015 Hedy Habra published a collection of lineated poetry and prose poetry entitled *Under Brushstrokes*, in which the prose poem "Afterthought" makes the following intertextual gesture (assuming that John William Waterhouse's painting *Lamia* may be considered as a "text"):

> If she weren't stilled by the painter's gaze, cast by John William Waterhouse in the role of Lamia kneeling in front of an unidentified knight posing as young Lycius, she would tell him how he once lit a candle within her that resisted melting.[48]

Holly Iglesias's "Conceptual Art" and Jane Monson's "Square of Light: The Artist is Present I" and "The Artist is Present II" explore art exhibitions or installations. Iglesias's prose poem responds to *The Lives They Left Behind*, an exhibition of suitcases and personal belongings found in the attic of the Willard Psychiatric Center in New York when closed in 1995. In "Conceptual Art," Iglesias enfolds the curatorial experience with the reimagining of lives based on abandoned belongings:

> An act of recovery, they say in curatorial tones, archiving the mundane, rooting through the baggage of inmates deposited long ago for safekeeping, anonymity the new caché, a hunger for narrative free of consequence. Within a small strapped case, the single shirt, carefully starched, his winter drawers and the geography text once memorized to win a ribbon that Mother tacked to the parlor wall, boasting of her genius boy. Before he began drooling in church, tweezing the hairs from his forearm, singing to himself as he walked to the foundry after a breakfast of oats and beans and splashing his cheeks with her cologne.[49]

Monson's prose poems refer to Marina Abramović's extended performance works, *The Artist Is Present* (2010) and *Rhythm 0* (1974). The first prose poem draws attention to the table at which Abramović sits and the white square of tape around it—the border at which most of the audience is said to have watched or hovered. The prose poem form heightens the reader's cognizance of this, as they must enter the box of text just as audience members entered the square of light to sit opposite Abramović.

> A table in an atrium; a square of light. Two chairs at the table face each other, the artist in one, the other empty, an open invitation. Anyone, from anywhere, can sit with her, for as long or as little as they like.[50]

Monson cleverly ends the prose poem by turning the table to enable the artist to "look" back as

> Lives leak, itch, burn, smile, wince, blink, twitch, close, open, sleep, wake, stutter through their eyes. She catches and collects every drop; becomes a diary of what they don't say.[51]

Similarly, in "The Artist Is Present II," Monson uses the compression of the prose poem form to create an uncomfortable feeling of intensity:

> Upon a table, she places 72 objects, some of which could give pleasure and others pain. The audience members are allowed to choose any thing and use it on her in any way they desire, while the artist sits by the table for six hours and waits to see what her changing company will do with a rose, treacle, knife, fork, salt, a gun, vase of water, feather, a glass frame . . .[52]

The reader is, as it were, obliged to watch what ensues and is implicated by sharing this space with Abramović and the audience:

> When one person points a gun at her head, another takes it away. When another cuts into her clothes, another pours treacle over her damp head. She is mocked with a fan, quick, slow, quick wind around her body, then crowned with a plastic tiara and forced to smoke the feather. A sitting Jesus.[53]

Finally, Joe Bonomo's *Installations* (2008) and Paul Hetherington's *Gallery of Antique Art* (2016) are notionally ekphrastic in the way they invent not only the art installations or artifacts to which they refer but also the repositories in which the art exists. Bonomo states:

> I imagined the same visitor at each installation, a curious museumgoer both eager and tentative . . . I simply dropped this guy into each room and watched the top of his head lift off. He'll leave that museum at the end of the day a very different man, the world having been represented to him in refreshing, startling ways.[54]

June Downey, Imagery, and Aesthetic Empathy

Visual imagery in poetic works tends to open up the space of writing and, as it does so, it often slows the movement of time because of the way in which imagery stimulates and activates fields of mental imagery in the reader, suggesting larger associations and evoking sometimes expansive scenes, giving the reader pause. The functioning of mental imagery has been much debated, but no matter how one understands the brain's way of producing and processing visual imagery, there is no doubt that, as Rudolph Arnheim writes, "Thinking calls for images, and images contain thought."[55] Arnheim also states that "[t]he kind of 'mental image' needed for thought is unlikely to be a complete, colorful, and faithful replica of some visible scene."[56]

Imagery drawn from reading a prose poem and internalized by the reader partly functions to allow that reader a sense that the confined literary spaces of prose poems may be somewhat balloon-like, expanding the reader's perception (instead of proceeding travelator-like from one narrated event to another like so much conventional prose). The reader must understand and appreciate prose poems from the inside if they are to enjoy a satisfying reading experience, and internalizing the reading experience in this way requires an imaginative journey of aesthetic empathy. One must be able to connect both emotionally and intellectually with the work and imbibe its key meanings and connotations.

Or, to pursue the metaphor of prose poems as rooms, one must enter inside in order to look around and understand the fittings and furniture. This process is discussed in Joanna Ganczarek, Thomas Hünefeldt, and Marta Olivetti Belardinelli's exploration of aesthetic empathy:

> In fact, works of art, in general, and works of figurative art, in particular, call for the act of "feeling into" another body or another environment for two main reasons: (1) all works of art are human artefacts, i.e. they have been produced by other human beings living in other historical, cultural, and personal environments, and (2) works of figurative art represent bodies or environments, and in particular often human beings or human environments . . . aesthetic "empathy" concerns human artefacts, especially those representing human beings or human environments.[57]

Prose poems are examples of such human artifacts. Importantly, the reader does not have to experience complete identification with a prose poem to imagine themselves *being spoken* by the work and, in many cases—and as we discuss below—*seeing through* the work. However, they are required to move far enough into the work's main tropes and ideas to be able to empathize with its concerns. This matters more in reading prose poetry than it does in reading other kinds of prose, because prose poems are usually so compact and condensed that readers who fail to "enter" a prose poem have few other readerly satisfactions available to them. Unlike novels and short stories, where there are satisfactions connected to narrative, plot, and character development available even to the relatively uninvolved reader, a prose poem is able to offer only a brief interlude of reading—along with the satisfactions of appreciating, and perhaps puzzling out, the imagistic, metaphoric, and metonymic content it may possess.

Reading a satisfying prose poem is a way into a compressed and intense period of engagement with a text, often not unlike an intense and intimate encounter with another person. Many prose poems conjure beguiling and suggestive spaces that ask for the reader's active participation in making them fully imagined. As R. K. Elliott states, "When we do make the expression our own, we are experiencing the poem *from within*."[58] If this does not occur, the reader is unlikely to invest enough in the work to make any complex sense of it.

While extended prose narratives often "hook" their readers by getting them to care about what will happen next, many prose poems engage their readers by prompting them to consider what it would be like if the prose poem's propositions were *actually and presently* the case—even when these propositions are obviously unrealistic in quotidian terms or are based on the author's reconstruction of a memory. And, while arguments such as Elliott's also apply more generally to poetry, the reader's experience "within" many prose poems is of particular importance because of their intimate, room-like confines.

The capacity for readers to connect empathically* with prose poetry is also linked to the way in which many prose poems require interpretation and readerly application in order to be understood and appreciated. (Aesthetic responses to complex language are partly driven by the yield of pleasure that is obtained from disentangling and clarifying its various layers of often simultaneously presented meaning.) Taking his cue from philosopher Ted Cohen, who writes, "There is a unique way in which the maker and the appreciator of a metaphor are drawn closer to one another,"[59] Edward Hirsch observes that "the maker and the appreciator of a metaphor are brought into [a] deeper relationship . . . because the speaker issues a concealed invitation through metaphor which the listener makes a special effort to accept and interpret."[60]

This assertion may be broadened to include the reader's "effort" to apprehend and enter all of the figurative language of a poem, whether that language is strictly metaphorical or not. Cohen claims: "In both tasks—realizing that the expression is intended metaphorically, and seeing what to make of it—the hearer typically employs a number of assumptions about the speaker: what the speaker believes, what the speaker believes about what the hearer believes (which includes beliefs about what the speaker thinks the hearer can be expected to believe about the speaker)."[61] In effect, Cohen's words constitute a succinct characterization of the journey of aesthetic empathy, as a reader (or, in Cohen's terminology, "hearer") enters into a—not necessarily benign—relationship with the language of a text.

However, this connection between reader and text only becomes aesthetic empathy when a text is embraced and to some extent embodied by the reader or, as early twentieth-century American psychologist and poet June Downey says, when

---

* The words "empathic" and "empathetic" are synonyms. While "empathetic" has been gaining popularity in common usage, "empathic" is the older term, which the Oxford English Dictionary dates from 1904. We do not intend "empathic" to be used in the specialized science fiction sense (from around 1959) where "empathic" is derived from "empath," that is, describing someone who can read other people's feelings via extrasensory perception.

reading becomes "a final assimilation of the projected experiences."[62] Thus, the concept of aesthetic empathy, as it recognizes the possibility for deep and complex empathy between reader and text, enables a consideration of the way imagery in prose poetry may function as an important conduit, allowing readers to enter a prose poem immersively.

Susan Lanzoni points out that "at the turn of the twentieth century, empathy was best known as an aesthetic theory that captured the reader's participatory and kinaesthetic engagement with objects of art" and that it "entailed an imagined bodily immersion in the shapes, forms, and lines of objects and the natural world."[63] In saying this she refers to Downey's early exploration of ways in which imagery functioned in poetry and remarks on Downey's interest in the early twentieth-century imagists, who were interested in "art that bears true witness . . . art that is most precise."[64]

The imagist movement was instigated not long before the First World War by T. E. Hulme, F. S. Flint, Hilda Doolittle (H.D.), Richard Aldington, and Ezra Pound, among others—with T. E. Hulme's 1909 poems "Autumn" and "A City Sunset" inaugurating the movement in practice.[65] Fired with enthusiasm for the visual arts, including Japanese prints, along with French symbolist poetry, Japanese verse forms, and Chinese T'ang Dynasty poetry, Pound published, in the journal *Poetry*, a now famous "note" under F. S. Flint's name entitled "Imagisme."[66] He advocated "[d]irect treatment of the 'thing,' whether subjective or objective," and Loizeaux writes that "[i]magism . . . desir[ed] the instantaneous revelation the visual image is thought to have."[67] The imagist movement emerged in a period, as Art Berman has commented, that was very much engaged with the notion that "the visual can provide direct and even prelinguistic knowledge."[68]

Downey "deemed the images in the work of key Imagist poets [T. E. Hulme, Ezra Pound, H.D., and Amy Lowell] crisp, clear and inventive; neither predictable nor stereotyped."[69] She characterizes Amy Lowell's imagination, for instance, as "delight[ing] not only in pictorial but in sculptural effects. Movement enters into its imaginal stuff, but it is movement *seen* rather than *felt*."[70] Downey also comments that in Ezra Pound's famous short poem, "In a Station of the Metro," "the reader is submerged in that feeling of poetic beauty which is one of the mysteries of experience."[71] She highlights how the imagistic language of these poets enabled the process of aesthetic empathy and was persuasive partly because it represented fresh and inventive ways of seeing. In its application to the short prose form, Murphy extends the analysis to include what she claims are tensions inherent in "the aspirations of Imagism, and how short prose pieces wrestle with mimetic possibility and insufficiency."[72]

Although imagism was one of the twentieth century's most short-lived poetic movements, it was seminal in the development of modernist and postmodern poetry. Just as many early modernist poets wanted to "see" the world in their work through visual imagery in the hope that they could reconnect with, or at least come closer to, a "true witness," as Pound phrases it, many contemporary poets continue to use imagery to ensure that their poems are memorable and "present" to the reader. While poetic imagery is used in a multiplicity of ways by poets, overall it has become so pervasive that Peter Jones's statement from the 1970s might equally be applied to twenty-first-century poetry: "The truth is that imagistic ideas still lie at the centre of our poetic practice."[73]

Evidence of the preoccupation of contemporary poets with imagery is everywhere, including the fame of poems such as William Carlos Williams's "The Red Wheelbarrow," from 1923, which is almost entirely a composite verbal image, and the influence of T. S. Eliot's imagistic "The Love Song of J. Alfred Prufrock."[74] Although, as Martin Scofield writes, Eliot "dissociated himself from the Imagist movement proper," Scofield also observes that "[s]omething of the Imagist clarity and concentration can be seen in Eliot's first two volumes and in *The Waste Land* . . . and the description of the fog as a cat in 'Prufrock' is virtually a little self-contained Imagist poem."[75]

As we discussed in chapter 5, later in the twentieth century, poets such as Robert Bly and James Wright made their names partly as a result of their involvement with the so-called Deep Image movement. They wrote poems that were in a direct line of descent from writers such as Hulme, despite Bly and others wanting to claim that "the Deep Image poem could be distinguished from the Imagism of the 1910s and 1920s by its use of the image to enact 'psychic leaps' between the conscious and the unconscious."[76]

Bly's prose poems typically have a strong visual component. "A Caterpillar on the Desk" is an example, taking the reader from a simple moment of observation to broader considerations about human responsibility. Here are the opening and closing sections:

> Lifting my coffee cup, I notice a caterpillar crawling over my sheet of ten-cent airmail stamps. The head is black as a Chinese box. Nine soft accordions follow it around, with a waving motion, like a flabby mountain. Skinny brushes used to clean pop bottles rise from some of its shoulders. . . . It is the first of September. The leaf shadows are less ferocious on the notebook cover. A man accepts his failures more easily—or perhaps summer's insanity is gone? A man notices ordinary earth, scorned in July, with affection, as he settles down to his daily work, to use stamps.[77]

Poetic imagery of this kind is able to act as a kind of empathy conductor, channeling the reader into and around the space that a poem or prose poem occupies. When absorbed in a work, the reader may be transported into an experience that is likely to have some broad features in common with what the writer brought to mind when composing the work—or that, at least, they hoped to evoke when constructing their images.

This is to say, in most cases, the linguistic prompts offered by a literary work will tend to yield readerly responses that are recognizably connected to the writer's imaginative projections, even if in their finest detail the reader's visualizations, and the ideas they draw from them, remain particular to that reader. The text of every poem or prose poem contains loosely precise instructions for readers, some of the most important of which is contained in its imagery. In prose poetry, these instructions are placed under pressure in their containment within a bounded form.

Prose Poetry and Seeing the Subjective

Imagery is of such central importance to the reading and understanding of poems of all kinds that even when Louise Rosenblatt characterizes the reader's aesthetic responses to poetic texts in theoretical terms, she speaks in richly imagistic language:

> So interwoven are the aesthetic responses to a text that when the response to one word is changed, it may affect the organization or structure of the whole work. Instead of a rigid stencil, a more valid image for the text seems to be something like an open-meshed woven curtain . . . One can imagine the reader peering through the curtain, affecting its shape and the pattern of the mesh by the tension or looseness with which he is holding it, and filling in the openings from his own palette of colours.[78]

Rosenblatt's emphasis on the importance of readers' individual responses to texts is certainly persuasive. However, if the understanding of poems is the result of individual acts of reading, and colored by the reader's subjective palette, contemporary prose poets also provide a great deal of color of their own, especially in the form of visual imagery, and practiced readers of such works are attuned to the complex meanings that imagery carries.

Here, for example, is the opening of a prose poem by Jenny Gropp. Its title, "Photo Graph Paper: American Push," is another marker of the influence of photography on prose poetry, as is the work's preoccupation with conjuring a sense of what one may call "still movement":

> I want everything to be frozen like a hive, spun like an ice cello hung and whirled round in the thick drop-down of winter.
>
> Off like the porch light, people standing grouped in the dark, shoulders rounded like couch corners. I give you all the trees in my heart, the will of children who curl like waves to lift a shell. Who lift dead fish for the same reason.[79]

It is worth noting the confidence with which Gropp employs similes and metaphors to restlessly transform the imagery of the poem, and to make unexpected connections—so that a frozen hive is connected to "an ice cello" and "the thick drop-down of winter." We not only "see" this work but watch it shift under our eyes, to the extent that the heart possesses trees and children are shaped like curled waves. The visual imagery functions to transport the reader almost instantaneously into an imaginative "space" that, at least for the duration of their reading experience, may empathically become their own.

This is true despite the extreme subjectivity of Gropp's poetic vision, which her imagery insists on—a subjectivity that is characteristic of a great deal of contemporary prose poetry. Such works seek to transform apparently personal experience and intensely personal visions into material that may connect with the reader. Mike Dockins's long prose poem in eleven parts, "Eleven Gin & Tonics," offers another example of this approach, providing powerful images joined to a strong and somewhat idiosyncratic vision. It opens confidently:

#1
The wall clock is concentrating on a Grand Unified Theory. I'm interested in physics, too: I listen to its ticking. The afternoon swings from the 5. I'm not wearing a tie, but if I were, it would be growing old, less effective in its choking. The jukebox won't talk to me. There are stars in my eyes. They sting.

#2
The earth can never produce enough limes. They grin at me from their little tin. I wonder if I look as good to them, or if the grins are only metaphors. Later, I'll ask them to dance.[80]

Dockins's strategies rely on tying his abstractions to concrete detail, on animating key details—such as the clock and the limes—so that they take on a (somewhat surrealistic) life of their own, and on providing sufficient visual imagery to allow the reader to "see" his somewhat strange ideas at work. He also employs occasional metafictional gestures, such as his question as to whether the grins of the tinned limes are metaphors. This prose poem's marked subjectivity does not need to deter readers because enough information is given, primarily through its images, to allow the reader to enter the poem and to read and "see" it, as it were, from the inside.

In a prose poem by Emily Brandt entitled "The Harbor," the reader is able to empathize with the work because the "house" of the prose poem gradually becomes emblematic of very many houses, something largely achieved through the accumulating detail, much of it presented as visual imagery ("a severed limb," "a body dull and steady as a rock," "a mother pulls mouse traps down from closet shelves," and so on). The poem begins:

In this house, cancer. In this house arthritis, a severed limb, hot wax. In this house, there's a cheater. In this house, travel low. In this house, a body dull and steady as a rock. In this house, a mother pulls mouse traps down from closet shelves, slaps a child's hands like hoards of rodent feet. In this house, a man girl-pulled her from bed and to the backseat of his car. In this house, the Christmas bulbs stay up til Valentine's, a schism in the rig. In this house, a dog that stings. In this house, the shower's always cold.[81]

The hypnotic repetitions of this poem have a dreamlike quality, and Downey believed "[d]reamlikeness, atmosphere, richness and fluidity of suggestion" were some of the poetic features that encouraged aesthetic empathy.[82] Many prose poems have the capacity to convey such qualities, although in contemporary prose poetry the "dreamlikeness" is frequently sharply inflected:

Diorama

Black in a black mirror—the glass panther. Even if you do not dream—the glass panther. On top of the Philco radio, in front of the rabbit ears—the glass panther. The credenza, the Barcalounger, the Formica table, the orange vinyl barstool, the chrome bar caddy, matching martini shaker, the Sputnik lamp—the glass panther. A puddle of India ink on a white patio floor. Rousseau moonlight, the bullet-shaped planter, plastic spear-shaped leaves, Sky King pedal plane, the ancient starlight, the rhinestone eyes of the glass panther.[83]

In this imagistic work by Richard Garcia—which he previously published as a less successful lineated poem[84]—the many things mentioned become a diorama in the imagination (thus twice transformed into a kind of artwork, as both "diorama" and prose poem), dominated by the persistent and ambiguous image of the glass panther. The swarming visual imagery (and the reference to the French postimpressionist Henri Rosseau's paintings, a number of which are rather eerily moonlit) allows the reader to "enter" the frame or scene of the prose poem even as it resists yielding certain kinds of information, such as whether this "diorama" is real and what its larger context may be. The work requires readers to feel and "see" their way into the work in order to imagine and make sense of it.

Lanzoni suggests the "meaning of empathy for [Downey] was close to the literal translation of *Einfühlung*" or, as Downey herself describes it, "a process of 'feeling-in,' in which motor and emotional attitudes, however originating, are projected outside of the self."[85] She also connects perception to patterns of behavior:

The aesthetic doctrine of empathy stresses, chiefly, behaviour patterns released through the sheer activity of perception, a much more evasive process than that of social identification. Moreover, while the response to art may be that of the participant (identification in the narrower and popular meaning of the term . . .), the truly aesthetic response does not stop there. It goes beyond introjection and projection to a final assimilation of the projected experiences, a complex integration.[86]

Downey characterizes aesthetic empathy in terms that emphasize the way in which both textual material and reader responses are meshed together in any act of complex reading. While different readers will inevitably respond with different levels of empathy to particular texts, texts with powerful imagery are, in general, more likely to elicit empathic responses in readers.

Excavating Autobiographical Memory in Prose Poetry

Imagistic prose poems may allow new readerly insights and empathy, but why do we care about their subjective ways of seeing when such experiences are at least one remove from our own? Part of the answer lies in the way that prose poets make use of memory material. If poetic imagery is able to appeal to and prompt readerly empathy, then the presence in prose poetry of autobiographical recollections rendered imagistically has the ability to solicit a connection between the reader's memories and sense of identity, and the poet's evocation of a past self. Huyssen writes of the way a photograph "resists quick forgetting, and as such serves as an entry point for memory, even if that memory may appear ghostly and uncanny,"[87] and such remarks may apply to the way many prose poems function too.

We are not arguing that prose poems necessarily deal with actual memories—although many of them do—but, rather, contemporary prose poets have written many works that, in Sidonie Smith's and Julia Watson's phrase, explicitly engage with "the uses of memory."[88] Such works often address the way in which language is only able to provide an incomplete bridge to others—as Ludwig Wittgenstein remarks in the *Tractatus*, "*The limits of my language* mean the limits of my world"[89]—and most of them link memory to visual images of the world.

This connection between imagery and memory is a recurrent one, from the ancient world to the present. A few examples are Plato's (ca. 428–348 BCE) conception of memories as impressions in a wax block "that we remember and know . . . as long as the image lasts," Aristotle's (384–322 BCE) likening of memory to "an impression or picture," Augustine's (354–430) articulation of "the treasures of innumerable images of all kinds of objects brought in by sense-perception," and John Locke's (1632–1704) characterization of memory as "the Power to revive again in our Minds those Ideas, which after imprinting have disappeared, or have been as it were laid out of Sight."[90] David Hume (1711–76) also described memory as a "faculty, by which we raise up the images of past perceptions."[91]

Studies conducted in recent decades have reaffirmed such connections. To give two examples, William Brewer writes of the importance of imagery to recollective memory and claims that the "measures of phenomenal experience during recall show that autobiographical recalls with high memory confidence are virtually always accompanied by high visual imagery," and David C. Rubin connects imagery to memory partly "because of its role in increasing the specific, relived, personally experienced aspect of autobiographical memory."[92] He states, "Concrete details make stories seem more accurate, thoughtful, and believable" and imagery and "[s]pecific [narrative] details . . . increase affect, intimacy, and immediacy."[93] However, Rubin notices a paradox at the heart of the link between imagery and autobiographical memory because, "imagery both increases the belief that memories are accurate and [because they are malleable] facilitates changes from initial perception."[94]

The malleability and unreliability of memory are now major strands in studies of autobiographical memory. Daniel Albright believes that the remembered self is "a matrix ramifying backward in all directions, a garden of forking paths that converge in the present."[95] Ulric Neisser observes that specific mental images accompanying generic memories "need not be an accurate representation of any particular experienced moment," and Martin Conway says that "there are no such things as autobiographical memories at least in the sense of discrete, holistic units in long-term memory."[96] Indeed, when Barclay states, "Perhaps the most important purpose [for reconstructing autobiographical information] is to adapt to the present by conveying authentic meanings instead of simply preserving the past,"[97] he might be talking about prose poetry.

Art Berman's remark, "The self is not exactly exercised in creativity, but evolved through the act of creativity,"[98] is a succinct way of acknowledging that poets (and other artists) inevitably remake and even invent their experience in writing about it. He characterizes the artist as positioning the self "at a critical junction of external events; at that junction, the external events integrate into an authentic artwork. The artist's personality has been the catalyst for the work, not its subject."[99]

In the reconstruction and reimagination of events readers are invited to interpose themselves in the gaps that memory elicits—and the poetic self one finds in prose poems is a simulation of a past self rather than an actual past self. Ana Margarida Abrantes posits that autobiographical memories can "represent the personal meaning of an event at the cost of historical accuracy. Autobiographical truth is hence not a finished concept, but a flexible construct which develops at the rhythm of one's self-definition."[100]

The poet and the reader experience the autobiographical memory newly when it is revived in prose poetry. Both are implicated freshly into the work as the past and present become an amalgam that reinflects a putative memory. Empathy between the reader and the prose poet's simulated self is built on a sharing of pertinent experiences, but these are related *kinds* of experiences rather than the same events. The reader contemplates and reassesses their own encounters in light of what they read. Thus, memory and prose poetry remain intimately connected, and many memories, like prose poems, work at the level of symbolism and abstraction. These features demand that readers "project themselves into the represented events" in order to comprehend them.[101]

But how does a prose poet excavate their memory for poetic creation? Interestingly, the process itself is sometimes discussed in metaphorical terms that link poetry and memory in a series of conceits. Bruce M. Ross likens memory and its retrieval to time spent in a waiting room, an inquiry at a Lost and Found department, and, finally, to ransacking old luggage:

> Every person possesses not only a waiting room of memories where old favourites are recalled but also a Lost and Found where recollections from the past appear without being recognized. Other less accessible memories are hidden in mental suitcases to which we have misplaced the keys; elsewhere suitcases are discovered empty that we thought were full. Piled in with the rest are convenient imitation packages of memories constructed out of dreams and fantasies that were never paid for with experience. Every baggage room full of memories is open day and night, for no living traveller rides free of the burden of old luggage.[102]

In such a light, many poets and prose poets might be identified as archaeologists of memory and the functioning of aesthetic empathy to be, in part, a subtle act of archaeological complicity between reader and writer.

An example is Paul Munden's prose poem "Arthroscopy/Sports Day, 1971," which explores memory in a series of imagistic flashes. The use of the year "1971" in the title suggests that this is a biographical moment compressed into a prose poem, a form of time retrieval. Here, the poet simulates a "Sports Day," forty-five years prior to the prose poem's composition:

> The smell of cut grass. The surgeon's view shows threadbare ground where the shotput circle splays to a heavily pockmarked V. A wayward flick of the wrist and it's the high jump. The bar being raised. Your lazy run quickens, each of us lifting a vicarious leg as you scissor the air. Watch the old footage, re-wind and re-believe you'll make it through. Try to miss your father's grimace as he bends and clutches his knee. Those slivers of loose cartilage. The elusive meniscus slipping offscreen.[103]

Time is cleverly warped in this prose poem. The memories are not only "backward-told" but also forward and sideways-told, so that the work may be read as a way of " 'holding open' . . . the moment."[104] Triggered by "the surgeon's view" of "slivers of loose cartilage," the high jump is relived via the narrator's memory of "old footage" that captured it. This prose poem turns on the image of the screen, as central to the reimagining of a traumatic memory. The surgeon's ultrasound screen is twinned with the screen of the home movie (and perhaps the rectangular form of this prose poem might also be viewed as a screen).

The work highlights shared experiences and different ways of viewing the high jump, encouraging the reader to see in a like manner, and thus to enter the text. In this way, the event can be replayed on high rotation. Munden's sophisticated use of time refers to the way prose poetry may be reread in much the same way as memory, or a film being rewatched. This work may be said to "see," and the reader to see into and through it. Acknowledging the reader's close connection to the narrator—in the sense that they are both watching the accident unfold—encourages an empathic readerly response. For example, the line, "lifting a vicarious leg as you scissor the air" depicts the viewer in empathic union with the high jumper and the narrator. This use of the second-person pronoun coupled with the slipperiness of time cleverly blurs identity so that the "you" is simultaneously father, narrator, and reader. In some small way, the knee injury is felt by all.

Munden's prose poem ends on a final image that is both physiological and confronting—its use of the word "meniscus." This thin, fibrous cartilage is in sharp focus for the reader, before it floats away: a metaphor for what lies between one thing and another, or between memory and its unreliability. The use of the screen metaphor aims to home in on Sports Day 1971 but, in the end, it is a conjuring of "old footage," spliced between multiple viewpoints, that tells a fuller story.

This work is also a nice demonstration of the prose poem form's relationship to film, which Jane Monson refers to in her interdisciplinary discussion of influences on the prose poem: "Of equal significance when thinking about the formation and definition of the prose poem are influences from other disciplines outside of poetry. The prose poem is not only at the behest of changing attitudes and ideas of what constitutes prose and poetry, but also part of experiments in architecture, urban environments, technology, photography, painting, advertising, journalism, social media and digitalised ways of communicating more generally."[105]

In the digital age, prose poetry resembles a still frame capture from a film, television, YouTube clip, home video or iMovie, all of which are often consumed, created, and/or filmed on portable digital devices. This comparison is based on the way in which both prose poems and still frame captures may represent moments or fragments that connect to something larger—in both literal and metaphorical ways. The frame and the prose poem contain boxlike images within defined spaces while simultaneously tearing a moment from an experience or narrative.

Murphy identifies the influence of "new reading practices" in the modernist period "with the growth of newspapers, specifically the *feuilleton* form, and new technologies that compete with literature—photography and cinema" in "rapidly modernizing cities."[106] Similarly, Monte, in his explication of Ashbery's "The System," notes the importance of its filmic qualities and their link to the mind's images, arguing that in a particular passage "the narrator admits to himself that all of the action of the poem was, in a sense, a film in his head, and yet makes gestures toward a world outside."[107] Gregory Robinson's volume, *All Movies Love the Moon: Prose Poems on Silent Film* (2014), features linked prose poems that refer to many silent movies, while also making other intertextual references, connecting the prose poetry form to cinematic history and some of its techniques.

Munden's prose poem, too, provides more than one single frame capture, drawing them from two different sources and requiring the reader to fill in the gaps.

This involves the process of aesthetic empathy because the reader must work with the imagery inside the prose poem while integrating it with further meaning from outside its frame.

Old and New Worlds

The presence of visual imagery in prose poetry—allied with its compression as a literary form and techniques such as metaphor, metonymy, and simile—permits readers to "see" into the work and begin to participate in what they read. While there remains disagreement about how mental imagery functions, and even debate about exactly what mental imagery may be, Stephen M. Kosslyn and others write that a "major problem in theorizing about the nature of mental images has been their inherently private nature";[108] nevertheless, imagery has been used by writers since time immemorial.

This is because of imagery's capacity to characterize, depict, and transfer to the reader visions of old and new worlds, and the stories of memory and identity that are crucial to all human communities. Visual imagery, combined with the prose poem's tendency to eschew closure while opening out its concerns for readerly inspection, invite readers to identify—however provisionally—with the prose poet. By extension, the reader is prompted to contribute to the text aspects of their own grappling for meaning.

Having said this, not all readers are as empathetic as others, and the distinction between voyeurism and empathy in prose poetry is important to an understanding of the way readers may enter a text. Voyeuristic readers maintain a degree of distance from the texts they encounter, while empathetic readers—who experience a work from "within"—allow themselves to be gathered into the space of the work. Bruce Bond contends that "the tension that empathic listening gives to a poem remains critical to its power, a quality of speaking and being spoken, of going more deeply inward as if somewhere in there were the path to others." He also writes that "[e]mpathy thus provides a model of what poetry longs to be, empathetic in the sense of listening as it speaks."[109]

Prose poetry is a literary form typically giving priority to poetic suggestiveness over narrative, and frequently situating its renderings of autobiographical memory in an immediate poetic present. Some prose poems even appear to see *for* a reader, as if they have eyes of their own. Or, to shift the metaphor, they convey a sense of being able to be seen into or through. Of course, what individual readers see in or through any particular prose poem will vary, but all readers who are seeing in this way are on a journey of aesthetic empathy—whether they know it or not.

CHAPTER 8

Metaphor, Metonymy, and the Prose Poem

Metaphor and Metonymy

Prose poetry typically employs a considerable amount of figurative language—as does lineated poetry and, to a lesser extent, discursive and narrative prose, including novels. Such figurations emphasize connotative (secondary, suggested or implied) meanings that extend a work's literal (or denotative) statements to suggest an array of overarching, associative, or subsidiary meanings and implications. Many of these secondary meanings significantly transform the interpretation of a work's language and imagery. For example, the familiar statement or adage "the pen is mightier than the sword" exploits metonymic techniques and, as a result, the statement does not mean what it literally says.

Metonymy takes place when something (sometimes a concept) is referred to by the name of something else associated with it, or—as the *Princeton Encyclopedia of Poetry and Poetics* (2012) states—it is a "trope in which one expression is substituted for another on the basis of some material, causal, or conceptual relation."[1] Thus, in the phrase above, "pen" is a shorthand way of naming the persuasive written word, writing more generally, and diplomacy, while "sword" stands in for, and is a way of naming, military power and warfare. One interpretation of the phrase is that persuasively expressed ideas are more powerful than an army.

Metonymy allows writers to use phrases or individual words in ways that suggest an array of meanings, enriching and adding complexity to their writing—and there are many kinds and examples of metonymy, just as there are many kinds of metaphor. Metonymy is especially important to prose poems because it complements, enhances, and complicates their literal and metaphorical meanings. As we have argued, the prose poem is fragmented and encourages leaps of thought, making metonymy—with its emphasis on meaning through association—particularly pertinent. The use of metonymic techniques is a key way for prose poets to refer to various ideas suggested, but not fully encompassed, by a prose poem.

As Andy Brown observes, authors of lineated poetry have a greater arsenal of poetic tools at their disposal, but the prose poet is able to hone an appeal to various kinds of absence:

The fact that all poets look for patterns in the signs of their poem is obvious, but its functions are foregrounded in the prose poem when the prose poet lacks recourse to other formal concerns (stanzaic shape, verse form, meter and other prosodic effects) most commonly associated with lineated verse. It is also most clearly seen in the rhetorical function of metonymy . . . The conjuring of the absent context is a necessary feature of words and of prose poems.[2]

Metonymic associations constitute one of the principal characteristics of human thought, which, as it moves rapidly from one thing or concept to associated things or concepts, is inclined to be digressive and ramifying. Thought locates meanings through a series of complex movements that penetrate, link, and sometimes transform linguistic (and imagistic, sensory, or embodied) connections and conceptual frameworks. Simultaneously, it distributes these connections and conceptual frameworks into new and developing contexts.

For example, Günter Radden and Zoltán Kövecses provide an account of the way metonymy has functioned to transform the meaning of the word *hearse*:

In medieval farming, the word [hearse] originally denoted a triangular harrow with pins and was then metaphorically applied to a triangular frame for supporting candles at church services. . . . [T]he burning of candles came to be metonymically associated with a special liturgical occasion, Tenebrae, the Holy Week before Easter. . . . In the church service of the Holy Week, all candles were gradually extinguished to commemorate the darkness at Christ's crucifixion. The burning candle was a metaphor for man's life, and, as an entailment, its extinction a metaphor for man's death. . . . The "funeral ICM [idealized cognitive model]" involves several parts, many of which were described by the word *hearse* . . . Among these parts, the moving carriage eventually appeared to be the most salient element.[3]

Such an account demonstrates how profoundly the evolution of language works through various associated complex metonymic (and metaphorical) processes. Words are connected to the tangible, experiential world, and many of them take on increasingly complex meanings as they evolve.

Jeannette Littlemore comments that metonymy may "be seen as a cognitive process which we use all the time" and states, "[m]etonymic thinking becomes more apparent when novel metonymies are produced, or . . . when we are exposed to new languages or enter new discourse communities."[4] Prose poetry, being neither traditionally lineated poetry nor traditional narrative prose, is rich with novel metonymies and represents a discourse community of its own. Individual prose poems do not, of course, work in the same way as the modification over time of the word "hearse," but such historical processes of metonymic transformation are not fundamentally dissimilar to the metonymic processes at work in many prose poems. In such processes, what one may call "drifts" of associative meaning occur. As language flows from image to association, and then to connected (or disjunct) images and associations, it constructs meanings through activating the effects of juxtapositioning and the linking of ideas. At the same time, some of the largely suppressed secondary meanings of words and their associations are also activated—along with the suggestiveness of sensory imagery that potentially bring whole conceptual "worlds" into play. As a result, metonymic processes illustrate how, as Sam Glucksberg writes, "in figurative language, the intended meaning does not coincide with the literal meanings of the words and sentences that are used."[5]

This is as true of metaphor as it is of metonymy. Metaphor is a word that came into English via French from Latin and Greek roots. It means a "transfer" or a "carrying over," and it has long been associated with poetry. Winifred Nowottny argues that "the vast power of metaphor in poetry . . . should be set in relation with simple linguistic facts. One reason why metaphor is common in poetry is that metaphor vastly extends the language at the poet's disposal."[6] Similarly, Antonio Barcelona defines metaphor as "a mapping of a domain onto another domain, both being conventionally and consciously classified as separate domains."[7]

Metaphors are used almost everywhere in language, and some metaphors are so commonplace we employ them without noticing. An example is "His heart is a stone." Through this metaphor the qualities of stones are transferred to the idea of a heart, and what is usually thought of as warm is understood to be inert and cold. In many instances, however, the functioning of metaphor may be more complex than such an example suggests because related but different metaphorical tropes may occur in a single work—each complicating the other—and in some cases, metaphorical suggestiveness may overwhelm literal (or denotative) meanings in a work. A pertinent example is Emily Dickinson's nineteenth-century poem that begins "I dwell in Possibility– / A fairer House than Prose–,"[8] where the word "Possibility" is hard to pin down, partly standing in for poetry, and suggesting a rather elusive, abstract, and beautiful place where the poet lives in the midst of poetic language and an attentiveness to the imagination and the natural world.

For a long time, metaphor and metonymy were considered to be more or less separate cognitive maneuvers—metaphor making links between differences that, at best, had analogical similarity and metonymy exploiting preexisting links between things or concepts. This artificial separation of metaphor and metonymy has now been disputed, as Barcelona summarizes in his survey of cognitive linguistics. He writes, "It is well known that metaphor and metonymy often interact with each other, sometimes in fairly intricate ways."[9] He identifies a developing area of research as "the extent to which the whole metaphorical network of a language is motivated by the metonymic one."[10] Similarly, Jiyoung Yoon observes that "the order of the conceptual operation between metonymy and metaphor may be somewhat fuzzy and arguably interchangeable."[11]

While the relationships between metaphor and metonymy as understood by cognitive linguists are too complex to explore in detail here, one of the examples of a metaphor we gave above—"His heart is a stone"—demonstrates that metaphoric and metonymic techniques often occur together. In this example, the "heart" is a succinct way of metonymically naming feelings and emotions associated with love and affection. Thus, for our purposes, the important issue to note is that some figures of speech may be both metaphorical and metonymic at once, complicating efforts to interpret them.

Even if readers do not always recognize figurative language, or consciously register how it functions, the primary effects generated by any particular work may largely depend upon such figurations. Indeed, in the case of prose poetry, connotative language associated with metaphoric and metonymic transformations may carry almost all the important meaning of a work. Simon Brittan suggests that "metaphor has always been, and still is, the main device of poetry,"[12] and because some figurative language and its associated connotative meanings are considerably more obscure or complex than the examples given above, they require active interpretation on the part of the reader.

This chapter will focus on reading and discussing examples of the metaphoric and metonymic features (and their interplay) in a range of contemporary prose poems, and by doing so, aims to demonstrate the centrality of such language use to prose poetry. In undertaking this analysis, we do not wish to suggest all prose poetry is equally metaphoric or metonymic. However, as Andy Brown notes, prose poets do not have the opportunity to exploit the resources (or concern themselves with the strictures) of the poetic line, the effects of meter, or the conventional "closure" of more conventional lineated poetry. In lineated or metrical poems, meanings are guided, inhibited, and directed to a significant extent by such considerations and, as we discussed in chapter 4, even free verse, because of its lineation, can invoke expectations of formal closure.

For instance, Barbara Herrnstein Smith writes, "the rhythm of a free-verse poem, as it is reflected in and reinforced by its lineation, is experienced as an expectation of the recurrence of certain distribution patterns of formal features."[13] Prose poets generally do not engage with such "formal features," and they look elsewhere for ways of introducing the poetic into their works. This is reiterated by Mary Ann Caws, who argues, "Having no necessary exterior framework, no meter or essential form, [the prose poem] must organize itself from within."[14]

Metaphor in Prose Poetry, and Some Metonymic Byways

As we noted in chapter 1, in defining prose poetry many poets, critics, and scholars resort to figurative language. Indeed, in the Clements and Dunham anthology, *An Introduction to the Prose Poem*, there is a section devoted to prose poems about the prose poem, the majority of which employ metaphors. In their preliminary remarks to this section, Clements and Dunham discuss these prose poems as "perhaps . . . the best kind of definition we have of prose poetry—the definition by self-reflexive example, which is no definition at all."[15] An example is Tom Whalen's "Why I Hate the Prose Poem,"[16] beginning:

> An angry man came into the kitchen where his wife was busying herself about supper and exploded.
> My mother told me this story every day of her life, until one day she exploded.

This work does not suggest that the angry man or the speaker's mother actually exploded; rather, as the prose poem asserts a little later, "it is not a story . . . It's a prose poem." In other words, the explosions are metaphors signaling, among other things, that a prose poem may be an occasion of significant (and, according to this work, sometimes sickening) literary disruption, and also a self-conscious reflection on its own form. This section of the anthology also includes Russell Edson's "The Prose Poem as a Beautiful Animal" and Rupert Loydell's "Towards a Definition," among other works.[17]

Furthermore, prose poetry has an abiding relationship with metaphor via the subset of prose poems identified as resembling folktales, parables, and fables—largely found in contemporary prose poetry from America. We have discussed some of these works in chapter 5, but it is worth reiterating that the fable is one of the categories of prose poem Robert Bly identifies in his essay "The Prose Poem as an Evolving Form," which, in turn, has a connection to Peter Johnson's rumination on whether "all prose poems are fables."[18] If Giambattista Vico's claim that many metaphors constitute "a fable in brief" is applied to prose poetry,[19] then this form's emphasis on the fable—and we would add, the parable—may help to demonstrate the form's symbiotic relationship with metaphor. Indeed, some prose poems, in being constructed as fables or parables through the use of an extended metaphor, are simultaneously all fable and all metaphor. W. S. Merwin's "Humble Beginning" is an example. It opens:

> When he had learned how to kill his brother with a rock he learned how to use a rock to begin stairs. For both of which secrets he thanked the rock.[20]

Prose poets make use of metaphors in a wide range of ways, some of them obvious and others obscure. An example of a self-evident metaphorical work is Kyle Vaughn's "Letter to My Imagined Daughter." The poem presents its main figure of speech at its opening and the rest of the poem develops this figure so the prose poem as a whole is suffused by its metaphorical import:

> If I could fold this lonely year in half and then in half again, until finally it became next year, I would keep folding until I came to where you are. I would keep folding until this year made a little paper car.[21]

A significant number of prose poems employ metaphor in this way, placing it at the center of their work. Such a poetic strategy makes it impossible to separate the metaphorical content of the poem from any denotative or literal content. In this case, the introduction of the main metaphor—that a year (an abstract idea) is a piece of paper (a concrete image) that then becomes a paper car (a more complex concrete image)—immediately means that the poem activates a number of conceptual domains at once. The first are the domains associated with the idea of a year and the folding of paper, and these domains are usually so remote from one another that the reader is obliged to make a significant leap of the imagination as the prose poem begins. Without such a leap, the work's meaning will not be carried over from one domain to the next.

However, once the reader begins to imagine a year as a piece of paper, the initial transformations of the metaphor—from year, to paper, to "next year" being reachable through further folding to the image of a "little paper car"—are easy enough to follow. The metaphor continues to be transformed when the work states that the car "would be soft, like a cloud in the air," and transformed again when it becomes "more like the sun"—after which the prose poem pursues and elaborates the metaphor of the sun (and the sun's rays), until it concludes with the image of the world spinning "like a red barber's chair, once around for every fast ray."[22] One needs to be mentally agile to follow these metaphorical transitions, yet the prose poem makes reasonably good sense at a metaphorical level, even as the metaphors become decidedly mixed.

A significant part of the work's appeal, however, is not metaphorical but is derived from the important metonymic meanings connected to the disparate metaphors and imagery. For example, the images of folding paper and making a paper car suggest the shared games of parents and young children, and these activities stand in metonymically for the whole domain of affectionate parent-child play. The image of a cloud in the air likewise suggests the activity of watching the sky, which almost all parents and children do together, often pointing out and discussing the shapes of clouds. Once again, the metaphor has important metonymic associations, this time connected to parent-child sharing and teaching. The final image of the spinning barber's chair stands in for those occasions when a parent takes a child for a haircut, and early childhood impressions of light through a barbershop's window.

In other words, there is a shifting constellation of metaphors in this prose poem that are approachable and emotionally involving, largely because, in metonymic terms, they evoke aspects of sympathetic, if hypothetical, parent-child interactions. This notional life is implied rather than being directly narrated, but it is no less compelling for that. More generally, this is an example of a prose poem that may be read as primarily depending on metaphoric transformations for its main poetic effects and impact, but that depends nearly equally on the metonymic associations that the metaphors carry with them.

The metaphors and metonyms in "Letter to My Imagined Daughter" are heightened by being contained in the paragraph of prose poetry. As this prose poem begins by invoking a piece of paper being folded, its rectangular shape makes visual reference to this folded paper—and even to the idea of a letter, mentioned in the title. Enclosed in a rectangular shape, the work asks the reader to see the further possibilities of the block of text as it is reshaped into a car, a cloud, a barber's chair, and the sun. The prose poem begins by not demanding much of the reader's imagination, but as it progresses, its transformations become more challenging, unexpected, and diverse. The way in which prose poems so frequently reach outward to embrace ideas and other references is also analogous to the image of the sun's rays presented by the prose poem—which may be read as partly a comment on the functioning of the prose poem form itself.

An example of a deeply metaphorical prose poem that prioritizes narrative and does not employ metaphors as obvious figures of speech is Jim Heynen's "The Boys Go to Ask a Neighbor for Some Apples."[23] This prose poem opens matter-of-factly and rather colloquially, telling the reader, "the boys went to one neighbor's farm to ask him if they might pick some of his apples." However, the boys cannot find their neighbor and only after some difficulty are they able to locate him in a dark corner of the barn:

> On his knees with his hands crossed on his lap. Praying to a piglet, a dog, a cat, and a bull calf. He had fed each of them their own kind of food, so they were content as he prayed.[24]

On one level, there is an apparent and disarming literalness about such writing. The reader may easily imagine an idiosyncratic farmer doing just as the poem suggests, and they may, as a consequence, read the prose poem as merely an illustration of human strangeness. And, indeed, it is *possible* to read it in this way. However, to do so would be to miss its deeper and richer dimensions, which depend on recognizing its metaphorical content.

The metaphorical dimension of the work is entirely implied rather than explicitly stated—although these implications are clear enough, especially when one arrives at the part of the poem where the neighbor says, "Little animals with four feet on the ground, teach the rocks to lie in their places, tell the oceans never to rise and the mountains never to fall. Little ones, give your gentle ways to me."[25] Such language has clear biblical overtones and shows the farmer instructing his flock as if they are disciples. The barnyard scene is also reminiscent of the Nativity scene, where Jesus was born among animals in a stable, and, furthermore, the apples may be construed as referring to the fruit of the tree of the knowledge of good and evil in the Old Testament's Garden of Eden.

However, in this prose poem, the best apples are given freely to the boys, and the boys are never tempted to pick them without permission. This work is reminiscent of the parable form in the Bible, and the manner in which it is set out in successive groups of sentences, rather than a homogeneous block of text, makes its appeal to narrative more obvious. Invoking the Bible, or making use of biblical metaphors in prose poems, also reminds one of the debate about whether the prose poetry form can be traced back to the Bible—or, alternatively, whether "[t]he term 'prose poem' has been applied irresponsibly," as the *Princeton Encyclopedia of Poetics* states, "to anything from the Bible to a novel by [William] Faulkner." The *Princeton Encyclopedia*'s position is that the term "should be used only to designate a highly conscious (sometimes even self-conscious) artform"[26]—although a variety of writers have made the connection between biblical texts and prose poetry. For example, Nikki Santilli devotes a section in her book to prose poetry and biblical style, asking, "What makes a biblical style valuable in writing prose poetry?"[27]

Jim Heynen's "The Boys Go to Ask a Neighbor for Some Apples" is not narrowly intertextual, but in a broader sense it is an intertextual work, drawing on the received situations and words of the Bible to make its most significant points. These are about respect for living things and for the land in general, about humility, and about a kind of neighborliness that goes beyond merely providing apples to boys.

In some ways, this poem is not so different from "Letter to My Imagined Daughter," because in both works the metaphorical dimension of the poem is developed simultaneously with the literal or denotative dimension. On a metonymic level, this prose poem's meanings derive from the way the limited barnyard scene conjures, and is analogous to, its biblical intertext. When the limited descriptive detail is read symbolically, it both rewrites and stands in metonymically for a significant part of the Bible story. As a result, in this case, metaphor and metonym become almost one and the same.

In some instances, prose poems provide a strong sense of narrative and place and, in doing so, appear to adopt the general approach and manners of prose fiction. However, they do so with a different intent. An example is "The Great Autumn Rains" by Tim Atkins, which begins with a storm:

> THE GREAT AUTUMN RAINS have arrived. Come and see. We were warned they were coming. For the last thirty minutes we have heard the thunder out to sea. The first drops are marking the tiles deeper red and the sky is so dark. Genki is sitting under the table. We won't see him moving.
>
> It's September and the heat is finally breaking. Everybody is ready. Soon we will have to wear socks again. We will have to get our sweaters from the back of the cupboard where Genki always makes his nest.[28]

This prose poem is part of a sequence of such works narrating the experiences of a father and daughter living in Barcelona over the course of a year. However, the emphasis of these works is on the evocation of poetic moments rather than on narrative development. The prose poem's primary significance is not as a contribution to an unfolding plot but as illuminations of how the poetic inheres in human relationships connected to quotidian experience.

This work also implicitly explores the nature of literary texts and the relationship of such texts to their readers in statements such as "Come and see. We were warned they were coming." These function as forms of disguised direct speech between father and daughter, and also as an address to the reader. The metapoetic nature of this address alerts the reader to the fact that literary works and their tropes are neither "real" nor transparent; they occupy the poetic space where the world, in being evoked in language, also disappears into the very utterance that evokes it.

What is left are words, sentences, and paragraphs as they engage with the reader's imagination and understanding of language, along with the gaps and spaces that the prose poem's truncated narrative refuses to fill. Such a work is also metonymic because, in speaking in heightened, almost rhetorical terms about "great autumn rains," it makes clear the way it stands in line with other works of literature using tropes on the occasions of storms and the pleasure of finding refuge from the weather. This prose poem speaks out of, updates, and to some extent also speaks for previous literary works, even as it finds new forms of expression—most specifically Juan Ramón Jiménez Mantecón's *Platero y yo* from 1914. Its condensed style also draws on techniques familiar from docupoetry and contemporary travelogues.

Such a prose poetry exemplifies ways in which prose poetry so often directly engages the reader's imagination. Frederick Luis Aldama writes that, in reading poetry

> we follow the poet's lead step by step, univocally, and where there are cuts that leave gaps in the poem we use . . . educated guess work—to fill in the gaps. . . . Yet the fact remains that the writing and reading of a poem implies the more continuous, frequent, and systematic use of the imagination. . . . [T]he poet uses the means of communication we call poetry more intensively as a direct appeal to the imagination of the reader than does the writer of novels or short stories.[29]

Prose poetry, when it initially appears as a paragraph of prose, can make this process especially intense, because the reader is doubly involved: first by the surprise of finding the poetic in a prose paragraph and then by the fragmentary—and thus imaginatively demanding—view of the world that a prose poem is likely to provide.

In some extreme cases, prose poems may be little more than the exploration of metonymic associations. Gertrude Stein's short prose poem "A Box" from *Tender Buttons* is a good example:

> Out of kindness comes redness and out of rudeness comes rapid same question, out of an eye comes research, out of selection comes painful cattle. So then the order is that a white way of being round is something suggesting a

pin and is it disappointing, it is not, it is so rudimentary to be analysed and see a fine substance strangely, it is so earnest to have a green point not to red but to point again.[30]

Michel Delville says of this work, "[t]he nonmimetic playfulness of Stein's poetic language bears striking resemblances to Jacques Lacan's definition of desire as an infinite extension of the metonymic chain, one which does not seek to bridge the gap between signifier and signified."[31]

However, metonymy usually functions most effectively in prose poetry when it is adding complex meaning to texts that do not endlessly defer meaning. An example of a work that places metonymic strategies at its heart is "1973" by Jen Webb:

He died when I was away from home, not knowing it would happen, not expecting that something so momentous could arrive without its having made an appointment, but he did anyway die, and me without my thoughts straight without my face on without the words to say ready on my tongue. The world is too big in his absence, it takes a week to cross the street a month to make that call. The world is too big and there is no space in it for all the words we failed to share.[32]

Ambiguity is evident from the first sentence, where Webb's strategy of refusing to anchor key phrases to either of the pronouns she introduces at the prose poem's opening makes it unclear whether it is the "I" or the "he" who did not "know [death] would happen." The suggestion is that they are twinned in their unpreparedness. The phrase, "without the words to say ready on my tongue" stands in metonymically for every failure to make sense of the event at the time and since, and the phrase even folds back onto the words of the prose poem, suggesting these are belated and still-unready words. Death's unpredictability is acknowledged in the drawing together of its first lines with a series of commas, and in the rush of overlapping fragments that almost seem to pant, as if they are a (metonymic) expression of a general sense of panic. Roger Robinson states, "to free a poem of its line breaks frees a poem of its breath,"[33] but, in this case, the freedom from line breaks liberates Webb to create complex, run-on, breath-like prose-poetic rhythms.

The work's reference to moments bigger than itself—to a larger frame—is evident from the repetition of the words "too big" and the use of fragments to metonymically connect to larger memories and moments. There is "no space" and yet, through the use of fragmented moments, the prose poem suggests a great deal. Significantly, too, this work resists closure by ending on words that are unuttered. The reader considers: What happened to the narrator? Who was the man and what was their relationship? These uncertainties are representative of a larger, absent whole that is referred to only in overlapping fragments of lamentation. By the prose poem's conclusion, an intimate's death and subsequent absence becomes a metonym for every significant absence the narrator has known since.

Intertextuality and Prose Poetry

Intertextuality is a term introduced by Julia Kristeva in "Word, Dialogue and Novel" (1966), and earlier in this chapter we identified examples of intertextual gestures in prose poems in Jim Heynen's "The Boys Go to Ask a Neighbor for Some Apples" and Tim Atkins's "The Great Autumn Rains." Kristeva states that "any text is constructed as a mosaic of quotations; any text is the absorption and transformation of another. The notion of *intertextuality* replaces that of intersubjectivity, and poetic language is read as at least *double*."[34] While intertextuality has been accused of supporting canon formation because it tends to reference and therefore bolster texts already within the canon, Kristeva's argument is that all literary works are intertextual in one way or another, whether or not they employ actual quotations, and whether or not they make explicit reference to other texts.

Many prose poems make use of intertexts that work subversively or playfully to create a new narrative from "classic" quotations or allusions. In such contexts, canonical quotations and references may appear as broken off from their original source and reassembled anew. For example, David Lehman's book *Poems in the Manner Of*, refers to a range of famous poets. A prose poem from this publication, "Poem in the Manner of Charles Baudelaire," draws attention to the continuing currency of Baudelaire's work while also adding a contemporary twist to the perspective he presents. It begins:

> The task of painting and installing a door is a charming respite for a soul fatigued from the struggles of life. The quality of the wood, the choice of the color, the need for precise measurements . . .[35]

Such intertexts may be broadly understood as metonymic because the quotations and allusions usually stand in for and represent other literary passages, or even other complete works, and summon the narratives, sensibilities, and attitudes associated with those works. Put simply, the part—often a fragment or fragments of text—stands in for a complex whole. Understood in this way, a conscious intertextuality is a powerful tool for writers of very short forms, such as prose poems, because of its capacity to carry across meaning from a wide variety of other and more extended sources. It is a shorthand way of invoking and transferring large ideas and wide frames of reference.

This transfer can take place even when a prose poet merely activates associations with a well-known writer's name. As Michael Riffaterre argues in his discussion of the prose poem and intertextuality: "Intertextuality is activated, actualized, whenever the reader's interpretation is stymied by anomalies he perceives in the text at the mimesis level. The problems they raise are solved as he realizes that while blocking his interpretation here and now in the text, they point to the solutions elsewhere, in the intertext."[36]

For instance, Roy Scheele mentions Marcel Proust's "fountain" at the beginning of a relatively short prose poem entitled "The Wake of Plenty" that evokes and describes a rural scene:

> The coral-footed pigeons chortle in the rafters of the loading shed, the sparrows billow up from the fall back on the road like the wrangling waters of Proust's fountain.[37]

This simple allusion immediately suggests a number of images of fountains in Proust's monumental *À la recherche du temps perdu* (*In Search of Lost Time*), including the famous lines from *The Captive*, in which Proust writes:

> The only true voyage of discovery, the only fountain of Eternal Youth, would be not to visit strange lands but to possess other eyes, to behold the universe through the eyes of another, of a hundred others, to behold the hundred universes that each of them beholds, that each of them is.[38]

In this way Scheele's intertextual gesture asks the reader to see again what he is describing—not just through new eyes but through an understanding that if, at least theoretically, there may be a hundred universes, then perhaps we should look again at the marvelousness of the one we know, and even understand his poetic evocation as a small "voyage of discovery." The intertextual allusion also reminds us—as did Atkins in his prose poem "The Great Autumn Rains"—that "The Wake of Plenty" is a literary work and part of a long line of literary works (all of them cognizant of other works and the worlds they conjure), and it increases the effect of defamiliarization that Scheele's lines already occasion. Sparrows "billow[ing] up from the fall back" challenge the reader to see these sparrows precisely and from an unusual point of view; the mention of "Proust's fountain" complicates and doubles this striking visual image.[39]

A related example is Santilli's discussion, in her essay "Prose Poetry and the Spirit of Jazz" (2018), of prose poet Tom Raworth's use of *À la recherche du temps perdu* in writing "Proust from the Bottom Up." Raworth recasts one of the key passages from the Enright/Kilmartin translation of Proust's masterwork:

> not traced by us is the only book that really belongs to us. not that the truth, they are arbitrarily chosen. the books whose hieroglyphs are patterns formed by the pure intelligence have no more than a logical, a possible upon us, it remains behind as the token of its necessary truth. the ideas printed in us by reality itself, when an idea—an idea of any kind—is let in dictated to us by reality, the only one of which the "impression" has been laborious to decipher

than any other, is also the only one which has been the most austere school of life, the true last judgement.[40]

Santilli observes, "If we have not read Proust's *In Search of Lost Time* . . . we are confused. If we have read it, we are not much more enlightened—just unsure whether the line of logic has been saved, ragged, or completely 'jazzed up.'"[41] This is a good demonstration of the way in which intertextuality reaches out to another text, asking the reader to access or read the intertextual prose poem through the frame of another—often canonical—work.

Prose Poetry and Postcolonial Intertexts

Appealing to the Western canon via the use of intertexts in prose poems takes on even greater significance when the poet is writing from a place steeped in the history of colonization. For this reason, American, Canadian, Australian, Singaporean, and New Zealand poets often write with an intention to address the canon in specific ways. Famously, Salman Rushdie used the term "writing back" in his 1982 article "The Empire Writes Back with a Vengeance."[42] The title of this piece refers to the well-known Star Wars sequel *The Empire Strikes Back* and was taken up by Bill Ashcroft, Gareth Griffiths, and Helen Tiffin in an early and major scholarly book on the status of postcolonial literature. In their discussion of the relevance of Rushdie's phrase, Ashcroft and others state:

> Directly and indirectly . . . the "Empire writes back" to the imperial "centre," not only through nationalist assertion, proclaiming itself central and self-determining, but even more radically by questioning the bases of European and British metaphysics, challenging the world-view that can polarize centre and periphery in the first place.[43]

Importantly, they are emphatic in their argument that it is reductive to set up simple oppositions or adversarialism between non-European and European cultures; postcolonial literature should, instead, offer alternatives. This is a point that John Thieme addresses in his summary of responses to canonical literature. He states:

> "Writing back," "counter-discourse," "oppositional literature," "con-texts": these are some of the terms that have been used to identify a body of postcolonial works that take a classic English text as a departure point, *supposedly* [emphasis ours] as a strategy for contesting the authority of the canon of English literature.[44]

Breaking down colonialism's barriers in its postcolonial manifestations through imaginative action and innovation, rather than erecting new walls, is one way forward. Prose poetry is well suited to taking such action in the sphere of creative writing because it is a flexible literary form in which postcolonial responses to the Western canon are able to be productively explored.

This is partly because prose poetry is a hybrid form that celebrates the blurring of boundaries and is well suited to registering the kinds of experiences that are neither complete nor fully coherent—nor entirely resolvable. When Michael Chanan writes, "Colonial (and postcolonial) melancholy arises from an unresolvable contradiction within the (post)colonial subject" and "colonial melancholy is a condition in which the concept of the nation is falsely embedded through the colonial relation,"[45] one may, for example, apply such statements to the Australian context. Australia is an independent nation and yet many would argue it is still in the process of finding ways to articulate an identity that properly and sufficiently acknowledges its colonial past.

Cassandra Atherton's prose poem "Albatross" is searching in its intertextual gestures. Atherton writes back to an Australian literary history built on British and American canonical texts while recasting her intertexts as part of a meditation on betrayal. References are broken off from their original contexts and manipulated into a new, fractured narrative highlighting the missing parts:

> You draw hearts from the top left, like you are drawing Hemingway's hills. Only the elephant is scarlet and hangs around my neck. In the throbbing hotel room I open my mouth for your tongue but you speckle kisses over the shadows between my breasts. Twilight bisects my left side from my right. I can't speak. All I can think of is "please, please." A triad without its final note.[46]

This brief work conjures ideas of broken identity within an intimate relationship, and an associated rupture in thought. The literary works it quotes and alludes to are Hemingway's short story "Hills Like White Elephants" (1927), Coleridge's poem "The Rime of the Ancient Mariner" (1798), and Hawthorne's novel *The Scarlet Letter* (1850). These quotations and allusions help to charge this prose poem with a considerable amount of condensed meaning.

In Hemingway's short story, the vulnerability of the female character and the precariousness of her situation are emphasized. Atherton connects Hemingway's image of hills like elephants to Coleridge's albatross—symbol of bad luck, bad faith, and damaged fate—in the way the elephant is "hang[ing] around [the narrator's] neck."[47] What's more, the inferred albatross is scarlet in color and, in referring to Hawthorne's scarlet letter, signifies the breaking of patriarchy's social and sexual taboos. Confirming this sense of rupture, the "hills" in the prose poem are likened to the top section of a heart, a shape never completed—like the missing note in the final "triad."

The movement of ideas in this work is also fractured, signaling that the intimacy it depicts is problematic and tainted. The inclusion of direct speech, which is thought rather than spoken, and the statement "I can't speak," refers to and recasts Hemingway's character's request to "please please please please please please

please stop talking."⁴⁸ It also gestures to Australia's unspoken history, in which women were so often not permitted a voice. This work is more ambitious in its intertextual references than many prose poems and exemplifies how intertextuality may make a very brief work wide-ranging and multifaceted. The intertexts stand in metonymically for an extensive range of readings and meanings.

Paul Hetherington's prose poem entitled "Antiquities" (2016) alludes to Jane Austen's *Emma* and Henry James's *The Turn of the Screw*:

> Within the restrictions of our common knowledge, spaces began to breathe—this courtyard in the city; that old quadrangle of orange trees; the pathway leading to a river bed with pebbles congregating like shiny vowels; the long slope where grassland furs a hill. We surveyed sunflowers in nodding conversations and admired antiquities: "Harriet Smith was the natural daughter of somebody"; "It was plump, one afternoon, in the middle of my very hour." We gathered them like a form of ardency, finding our own inflections in these words. Among our vernacular phrases, the nineteenth century murmured in our ears.⁴⁹

This work gives priority to "words" and "inflections" and, in two intertextual moments, recasts references to classic texts, finding resonances in their contiguity for a contemporary reader. Indeed, the juxtaposition of the Austen quotation, "Harriet Smith was the natural daughter of somebody," with the James quotation, "It was plump, one afternoon, in the middle of my very hour," changes their original meaning and introduces a splintered twenty-first-century "conversation" between these disparate quotations. They haunt the prose poem, inflecting its implications and offering different kinds of narrativization, amounting to more than just a juxtapositioning of fragments.

In *Emma*, Harriet Smith is presented as illegitimate and struggles to finish a full sentence or know her own mind. Her dialogue is full of dashes and broken thoughts, for example, when Mr. Martin proposes to Harriet in a letter, and Emma gives her opinion about the situation (while simultaneously declaring that she does not wish to influence the outcome), Harriet says,

> Oh! no, I am sure you are a great deal too kind to—but if you would just advise me what I had best do—No, no, I do not mean that—As you say, one's mind ought to be quite made up—One should not be hesitating—It is a very serious thing.—It will be safer to say "No," perhaps.—Do you think I had better say "No"?⁵⁰

In this way, Harriet's illegitimacy and fragmented speech defer meaning. Hetherington is questioning and playing with concepts of authenticity, and his use of a single line from the text further fractures meaning in a postmodern approach, emphasizing spuriousness and simulacra. Hetherington's use of the quotation from

The Turn of the Screw also gently and affectionately parodies the canon in referring to Shakespeare, who is at its center:

> When the Governess in Henry James's *The Turn of the Screw* sees her first ghost, that of the wicked valet Peter Quint, the words she uses to describe the event—which initially persuades her that her "imagination" has "turned real", in the person of her handsome employer—are words in which *Hamlet* is remembered.[51]

Thus, these canonical authors' words inform Hetherington's prose poem in a variety of ways, and juxtaposing them in this revisionistic technique encourages a perspective of multiple viewpoints. As he recontextualizes British and American texts that provide a literary inheritance for Australian writing, Hetherington urges us to find our "own inflections in these words."[52]

Jahan Ramazani states that "postcolonial poets have arguably made profoundly important contributions to literature in English. They have hybridized European with indigenous forms, inventing new literary structures for cultural expression in lyric and experimental styles. . . . They have recast their cultural inheritances . . . They have found new ways of aesthetically embodying, probing, and dramatizing the divisions and complexities of postcolonial worlds."[53] While this is certainly true, postcolonial prose poetry has yet to attract much scholarly discussion, and it is largely overlooked in *The Cambridge Companion to Postcolonial Poetry* (2017). However, Samuel Wagan Watson's prose poem "Parallel Oz" is mentioned in the Australian/New Zealand chapter. Wagan Watson is identified as a poet who presents "Australia as a place haunted by its own (denied) Indigeneity . . . characteristically deform[ing] popular culture to produce unsettling allegories of the politics of post/colonial Australia."[54]

The prose poem form of "Parallel Oz" (a work also published in 2012 under the title of "There's No Place Like Home") intensifies this haunting, not only because its slipperiness and hybridization resist definition but because of the absence of line breaks, which in this work are able to capture a sense of the pressing, almost claustrophobic nature of the postcolonial condition:

> It's the Lucky Country's closet; a dark interior with frontier skeletons . . . The yellow-brick road is pock-marked with massacre sites and the Wizard, the Wizard of Parallel Oz; he holds Dorothy hostage to a mutual obligation agreement. The Straw Man has the grazing monopoly, the Tin Man has the mines, and the Lion waits in the spinifex, with the long-grass drinkers.[55]

For Wagan Watson, the prose poem form is a way of speaking back directly to a nation where many indigenous Australians still inhabit what feels like an alternative or "parallel" reality. His adaptation of tropes from the film *The Wizard of Oz* speaks back ironically and with postmodern verve to mainstream Australian culture, and phrases such as "frontier skeletons" and "massacre sites" metonymically conjure the extensive history of frontier wars that is still being written.

The Singaporean poet Desmond Kon Zhicheng-Mingdé has also written prose poems that use English canonical intertexts that have a complex significance in postcolonial Singapore. His "dame de compagnie :: lady of company" is an example. The opening of this work draws attention to various authoritative critical texts, as well as the well-known American literary journal the *Paris Review*:

> There's a new book on the table from the library. It's something on Austen. Thirty-three writers talk about why they read her. There's even a foreword by Harold Bloom, who Gigi remembers as being something of a genius. She'd read his interview once in "The Paris Review", and it'd kept her up all night, thinking about what he'd said. This new book seems somewhat gratuitous in its dripping praise for a novelist so widely read.[56]

Zhicheng-Mingdé problematizes the authority of these texts, not only by introducing the notion of the "gratuitous" but by shifting his focus to the importance of "gossip," which he introduces by referring to "the essay by Virginia Woolf," and how she thinks "our knowledge of Austen is derived from a little gossip, a few letters, and her books." In this way, the authority of canonized texts and their associated critical traditions undergoes a reassessment:

> It's Woolf's mention of gossip that Gigi finds disturbing. Gigi doesn't like gossip, but what Woolf writes after is what gets her thinking: "As for the gossip, gossip which has survived its day is never despicable; with a little rearrangement it suits our purpose admirably."[57]

The clear implication is that in a postcolonial context, the "gossip" of the former colonial power may be repurposed and reinflected, including in contemporary literatures.

Prose poems by Atherton, Hetherington, Wagan Watson, and Zhicheng-Mingdé all find modes of poetic utterance that foreground ways in which language, in its various forms and contexts, is both an impediment to and an enabler of communication. These works—like Jen Webb's prose poem discussed in the previous section—demonstrate how prose poetry so often inhabits an in-between and yet widely suggestive space between traditional narrative prose and conventional lyric poetry. This in-between space is sometimes the space between different texts and various canonical notions. As intertextual prose poems engage with literary works that have preceded them, so they remind the reader that the literary tradition is continuously being reexamined, reinterpreted, and rewritten.

Many prose poets adopt similar intertextual strategies. Margaret Atwood's "In Love with Raymond Chandler" celebrates and affectionately parodies Chandler's work, stating, "An affair with Raymond Chandler, what a joy! Not because of the mangled bodies and the marinated cops and hints of eccentric sex, but because of his interest in furniture."[58] Following Chandler's writing, in which tantalization and suspense is crucial, the prose poem suspends bodily ideas of what this "affair" might bring by dwelling mainly on furniture until the work's final line. It is playful and irreverent, and depends for its full effect on the reader's acquaintance with at least some of Chandler's texts, his prose style, and his narrative techniques.

David Shumate is well known for the way he plays with the relationship between the narrator of his prose poems and authors or characters from canonical intertexts. In "Kafka" Shumate reworks the opening line of *The Metamorphosis* to begin his poem: "I wake to find I have become Kafka."[59] He then imagines what it might have been like for Kafka to write his famous novella, breaking the narration to make asides such as, "I'm not used to being Kafka yet."[60] In "Don Quixote," Shumate opens with the line, "Now and then Sancho Panza telephones me from the Yucatan where he is vacationing with his lover while I take care of his master."[61] In "The Rain," he even empathizes with God: "I suppose after the heavens and the earth I too would have created Adam and Eve. Or some pair of innocents like them."[62] Other prose poems include Hemingway, Fitzgerald, Neruda, Ferlinghetti, and also a range of famous painters. Shumate juxtaposes the ordinary with the fabulous in moments where the writer not only meets but occasionally inhabits some of his most important literary and artistic personalities.

Hadara Bar-Nadav's prose poem "And Leaves the Shreds Behind" draws on Emily Dickinson's poem "She sweeps with many-colored Brooms—" for its title and for the phrase "littered all the East."[63] The work may be read successfully without knowledge of Dickinson's oeuvre, or of the specific poem it refers to, but as Dickinson's humor and main metaphor (of evening and sunset being a housewife sweeping with a broom) is transformed by Bar-Nadav into a kind of existential keening about memory and grief, so her work achieves additional power by contrasting so significantly with its source text—which is metonymically summoned in a rather ghostly way by the poem's direct quotations.

Alicita Rodríguez's "A Weekend in the Country" plays with the very idea of intertextuality, throwing together a cast of fictional characters, including Adam and Eve, Dr. Frankenstein, Gregor Samsa, Don Quixote, and Gatsby.[64] The work makes fun of the very intertextuality it exploits, commenting with multiple ironies—only available to those who recognize the prose poem's characters and have read Cervantes's masterpiece—that "Don Quixote . . . had done a lot of reading, and he knew fiction when he saw it."[65] Suzanne Burns writes a prose poem entitled "Out There,"[66] making intertextual reference to the television series *Sex and the City* (and also, in passing, to the poet Joseph Brodsky). Lauren Russell's book, *What's Hanging on the Hush* (2017), contains many prose poems with playful intertexts. The notes at the end of the collection explain the sophisticated way Russell writes back to the canon: "'Regulator, I Married Him,' 'Primacy and Preference,' and 'Meta' involve same-letter substitutions of nouns in passages from

Charlotte Brontë's *Jane Eyre*, Jane Austen's *Pride and Prejudice*, and a translation of Franz Kafka's *The Metamorphosis*, respectively."[67]

Daniel M. Shapiro conjures a world of politics and popular culture in "Richard M. Nixon Attends 'Star Wars' Premiere, Brea Mann Theatre, 5/25/77."[68] His prose poem uses a variety of allusions to the film to illuminate and refresh ideas about the Watergate scandal, as Nixon is represented as a character who comments directly on the film's characters and actions to his wife, Pat, in ways that reflect various perspectives on his actions during his presidency. The two main metonymic gestures in the work—Nixon himself and the *Star Wars* film—stand in for different, and perhaps alternative, strands of American life, and the poem achieves many of its effects and its rather droll humor by implicitly contrasting Nixon's rueful view of Watergate with popular culture's vision of a future where the film's central characters have powers that Nixon lacked as US president. The final line, "Seconds later, Vader releases his grip as an afterthought, a defiant wave," also references Nixon's final gesture after his resignation: his trademark victory wave.[69]

Mark Strand, in "Chekhov: A Sestina," writes a tour de force of a prose poem in which he contemplates and evokes a Chekhovian world.[70] In doing so, he examines a variety of broad human aspirations and foibles. Throughout Strand's ruminations, all of Chekhov's works are, as it were, standing metonymically in the wings.

Language Transactions and Transfers

In prose poetry, metonymic associations and metaphorical transformations tend to nestle together into the prose poetry paragraph and to feed exponentially off one another. As they do, they defeat expectations of either narrative closure or poetic closure because not only are prose poems usually open forms—for reasons we have previously discussed—but such figures of speech open up suggestive tropes that have a life beyond the prose poems that contain them. Metaphorical and metonymic meanings often spill over from the reading experience into the world as new constructions of thought, thus opening up their poems to further consideration.

I. A. Richards suggested as long ago as 1936 that metaphor "is a borrowing between and intercourse of *thoughts*, a transaction between contexts. *Thought* is metaphoric," he contended, "and proceeds by comparison, and the metaphors of language derive therefrom."[71] Unique metaphors often live on in the minds of readers, whether (using examples we have cited in this chapter) it is the idea that a year may be a folded page or that a farmer may make disciples of his farm animals. Such metaphors have the potential to resonate beyond any particular work, and open into what they imply to be language's limitless and protean variety. Prose poems have a powerful ability to suggest the shifting infinitudes of language (released from more utilitarian and quotidian purposes) and to invoke the possibility of endlessly inventive modes of thought.

Prose poems underline the distinction between literal or denotative uses of language and metonymic or metaphoric uses, because these works highlight the way in which poetic language *always* tends toward the metonymic and metaphorical. Prose poems such as Jim Heynen's "The Boys Go to Ask a Neighbor for Some Apples" emphasize how even works that may, at first glance, appear to be mainly composed of straightforward narratives have figurative transformations at their heart. And this also answers one of the puzzles about prose poetry—the question of how some of the more prosaic prose poems may be understood as poetic. A large part of the answer is in the ways in which they activate metaphoric and metonymic figures of speech to insist on the connotative dimensions of their utterance.

Many of the most impressive effects of language involve the transfer of qualities from one thing or idea to another thing or idea. This may be the carrying over of meaning from preexisting texts—such as Hemingway's short story "Hills Like White Elephants" and Hawthorne's *The Scarlet Letter*—into a new poetic context (in the prose poem "Albatross"); or (as in the prose poem "Letter to My Imagined Daughter") it may involve the transfer of the passage of years into the image of folding paper. And, in terms of metonymic associations, one may note, too, that the fragility of a folded paper car is superbly appropriate to the rather tenuous, not to say fragile idea of an "imagined" child—a subsidiary and relatively undeveloped metonym in this work but a significant one.

The prose poems just mentioned exemplify how, in narrative terms, prose poetry is incomplete and is only completed by its suggestive, figurative tropes. Both "Albatross" and "Letter to My Imagined Daughter" open out to embrace wide frames of reference that require the reader to move beyond, and then back inside the boundaries of each work in a to-and-fro imaginative process—the effect of which is that the works receive a considerable supplement of information and meaning from the external conceptual domains they refer to. In prose poetry the compressed form and frequent activation of such strategies create worlds in which a "whole" story is only ever gestured at, and in which fragmentation and metonymic suggestiveness so often create a sense of openness that poses unanswerable questions.

It may not be an exaggeration to suggest that—and our analyses in this chapter demonstrate aspects of this process at work—a great deal of prose poetry *depends on* and continually exploits as its primary poetic mechanism metonymic (and associated metaphorical) strategies in order to complete itself. Andy Brown asserts this in his application of Santilli's arguments about metonymic structure in prose poetry to Seamus Heaney's *Stations*. He states:

> In a prose poem then, the lack of context on the page (a decontextualised "spot of time") sends readers off in search of it. Readers are "denied passivity"

and are obliged "instead to participate in the lawlessly expansive creation process in order to arrive at a point of interpretation." Santilli argues that this has resulted in a "shift in roles: the writer writes the work, but the reader writes the text by taking control of context."[72]

Prose poetry makes a virtue of brevity, absence, and gaps in narrative, and fills in missing details with its various poetic figures. As it does so, it denies its accountability to the literal and denotative, and refuses to be driven by everyday demands and functional requirements. This may be understood as the prose poem's tendency toward subterfuge, because the prose form and narrative tendencies frequently *present to the reader* like a form of short, functional prose, even as it plays with representation, ideas of the real and the illusory, transformations of the quotidian, and deceptive narrative voices—nothing less than a tantalization of our understanding of the real/unreal divide.

In this way, prose poems may be read as provisional poetic articulations that quiz and transform everyday understandings and assumptions. In their fragmented, incomplete, and unclosed state they even remind the reader that subjectivity itself, articulated and understood through language, is mostly only understandable in fragmentary moments—experiences informed by, and yet separated from, any whole-of-life narrative. Prose poems are one way of constituting such subjective and fragmentary experiences, and prose poetry's metonyms and metaphors are especially important to this articulation. They function as tightly spaced conduits into ramifying associations and meanings, closely connected to those associative and analogical modes of human thought that are central to subjective experiences in general.

Prose poetry and human subjectivity are also connected through their awareness of absence and indeterminacy. The prose poem as fragment signals that completion and closure are, after all, primarily literary matters; that in the larger domain of subjective experience, new meanings are always being made, and new interpretations and possibilities opened up. Unlike much conventional narrative prose, prose poetry's condensed narrative gestures imply and enact multiple simultaneous and sometimes hidden narratives. They emphasize the multivalency of human experience and its frequently unstable complexities. In this way, prose poems that use intertexts from the Western canon are able to embrace postcolonial perspectives by recasting fragments of "classic" texts to create new works.

Consequently, prose poetry is an avenue for bridging the divide between our desire for narrative satisfaction, lyric coherence, and reassurance on the one hand and the less polished and finished subjectivities we know on the other. Our awareness of these subjectivities tells us a great deal about what it is to be human in the twenty-first century. Prose poetry as a form speaks to these subjectivities in its multifaceted contradictions, irresolutions, and intensities. And it is particularly well suited to articulating some of the conundrums and indeterminacies associated with postmodernity. Margueritte Murphy argues, "The prose poem is potentially or formally 'postmodern' according to Lyotard's definition: 'the unpresentable in presentation itself.'"[73]

In sitting outside of canonized generic categories—while referencing the canon and its multiple genres, in making a virtue of fragmentariness, and in understanding the power and persuasiveness of intensely metaphoric and metonymic tropes—prose poetry claims a freedom to carry multiple and charged meanings, to complicate its discursive gestures, and to reinterpret and refresh the literary canon itself.

CHAPTER 9

Women and Prose Poetry

Laying the Groundwork

The critical tradition relating to English-language prose poetry over the last fifty years or so has tended to highlight the work of male prose poets. Men have done a great deal of anthologizing and writing about the form in the United States and have also been prominent as editors of journals. In the last couple of decades this emphasis has begun to change, driven largely by the scholarship of women, including Holly Iglesias, Jane Monson, Nikki Santilli, Margueritte Murphy, Mary Ann Caws, and Carrie Etter. However, the tradition of English-language prose poetry by women is yet to be fully investigated, and while we have featured and discussed numerous prose poems by women in this book, we also wish to explore more explicitly what women's prose poetries may be—not only in terms of content and approach but in terms of technique and emphasis.

Holly Iglesias's seminal text, *Boxing Inside the Box: Women's Prose Poetry* (2004), is the most comprehensive study of women's prose poetry to date, and we will begin by reiterating a few of Iglesias's main points to frame our discussion. She advocates for the liberation of women prose poets, using the prose poem box as a metaphor for their containment: "It doesn't take a visionary to see the box, just experience inside one. And it doesn't take a theorist to explain captivity, or conversion, or a life sentence in narrative. As Gertrude already told us a box is a box is a box. Dainty containment, the domestic box. Male fantasy and fear, her tight box."[1]

Beginning with Carolyn Forché's famous and disturbing prose poem about male power and brutality, "The Colonel," and ending with C. D. Wright's hybrid prose poem essay, "The box this comes in: (a deviation on poetry)," Iglesias's book celebrates women prose poets by giving them space and prominence. Many of the book's contentions are expressed in creative and experimental ways, highlighting the possibility of combining critical and creative works in new combinations—*Boxing Inside the Box* intersperses essays, poetry, poetic prose, and quotations. These elements function together to challenge patriarchal language constructs and lines of authority, and Iglesias reclaims women scholars and poets who have been excluded from significant creative and critical publications, with a specific focus on prose poetry. Susan Griffin is a compelling example. Her book *Women and*

Nature: The Roaring Inside Her (1978) is written in what Iglesias identifies as prose poetry—drawing on Griffin's statement in her preface that she has written in an "unconventional" mode, and that "my prose in this book is like poetry, and like poetry always begins with feeling."[2]

Women and Nature is a prose-poetical examination of ecofeminism, and Iglesias makes the point that while it was published only two years after the publication of Michael Benedikt's *The Prose Poem: An International Anthology*, it did not gain anything like the same recognition. The book has gained in popularity in recent years—especially since Darren Aronofsky announced his film *Mother!*, which was influenced by it—and Iglesias gives Griffin particular prominence, alongside Rosmarie Waldrop, to underscore the importance of their work in the field and emphasize their struggle for recognition.

In a section entitled "Denouement" (possibly a play on a traditional masculine narrative that moves from a denouement to a conclusion), she places a string of brilliant women poets and their comments on poetry in the middle of the page, creating an informal lineage. One of the quotations is Maxine Chernoff's "I linger in the shadows. I learned how to do that by writing prose poems."[3] Amy Moorman Robbins makes the point that, in this statement, Chernoff "succinctly underscores Iglesias' argument about the form and its metonymic relationship to the containment of women and their histories, and Chernoff's suggestive linking of gendered subjectivity to lingering in shadows functions as a keynote to Iglesias's work."[4]

Historically, as we've mentioned, the prose poem form has largely been understood in terms of a male trajectory. Therefore, "finding a line of conversation,"[5] or a lineage of women—which Chernoff deems important for her creative practice—requires some rethinking of the way in which the form has often been understood or critically appraised in recent decades.

The neglect of many women prose poets did not occur because women weren't writing prose poems; it is just that many women weren't writing the kinds of prose poems that fit the prevalent critical view of what successful prose poems might look like. For instance, until recently, Chernoff was one of few women broadly identified as having written neo-surrealist prose poems in America, despite many women having written prose poems with neo-surrealist features. In her essay "Gendre: Women's Prose Poetry in the 1980s," Ellen McGrath Smith reflects that while prose poetry in general has been gaining momentum, discussion of the prose poem form defers to "a predominantly patriarchal lineage . . . traced along masculinist lines: Baudelaire or Bertrand [France] . . . Wilde, Sharp, or Dowson [Britain] . . . Emerson, Whitman, or Poe [premodernism America] . . . William Carlos Williams or Sherwood Anderson [modernist America]."[6]

As we mentioned in chapter 1, Iglesias discusses the way in which the names and "template" of male neo-surrealist prose poets, such as Russell Edson, Charles Simic, and David Ignatow, became almost synonymous with the American prose poetry tradition. As part of this template, humor—"especially wit characterized by a distancing irony"[7]—has often been given priority by (male) editors, which has led to the exclusion of many women prose poets from journals and anthologies and the associated critical discourse. As Iglesias remarks, women's prose poetry is often "at once lyrical and strident,"[8] and she identifies a potential point of rupture between ideas of what a prose poem should be and other short forms of poetry. The "lyric"—a word so often used to denote short, lineated poems—and the prose poem have been viewed by some editors and critics as more or less mutually exclusive.

Yet, as Steven Monte comments, "verse poetry is potentially as generically mixed or dialogic as the prose poem."[9] There may be antilyrical poems in verse or free verse, and there may be lyrical prose poems. Significantly, in recent times, books by Anne Carson, Claudia Rankine, and Maggie Nelson have been identified as containing "lyric prose poems,"[10] or as straddling the lyric essay and prose poem forms.

Rewriting Narrative Assumptions in Women's Prose Poetry

Joy Fehr, in her article "Female Desire in Prose Poetry: Susan Holbrook's 'as thirsty as' and Hilary Clark's 'Tomato,'" focuses specifically on prose poetry for the way it "subverts the longer line of traditional narrative."[11] The first part of her article provides a rich literature review about "female sexual desire and its appearance in language."[12]

Fehr discusses Luce Irigaray's "conceptualization [of the way] . . . female sexual pleasure appears in language as multiple beginnings, succinct diction, fragmented sentences, and illogical reasoning as well as a refusal to follow sequential patterns (beginning, middle, end) and a resistance to fixed definitions and positions."[13] Fehr extends this conceptualization to prose poetry, discussing the form's suitability for voicing women's experience: "The tension that results from the conflation of prose and poetry, from the challenge of the line(s) [in prose poetry], presents even more opportunities for women to disrupt conventional forms and to resist the patriarchal containment that often is implicit in those [separate] forms."[14]

We have already mentioned that a poetic form using sentences instead of lines has the potential to disrupt readerly expectations, and Fehr more specifically argues—using Irigaray's language—that Holbrook's and Clark's prose poetry "upsets the linearity of a project, undermines the goal-object of desire, diffuses the polarization toward a single pleasure, disconcerts fidelity to a single discourse."[15] The prose poem's use of gaps and spaces, and its fragmentation, may rupture patriarchal linearity and closure, and Fehr concludes: "Holbrook and Clark deploy an associational erotic that weaves in and out, between and around passages and words to speak a female sexuality."[16] In prose poetry, words and ideas often radiate or ramify outward, challenging the kind of traditional narrative structure that builds in a relatively linear fashion toward a denouement and conclusion. It offers different possibilities for readerly pleasure.

Nicole Markotic discusses these possibilities in "Narrotics: New Narrative and the Prose Poem":

> For me, the prose poem is a poetic strategy embedded within the structure of narrative, and a feminist response to patriarchal language and forms. By embracing both prose syntax and poetic disruptions, the prose poem defies conventional linear grammar and refuses to satisfy my desires for either poetry or story. My desire is for so much more than causal, linear, rational and persuasive normative sentences. . . . I try to live between the promise of narrative and the fulfillment of the habit of fiction.[17]

Markotic is interested in prose that "rumbles inside the belly of poetry."[18] She states, "Readers, seduced by the sentence structure, discover themselves trespassing an erotics of prose, trangressing away from familiar and known fiction offerings."[19]

In "The Gender of Genre: Margaret Atwood's Unnameable Prose," in *The American Prose Poem*, Michel Delville begins with a discussion of Chernoff's use of the "subjective space in which the I-persona remains 'credible' in its own right" in order to frame a discussion of lyricism in Atwood's parodic writing.[20] Delville makes the case:

> Characteristically, Atwood's narrative revisionism—for all its apparent formal and thematic heterogeneousness—often goes hand in hand with a more specifically feminist concern with the different textual and, ultimately, existential constraints under which the female self is compelled to live.[21]

Atwood writes back to the containment and silencing of women in male-scripted narratives. However, reading her work as either microfiction or prose poetry has the capacity to affect its interpretation. Delville suggests that when Atwood's work is categorized as prose poetry, it can be read as challenging—and possibly parodying—traditional ideas about lyricism's "voicing" strategies. Reading her writing as prose poetry, rather than fiction, illuminates her characteristic use of tropes of evocation and suggestiveness as she leaves interpretation to the reader—and, as Delville observes, "diagnose[s] the various ways in which her personae *fail* to become aware of their real causes of oppression."[22]

And, in this context, it is worth remembering that, as Monson writes, "the first full-length collection of prose poems in the UK, at least of a relatively mainstream publication [Smith|Doorstop]" only took place in 2005.[23] This was Patricia Debney's *How to Be a Dragonfly* (2005). The volume begins with a preface by Philip Gross entitled "Coming to Prose Poetry," which introduces and contextualizes the form for readers. Debney's prose poems in this collection are focused on transience and transformation in the natural world, and in "Bluebell Wood," the narrator is waiting to catch bluebells "danc[ing]":

> We long to catch it at its zenith, the moment when the purple mist seems most likely to rise up and swirl, whirl patterns around the trunks of trees.
>
> We walk, hoping for a glimpse, a patch, of perfection.[24]

In the remainder of this chapter we provide three case studies focusing on different approaches to, and varieties of, prose poems written by women. However, as the writers we have just discussed illustrate, there is far more diversity in prose poetry by women than we have the space to cover. While we have mentioned, quoted, or explicated prose poems by various women in other chapters, it is worth acknowledging some of them again for their new and often hybrid prose poems: Patience Agbabi, Nin Andrews, Linda Black, Elisabeth Bletsoe, Dionne Brand, Suzanne Buffam, Laynie Browne, Zarah Butcher-McGunnigle, joanne burns, Vahni Capildeo, Mary Jean Chan, Killarney Clary, Sarah Crewe, Kimiko Hahn, Lucy Hamilton, Claire Harris, Holly Iglesias, Maria Jastrzebska, Bhanu Kapil, Mary A. Koncel, Karen An-hwei Lee, Jane Monson, Harryette Mullen, Mariko Nagai, Marlene NourbeSe Philip, Khadijah Queen, Lauren Russell, Julia Story, Wendy Taylor Carlisle, Nikki Wallschlaeger, C. D. Wright, and Jenny Xie.

Experimental Prose Poetry

We have briefly discussed Ron Silliman's manifesto, "The New Sentence," and his essay "New Prose Poem" in relation to neo-surrealist prose poetry. We have also flagged the role of the so-called language poets as a significant part of the trajectory of the development of the contemporary prose poem. However, it is perhaps even more pertinent to invoke the tenets of the language poets and what is often referred to as post-avante-garde (or post-avant) poetics in a discussion of women and prose poetry. This is because language poetry centers on liberating language from its hegemonic structures. It aims to do this, broadly, by "plac[ing] its attention primarily on language and ways of making meaning, that takes for granted neither vocabulary, grammar, process, shape, syntax, program, or subject matter."[25] We have seen this idea put into practice in Harryette Mullen's abecedarian *Sleeping with the Dictionary*, and another example is Cheryl Pallant's "Yonder Zongs," which uses oulipian constraints to try to liberate writing from the restrictions of literary tradition and convention.[26]

Because language poetry has been called "multifacted and diffuse,"[27] and has also been controversial, it is important to give a brief definition to frame the discussion in this section. In 1978, Charles Bernstein and Bruce Andrews created $L=A=N=G=U=A=G=E$, "a forum for poetics and discussion."[28] Bernstein defines language poetry as:

a term that has come to stand for a rather raucous period in American poetry from the mid-70s onward in which a group of writers . . . engaged in a large-scale collective effort to champion poetic invention both in our own work and the work of other English language poets of the 20th century. . . . [The forum was] interested in both an historical and an ideological approach to poetics and aesthetics and also a stand of dissent, both to prevailing poetry norms but also to U.S. government policies. We questioned all the "given" features of poetry, from voice and expression to clarity and exposition; and in the process, came up with many different, indeed contradictory, approaches to poetry and poetics. Our desire to link our poetry and poetics with the contemporary critical, philosophical, speculative, and political thinking—with a visceral connection to the civil rights movement, feminism, and the antiwar movement—has become a significant mark of our work, and one that has perhaps given rise to our various collective names, which have been both praised and condemned.[29]

Ron Silliman has long been identified as one of the original language poets, although he said in 2012, "Am I a language poet? In that sense, was I ever?"[30] He extends Bernstein's views in the statement quoted above, challenging the basis of most literary writing in a capitalist society:

What happens when a language moves toward and passes into a capitalist stage of development is an anaesthetic transformation of the perceived tangibility of the word, with corresponding increases in its descriptive and narrative capacities, preconditions for the invention of "realism," the optical illusion of reality in capitalist thought.[31]

He adds, "Recognition of a capitalist mode of reality passed through the language and imposed on its speakers finally will require a thorough re-evaluation of the history, form and function of the poem."[32] More recently, he noted that since 1994 and the rise of the internet, the "world [is] very different, in terms of the social structures that organize the composition, publication, distribution & reception of poetry,"[33] and suggested that the development of new technologies has changed the context for the practice and understanding of language poetry. In 2017 the poet Ben Lerner took issue with some of the tenets of language poetry, referring to its political commitment to "deconstructive strategies." He asks, "But who among us still believes, if any of us ever really did, that writing disjunctive prose poems counts as a legitimately subversive political practice?"[34]

However, language poetry's influences remain important to various recent volumes of prose poetry, and there is an acknowledgment in the critical work associated with language poetry that intergenerational influences are strong. The challenging *Human-Ghost Hybrid Project* (2017), written collaboratively by Carol Guess and Daniela Olszewska, is described as a "hybrid text with two authors, its sentence structure grounds us as readers, but the narrative is nonlinear, at times absurd, reading almost like a mad libs with unexpected nouns and verbs filling each otherwise familiar sentence."[35] This demonstrates the continued interest in language poetry for some contemporary women poets and the enduring appeal of the techniques of rupture and disjuncture. Furthermore, Anne Boyer's experimental book, *The Two Thousands* (2009), uses some of the techniques evident in Lyn Hejinian's and Bernadette Mayer's prose poem autobiographies, *My Life and My Life in the Nineties* (2013) and *The Desires of Mothers to Please Others in Letters* (1994), respectively. Similarly, Fanny Howe likens Dawn Lundy Martin's recent prose poems to the work of West Coast language poet Leslie Scalapino because of their exploration of trauma and human suffering.[36] Martin delivered the Leslie Scalapino Memorial Lecture in Innovative Poetics in 2016. Interestingly, Boyer's book is available for free on the internet, which, in itself, is part of a relatively new wave of writing that is primarily being published online as an alternative to traditional publishing and distribution methods. While we discuss Boyer's and Lundy Martin's prose poetry below, we will first turn to some of the original women language prose poets.

As we've mentioned, Iglesias gives significant space to Rosmarie Waldrop and C. D. Wright in her study of women prose poets. More recently, she has stated:

> C. D. Wright, Rosmarie Waldrop, Susan Howe, Marie Harris, Amy Gerstler, Maxine Chernoff, Nin Andrews, Mary Koncel: these women made me want to write prose poems and they made me want to write about women writing prose poems even when writing prose poems looked like a straight path to obscurity.[37]

Despite this, Silliman takes issue with Iglesias because Hejinian is only mentioned once in Iglesias's *Boxing Inside the Box: Women's Prose Poetry*. There are other language poets, such as Rae Armantrout, Carla Harryman, Tina Darragh, Lynne Dreyer, Diane Ward, Harryette Mullen, Leslie Scalapino, Mei-mei Berssenbrugge, Erica Hunt, Bernadette Mayer, Hannah Weiner, and Laura Moriarty[38]—some of the most important women writers to have worked in this field. Silliman endorses Delville's and Fredman's books (*The American Prose Poem* and *Poet's Prose*), which devote significant time to the language poets. Of the two, Delville gives the most space to women, whereas Fredman highlights the work of David Bromige, Silliman, and Michael Davidson, with a section on David Antin.

In addition to their experimentation with the sentence and paragraph in prose poetry, books of prose poetry written by language poets—and many of the prose poets who have been significantly influenced by them—frequently contain works that are much longer than a page. As we have outlined in chapter 1, prose poems longer than one page tend to lose some of their visual and verbal tension, as well as releasing the "anxiety" associated with a sense of constrained or compressed space. Their greater length creates various other effects, including a sense of visual expansion and even weightiness, and often a sense of discursiveness or meandering.

In chapter 1, we discussed Fredman's preference for the term "poet's prose" instead of "prose poetry" and Delville's argument that the prose poem is "a form of poetic prose,"[39] and these comments are especially pertinent to discussions of prose poems that extend beyond a page. Language poets, in particular, may be seen to interrogate and cross the boundaries between poetic prose and prose poetry. Indeed, language poetry is often and necessarily hybrid, interspersing prose poems with sections of prose, script-writing, and performance pieces. For example, Laura Hinton argues that Carla Harryman's writing includes a "poet's prose that is neither prose nor poetry but 'new genre,'" and that it "rejects location and internal placement."[40] Many language poets write works that fall outside of any clear definition of prose poetry and are hard to classify.

Hejinian's *My Life* is considered to be one of the most compelling achievements of the language poets. In 1980, at the age of thirty-seven, she published a series of thirty-seven "new sentence" prose poems composed of thirty-seven sentences each. She revised the book when she turned forty-five, extending the poems so that each comprised forty-five poems of forty-five sentences. In 2003, Hejinian published this revised work alongside a new ten-part work in a volume entitled *My Life and My Life in the Nineties*. Working with the initial constraint of her age, and then working with it a second time in revision, Hejinian demonstrated an open-ended approach to both composition and publication. In republishing her revised prose poems, Hejinian challenged the finality of publication.

The poems in *My Life* are generally between three and four pages each, creating a visual rhythm throughout the work; all are fully justified and appear as large rectangles on the page. The individual sentences work against this homogeneity and continuity, rupturing readerly expectation in their sometimes disconcerting combinations of words and the sentences that contain them. The reader is taken out of their comfort zone because many sentences relate to one another in ways that Silliman in "The New Sentence" identifies as polysemous, ambiguous, or syllogistic: "Its effects occur as much between, as within, sentences."[41] Marjorie Perloff points to the way in which Silliman's manifesto "envisions a paragraph that might organize sentences even as a stanza organizes lines."[42] The "new sentence" is "an independent unit, neither causally nor temporally related to the sentences that precede and follow it. Like a line in poetry, its length is operative, and its meaning depends on the larger paragraph as an organizing system."[43]

Hejinian's *My Life and My Life in the Nineties* uses a related approach to the construction of autobiography. Delville argues that "what Hejinian's subversive use of autobiographical or diary writing sets out to achieve is a complex dissemination of private experience and its reinscription into a network of gender relationships and cultural and ideological principles."[44] Indeed, Hejinian rewrites her life even as she is living it, and the fully justified text blocks serve, in part, to critique conventional constructions of domesticity and the private lives of women.

However, it is important to note that each of her poems begins with the title reproduced in an empty block of space at the top left of the poem's layout. Thus, the beginning of each poem appears as a bisected box where one half is white space and the other half is text—and each poem may be read as giving simultaneous priority to white or negative space and the black text, both elements in the work functioning as metaphors for memory. In this excerpt from "Yet we insist that life is full of happy chance," the poem both attempts and rejects cohesion:

Yet we insist that life is full of happy chance   The windows were open and the morning air was, by the smell of lilac and some darker flowering shrub, filled with the brown and chirping trills of birds. As they are if you could have nothing but quiet and shouting. Arts, also, are links. I picture an idea at the moment I come to it, our collision. Once, for a time, anyone might have been luck's child. Even rain didn't spoil the barbecue, in the backyard behind a polished traffic, through a landscape, along a shore. Freedom then, liberation later. She came to babysit for us in those troubled years directly from the riots, and she said that she dreamed of the day when she would gun down everyone in the financial district. That single telephone is only one hair on the brontosaurus. The coffee drinkers answered ecstatically. If your dog stays out of the room, you get the fleas. In the lull, activity drops. I'm seldom in my dreams without my children. My daughter told me that at some time in school she had learned to think of a poet as a person seated on an iceberg and melting down through it. It is a poetry of certainty. . . .[45]

The poem turns on a number of self-reflexive expressions, many about chance or coincidence. Even the title emphasizes the words "happy chance" as a masthead, suggesting that the reader would do well to embrace the work's looser connections between contiguous sentences.

Such strategies challenge the more conventional structures of most autobiographical writing, rupturing the reader's expectations and suggesting that much of life's activities, apparent meanings, and their associated stories have a more or less arbitrary relationship to one another. In Hejinian's work, the interplay of disparate experiences, recollections, and feelings is often surprising and, indeed, she makes a virtue in her work of juxtapositions and collisions that simulate disjuncture in memory. Her often extended prose poetry form squeezes these collisions into long, recurring rectangles, creating a sense of a sometimes jarring and constrained meandering. The reader is required to grasp at related tropes and ideas in order to create meaning—such as linking the open window at the beginning of the poem we have quoted from with words that occur subsequently: "Freedom then, liberation later."

However, any attempt to closely analyze a "new sentence" prose poem runs the risk of imposing meanings on the work. Meanings tend to be slippery in works that exploit the humorous and elegiac while also highlighting fractures of thought. For example, Heijinian writes: "That single telephone is only one hair on the brontosaurus."[46] This is disjunctive and wonderfully witty. It is an example of Hejinian's understanding of the gaps and insufficiencies that occur in any attempt to find an equivalence between thing and word. In "The Rejection of Closure" she comments: "Children objectify language when they render it their plaything, in jokes, puns, and riddles, or in glossolaliac chants and rhymes. They discover that words are not equal to the world, that a shift, analogous to parallax in photography, occurs between thing (events, ideas, objects) and the words for them—a displacement that leaves a gap."[47]

Hejinian rejects both the patriarchal voice and established lines of authority in her conceptualization of an "open text," which "emphasizes or foregrounds process."[48] In such a text, she says, "The writer relinquishes total control and challenges authority as a principle and control as a motive." In this way, Hejinian also eschews the usually fairly stable "I" of autobiography for the image of the poet-autobiographer as a "person seated on an iceberg and melting through."[49]

Anne Boyer's writing is also influenced by the techniques of the language poets. Her book *Garments Against Women* uses sketches, fables, and prose poems to discuss freedom and survival. In a manner somewhat reminiscent of Hejinian's work, Boyer uses an autobiographical mode to highlight the way women and their work are constructed by patriarchy, their lives fraught with negotiation and negation. Sewing and motherhood, two of the concerns of this book, symbolize a private and domestic sphere that has long been trivialized. The ambiguous use of the word "against" conjures the image of clothes being held up against a woman's body, referring to the way women are often judged according to their dress and appearance.

Garments can be constricting or loose, and they can be altered or even made into something else. Boyer chooses prose poetry for this exploration because it allows her to stitch together paragraphs and shape or modify them to dress her ideas about women and work. Her own work is metaphorical, extending into an examination not only of the garments or remnants of her time but of "the political economy of literature and of life itself":[50]

> When I am not writing I am not writing a novel called *1994* about a young woman in an office park in a provincial town who has a job cutting and pasting time. I am not writing a novel called *Nero* about the world's richest art star in space. I am not writing a book called *Kansas City Spleen*. I am not writing a sequel to *Kansas City Spleen* called *Bitch's Maldoror*. I am not writing a book of political philosophy called *Questions for Poets*. I am not writing a scandalous memoir. I am not writing a pathetic memoir. I am not writing a memoir about

poetry or love. I am not writing a memoir about poverty, debt collection, or bankruptcy. I am not writing about family court. I am not writing a memoir because memoirs are for property owners and not writing a memoir about prohibitions of memoirs.[51]

This excerpt uses the technique of paralipsis where, by saying she is not doing various things, Boyer conjures those things. She writes even as she claims not to be writing, and her use of intertexts wittily establishes a contrast between high art and popular culture. Her reference to *Kansas City Spleen* and *Bitch's Maldoror* is particularly arch in its conflation of Boyer's city of Kansas with Baudelaire's *Paris Spleen* and Comte de Lautréamont's well-known novel (or extended prose poem) *Les Chants de Maldoror*—both published in the late 1860s. Boyer co-opts these texts for the use of women flaneurs (or the *flâneuse*), protesting at the idea that the experience of the meandering poet belongs to men. She writes, "the flaneur is a poet is an agent free of purses, but a woman is not a woman without a strap over her shoulder or a clutch in her hand."[52] Importantly, Boyer promotes the contemporary *flâneuse* as a working-class feminist psychogeographer.

The epigraph to Boyer's poem is a quote from Mary Wollstonecraft's novella *Maria: or, The Wrongs of Woman* (1798). This epigraph emphasizes the importance of women writing and speaking out, and also the significance of the mother-daughter connection. For Wollstonecraft, this is her relationship to her daughter, who was to become Mary Shelley. For Boyer it is her daughter, who says that even in a world devoid of things (except people, trees, and dirt), "We would make things with trees and dirt."[53] Boyer's own writing is a form of such making yet, as Boyer writes, she also meditates on not writing, to the extent that her work becomes a meditation about the costs and compromises associated with her art. She says, "It is easy to imagine not writing, both accidentally and intentionally. It is easy because there have been years and months and days I have thought the way to live was not writing."[54] Boyer asks the reader to consider the costs associated with writing, the marginalization of women and many of their cultural activities within a patriarchal society, along with the decreased value of their labor in the marketplace. This is similar to the way "Hejinian's use of procedural form [where poetic constraints are largely determined in advance] in *My Life* highlights the arbitrary, repetitive nature of postindustrial labor, and her treatment of commodities highlights the reification of labor."[55]

Boyer presents writing as work and toil, and her use of the prose poem form underscores her exploration of women's work as a celebration of the quotidian. On the surface the paragraph looks ordinary—much the same as sewing—but when you engage on a deeper level, it grows into something extraordinary and unexpected. In this way, Boyer's prose poetry paragraph is confining but also surprisingly large in the way it reaches out to embrace other books, metaphors, and histories. When she asks toward the beginning of the book, "Also, how is

Capital not an infinite laboratory called 'conditions'? And where is the edge of the electrified grid?,"[56] she could be referring, in part, to the prose poetry box and the "conditions" and "capital" placed on writing poetry: they could all be identified as part of what hides in plain sight. Boyer's meditation on gender, creativity, and work is chastening but also savagely humorous—like Chernoff's prose poetry, but with very different inflections, it is prose poetry as mise en abyme.

Dawn Lundy Martin's book *Life in a Box Is a Pretty Life* uses the box-shaped prose poetry paragraph to explore incarceration and resistance. Significantly, it's also a response to artist and photographer Carrie Mae Weems's "Framed by Modernism" series, which gives further relevance to the symbolic significance of the frame and the box. In an interview, Martin stated:

> The investigation of the box in the poems is really about a question of freedom, of agency. Is there any way to live in the world and be free? To make our own choices? So I imagine the box as not a single entity but a series of enclosures—actual, relational, and cultural—that prevent us from real feeling.[57]

Throughout her work Martin intentionally leaves gaps, spaces, and ellipses for the reader to fill—and some of the most significant absences are underlined, such as in the incomplete phrase, "WE ARE _____ WITH GLEE."[58] Such gaps encourage the reader to make their own connections inside and outside the box-shaped paragraph, empowering the reader. However, her work also breaks open its boxes, revealing that when the frame of the prose poem is ruptured, there is no "inside" or "outside" because everything inhabits the same space. Any sense of a hierarchy that may be inferred from text being placed in a box, or from words being underlined, is thus diffused and equalized.

Martin explores prose poetry's ability to enact social change and its resistance to closure. By exposing the limits of articulation concerning the black, queer female experience, and in condemning the history of racist science, she seeks to upset frames that constrain discussion or represent forms of incarceration. In discussing race in contemporary society, she is, by extension, tackling the persistence of racist historical representation. In this excerpt from the title prose poem, she considers personal and collective freedom:

> Life in a box is a pretty life, arrangements and things. We all have the same type of feeling. There's some drifting. *Breathe into my bag.* Flowers. To fight is to lie down among the dead. [Unstable space.] [Claims historical.] History is littered with severed cocks. A want to be buried there—those ruins.[59]

Martin's book *Discipline* has been likened to Leslie Scalapino's poetry for its emphasis on vulnerability and trauma. In charting the death of her father—"I waited all my life for my father to die and when he did I felt empty"[60]—she focuses on the importance of the body and the importance of certain bodies over others.

Bodies give us joy, but bodies also fail us. At various junctures, blocks of binary code gesture toward alternative language systems and the possibility of new modes of communication.

Lyric Prose Poetry

While the term "lyric poetry" once referred almost exclusively to short, lineated poems, it has increasingly been used in recent decades to name different forms and varieties of poetry that may or may not be lineated. In its original form—as it survived as remnants of poetic practice in archaic Greece (ca. 800–480 BCE)—lyric poetry was understood as musical verse written in meter that often employed the first-person voice or lyric "I." Two of the most famous writers of such poetry are Archilochus (ca. 680–ca. 645 BCE) and Sappho (ca. 630–ca. 570 BCE), both of whom sometimes seem to speak directly of personal matters.

However, there has been considerable debate about whether their poetry is autobiographical in any modern sense, although both appear to draw directly on personal experience for some of their work—Sappho, for instance, alludes to family members in her poetry. While the lyric "I" has almost become a defining feature of the traditional lyric lineated poem, in the words of S. R. Slings, the "I is the I of the performer, which moves through a continuum, in which the biographical I and the fictional I are the two extremes: most of the time it is neither."[61] In contemporary lyrical prose poetry, "personal" and autobiographical material is often present but, as with ancient writers, the "I" of such poems may not simply be conflated with the voice of the person who writes.

Anne Carson, Claudia Rankine, and Maggie Nelson are three of the most celebrated contemporary poets writing prose poetry that engages with the lyric form—partly through their employment of the first-person pronoun and their exploration of autobiographical tropes. Importantly, while all have been identified as writing prose poetry, they also disturb this identification by incorporating other forms and genres into their writing—or elements of them—including essay, drama, fiction, performance, translation, sketch, vignette, notebook, and mixed media. In their more essayistic moments, their prose poetry moves toward poetic prose. Rankine identifies this in her two books *Citizen* and *Don't Let Me Be Lonely*, refashioning the lyric as an "American Lyric" in the subtitles of these books. Similarly, Carson and Nelson transform the lyric and complicate any understanding of the lyric "I" through focusing on various forms of the loss and reconstruction of the self, and on the creation of an "I" that is constantly transforming.

The use of the lyric "I" by contemporary writers has sometimes been viewed as simplistic, naive, or even as politically complaisant or incorrect—by language poets, in particular. Ben Lerner best summarizes such views in his analysis of Claudia Rankine's and Maggie Nelson's poetry:

Language poetry's notion of textual difficulty as a weapon in class warfare hasn't aged well, but the force of its critique of what is typically referred to as "the lyric I" has endured in what Gillian White has recently called a diffuse and lingering "lyric shame"—a sense, now often uncritically assumed, that modes of writing and reading identified as lyric are embarrassingly egotistical and politically backward.[62]

Yet Carson, Rankine, and Nelson use the lyric on their own terms, exploring absence, disjuncture, grief, and silence in writing that blurs the bounds of prose and poetry. Their hybrid prose poetry is constituted as remnants or fragments of what is broken.

While Anne Carson's *Autobiography of Red* is subtitled "A Novel in Verse" and uses lineation to reimagine the myth of the monster Geryon, her long lines can be likened to sentences of prose poetry. For example, in "XLIV: Photographs: The Old Days," every second line reaches toward the right margin:

Herakles standing at the window staring out on the dark before dawn.

When they made love

Geryon like to touch in slow succession each of the bones of Herakles' back

as it arched away from him into

who knows what dark dream of its own, running both hands all the way down

from the base of the neck

to the end of the spine which he can cause to shiver like a root in the rain.[63]

The visual effect of these severed lines promotes the idea of brokenness, and as Carson appeals to the conceit that many of her poems refer to photographs, she emphasizes what is fragmentary and unreliable in human memory and subjective experience. Her poetic narrative and lyric "I" are irrevocably fractured.

After Herakles seduces and then abandons a broken-hearted Geryon, his photographs become a poignant misrepresentation of their relationship, offering only one point of view. Leila Talei observes, "Geryon is aware of the disturbing nature of photography . . . photos are the prisons of living memories that convey a sense of becoming."[64] Furthermore, just as photographs are fragments of a moment, Talei points to the way Geryon sees his lover as a series of parts as he moves "in slow succession" down his spine, focusing on each piece of him. These concerns are all relevant to the prose poem form, which so frequently focuses on parts rather than on the whole. It also explores the connection between prose poetry and photographs, which we have discussed in chapter 7.

When Carson returns to Geryon's story in *Red doc>*, she chooses to write in mostly narrow, rectangular boxes of poetry that run like a long stripe down the middle of the page. Their full justification is reminiscent of the prose poem:

> LOVE'S LONG LOST
> shock the boy the man he
> knows him. Knew. The
> lion head the sloping run a
> lavishness in him made you
> want to throw your soul
> through every door.
> Memory sucks it all
> backward . . .[65]

As Geryon (now G) and Herakles (now Sad but Great) take a road trip, the preponderance of thin, centered poems could be read pictorially as somewhat reminiscent of the dividing line down the middle of the road. The full justification for many of the poems and large left and right margins leave only a few words on each line, encouraging a speedy reading—even if the work demands considerable time for a reader to appreciate it fully. The thin poems also stand for bite-sized glimpses of life, fragments of existence and a fractured lyric "I."

Red doc> explores the relationship between prose and poetry, which is evident from Carson's well-known metaphor, which she chooses to center on the page:

> what is the difference between
> poetry and prose you know the old analogies prose
> is a house poetry a man in flames running
> quite fast through it
> or
> when it meets the mind waves appear (poetry) or
> both are defined by
> length of lines *and there are times*
> *your life gets like that* . . .[66]

Carson's *Short Talks* and *Nox* contain more easily identifiable prose poems. *Nox* is Carson's most obvious autobiographical work. It is an elegy to her brother and riffs on ideas of the box and of the limits of language. This concertina book of gnomic prose poems and collage is presented in a display box, reminiscent of a coffin, Bible, or stone tablet. In it, she lays out fragments of her brother's life, who was lost to her even before he died. The box and the prose poem become a way of grieving a double absence as Carson begins, "1.0 I wanted to fill my elegy with light of all kinds."[67]

Carson lets her readers into a personal space while also distancing them from it. The prose poem form underscores the gaps and spaces in her brother's narrative, suggesting that the moments Carson explores are only small aspects of a complex life. In framing the text, the prose poetry box demonstrates the limits of what can be said in heightened moments of emotion. Carson demonstrates that expressions of grief are as much about what is not said as about articulation.

Finally, Anne Carson's first collection, *Short Talks*, is composed of prose poems as ruminations on a variety of subjects, many of which deal with absence. For example, her "Short Talk on Defloration" turns on compressed imagery and is upfront about the lyric "I":

> The actions of life are not so many. To go in, to go, to go in secret, to cross the Bridge of Sighs. And when you dishonoured me, I saw that dishonour is an action. It happened in Venice; it causes the vocal cords to swell. I went booming through Venice, under and over the bridges, but you were gone. Later that day I telephoned your brother. What's wrong with your voice? he said.[68]

Even in this interior moment, Carson destabilizes the lyric by questioning the nature of "voice" in the prose poem.

Claudia Rankine has stated that her "American Lyric" is about "pull[ing] the lyric back into its realities"[69]—by which she means, in part, that she wants to explore racism and the lived experience of racial discrimination. Her American lyric resets the inward-turning stance of confessional poetry by turning her meditations outward and asking the reader to recognize the endemic internalization of racism, which she suggests has become normative. The lyric, then, is politicized by Rankine, who includes her own subjectivity insofar as it serves to ask urgent questions of the reader. Any idea that the lyric is privileged, frivolous, or "egotistical and politically backward" is deconstructed in such work.[70] Rankine uses prose poems like building blocks, where one moment builds on the next, like evidence in a case she presents to the public. The prose poetry form is useful for testimony in the way it may visually resemble a paragraph of nonfiction or part of an article in a newspaper. Rankine's use of the prose poetry form is both weighty and democratic in its emphasis.

Don't Let Me Be Lonely: An American Lyric begins with personal tragedy but builds to expressions of local and global tragedy. It begins by considering the death of a friend from cancer and ends with the capture of Saddam Hussein, sparking a final rumination on what it means to be present, to be "here": "We must both be here in this world in this life in this place indicating the presence of."[71] This passage is accompanied by a black-and-white photograph of an advertisement over a road that has the word "HERE" capitalized on a white background. Loneliness, then, is existential and stems from people's failure to connect as equals. Rankine uses the free-line to express these sentiments earlier in the book, where six sentences hang in the middle of the page at the left margin, engulfed by white space:

Define loneliness?

Yes.

It's what we can't do for each other.

What do we mean to each other?

What does a life mean?

Why are we here if not for each other?[72]

Rankine's use of imagery, most notably the repeated evocation of a television showing white noise, implicates the media's influence in the daily struggle to make meaning and connections. It compares the square television screen to the prose poetry box or frame, exposing the stream of toxic images being projected into people's homes. Rankine notes the way the media manipulates events in the news and damages people's sense of self-worth:

> It occurs to me that forty could be half my life or it could be all my life. On the television I am told I don't want to look like I am forty. Forty means I might have seen something hard, something unpleasant, or something dead. I might have seen it and lived beyond it in time. Or I might have squinted my eyes too many times in order to see it, I might have turned my face to the sun in order to look away. I might have actually been alive . . .[73]

In her award-winning book *Citizen* (subtitled *An American Lyric*), Rankine uses the second-person present in a conversation that both implicates readers and calls them to action. As Kelly Caldwell argues:

> If, traditionally, the lyric's territory is that of the first-person pronoun, Rankine opens up the potentially sealed or homogeneous lyric unit to the grammatical and subjective confusion of the second person (the primary figure is designated throughout as "you"). Against the traditional aestheticist notion that the lyric is apolitical, Rankine broadens the lyric's scope into a space for staging various negotiations between—in *Citizen*'s words—the "self self" and the "historical self."[74]

Rankine uses her position as a black citizen of the United States to meditate on the relationship between private and public identity, on black bodies in public spaces and on the body politic. This is best explored in her discussion of split subjectivity and racial injustice in postmodern society:

> A friend argues that Americans battle between the "historical self" and the "self self." By this she means you mostly interact as friends with mutual interest and, for the most part, compatible personalities; however, sometimes your historical selves, her white self and your black self, or your white self and her black self, arrive with the full force of your American positioning.[75]

In a similar way to *Don't Let Me Be Lonely*, each prose poem in *Citizen* builds on the next. Moments of prejudice or racial microaggressions (the term microaggression, coined by Harvard University psychiatrist Chester Pierce, means "subtle, stunning, often automatic, and nonverbal exchanges which are 'put-downs' of blacks by offenders"[76]) continually build to become a much larger discussion of dislocation, disconnection, and a failure of community and citizenship.

Despite being published by Wave Books—a poetry press—Maggie Nelson identifies her book *Bluets* as having "essayistic logic" and no line breaks, arguing that this means it is prose rather than poetry. Nevertheless, she is generally unconcerned with how others label her writing. Nelson's books cover a wide spectrum of genre and form and, like Carson and Rankine, she is known for her experimentation, hybridity, and use of autobiographical tropes. Nelson has written a book of criticism entitled *Women, the New York School, and Other True Abstractions* in which she reinvigorates writing on the New York school by focusing on reading the work of women such as Joan Mitchell, Barbara Guest, Bernadette Mayer, Alice Notley, and Eileen Myles from a feminist perspective. Nelson refers to this work in *The Argonauts*: "Once I wrote a book about domesticity in the poetry of certain gay men (Ashbery, Schuyler) and some women (Mayer, Notley). I wrote this book when I was living in New York City in a teeny, too-hot attic apartment on a Brooklyn thoroughfare underlined by the F train."[77] *Bluets* and *The Argonauts* both demonstrate the importance of theory and philosophy to Nelson's writing. In these books, she engages with writers, artists, and thinkers through a form of creative dialogue and a series of intertextual moments.

Bluets is divided into 240 fully justified blocks of prose poetry, none longer than two hundred words. These small moments have been called propositions. Importantly, while there is a progression in numbers chronologically, there is not a similar progression in the subject matter of the fragments themselves. This is deliberate, as Nelson states that she shuffled them around "countless times" prior to publication.[78] Thomas Larson identifies this as a "Nomadic mosaic" where "[a]s one reads, the book, despite its progression, loses its linearity and feels circular, porous, a tad unstable."[79]

Nelson gives female desire prominence in *Bluets*. In one sense, her ex-lover is absent from the text, given that their relationship occurred in the past. However, he haunts her words subtextually, and his presence and her relationship with him are reconstituted through her exploration of female subjectivity. At times she evokes intimate experiences with poignancy and humor:

> 116. One of the last times you came to see me, you were wearing a pale blue button-down shirt, short-sleeved. *I wore this for you*, you said. We fucked for six hours straight that afternoon, which does not seem precisely possible but that is what the clock said. We killed the time. You were on your way to a seaside town, a town of much blue, where you would be spending a week with the other woman you were in love with, the woman you are with now. *I'm in*

love with you both in completely different ways, you said. It seemed unwise to contemplate this statement any further.[80]

Used in this way, the prose poem form scrutinizes and disrupts the primacy of male subjectivity, and its compression becomes a metaphor for the sometimes chastening constraints of language.

The Argonauts is a hybrid work that employs fragments, poetic prose, and prose poems as part of its structure. Divided into anecdotes instead of propositions with a fractured chronology, it is a love story written in response to the work of Roland Barthes and other theorists, artists, and thinkers:

> A day or two after my love pronouncement, now feral with vulnerability, I sent you the passage from *Roland Barthes by Roland Barthes* in which Barthes describes how the subject who utters the phrase "I love you" is like "the Argonaut renewing his ship during its voyage without changing its name." Just as the *Argo*'s parts may be replaced over time but the boat is still called the *Argo*, whenever the lover utters the phrase "I love you," its meaning must be renewed by each use, as "the very task of love and of language is to give to one and the same phrase inflections which will be forever new."
>
> I thought the passage was romantic. You read it as a possible retraction. In retrospect, I guess it was both.[81]

Described by the publisher as "autotheory," like *Bluets*, Nelson politicizes the personal in this book, interrogating society's ideas about gender and sexuality. She inflects her intertextual moments with her experiences as a woman, using fragments and the prose poem form to emphasize the fractured nature of memory and subjectivity.

Nelson's books are partly autobiographical, like Carson's and Rankine's, but they are not simple accounts of the writer's life. Lerner has argued, "*Bluets* and *Don't Let Me Be Lonely* open with a mixture of detachment and emotional intensity that simultaneously evokes and complicates the status of the 'lyric I.'"[82] The books and prose poems by Carson, Nelson, and Rankine are hybrid, and in their different ways they make use of prose poetry to explore insider/outsider status, absence, and presence. Their prose poems emphasize not only what is inside its frame but what is left out—implied but never explicitly stated.

Contemporary Rape Narratives in Prose Poetry

Many women prose poets who write about gender roles publish their writing on the internet as well as in print, reaching a considerable number of readers. They often use humor and satire to challenge the oppression and victimization of women and to rework traditional lyricism as a powerful means of expression for women.

A long prose poem by Raquel de Alderete on Tumblr attracted more than fifty thousand comments. It focuses on the internalization of patriarchal assumptions by men and women that lead to gender discrimination. She achieves this in the confined quarters of the prose poem with the anaphoric binary, "it's not" / "it's that." The opening of this prose poem juxtaposes what appear to be relatively benign skills, such as doing the laundry, with the insidious nature of unexamined gender bias:

> it's not about that i know how to do laundry. it's that when i was four i knew how to fold clothes; small hands working alongside my mother, while my older brother sat and played with his toys. it's that i know what kind of detergent works but my father guesses. it's that in my freshman year of college i had a line of boys who needed me to show them how to use the machine. it's that the first door they knocked on belonged to me. it's that they expected me to know.[83]

This prose poem demonstrates that gender lines are drawn early as the narrator is given a "plastic kitchenette for christmas," an act that gains momentum in the prose poem and results in her being expected to bake cakes and being told by a boy that she isn't "wife" material when she "burns popcorn." Significantly, another opposition is drawn here when the same boy "burns popcorn" and he simply "laughs":

> a boy burns popcorn in the dorm microwave and laughs. a week later, i do the same thing, and he snorts at me, "just crossed you off my wife list." it's that i had heard something like this so many times before that i laughed, too. . . . it's that i'm weak and i don't know if it's because i just am or i was trained to be. it's that we need to sit pretty with our pretty smiles and our pretty words trapped pretty and silent in our throats.[84]

Alderete exposes the way people practice everyday forms of sexism often without realizing it. The narrator has been conditioned to laugh at the denigration of women and the reader is invited to join the narrator's amusement at the discrimination she experiences. This levity is immediately undercut as the sentences outlining women's silencing are laced with bitterness. Many women's narratives in a patriarchal society include marriage as a central trope, and Alderete names and contains attitudes associated with marriage and allied assumptions about gender roles, suggesting that while discrimination can look benign, or appear familiar (like the prose poetry paragraph), it is highly complex (like the poetry the paragraph contains).

Prose poems by Patricia Lockwood, Thylias Moss, Kristin Sanders, Claire Louise Harmon, and Khadijah Queen give voice to instances of sexual assault and experiences of toxic masculinity. Significantly, the prose poem form is able to provide more than testimony, liberating the narrator from her status as victim in a series of subversions. First, it compresses and ruptures the experience it recounts; second, the use of anaphora and savage humor reverberates in a tighter space than a lineated poem; and third, it resists closure, demonstrating the ongoing relevance of these issues. Furthermore, the prose poem is an effective form for testimonials and protest poetry because it can attract a significant public readership who, when they begin reading, may not be aware that they are encountering a form of poetry.

Patricia Lockwood has been dubbed the "Poet Laureate of Twitter" for her invention of ironic sexts on this online forum.[85] She has commented that it is mostly men in their responses to her tweets who misunderstand her satire and comedy, failing to see how unsexy they really are. This lends her writing a subversiveness that reaches beyond its online frame, as her inversion of common tropes sparks gendered responses. This has gained her supporters, who identify "her sexual-political target" as "all manner of straight-male privilege, every objectifier and braggart, whom she outflanks."[86] Lockwood uses the same satire and "bleak humor" in many of her poems and prose poems, published online and in print.[87] Her use of the prose poem form heightens the irony of the content, so that the visually subversive form works as a metaphor for men's fetishization and objectification of women.

Lockwood's most famous work, "Rape Joke," went viral in 2013. It was selected by Terrance Hayes for the 2014 edition of *The Best American Poetry*. He points to the prose poem's use of black humor, which lends the titular "joke" poignancy: "[T]here's a blade at the heart of the joke, but there's also a kind of suffering, and an awareness of that suffering, which gives it a kind of empathy for people who are exposed to it. The whole poem is a big question, isn't it?"[88]

Lockwood's "Rape Joke" posits itself as a joke that responds to the social silencing of rape.[89] It is a long prose poem that turns on its black humor and its use of the anaphora, "the rape joke," to undermine its status as any real "joke":

The rape joke is that you were 19 years old.

The rape joke is that he was your boyfriend.
. . . .
The rape joke is that he was seven years older. The rape joke is that you had
known him for years, since you were too young to be interesting to him.
You liked that use of the word *interesting*, as if you were a piece of
knowledge that someone could be desperate to acquire, to assimilate, and to
spit back out in different form through his goateed mouth.[90]

Lockwood uses the prose poem box in juxtaposition with what has been identified as the prose poem's free-line (discussed in chapter 4), to play with notions of containment and liberation. Moreover, the free-line extends the prose poem, allowing the expansion of her ideas as she demonstrates the broader social and political significance of what starts out as personal trauma.

The final part of the prose poem positions the reader to smile—most obviously at the moment when the narrator is given a Beach Boys album, *Pet Sounds*—and to simultaneously feel conflicted for being amused by any part of a rape narrative. The prose poem form does all of this in close quarters and ends by implicating the reader:

Can rape jokes be funny at all, is the question.

Can any part of the rape joke be funny. The part where it ends—haha, just kidding! Though you did dream of killing the rape joke for years, spilling all of its blood out, and telling it that way.

The rape joke cries out for the right to be told.

The rape joke is that this is just how it happened.

The rape joke is that the next day he gave you *Pet Sounds*. No really. *Pet Sounds*. He said he was sorry and then he gave you *Pet Sounds*. Come on, that's a little bit funny.

Admit it.[91]

The direct address that concludes the work is a forceful and ambiguous note that expands to encompass a range of possibilities. The words "Admit it" could refer to the gift of the *Pet Sounds* album, but it has other more serious implications too. As Elizabeth Lanphier says, "the poem also makes a demand: It draws its reader in as part of a moral community that 'gets the joke' and holds the reader accountable within an ethical relationship to receive and respond."[92]

Lockwood's is not the only well-known prose poem to chronicle rape. It is worth mentioning Thylias Moss's "Goodness and the Salt of the Earth," which was anthologized in *Models of the Universe* and also uses the second-person pronoun and the device of repetition—this time wholly within a prose poem box. It writes back to the scriptures, specifically the story of Lot and his wife, to expose the poor treatment of women historically and to suggest that little has changed:

Somebody's husband raped you while you were supposed to be in the choir pounding a tambourine, not a chest . . . You got pregnant. Good. Had an abortion. Good. That's what the Lord said in Genesis, he saw the world and what was happening, and it was still good. So you were good and turned the pages, read every line, and Lot's wife, that good woman, turned to salt because she was polite and couldn't leave without saying good-bye.[93]

The use of these repetitions within the prose poetry box is intensely powerful, due to their close proximity to one another. And here, the repetition of the word "good" undermines the word's meaning, functioning instead to question the goodness of any situation where the writer or reader, in the implied second-person address, experiences the aftermath of a rape and an ensuing abortion.

Similarly, Kristin Sanders uses the anaphoric "thank you to . . ." in both earnest and sarcastic ways throughout her prose poem "Country Song of Thanks."[94] It is a long work, like Lockwood's, but doesn't contain any free-lines. The words are compressed into a prose poem box with some long run-on sentences. These moments are conveyed in a stream-of-consciousness mode to emphasize the distressing scenarios that are being broached, suggesting something raw.

Bookended by the narrator's sexual assault in Las Vegas, this experience sparks a chronicling of males who have either abused or supported her:

> Thank you to the man in Las Vegas who ripped my tampon out and went down on me anyway who waited who didn't put it in me when I said no let's wait till you come out to California since I was a virgin and of course he did not know that I was a virgin . . . Thank you to the boys who saw me walking wearing that outfit like a real slut. Thank you to the boys who saw me dancing that way like a real slut. Thank you to the boys who heard me talking that way like a real slut. Thank you to the boys who slept in my bed thank you to the boys who slept on my sofa thank you to the boys who slept in a hotel room a tent a train car with me. . . . Thank you that the worst image is the way the blood dripped down my leg when I went to the bathroom after he had ripped my tampon out and how I thought for one moment that I had been because there was blood from some wound and the blood from this wound was running down my thigh until I realized it was menstrual blood so I wiped it up with tissue and put my pants back on and left the room and was not raped.[95]

This prose poem is almost choked with the word "thank you," which becomes deeply ironic, signifying the pervasive nature of the experiences chronicled and creating an overwhelming testimony about the problematic nature of women's experiences in contemporary society. Sanders uses key tropes to expose the sexual shaming of women, and questions the semantics of how we understand, and name, personal trauma and sexual assault. The last sentence opens out to embrace questions of society's moral and ethical responsibilities concerning such matters.

Khadijah Queen's chapbook, *I'm So Fine: A List of Famous Men & What I Had On*, is a book of prose poems that chronicles the way in which girls and women are objectified in contemporary society. Hope Wabuke characterizes the work as "a vivid, visceral articulation of living under this constant threat of sexual assault and sexual harassment our rape culture normalizes; of living with the trauma of having been sexually assaulted or harassed."[96] In this book Queen charts what the narrator was wearing when encountering a range of men at different points in her life. The repetition of items of clothing and the importance ascribed to them shows how girls and women so often internalize the importance of gender stereotypes and their exposure to male aggression:

> it was fun at first my sister's friend Catharine had DD's and never wore underwear so we got in free everywhere and we saw a bunch of Lakers and then she had to go and get drunk and we had to save her from this boxer dude who was trying to take her home she didn't know what the f she was doing I stayed with her while our younger sisters went to get the car then the guy grabbed her by the arm I could see it turning red I wouldn't let go of her hand I called for help no one came . . . and finally finally a bouncer came and told the guy to leave and the boxer guy looked at me and acted like he was going to walk off then turned around and lunged I thought he was going to hit me in the face.[97]

Queen uses uppercase bold text to begin each poem and a large round font to narrate the events, disrupting the narrative with numbers in bold font.[98] In addition to this, all of the prose poems in Queen's book have short, vertical lines at each margin, demarcating the text from the generous amount of white space around it, creating a greater sense of enclosure and emphasis. The final prose poem in the chapbook ends by lamenting that encounters with men are so often understood in crudely sexual terms:

> I had on suede knee boots and a trench because it was fall and we ended up walking somewhere in Manhattan after Thai food holding hands and a random guy telling him You Doing it Big! And why couldn't all this be only about name-dropping and brand names and puddintang **ASK ME AGAIN I'LL TELL YOU THE SAME**[99]

In her postscript to the full-length collection of *I'm So Fine: A List of Famous Men & What I Had On; A Narrative*, Queen states, "Some men can't stop telling me who I am or what exactly is so incredible about me or what they had to take or offer without asking."[100] The postscript is written as a long piece of poetic prose that uses enjambments between some paragraphs to link driving concerns about identity and to claim the space for the poet. It ends on the image of a rose being drawn with "layer[s of] new petals."[101] Here Queen emphasizes "the lines unbroken," a self-reflexive moment reminiscent of the way the prose poem, with its lines that turn at the right margin, is an example of "endless making."[102]

Prose Poetry and Feminism

Prose poetry originated in nineteenth-century Paris as a subversive literary form that challenged poetic conventions and social mores. However, it originally spoke almost exclusively for male viewpoints and was part of a nineteenth-century French literary culture that largely silenced women. In the twenty-first century, particularly in the hands of women writers, the form is now being used to critique conventional, stereotypical, or sexist views of society and human relationships, making many prose poems at once highly contemporary and highly political. Women prose poets are using the form to find new and complex ways of speaking about ongoing issues of oppression, and to challenge limiting ideas of what prose poetry itself might do and how it might be defined.

In this way, prose poetry may be understood as one of the contemporary literary forms that most clearly expresses feminist ideas and intent. The examples we have discussed in this chapter demonstrate that as women explore their experiences through prose poetry, in sometimes raw and confronting ways, so prose poetry's characteristic brevity and condensations begin to expand in many directions—critiquing patriarchy and its assumptions, denouncing sexual assault, challenging readers to question or overturn their assumptions about gender roles, and making new ground for women to write creatively. This is such an important aspect of prose poetry that it may continue to be one of its key defining features in the century to come. Contemporary prose poetry is a powerful literary vehicle for social and political change, and although W. H. Auden once wrote that "poetry makes nothing happen,"[103] it may be that women prose poets are in the process of proving him wrong.

CHAPTER 10

Prose Poetry and the Very Short Form

The Very Short Form

Very short literary forms are proliferating online and in print. While novels, short stories, lineated lyric poems, and dramatic works have been at the center of literary practice for centuries, contemporary writers are reinvigorating our understanding of genre and form—and some of their writing does not sit comfortably within conventional literary classifications. To an extent, and as we have discussed, this is true of prose poetry in general, and it is certainly true of hybrid works that contain, reframe, or transform prose poetry. We provide and discuss examples of innovative hybrid works in this chapter.

This is not to suggest that all hybrid prose-poetical works are products of the late twentieth- or early twenty-first century. There are many early examples of hybrid works that make use of poetic prose (or prose poetry, if one defines the term very generally). These include Friedrich Hölderlin's hybrid novel/prose poem *Hyperion* (1797–99); Edgar Allan Poe's nonfiction work *Eureka: A Prose Poem* (1848); Stéphane Mallarmé's combination of prose poetry and critical essays and reflections, *Divagations* (1897); William Carlos Williams's prose poetry sequence *Kora in Hell: Improvisations* (1920); Elizabeth Smart's short "poetic" novel, *By Grand Central Station I Sat Down and Wept* (1945); and Karl Shapiro's *The Bourgeois Poet* (1964), which consists of three sections and ninety-six parts of poetic prose.

However, many contemporary hybrid works that make use of very short prose forms are especially notable for their emphasis on an irredeemable sense of fracture, and such works are increasingly being accepted as central to the literary world—Claudia Rankine's *Citizen: An American Lyric* is an obvious example. This recent growth in the popularity and esteem of very short literary forms provides a new and positive context for understanding prose poetry and its scholarship.

William Nelles claims that "while such poetic forms as the sonnet, haiku and epigram have been recognized as prestigious genres, serious criticism of very short prose works [and we would add, prose poetry] has been slower to develop."[1] He believes this is because of "the stigmatization of the very short work," which he identifies as extending as far back as the ancient Greek philosopher Aristotle's statement that "Beauty is a matter of size and order, and therefore impossible . . . in a very minute creature . . . the longer the story, consistently with its being comprehensible as a whole, the finer it is by reason of its magnitude."[2] Although the stigma Nelles identifies has been attached more commonly to short forms of prose rather than to poetry, prose poetry's use of sentences and paragraphs may help explain its relative neglect. The mode of prose has often been understood to be less elevated than poetry.

We have argued that prose poetry gained legitimacy from Charles Simic's 1990 Pulitzer Prize for *The World Doesn't End*, while Claudia Rankine's awards and honors for *Citizen* renewed the attention given to hybrid works containing prose poetry. Similarly, the contemporary resurgence of short fiction and the rise of very short stories were given prominence in 2013. Lydia Davis won the Man Booker International Prize for a body of work featuring both microfiction and prose poetry, and Alice Munro, whose epiphanic short fiction employs literary strategies similar to those found in some prose poems, was awarded the Nobel Prize for Literature. Also in this year, George Saunders's collection of short stories *The Tenth of December* was published. It received the Folio Prize and the Story Prize.

Marc Botha writes, "the antecedents [for contemporary short literary forms] . . . include the aphorism, parable, fragment, digression, paradox, anecdote, joke, riddle, epigram, exemplum, emblem, myth, fable, tale, tableau, vignette, character, sketch, prose poem, miniature, and indeed, short story."[3] There have been various well-known examples of very short stories from the twentieth century, including Ernest Hemingway's *In Our Time* (1925), Jorge Luis Borges's *The Book of Imaginary Beings* (1969), and Franz Kafka's *Parables and Paradoxes* (1961).[4] Contemporary names for very short forms include, but are not limited to, microliterature, microfiction, flash fiction, sudden fiction, nanotales, palm-of-the-hand stories, SmokeLong, drabbles, and short-shorts. The differences between all of these forms of (mainly) fiction are often debated, and these debates often focus on the length of works.

The further distinction between the relatively broad categories of microfiction and prose poetry most often troubles writers and critics. In his discussion of short forms, Michel Delville cautions against any "attempt to distinguish between the prose poem and the recent 'new' genres of the 'short short story' or 'sudden fiction.'"[5] He provides examples of short writing that "can be assigned different hermeneutic priorities and read as a short short story or a prose poem."[6] However, while distinguishing between various forms of very short fiction may present legitimate difficulties, if we return to questions of literary form and genre, it is important to make a clear distinction between prose poetry and microfiction.

The most conspicuous difference between these kinds of writing is that prose poetry is a form of poetry and gives priority to poetic techniques and their effects, while microfiction and its counterparts (such as flash fiction) give priority to techniques traditionally associated with narrative prose. Compelling discussions of the short form began and remain in blogs such as Nancy Stohlman's, where she outlines differences between the two forms: "Prose poems . . . [rely] heavily on poetic devices such as heightened imagery and precision of language" and flash fiction makes use of "devices . . . such as story arc and tension."[7]

Similarly, in an interview with Michael Loveday on the website Page Chatter, Carrie Etter says that "successful flash fiction almost always has some semblance of a narrative arc, even if it's simply the protagonist facing a conflict and responding to it . . . whereas in prose poems any narrative is in the service of an overall idea that the poem circles or inhabits."[8] Additionally, prose poet Ian Seed makes an important distinction: "at the end of a piece of flash fiction you feel satisfied in some way, at the end of a prose poem you feel more like a dog barking at the shape of air: you still want a resolution."[9]

Many scholars and writers have argued that microfiction and prose poetry are flexible forms: Stohlman identifies this flexibility as being due to their "somewhat fluid . . . boundaries"; H. K. Hummel and Stephanie Lenox "define the short form as creative prose that relies on compression. It can be found in all genres, and it straddles the fence between genres as well"; and Botha emphasizes microfiction's suitability for "representing a wide range of subjects while remaining responsive to the shifting contexts of literary production and reception."[10]

The Very Short Form and Digital Platforms

The very short form takes the adage "less is more" as one of its defining tenets. The current resurgence and development of such forms partly reflect the teaching of creative writing in universities, where maxims such as "show don't tell" focus on being highly selective with words, paring back adjectives and adverbs and eliminating verbosity. The popularity of the very short form has been understood as a response to "the rise of digital media . . . [which] privileges short texts and inculcates 'hyper attention.'"[11]

Kyle Booten, with Sarah Warshauer Freedman and Glenda A. Hull, argue that "[w]hile microfiction exists outside of digital media, it has found a natural home in the context of digital platforms,"[12] largely due to its compactness and its easy consumption on digital devices. Similarly, one of the key proponents and anthologizers of very short fiction, Robert Shapard, also discusses its compactness and ability to fit onto small screens as an important reason behind the reinvigoration of the form. As it is highly portable and usually brings with it a fractured, compressed intensity, the very short form can be said to respond to the conditions of postmodernity.

These forms are suited to registering the disparate, the diverse, and the "broken" in contemporary society due to their fragmentary nature and the multivalency that often characterizes them. However, while prose poetry—in works by Gertrude Stein and Sherwood Anderson, for example—has been linked to discussions of early twentieth-century modernism, scholarship on the connection of prose poetry and microfiction to postmodernity is fairly scant. Michèle Roberts's introduction to Deborah Levy's *Black Vodka* is one example, in which she contends, "The short story form, in its brevity and condensation, fits our age" and is suited to "the short attention span of modern readers, the gaps and fragmentedness of modern consciousness."[13]

This comment about short attention spans raises some interesting questions. Highly condensed forms often make readers work hard to fill in textual gaps or absences and to interpret ambiguity, encouraging multiple readings of each work. Botha, invoking Nelles in his discussion, asks:

> Is the increasing prominence of microfiction as a contemporary literary genre indicative of the fact that even the short story cannot convey the speed and immediacy of contemporary life, and that only the extremities of narrative scale are able to communicate the relentless intensity of the present and future? If the short story is the genre of today, might the very short story—which is as comfortable on the screen as it is on the page . . . be the genre of tomorrow?[14]

Contemporary culture may require very short literary forms, including the prose poem, in order to speak more truthfully about the crises at the heart of postmodernity, which are often identified as centering on identity, the interpenetration and mixing of cultures, and the need to find authentic ways of speaking beyond the persistent noise of technology and the twenty-four-hour news cycle. Brigitte Byrd notes:

> We can be reached anywhere, at all times. We are expected to check our phone messages and emails daily, all day long. We all work, sometimes more than one job, manage our writing careers . . . and care for our families. We are constantly under pressure. We cannot stop writing. And there it is. Compact, controlled, melodic, polyphonic, lyric, heroic. The poem in a box. The prose poem.[15]

These are issues explored by Harryette Mullen, whose prose poems demonstrate her "interest in the collision of contemporary poetry with the language of advertising and marketing, the clash of fine art aesthetics with mass consumption and globalization, and the interaction of literacy and identity."[16] She describes *Trimmings* (1991) and *S*PeRM**K*T* (1993) as "serial prose poems that use playful, punning and fragmented language to explore sexuality, femininity and domesticity."[17] Where Gertrude Stein's poetry responds to the crisis of modernity, Mullen's prose poetry joins with Stein's "meditation on the interior lives of women and the material culture of domesticity" while also being a response to postmodern culture and consumption.[18]

Prose Poetry and Contemporary Culture

Prose poetry challenges assumptions about what may be "said" in writing. It questions whether a good deal of human experience in the twenty-first century—whether in America, Europe, or Asia—is likely to be best expressed through the creation of hybrid and fragmented literary forms reflecting the intercultural meshing taking place in many modern nations, and the accompanying breakdown or destabilization of previous norms. If cultures are to some extent hybrid, their literature—and language use more generally—tend to reflect this reality. If most people's subjective experiences are characterized by considerable fragmentation, their writing and art will often possess such characteristics.

Prose poetry enables the intense expression of many things at once—dislocation, the multivalent, the intimate or lyrical gesture, the indeterminate, and a limited narrative discursiveness—and signals that the "prosaic" and the "poetic" are frequently bound together. Therefore, prose poetry is able to encompass very diverse expressions of the crammed and sometimes clashing nature of contemporary experience, much of which is unsuited to traditional literary forms. Prose poetry also partakes of postmodernism's tendency—as Marjorie Perloff writes of Andreas Huyssen's analysis in *After the Great Divide* (1986)—to break down "the Modernist 'frontier' between high art and mass culture."[19] This, in turn, relates to what Gerry LaFemina terms the "schism between elitist language of poetry and the more urbane realm of prose."[20]

Prose poetry is often characterized by what Clements and Dunham argue is an ability to "take . . . on the structural conventions of other discourses"—a feature common to many postmodern poetries.[21] We discussed prose poetry's capacity for camouflage in chapter 4, pointing out that, on a first encounter, the prose poem looks like one or more standard paragraphs of prose fiction but reads like a poem. While this can be interpreted as a kind of subversion, in the light of the contemporary prose poem's connection to postmodernity, it has now become important to move beyond Simic's assertion that the prose poem "must remain a pariah and an object of ridicule to survive," and also to leave behind any assertion that the form is in some way, as Andrew Zawacki states, a "schizophrenic genre."[22]

Robert Vas Dias discusses the implicit connection between prose poetry and postmodernism when he states: "Concepts such as the non-linear, non-hierarchical development of the poem/prose poem, a preference for open-ended writing rather than an obvious closure, the use of counter-expectation or absurd, subversive propositions, and a dissociative, discontinuous structure, all are characteristic of much contemporary and post-modernist prose poetry."[23]

An example of a writer who fits Vas Dias's characterization is Amy Gerstler, who has been identified as a "quintessentially postmodern poet" for her "use of the prose poem, the abundance of surreal imagery in her poetry, her compression of language . . . and her work involving comic re-vision of American popular culture."[24] In "The True Bride," Gerstler critiques conventional gender roles in a parody of the Grimms' fairy tale of the same name, while "mingling it with memories of *The Fall of the House of Usher*, *The Blithedale Romance*, *Psycho* and *The Collector*."[25]

Gerstler's titular prose poem in this collection is voiced by the bride's fetishistic husband who loves his wife's infirmness and disability, for the way it makes her eternally passive:

> Elaine sleeps most of the day. She's the prettiest invalid I've ever seen, and I collect them. Her name means *illumination*, which I think refers to her skin: luminous and unused as a newborn's. Her breath smells lofty as an attic with cedar beam ceiling, ancient papers, forgotten bottles that once held medicine or scent. Limp Raggedy Ann dolls, and old bath toys.
>
> I've always been attracted to crippled women. I'm convinced that if they were pruned in early girlhood, the beauty of what survives (face, neck, hands) is intensified. My potted palm grows greener and puts forth new shoots after I nip off a few ailing fronds.
>
> Elaine's legs are all that's wrong with her. Her mother was rushed one day when Elaine was three, and prepared her salad carelessly. Germs on the unwashed romaine lettuce gave Elaine polio. Earmarked her for me.[26]

It is clear from this work's focus on what Terence Diggory identifies as the "chaotic inner-contemporary life" that the narrator is deranged.[27] In his mind, his wife exists only in his creation of her, and the question of whether she is merely one of his dark fantasies is implied—not unlike the postmodern novel *American Psycho* (1991). Indeed, the husband in "The True Bride" controls his wife within the prose poem's bounds in a manner that disturbingly "evokes the weirdness and smarts of the Western metropolis toward century's end."[28] It is what is hidden or implied in this prose poem, as much as its voicing, that makes it postmodern.

This prose poem contains many of the features Vas Dias identifies, especially at its conclusion where the husband fantasizes about "An army of true brides like her, hobbling women, are crossing a desert. The sand is yellow. They limp and crawl over the dunes."[29] This ending is dissociative, subversive, almost parodic, and lacks closure, making the reader work to interpret the implications of the husband's words. The focus on and fetishization of body parts emphasizes the fragmentary nature of both the prose poem and postmodernism, and the uneasily emancipatory quality of incompleteness. Identifying Gerstler's prose poems as postmodern, Rise B. Axelrod and Steven Gould Axelrod argue, "In images and sentences that speak to each other at odd angles, and in common cultural motifs set awry, Gerstler's texts evoke pairings that are inimical, furious, doomed, or ambiguous."[30]

Similarly, in Evie Shockley's "my life as china" (2011), the fragmentation of the work and the condition it evokes are signaled by the use of sets of double colons. Where Gerstler's "The True Bride" provides a "discontinuous, disenchanted discourse of marriage,"[31] Shockley's use of double colons both links and separates the phrases and clauses with squares of space, demarcated by four dots. The prose poem turns on the conceit of the African American woman's experience as a piece of china—and the use and repetition of the lowercase "i" deconstructs and diminishes the first-person pronoun, until the capitalized "I" appears in the penultimate line:

> i was imported : : i was soft in the hills where they found me : : shining in a private dark : : i absorbed fire and became fact : : i was fragile : : i incorporated burnt cattle bones' powdered remains : : ashes to ashes : : i was baptized in heat : : fed on destruction : : i was not destroyer : : was not destroyed : : i vitrified : : none of me was the same : : i was many : : how can i say this : : i was domesticated : : trusted : : treasured : : i was translucent but not clear : : put me to your lips : : I will not give : : I will give you what you have given me[32]

Clarissa Richee observes, "The poem begins with the importing of the material as a direct allusion to the importing of Africans to America; it then continues through the violent steps of being crushed, burned, and reformed into something new."[33] As these fragments reimagine African American women's history and experiences, they become a metaphor for broken identity. Yet strength is demonstrated by the china's resilience, and by the repetition of the word "will" as the prose poem finally moves into the future tense. This block of text, tattooed with colons, provides robustness in its shape and a forceful compression, concluding with (somewhat ambiguous) tropes of resolution and hopefulness.

Similarly, both Nin Andrews and Brenda Iijima use the prose poem as a vehicle for the exploration of a range of important political views. In their books, the block of text becomes a powerful visual statement of strength and unity. Andrews's *Miss August* (2017) tackles racism and issues of sexual identity and mental illness. Set in the late 1950s and early 1960s in Chinquapin Hill Farm in Lessington, Virginia, Andrews explores Jim Crow laws enforcing racial segregation. The book is narrated by three characters and offers multiple and alternating perspectives. The following excerpt is narrated by Gil Simmons:

> Sarah Jane used to tell me things about slavery that I didn't learn from school or my folks. She talked in a whisper even when the door was closed. She said her neighbor, Miss Alice, told her that if a slave tried to run away, he could be beaten or even lynched. She said Miss Alice once saw buzzards circling before she saw a colored man, hanging from a tree limb, left there for the birds to eat. When I asked my daddy if that was so, he asked, *Who have you been talking to?* Then he paused and added, *There have always been bad folks, Gil. But the South is a refined culture where people take care of each other, no matter who they are and how they fit into society. Coloreds included.*[34]

Brenda Iijima's chapbook, *Some Simple Things Said by and about Humans* (2014), contains poems about animal welfare. "White Tigers," for instance, exposes captive inbreeding of the rare animals:

At the Cincinnati Zoo, formerly "the world's leading purveyor of white Tigers" over 70 white Tigers have been born Zoo officials sold Tigers for $60,000 a piece The 1980's were the years of peak production/mating White Tiger mill? Proliferation? Psychology of the white Tiger stuffed Animal as it poses for the *Uniqlo* commercial.[35]

Iijima's "Dolly the Sheep" uses three boxes to discuss cloning and begins:

Museum of Scotland

Dolly|DOLLY© Dolly|DOLLY© Dolly |DOLLY© Dolly |DOLLY©
Dolly|DOLLY© Dolly|DOLLY© Dolly |DOLLY© Dolly |DOLLY©[36]

Additionally, there are works of prose poetry that explore the possibilities of the prose poem as literary nonfiction, such as Prageeta Sharma's *Grief Sequence* (2019) and Charles Barde's *Diary of Our Fatal Illness* (2017), exploring the loss of a loved one; Dan Beachy-Quick's *Of Silence and Song* (2017), interrogating midlife crisis; Nancy Lagomarsino's *Light from an Eclipse*, observing her father's Alzheimer's disease (2005); Kate Schmitt's *Singing Bones* (2014), examining depression; and Allison Benis White's *Small Porcelain Head* (2013), grappling with her friend's suicide.

In such ways, prose poetry can advocate for truly complex and fluid ideas connected to society, politics, race, gender, and sexuality. The employment of prose poetry's often tight margins, combined with the flexibility and adaptability of the prose poem form, may even be said to encourage critiques of and emancipation from the stricter or more straitening societal structures and boundaries that have traditionally governed and even oppressed individual and cultural identity. Perhaps, in this sense at least, prose poetry remains a subversive literary form, challenging stereotypes and opening up new modes and manners of discourse.

Prose Poetry, Consumerism, and the Right Names

As we have stated, the differences between prose poetry and other very short literary forms is widely debated. Alan Ziegler comments, "Emotions can run high regarding nomenclature [as applied to short literary forms]; the claim implicit in a name may raise the hackles and bring out the shackles"[37]—and yet, some writers, editors, and publishers use prose poetry and microfiction (and any of its variations) more or less interchangeably.

There are many collections that couple these forms together, such as Ziegler's *Short: An International Anthology of Five Centuries of Short-Short Stories, Prose Poems, Brief Essays, and Other Short Prose Forms* (2014), R.E.N. Allen and Grant Loewen's *Prose Poems and Sudden Fictions* (2006), and Liesl Jobson's *100 Papers: A Collection of Prose Poems and Flash Fiction* (2008). Spineless Wonders, an Australian publisher which specializes in the short form, lets the reader decide whether they are reading microfiction or prose poetry by labeling their anthologies "microlit"—a term they argue encompasses all very short forms, including prose poetry and microfiction. They give no indication of the category into which each of the works they publish falls, other than stipulating a limit of two hundred words for all inclusions.

Rachel Barenblat comments on the similar appearance of very short forms on the page or screen: "Prose poems, microfiction, 'short-short' stories: regardless of what you call them, these [are] small (usually), blocky (sometimes), paragraph-style pieces of writing."[38] While she argues that "[t]he line between the prose poem and the short-short is invisible, if not non-existent,"[39] she undercuts this statement by characterizing these forms differently. She refers to the experience of many writers who believe they have written a prose poem, only to have it published in a journal or anthology as microfiction, or vice versa. This is also noted by Ziegler, who mentions the example of Jayne Anne Phillips's piece "Happy," which was initially published as a prose poem in the *Paris Review* and then republished in a collection of her short stories.[40] Similarly, while some scholars refer to Elizabeth Bishop's "The Hanging of the Mouse" as poetry or prose poetry, others label it a story, tale, or even an "animal fabliaux."[41]

Despite such confusions, as prose poetry has grown in popularity it has become more easily identified by writers, editors, and publishers. In an interview in *The Double Room: A Journal of Prose Poetry and Flash Fiction*, Denise Duhamel states:

> the difference (for me) between the forms is the psychological approach I adopt to the method of composition in either case. . . . I feel it is important for a writer to articulate and/or define forms—even if the end result remains inconclusive. The more we attempt to define and articulate, the more we clarify and discover our own aesthetic sensibilities and compositional practices.[42]

Moreover, the majority of journals ask writers to make decisions about the appropriate category for their writing by requiring them to submit to either a fiction or poetry editor, or via an online portal that separates poetry from fiction. In this way, anthologies or journals that publish varieties of very short fiction tend to be relatively homogeneous in ways collections combining prose poetry and short fiction are not.

For instance, in *Landmarks: An Anthology of Microlit* (2017), Danielle Wood's "Hare" is situated close to Chloe Wilson's "Arm's Length." There is no information about which work is microfiction and which is prose poetry—although an excerpt from Wood's demonstrates it is a piece of short fiction due to its narrative drive:

> It's New Year's Day and resolve hangs in the air alongside the tinderbox threat of bushfire. Circling the home paddock on the mower, she watches the falling

shafts of grass, thistle, caltrop, boneseed. Then: look! A hare! A wire-sprung twist of fur and fright, zigzagging for the fence line![43]

Wilson's piece turns on wordplay rather than a narrative arc. There is action in this prose poem but its momentum is conveyed poetically through the use of repetition and metaphor. Interestingly, unlike some American prose poems that present dialogue in more conventional ways, Wilson italicizes her dialogue so she doesn't break the rhythm or sunder this prose poem's box. It begins:

> They said *keep that boy at arm's length*. But whose arm? The arm of an orang-utan, or a tyrannosaurus rex? A rat's arm? A baby's arm? A spider's arm—and if so, which one of the eight should she measure? *Your arm*, they said. So she took a saw and severed her arm at the shoulder.[44]

Similarly, Robert Alexander's *Richmond Burning* (2017) contains a selection of short works including prose poems and flash fiction. For Alexander, the labeling of short works into specific genres, forms, or modes is unimportant, so the book is committed to showcasing a variety of short forms that the reader can choose to identify, or not. Alexander's "September" and "Like Our Shadow-Selves" are examples of two different short forms. "September" is a prose poem eschewing a strong narrative trajectory in order to focus on kingfishers. It circles around a series of images:

> Last day of the summer, the sky clear after weeks of rain, a slight breeze tapers to calm. Late morning sun through the leaves, a pair of kingfishers arc from tree to tree along the shoreline, purple aster and joe-pye weed, mountain ash with its ripe red berries. In the bayou there's a single water-lily, pure as any lotus-blossom, a couple of small flies feeding on its petals—then off to the side a splash, the kingfisher rises to a branch, minnow in its beak.[45]

"Like Our Shadow-Selves" is a longer, more narrative-driven piece of flash fiction:

> It was the summer the Corps of Engineers were rebuilding the harbor break-wall, after a lapse of half a century, and the beavers were building a new lodge inland at Sable lake. Each morning, if I arrived early enough, I'd see the male or sometimes the female with her yearling, nibbling small branches along the shore in the early morning light—but on days I was a little late, and they'd already, being nocturnal creatures, gone to bed, I'd take a closer look at the progress they'd made on their low mud-daubed hut.[46]

These examples confirm that prose poetry and very short forms of fiction are usually identifiable and fairly easily distinguishable. Nevertheless, many readers of very short forms enjoy all varieties and are not necessarily interested in the finer points of nomenclature or genre. As a result, when writers or enthusiastic readers become involved in labeling writing, this labeling may become blurred or skewed. This may be because they wish to maximize their readership, or because they don't care much about nomenclature, or because they don't know any better. The following analysis of very short forms on digital platforms illustrates the point:

> Tumblr users tend to use tags to describe the genre of their posts. Generally, however, they do not use tags in mutually exclusive ways. Just because a text is a story does not mean it cannot also be poetry. Out of 2,000 ten word story microworks, 47 percent were also tagged as "poetry" or "poem." (Variations on "prose poem," however, were relatively rare, occurring only 14 times).[47]

In online tags, the term "prose poem" still struggles for currency in the face of the more familiar terms "fiction" and "poetry." This, in turn, influences the reception of work because, like some readers, writers do not always classify their writing according to the most identifiable features of the literary forms they employ. A looseness of categorization is also often apparent in self-published books, many of them available online. Lehman suggested in 2003 that "a practical way of proceeding is to make a division between work that the writer conceives as fiction and work that is conceived as poetry. Writers are under no obligation to classify their writing for us. But their intentions, if articulate, could be thought decisive."[48]

Prior to the current information age, writers could (and did) comment on their work publicly. Nomenclature and labeling—whether by publishers or writers—was important, not least because writers' intentions have, to a significant extent, always been gauged by paratextual indexes. However, with the advent of various forms of social media—and of the internet more generally—individual writers have the capacity to actively jostle for media attention, and many authors are encouraged by their publishers to establish an active online profile to help promote their books.

In this context, discrepancies, idiosyncracies, or inconsistencies in labeling works by an agent, editor, publisher, or author may have a significant impact in the identification of a book's form. In discussing prose poetry, Murphy observes: "Such features as title and subtitle, preface and preamble, help us to recognize a text as a prose poem as well as the typographical presentation of the text on the page, and the fact of its inclusion in a volume marked as 'poetry' or 'poems.' To consider authorial intention is here unavoidable as these indices designate the author's conscious choice of genre."[49]

However, Amy Balog's *The Mirror that Lied (A Prose Poem)* (2017) is a good example of how an author's or publisher's indication of their "choice of genre" may not always be reliable.[50] The book begins with what one might possibly define as part of a prose poem. However, the work continues with a fairly standard fictional narrative that does not employ any obvious poetic techniques or devices. While the writer or publisher clearly intends to market this work as a prose poem, this labeling sets up readerly expectations that the work does not fully meet. And even some anthologists define the term "prose poetry" in ways that make it hard to identify any significant difference between various forms of poetic prose and prose poetry as a distinct literary form. Ziegler comments on the problems associated with inaccurate or loose naming of works when he says, "One advantage of not designating a genre—or of using a nondescript term like *paragraph*, *piece*, or *text*—[is that] . . . [e]ach piece makes a *prima facie* case for itself, with no room for rebuttal based on merely formal expectations."[51]

However, Ziegler's suggestion may be impractical because of the connection between the categorization of a literary work and many marketing (and purchasing) decisions—with labels, categories, and keywords used as a way to connect books to their projected target audiences. Publishers usually reserve the right to label books in the manner they believe provides them with the best chance of sales and/or publicity, and this labeling may also sometimes be partly dictated by the way in which booksellers shelve their titles, or by the search engines and their keywords provided by online stores. For example, on Tupelo Press's website, Christopher Merrill's book *Boat* (2013) is identified from a search on the term "prose poems," and the form is also highlighted in the quotation from a book review cited in its description: "The poems assume forms as diverse as traditional narrative and prose poems as well as translations."[52]

Without identifiers, or with the wrong ones, a book may be consigned to obscurity (even the Dewey decimal system—still the most widely used method for organizing books in libraries—relies on accurate information in order to classify books). Labels can also restrict the accessibility of books in other ways too. For instance, publications that straddle genres or contain multiple literary forms may have trouble finding their right place in the market. Kristina Marie Darling, in her conversation with Joshua Edwards of Canarium Books, states, "The channels of distribution for literary texts—ie, the ways we buy, sell, promote, and categorize books—assume that there is a clear boundary between genres,"[53] which is not usually the case with experimental and hybrid texts. Thus, while labels and keywords assist readers in identifying their literary preferences, they may not always serve unorthodox works well.

Publisher Shane Strange claims that where the very short form is concerned, "the identification of texts as 'prose poetry' or 'micro-fiction' seems arbitrary or the result of forces beyond formal consideration, and yet these formal identifiers persist, are negotiated and fought over. This, I should say, is not necessarily an unwelcome position. If anything it tells us about the effects of the critical gaze in understanding/co-opting/reifying formal innovation. . . . Or, it tells us that however liberating or innovative the form might appear . . . it never really escapes the reach of formal consideration, no matter how the practitioner sees it."[54]

We argue that nomenclature and labeling matters a great deal, and it is important for prose poetry—as a very short literary form among numerous other very short forms—to be recognized and categorized as poetry (or, preferably, "prose poetry") rather than fiction, not least because readers approach these forms in different ways. As online shopping and reading sites continue to grow in sophistication, readers will increasingly be able to search precisely for specific forms of writing, allowing many hybrid and experimental forms to be named for what they are, while being linked to the broad "genre" category that is closest to the work. Indeed, with the vast amount of creative writing online, or available through online booksellers, accurate labeling is perhaps the primary way of ensuring that contemporary writers have the best possible chance of finding sympathetic readers.

Shape-Shifting Prose Poetry

Considerations of the prose poem's boxed or rectangular shape—however fruitful—sometimes overshadow discussions of its other formal features. As scholars and poets have grappled with definitions of the prose poem, often using metaphors to try and pin down or elucidate its characteristics, they do not always remark on its various shapes and styles. Yet prose poetry lends itself to operating at the borders of its own form. It is inherently protean, although appearing contained, and tends to shift and adapt to accommodate diverse writerly needs—to the extent that some prose poems appear anomalous. General examples of such "anomalies" include those prose poems that use line breaks (discussed in chapter 4), long prose poems, prose poems that radically minimize or maximize their margins, and works that mix prose poetry with other kinds of writing—often with discursive prose.

Some of the most nuanced discussions of prose poetry's relationship with prose are contained in introductions to a number of prose poetry anthologies. In the introduction to *Models of the Universe* (1995), David Young states, "the distilling and mimicking of the normal behavior of prose allows prose poems to offer us life stories reduced to paragraphs, essays the size of postcards, novels in nutshells, maps on postage stamps, mind-bending laundry lists, theologies scribbled on napkins."[55] In *An Introduction to the Prose Poem* (2009), Clements and Dunham break their anthology into twenty-four "varieties of the prose poem"—although the boundaries between these different sorts of works are sometimes fluid—and in *Great American Prose Poems*, David Lehman also identifies different kinds of prose poetry:

> There are prose poems in the form of journal entries (Harry Matthews's *20 Lines a Day*), radically foreshortened fictions (Lydia Davis's "In the Garment District"), a fan letter (Amy Gerstler's "Dear Boy George"), a rant (Gabriel Gudding's "Defense of Poetry"), a linguistic stunt (Fran Carlen's "Anal Nap," in which only one vowel is used), an essay (Fanny Howe's "Doubt"), a political parable (Carolyn Fourche's "The Colonel"), and other inventions . . . Mark Strand's "Chekhov: A Sestina" demonstrates that prose can accommodate the

intricacies of that verse form, just as "Woods" in Emerson's journals can serve as a "prose sonnet."[56]

Furthermore, Robert Alexander, Mark Vinz, and C. W. Truesdale, in selecting prose poems for *The Party Train: A Collection of North American Prose Poetry*, identify "some of the following kinds of prose poem: The Object Poem; The Surreal Narrative; The 'Straight' Narrative; The 'Character' Poem; The Landscape or Place Poem; The Meditative Poem; The 'Hyperbolic' or 'Exaggerated' Poem."[57]

In other words, individual prose poems manifest in a great diversity of ways and may also be combined with other literary forms to create hybrid works. Beckel states that the prose poem, "with its shameless, joyful borrowing of craft and conceits from other types of poetry, other genres, and even everyday language encounters like letters, emails, conversations, lists, and questionnaires, makes it particularly well suited to techniques such as epistolary and ekphrastic writing."[58]

As prose poetry uses the sentence and paragraph, it most often draws on prosaic modes and more everyday forms. The epistle or letter is one quotidian form prose poets have often used. While epistolary verse dates back to ancient Greece and Rome with, for example, Horace's *Epistles* and Ovid's *Heroides*, the epistolary prose poem can be traced to the fictional letter form in eighteenth-century France and, to some extent, to epistolary novels such as Aphra Behn's *Love-Letters Between a Noble-Man and His Sister* (1684–87) and Samuel Richardson's *Pamela* (1740) and *Clarissa* (1747–48), among other works. As Julia K. De Pree argues, "The epistolary qualities of brevity, open-endedness, and fragmentation establish a link between the fictitious letter and the prose poem. As the vehicle of lyricism during the French Enlightenment, the letter may be read not only as a textual 'ancestor' of the prose poem, but as a kind of prose poem in its own right."[59]

As the epistolary prose poem has proliferated, questions that once occupied readers and scholars about whether they are encountering "real" or "fictional" letters, and whether these are actually poems, are now rarely considered. This is evident in Alice Jones's discussion of her epistolary prose poem, "Reply" where she states: "The epistolary form felt apt, given the prose poem's block of text is just the right size to fit on the back of a postcard. And after Emily Dickinson's 'Letter to the world,' isn't every poem a letter from writer to reader? This poem takes that imaginary reach across a gap and makes the letter real."[60]

Contemporary examples of epistolary prose poems, ranging across both fiction and nonfiction, include E. Ethelbert Miller's series, "The Fictional Letters of Don Millo Written to the Colored Poet Micky at the end of the 20th Century," which begins, "Dear Micky, I got the real dope. I'm going with this new book—no film offers yet";[61] Amy Newman's witty prose poems in *Dear Editor: Poems* (2011), where most prose poems begin, "Dear Editor: Please consider the enclosed poems for publication"; Susan Briante's six open letters in *Utopia Minus* (2012), written to people such as the president of the United States and Eileen Myles; Julia Bloch's

Letters to Kelly Clarkson (2012), which are addressed to the *American Idol* star and explore the emptiness of celebrity and the female body as spectacle; Sugar Magnolia Wilson's historical "Dear Sister" series; Bernadette Mayer's celebrated *The Desires of Mothers to Please Others in Letters* (1994), which documents her third pregnancy; and Laynie Browne's homage to Mayer's book *The Desires of Letters* (2010), which continues the conversation about writing and mothering.[62]

In these epistolary prose poems, the opening address to someone other than the reader, coupled with the lack of response from the addressee, makes reading these poems a complex experience. De Pree writes, "This complexity has to do with the attempt to create presence on the page while simultaneously affirming a separation in time and space."[63] The epistolary prose poem with its compressed TimeSpace and awareness of accompanying gaps and spaces intensifies the reading experience. In addition to this, the letter form easily hides the prose poem in its sentences and paragraphs. As Kathleen McGookey argues of her own epistolary prose poem "Ordinary Objects, Extraordinary Emotions," "When a reader expects one thing (a straightforward rejection letter) and the prose poem delivers something oddly different . . . a little chill runs down my spine."[64]

Lydia Davis's "Letter to a Funeral Parlor" (2013) is an excellent example of an epistolary prose poem. It begins:

Dear Sir,
   I am writing to you to object to the word *cremains*, which was used by your representative when he met with my mother and me two days after my father's death.

And ends:

   At first we did not even know what he meant. Then, when we realized, we were frankly upset. *Cremains* sounds like something invented as a milk substitute in coffee, like Cremora, or Coffee-mate. Or it sounds like some kind of a chipped beef dish. . . .

   There is nothing wrong with inventing words, especially in a business. But a grieving family is not prepared for this one. We are not even used to our loved one being gone. You could very well continue to employ the term *ashes*. We are used to it from the Bible, and are even comforted by it. We would not misunderstand. We would know that these ashes are not like the ashes in a fireplace.

   Yours sincerely.[65]

This prose poem's language is rhythmic and the work turns on various kinds of verbal play. It concludes in an open-ended fashion with a rumination on the denotative and connotative associations of the word "ashes." Davis is a writer who has responded publicly to the classifying and labeling of her work:

When I first began writing seriously, I wrote short stories, and that was where I thought I was headed. Then the stories evolved and changed, but it would have become a bother to say every time, "I guess what I have just written is a prose poem, or a meditation," and I would have felt very constrained by trying to label each individual work, so it was simply easier to call everything stories.[66]

However, the title *The Collected Stories of Lydia Davis* (2013) is to some extent challenged when readers encounter the prose poems in this book and, more generally, the title has generated discussion about the appropriate classification for different short forms of literature.

If Davis's book is called fiction by its author and publishers, Claudia Rankine's poetry books often defy categorization. Many are hybrid works that contain prose poetry, and they destabilize readerly expectation. For instance, Ira Sadoff makes the point that while *Don't Let Me Be Lonely* is "mysteriously call[ed] a poem/essay" by her publisher, it is "[o]ne of the most adventurous, ambitious and uncategorizable uses of the prose poem form."[67] Likewise, her *Citizen: An American Lyric* (2014) was a somewhat contentious winner of the Forward Prize for poetry because it contains so much prose—along with poetry and prose poetry. Other poets working in ways that may challenge readers' assumptions about the boundaries between prose, lineated poetry, and prose poetry include Kimiko Hahn, Lyn Hejinian, Leslie Scalapino, Barry Silesky, and Rosmarie Waldrop, all of whom John Bradley identifies as "innovators who experiment with form, as well as content . . . blurring the lines between poetry and prose and essay and drama and almost every genre you can think of, [and] like it or not, are opening up new territory for the prose poem."[68]

We would add other authors who make use of mixed poetic forms or hybrid works partly composed of prose poetry,[69] including Diane Williams (*Vicky Swanky Is a Beauty*, 2012), Anne Boyer (*Garments Against Women*, 2015), Laynie Browne (*The Scented Fox*, 2007), Amy Sara Carroll (*Fannie + Freddie: The Sentimentality of Post-9/11 Pornography*, 2013), Tania Hershman (*Nothing Here Is Wild, Everything Is Open*, 2016), Maria Jastrzebska (*The True Story of Cowboy Hat and Ingénue*, 2018), and Meghan Privitello (*A New Language for Falling Out of Love*, 2014). A variety of other books are also worth noting for their unusual or idiosyncratic approaches to articulating concepts of identity and self in mixed poetic forms, including prose poetry: Mary Jean Chan's *Flèche* (2019), Sarah Howe's *Loop of Jade* (2015), Khadijah Queen's *I'm So Fine: A List of Famous Men & What I Had On* (2013), Sabrina Orah Mark's *The Babies* (2004), Barbara Tran's *In the Mynah Bird's Own Words* (2002), Ocean Vuong's *Night Sky with Exit Wounds* (2017), Jenny Xie's *Eye Level* (2018), and Karen An-hwei Lee's *In Medias Res* (2004) and *Ardor* (2008).

These books are often hybrid in their use of images, essays, fragments, marginalia, or sections of prose and odes, all of which are variously juxtaposed with works of prose poetry. Zarah Butcher-McGunnigle's *Autobiography of a Marguerite* (2014) is described as a "book-length poem" on its dust jacket, yet it is an unusual volume. The first thirty-nine pages are series of connected prose poems, some fully justified and some with a ragged right margin. This gives way to works composed largely of a series of single and double lines, with footnotes incorporated into each work. The final section returns to a series of prose poems of an ekphrastic nature, coupled with color photographs. The book as a whole may also be read as a form of creative nonfiction, based on the author's autoimmune illness.

Abigail Zimmer's chapbook, *Child in a Winter House Brightening* (2016), is described by the publisher as a "hybrid long poem" and contains some prose poems that feature a forward slash between phrases and clauses, trying to make a virtue of both line breaks and the paragraph form:

> Inside a pail of water freezes / the child holds a pail of water / cracks the ice which flies across / the house the swan in flight / now knows to feather out and up / the holding flies inside the child.[70]

This technique is not unique to Zimmer. A range of prose poets have employed the forward slash in their prose poetry, including Ocean Vuong (as we discussed in chapter 4) and Donte Collins in "Whiteness Shops for a Prayer."[71]

Mariko Nagai's *Irradiated Cities* (2017) juxtaposes the author's photographs of Hiroshima, Nagasaki, Tokyo, and Fukushima with prose poems using colons as a poetic device, a technique also employed in Evie Shockley's "my life as china" (discussed earlier in this chapter). These colons begin and end every one of Nagai's prose poems and are also scattered throughout her works. Most importantly, the book ends on two colons—a final moment of open-endedness connecting what is to come with what has already been:

> : how long until we run out of notes in the music? : here, in Fukushima, there is no *after* : there is no *after* and *everafter* in this land of the fortune, in this land by the sea, in the land of the displaced : not yet : maybe not for a very long time : it has been a year : it has been two years : it has been four years : it has been five years : we are still in the *before* the *after* : *before* the *before* the *after* ::[72]

Linda Black's *Inventory* (2008), Oz Hardwick's *An Eschatological Bestiary* (2013), Jacqueline Saphra and Mark Andrew Webber's *If I Lay on My Back I Saw Nothing but Naked Women* (2014), Hilda Sheehan's *Frances and Martine* (2014), Jessica Singh's *When Love Lived Alone* (2017), and Bella Li's *Argosy* (2017) and *Lost Lake* (2018) are examples of prose poetry books that include illustrations or artwork. These works sometimes make it difficult for the reader to immediately identify them (in visual terms) as prose poems, or they require the reader to integrate their "reading" of visual art with their reading of prose poetry. More generally, because in a hybrid work the prose poem is only a part of the work's content, the reader's capacity to identify all of the literary (and visual) forms at play is an important part of the work's full appreciation. Hybrid works intensify and complicate the reading experience, and in many such cases the prose poem could be said to be hiding in plain sight, among fragments, more discursive prose and images.

Another variation on the prose poem form is the prose poetry sequence. These have been written since the nineteenth century—Arthur Rimbaud's *A Season in Hell* is one of the earliest, most idiosyncratic, and most influential examples. Sequences have played a significant part in the development of the form because they have been a way of exploiting various effects that are able to be achieved through juxtaposing linked (or disparate) prose poems—sometimes creating mosaiclike effects. Allen Upward's sequence "Scented Leaves—From a Chinese Jar," an example of poetic chinoiserie first published in 1913, is one of the best known of the early modernist sequences in English—although it is not entirely prose poetry, as it also contains lineated poems.[73]

Many long prose poetry works are divided into sections that allow their individual parts to have a degree of autonomy while contributing to the whole. William Carlos Williams's *Kora in Hell: Improvisations* (1957) and Anne Carson's *The Albertine Workout* (2014) are broken into sequences and, as we discussed in chapter 9, Lyn Hejinian's *My Life and My Life in the Nineties* (2013) has a line structure that corresponds with the poet's age at the time of writing—indicating the way longer prose poems are so frequently constructed from a series of smaller sections or parts.

In the last three decades, the range of popular examples of extended and book-length sequences includes: "Lake," in Andre Bagoo's *Pitch Lake* (2018); Joe Bonomo, *Installations* (2008); Suzanne Buffam's *A Pillow Book* (2016); many of Anne Carson's works, including *Short Talks* (1992);[74] Dionne Brand, *The Blue Clerk: Ars Poetica in 59 Versos* (2018); Emma Glass's *Peach* (2018); Paul Hetherington's *Palace of Memory* (2019); Jeff Hilson's *Bird bird* (2009); Lily Hoang's *Changing* (2008); Peter Johnson's *Love Poems for the Millennium* (1998); Harryette Mullen's *Recyclopedia: Trimmings, S*PeRM**K*T, and Muse & Drudge* (2009); Maggie Nelson's *Bluets* (2009); Brynne Rebele-Henry's *Autobiography of a Wound* (2018); Prageeta Sharma's *Grief Sequence* (2019); Donna Stonecipher's *Transaction Cities* (2018); Alison Strub's *Lillian, Fred* (2016); Anne Waldman's *Voice's Daughter of a Heart Yet to Be Born* (2016); Rosmarie Waldrop's *The Reproduction of Profiles* (1987); C. D. Wright's *Deepstep Come Shining* (1998); Ania Walwicz's *Palace of Culture* (2014) and *Horse* (2018); and Andrew Zawacki's *Masquerade* (2001).[75]

Maureen Seaton has described velocity in the prose poem sequence as very fast but with abrupt pauses: "Some of my prose poems feel fast, like strapping myself into a roller coaster and riding it all the way down, left to right, top to bottom, until the wild mouse crashed into the final image. Or like driving my imaginary friend, my Nissan Skyline GT-R, on Route 40 through New Mexico. I loved the way that felt. Opening a vein. Baffling the radar. I also loved stopping (like at the top of a Ferris wheel), taking a breath while balancing mid-air, then off I'd go again: poems with several prose stanzas, boxes on boxes filled with jetsam and doubloons."[76]

Composed of "two interlocking sequences," Carrie Etter's *Imagined Sons* (2014) "presents ten 'Catechisms,' modified from the familiar religious lessons, and 38 prose poems in which a speaker (designated 'Birthmother' and identifiable with the poet only via extratextual knowledge) imagines meeting, or almost meeting, the son she gave up for adoption at birth, some eighteen years later."[77] The catechism sequence is lineated and functions like a Greek chorus in its structure, while the longer "Imagined Sons" sequence is composed of elegiac and often dreamlike prose poems. The prose poem form and use of a prose poetry sequence works to simultaneously compress time and signal its passing. In "Imagined Sons 5: Reunion," set in Etter's birthplace of Normal, Illinois, the narrator returns to her high school and nothing appears to have changed, apart from the important and haunting addition of her imagined son in this frame, who shames her along with her peers:

> I walk into my old high school and run a hand over the lockers as I try to remember which was mine. Turning a corner, I see a classmate, Mark, somehow appearing just as he did at seventeen. As I approach, he mutters, "Slut," and stepping into the stairwell I see a gauntlet of old classmates lined up to greet me thus. I hurry down, cringing, and see one face I don't recognise at first.
>
> It's you, grown to the age I was when I gave you up. Your hands clench, your face flushes as you chant, louder than the others, *"Whore, whore, whore."*[78]

Vahni Capildeo's *Measures of Expatriation* (2016) won the Forward Prize for Best Collection, the Poetry Books Society Choice award, and was shortlisted for the T. S. Eliot Prize, all in 2016. It comprises lineated poems, prose, and prose poems. In "All Your Houses: Notebook Including a Return," Capildeo creates a polysemous hybrid sequence in sixteen parts:

> XI
>
> My mother's family comes from the East: from the East of Trinidad: Sangre Grande. The source of stories of fear and of pragmatism shifts the mind East. The second youngest girl recalls the praying mantis . . .
>
> Why in a conversation with someone who is not well and asks me—
> Do you believe in God? do I say—No, not really, when at other times to other people I say and mean that I believe in *gods*?
> Why does she look at me without much surprise while telling me

that like all atheists I am on the path to the devil and that my name will be forgotten after I die? . . .

To be looked at as if one is neutral ground. To identify with the narrative voice when one reads novels. To have no child in a house where the women are women together. What about the instantaneous alerts of kindness? What about belly dancing? Salmon strips of light in the sky? . . .[79]

Jeremy Noel-Tod identifies Capildeo's writing as works "in which prose and verse are interwoven."[80] He emphasizes her playfulness with boundaries and language by drawing attention to statements she has made about her own creative practice: "In my own writing," she has said, "I try to create changes of modality in one book, not make collections of 'prose poems' and 'poem poems.'"[81] Certainly her work mixes reflective or meditative prose and lineated poetry with more obviously prose-poetical gestures, creating a kind of work that is different from, yet bears some relationship to, Mallarmé's combinations of various mixed modes of writing in *Divagations*.

John Ashbery's highly influential *Three Poems* (1972) has been the subject of much debate in prose poetry scholarship, largely centered on whether the "three poems" are indeed prose poems or if they belong to another form or genre. Fredman believes that they unite "the two extreme forms of American poetry, the long poem and the poet's prose," and also claims that "the repetition and tonal invariance of the writing . . . break up into what Ashbery calls 'an endless process of elaboration,' of differentiation."[82] Monte writes, "From the perspective of today . . . *Three Poems* frames itself more as an Ashbery long poem than as a prose poem or prose-poem sequence." Murphy states, "The length of Ashbery's 'three poems' may . . . represent an expansion rather than a renunciation of this eclectic genre, the prose poem, a drive to include more and more discourse."[83] Noel-Tod takes up this issue in his introduction to *The Penguin Book of the Prose Poem*, also writing of "the prose poem's genius for expansiveness."[84]

Yet Ashbery's *Three Poems* may not easily be described as prose poetry. Ashbery did write prose poems, such as "A Linnet" and "The Bobinski Brothers," published as "Two Prose Poems" in the *London Review of Books* in 2000, and he sensitively translated Rimbaud's *Illuminations*. However, the beginning of "The New Spirit," for instance, combines three broken lines with two fully justified paragraphs of text:

I thought that if I could put it all down, that would be one way. And next the thought came to me that to leave all out would be another, and truer, way.

clean-washed sea

The flowers were.

These are examples of leaving out. But, forget as we will, something soon comes to stand in their place. Not the truth, perhaps, but—yourself. It is you who made this, therefore you are true. But the truth has passed on

to divide all.[85]

Another of the *Three Poems*, "The System" does not contain any broken lines and, instead, turns on fully justified paragraphs of varying lengths that are divided by a generous space between paragraphs. "The Recital" is comprised of paragraphs without any space between them but with indents at the opening of their paragraphs.

While each of the *Three Poems* is divided into sections or paragraphs, nevertheless these works encourage the reader to approach each text as a single long piece. On the continuum between prose poetry and poetic prose, *Three Poems* is more akin to poetic prose (with some inclusions of lineated poetry) because of its meandering qualities and slow-building tension—what is characterized by David Herd as "the sentence perform[ing] the process whereby . . . the search for meaning tends to carry one further and further from the experience or fact one was trying to understand in the first place."[86]

The Contemporary Prose Poem and the Future

Overall, the twenty-first-century prose poem is in flux during a period when many literary forms are being challenged or reimagined. The forms being reshaped include the novel, the essay (and lyric essay), and microliterature of all kinds. The prose poem is a relatively "new" form, especially in English, and consequently it has a lot of room to move. Its literary foundations are still being established, and its technical characteristics continue to be expanded and defined. There are now two illustrated books for junior writers: *Prose Poems (Poetry Party)* (2015), aimed at four- to eight-year-olds, and *Penelope and Pip Build a Prose Poem (Poetry Builders)* (2012),[87] targeted at seven- to nine-year-olds, which define and include tips for writing prose poetry. And a number of students between eleven and nineteen have prose poems published in *England: Poems from a School* (edited by Kate Clancy, 2018).[88] These kinds of publications suggest, for the next generation, that prose poetry may become more generally approachable and easier to pin down.

There have been many claims made for the prose poem, but it has simultaneously suffered from various kinds of diminishment. It has been called contradictory, oxymoronic, or cross-generic,[89] or it has been defined so broadly that almost any kind of modern poetic prose has been given its name. The prose poem is indeed many things at once, but it is also a form with clear and distinctive features, as we have outlined throughout this volume—and it is nothing less than the most important new poetic form to emerge in English-language poetry since the advent of free verse.

Prose poems are fragments that resist closure, with a characteristic compression and brevity giving priority to the evocative and the connotative. Prose poetry functions analogically, metonymically, and metaphorically, and frequently explores unseen or unconscious forces. It is often dreamlike, or it makes meanings glancingly—laterally indicating issues other than those it explicitly encompasses. It refashions prose for poetic ends, often exploiting the compressed, rectangular paragraph, and sometimes making use of a variety of typographical features to emphasize that it represents no ordinary species of prose. It presents many surprises and unsettles, or makes strange, the reading experience. It moves quickly through its themes, yet its poetic tropes have the capacity to slow the reader's apprehension of time. Its complex rhythms invigorate its sentences, and it uses visual imagery to present scenes of great immediacy.

Because the prose poem is now a major and developing form that has moved well beyond the early groundwork of the French symbolists, and of modernist writers such as Amy Lowell and Gertrude Stein—not to mention T. S. Eliot's "Hysteria"—its contemporary practitioners are able to size up many earlier examples and to confidently extend the form in various directions. In doing so, they are increasingly taking the importance of prose poetry for granted and finding within it a wide variety of new possibilities for literary innovation and invention. This activity is strengthening the prose poem daily, as its potential for expressing a diverse range of ideas and emotions is being discovered—not through theory but through the differing practices of numerous writers all over the world.

The prose poem's time has come. The old, doubtful divide between prose and poetry was seriously undercut in the mid-nineteenth century by Baudelaire (in France) and Whitman (in the United States), among others. At that time, the sometimes uneasy, sometimes acrimonious negotiations and debates among writers of a new "free" verse and writers of a subversive prose poetry, on the one hand, and writers of traditional verse, on the other, began in earnest. In the late twentieth and early twenty-first centuries, this has resulted in greater clarification of how literary forms and genres may be understood, defined, and expressed. Every serious writer of prose has always known that prose may be "poetic"; what prose poetry has shown is that prose may, in every meaningful way, be poetry. As it demonstrates this, prose poetry is extending the bounds of the "poetic" and claiming a new, secure place for poetry among the demotic and the vernacular that lineated free verse never fully claimed.

Prose poetry tells us that if the old genres still hold—rather shakily—as a general framework for understanding literary works, they have nevertheless become too imprecise and sometimes too prescriptive to define the diversity and complexity of twenty-first-century literature overall. It is no exaggeration to suggest that prose poetry (along with other forms of microliterature) may be a literary form that most decisively charts the future of the word in a post-technological, post-postmodern society. Fixed beliefs and monocultural assumptions have largely passed; so much of everyone's experience is defined by provisional and unfixed encounters and relationships.

Most people's lives are characterized by the experience of almost endless, fractured images, sound bites, and conflicting statements. Reality itself is now a highly elusive concept when so many layers of representation and interpretation sit between the subjective self and the "external" world. Individuals often grapple with the idea that anything may be unitary or knowable—whether that is the self, another person, or the world at large—and almost everyone agrees that the "other" is multiple. Indeed, there may be no "other'" at all but only fragments and facets of diverse "others." In such circumstances, language must attempt to come to terms with the fracturing of self and consciousness. Because most people can no longer believe in the old narrative verities, they must find ways of grappling with a fractured subjectivity, breaking up conventional narratives and their assumptions, and evoking the urban realities that present cacophonous, irreducible amounts of information, continuously and simultaneously.

Anne Caldwell and Oz Hardwick argue, "Prose poetry provides a playful and condensed space for creative work to be shared, both in print and online, through smartphones, tablets and social media platforms . . . Prose poetry: a form that both combines and resists; a developing photograph; a hall of mirrors with the lights switched off; a Promethean form for unstable times."[90] Prose poetry, indeed, permits and enables writers to address the twenty-first century in its own terms— through short, sometimes inveigling, sometimes confronting (or even shocking) paragraphs. It may disrupt, seduce, disturb, or dismember. It consists of works that evoke the world's contemporary puzzles and contradictions, its multicultural realities, its often disjunctive imagery, and even its multilingual characteristics.

An impressive example, Mary Jean Chan's "Written in a Historically White Place (I)", is a moving but erudite multilingual prose poem, challenging the privileged monoglot reader with the inclusion of unglossed Chinese characters. The reader who is unfamiliar with Chinese must stop to find a way of translating the characters if they want to unlock meaning in the poem, interrupting the flow of the prose poem:

> The reader stares at my 皮膚 and asks: why don't you write in 中文? I reply: 殖民主義 meant that I was brought up in your image. Let us be honest. Had I not learnt 英文 and come to your shores, you wouldn't be reading this poem at all. Did you think it was an accident that I learnt your 語言 for decades, until I knew it better than the 母語 I dreamt in? Is anything an accident these days? Dear reader, you are lucky to have been the centre of my 宇宙 for the past twenty years. One summer, a taxi driver in Shanghai asked me whether I was my lover's tour guide, declaring that she was from 大英帝國. How does that make me feel? Can you tell me what it is that I should do next?[91]

Chan's prose poem places the reader in a situation many non-English speakers find themselves in as migrants or as visitors to English-speaking countries, and, importantly, she is also referring to the colonial experience. She states:

> I have a poem in my collection where there are Chinese characters inserted into a prose poem, but I don't explain them. So, monolingual readers encounter that poem as an erasure poem. Those characters would be like blanks that they wouldn't be able to comprehend. That's my offering to the reader. What do you do when you encounter a language you don't speak? Just as I've had to master English.[92]

Prose poetry creates brief language parcels that wrap and conjure subjective human experience in language that evokes the elusive, the unconscious, the uncanny, and the unresolved. As prose poetry does this, it finally dismantles the old, persistent idea that poetry is the most elevated form of language among the world's literatures. Prose poetry insists, while it may reserve the right to speak in elevated—and even lyrical—modes, that it has followed Yeats into "the foul rag and bone shop of the heart."[93] It has also gone beyond, into the waste grounds and into the unknown places. Poetry, when it is prose poetry, returns to one of its origins—the use of language to probe the ineffable. In a secular world, the ineffable is everywhere distributed among the urban lots and suburban sprawl that postmodernity has delivered to so many of its inhabitants. Some of the old shrines still exist, but poetry has long-since escaped the confines of prayer and an idealized natural world, and since the nineteenth century it has increasingly also eschewed the lyrical. As it ramifies, a significant part of the poet's task is to locate the heart of loss and the confusion of memory that constitutes almost everyone's contemporary experience.

Prose poetry is unlike microfiction in that it represents an idea of what may be encountered beyond narrative and beyond the constructs of plot. Yet it takes narrative tropes and reworks them assiduously, knowing that in the absence of the confident lyric voice, narrative gestures are one way of conjuring situations, however improbable, to which the poetic may adhere. Prose poetry speaks of how the poetic belongs to all circumstances, and of how the common language of prose may be used to dig it out—and this is a sharpened common language that winkles and delves more closely than everyday prose is able to do. It recognizes that the metaphoric and metonymic belong to everybody's ways of speaking, and heightens and hones these forms of expression. It understands that what we see is a considerable part of what we know, but that what we see is unreliable; thus, it gives us many shifting images, as if we are looking through a complex album of highly suggestive photographs, never quite able to pin down the images.

Prose poems know, too, that fragmented forms, while essential to understanding the post-postmodern world, cannot give a whole story. As a result, they gesture to larger frames of reference that are often out of reach, indefinable, or unrealizable. They recognize that larger contexts must be invoked as a sign that, in metonymic terms, the part and the fragment stand in for the absent "all." As prose poetry explores many different ideas and takes many directions, so it remembers that only through multiple attempts at speaking will a sense of a whole experience begin to be inscribed—even as that "whole" forever slips away from every work that tries to catch it. Prose poetry suggests that just as prose and poetry are not meaningfully separate genres, so many significances belong in the interstices between what has been hallowed (old ideas of genre, for example) and what is elusive and yet to be fully understood.

The prose poet belongs to an emerging tradition that is beginning to say a great deal about the world and about literature, using innovative, complex, and connotative forms of expression. Furthermore, prose poets are helping to define the literatures to come and the genres and forms that those literatures will create. Prose poetry offers to express what we know beyond the daily posts on social media and the prosaic mundanities of ordinary self-narration. It continually promises to transform our perceptions.

Acknowledgments

We would like to thank all of the people who supported us in myriad ways during the writing of this book. While we cannot name everyone who helped us, we would like to mention the following people, who offered key advice or tangible support, provided us with research material or specific guidance, or showed us conceptual paths we might follow: Robert Alexander, Holly Amos, Tim Atkins, Kevin Brophy, Owen Bullock, Anne Caldwell, Vahni Capildeo, Martin Dolan, Carrie Etter, Charles Forgan, Tania Hershman, Paul (Oz) Hardwick, Katie Hayne, Holly Iglesias, Peter Johnson, Gian Lombardo, Steven Matthews, Alyson Miller, Jane Monson, Margaret Moores, Paul Munden, Niall Munro, Mariko Nagai, Catherine Noske, Alvin Pang, Peter Robinson, Nikki Santilli, John Skoyles, Ian Seed, Shane Strange, Marc Vincenz, Jen Webb, and Gary Young. We also received support from the Faculty of Arts and Design (and its Centre for Creative and Cultural Research), the University of Canberra, and the School of Communication and Creative Arts, Faculty of Arts and Education (and the Contemporary Histories Research Group), Deakin University.

Some of the ideas in this book received their first, preliminary exploration in articles published in the following journals: *Axon: Creative Explorations*; *Coolabah*; *Creative Approaches to Research*; *New Writing: The International Journal for the Practice and Theory of Creative Writing*; *TEXT: Journal of Writing and Writing Courses*; and *Western Humanities Review*. We would like to thank the journal editors.

We are especially grateful to Anne Savarese, commissioning editor for this book, who showed confidence in our publishing proposal from the time she received it, and who encouraged and guided us throughout the writing and publishing process. We would also like to thank Ellen Foos and Cathryn Slovensky for their meticulous work as production editor and copyeditor, respectively, Jenny Tan, Laurie Schlesinger, Erin Suydam, Alyssa Sanford, Katie Lewis, and the rest of the Princeton University Press team for their expertise, advice, and support.

Celeste Thorn has been an indefatigable and indispensible part of our project, so much more than an occasional research assistant, who frequently went "above and beyond" and was instrumental in the extended process of obtaining permission to reproduce the many prose poems and other creative works we have quoted.

We also depended on the support from our families, especially Michelle Hetherington, Suzannah Hetherington, and Rebecca Hetherington; and Glenn Moore, Eva Atherton, John Atherton, and Debra Atherton.

Finally, we would like to thank all of the prose poets, editors, publishers of prose poetry, and prose poetry scholars who were working in the field before us, so many of whom cooperated willingly in our enterprise and whose works informed and energized our writing.

Grateful acknowledgment is made for permission to reprint the following previously published material:

Kaveh Akbar, "Calling a Wolf a Wolf (Inpatient)," in *The Adroit Journal*, 2017. Reprinted with permission of the author and *The Adroit Journal*.

Robert Alexander, excerpts "September" and "Like Our Shadow-Selves," from *Richmond Burning*, published by Red Dragonfly Press. Copyright © 2017 by Robert Alexander. Used with permission of the author.

Hala Alyan, "Oklahoma," *Poetry Magazine*, 2017. Reprinted with permission of the author.

Jack Anderson, "Thimbleism," from *Traffic: New and Selected Prose Poems*. Copyright © 1975 by Jack Anderson. Reprinted with the permission of The Permissions Company, LLC, on behalf of New Rivers Press, www.newriverspress.com.

Nin Andrews, excerpt from "Southern Culture," from *Miss August*. Copyright © 2017 by Nin Andrews. Reprinted with the permission of The Permissions Company, LLC, on behalf of CavanKerry Press, www.cavanberrypress.org.

Simon Armitage, "The Christening," from *Seeing Stars: Poems*. Copyright © 2010 by Simon Armitage. Used by permission of Alfred A. Knopf, an imprint of the Knopf Doubleday Publishing Group, a division of Penguin Random House LLC. All rights reserved.

Simon Armitage, Excerpt of "The Christening," from *Seeing Stars: Poems*. Copyright © 2010 by Simon Armitage. Published by Faber & Faber Ltd., and used with permission.

Simon Armitage, Excerpt of "The Christening," from *Seeing Stars: Poems*. Copyright © 2010 by Simon Armitage. Published by Faber & Faber Ltd., and used with permission of the author and David Godwin Associates.

John Ashbery, "The New Spirit," from *Three Poems*. Copyright © 1972 by John Ashbery. Reprinted by permission of Georges Borchardt Inc., on behalf of the Estate of John Ashbery.

Sally Ashton, "Origins of Sublime." Originally published in *Sentence: A Journal of Prose Poetics*, volume 2, edited by Brian Clements. Copyright © 2004 by Sally Ashton. Used with permission of the author.

Cassandra Atherton, "Albatross," from *Pre-Raphaelite*, published by Garron Publishing. Copyright © 2018 by Cassandra Atherton. Used with permission of the author.

Marc Atkins, "Afterwords," from *The Logic of the Stairwell and Other Images*, published by Shearsman Books. Copyright © 2011 by Marc Atkins. Used with permission of the author.

Tim Atkins, "The Great Autumn Rains," in *Koto Y Yo (Koto & I)*, published by Lulu. Copyright © 2016 by Tim Atkins. Used with permission of the author.

Mary Jo Bang, "Mask Photo," in *A Doll for Throwing: Poems*, published by Graywolf Press. Copyright © 2017 by Mary Jo Bang. Used with permission of Graywolf Press.

Claire Bateman, "Distinction," in *Clumsy*, published by New Issues Press. Copyright © 2003 by Claire Bateman. Used with permission of the author.

Charles Baudelaire, excerpts from "Good Dogs," "To Each His Chimera," and "A Joker." Translation © 2009 by Keith Waldrop. Published by Wesleyan University Press and reprinted with permission.

Yasmin Belkhyr, "Interlude with Drug of Choice," in *Pinwheel*, Spring 2016. Copyright © 2016 by Yasmin Belkhyr. Used with permission of the author.

Fiona Benson, "Demeter," in *Granta*, volume 126. Copyright © 2014 by Fiona Benson. Used with permission of the author.

Emily Berry, excerpt from "Some Fears," from *Dear Boy*. Copyright © 2013 by Emily Berry. Published by Faber & Faber Ltd., and used with permission.

Linda Black, "The Most Exciting Beliefs Could Be Written in Verse," from *Son of a Shoemaker*, published by Hearing Eye. Copyright © 2012 by Linda Black. Used with permission of the author.

"The Morning Glory," from *The Morning Glory* by Robert Bly. Copyright © 1975 by Robert Bly. Reprinted by permission of Georges Borchardt, Inc., for Robert Bly.

"Warning to the Reader," from *Eating the Honey of Words* by Robert Bly. Copyright © 1999 by Robert Bly. Reprinted by permission of Georges Borchardt, Inc., for Robert Bly.

Robert Bly, "Warning to the Reader," from *Eating the Honey of Words: New and Selected Poems*. Copyright © 1999 by Robert Bly. Reprinted with permission of HarperCollins Publishers.

Roo Borson, "City," from *Intent, or the Weight of the World*, published by McClelland & Stewart. Copyright © 1989 by Roo Borson. Used with permission of the author.

Anne Boyer, excerpts from *Garments Against Women*, published by Ahsahta Press. Copyright © 2015 by Anne Boyer. Used with permission of the author.

From *Collected Writings of Joe Brainard*, edited by Ron Padgett, with an introduction by Paul Auster (Library of America, 2012). Copyright © 2012 by The Estate of Joe Brainard. Reprinted by permission of Library of America, www.loa.org. All rights reserved.

Emily Brandt, "The Harbor," originally published in The Literary Hub. Copyright © 2016 by Emily Brandt. Used with permission of the author.

Kevin Brophy, "The Night's Insomnia," from *Radar* by Kevin Brophy and Nathan Curnow, published by Walleah Press Poetry. Copyright © 2012 by Kevin Brophy. Used with permission of the author.

Suzanne Buffam, *A Pillow Book*. Copyright © 2016 by Suzanne Buffam. Used with permission of Canarium Books.

Suzanne Buffam, *A Pillow Book*. Copyright © 2016 by Suzanne Buffam. Used with permission of House of Anansi Press.

Anne Caldwell, "Wild Garlic and Detours," from *The Valley Press Anthology of Prose

Poetry, edited by Anne Caldwell and Oz Hardwick. Copyright © 2019 by Anne Caldwell. Used with permission of the author.

Anthony Caleshu, "With Your Permission, Allow Me to Perform Exemplary Surgery on Your Brain," from *A Dynamic Exchange Between Us*, published by Shearsman Books. Copyright © 2019 by Anthony Caleshu. Used with permission of the author.

Vahni Capildeo, "XI," in *Measures of Expatriation*, published by Carcanet Books. Copyright © 2016 by Vahni Capildeo. Used with permission of Carcanet Press Limited.

From *Autobiography in Red: A Novel in Verse* by Anne Carson. Published by Jonathan Cape. Reprinted by permission of The Random House Group Limited. Copyright © 1999.

Excerpts from *Autobiography in Red: A Novel in Verse* by Anne Carson. Copyright © 1998, by Anne Carson, used by permission of Alfred A. Knopf, an imprint of the Knopf Doubleday Publishing Group, a division of Penguin Random House LLC. All rights reserved.

From *Red doc>* by Anne Carson. Published by Jonathan Cape. Reprinted by permission of The Random House Group Limited. Copyright © 2013.

"Wife of Brain" and "Love's Long Lost," from *Red doc>* by Anne Carson. Copyright © 2013 by Anne Carson. Used by permission of Alfred A. Knopf, an imprint of the Knopf Doubleday Publishing Group, a division of Penguin Random House LLC. All rights reserved.

"On Hedonism" and "On Defloration," from *Plainwater: Essays and Poetry* by Anne Carson. Copyright © 1995 by Anne Carson. Used by permission of Alfred A. Knopf, an imprint of the Knopf Doubleday Publishing Group, a division of Penguin Random House LLC. All rights reserved.

"On Hedonism" and "On Defloration," from *Plainwater: Essays and Poetry* by Anne Carson, published by Knopf, an imprint of the Knopf Doubleday Publishing Group, a division of Penguin Random House LLC. Copyright © 1995 by Anne Carson. Used by permission of Aragi Agents.

From *Will You Please Be Quiet, Please?* by Raymond Carver. Published by The Harvill Press. Reprinted by permission of The Random House Group Limited. Copyright © 1995.

Will You Please Be Quiet, Please? by Raymond Carver. Copyright © 1976, Raymond Carver, copyright renewed 1989, Tess Gallagher. Used by permission of The Wiley Agency (UK) Limited.

Gary Catalano, "Incident from a War," from *Fresh Linen: Sixty Prose Poems 1980–1986*, published by the University of Queensland Press. Copyright © 1988 by Gary Catalano. Used with permission of University of Queensland Press.

Mary Jean Chan, excerpt of "Written in a Historically White Place (I)," from *Flèche*. Copyright © 2019 by Mary Jean Chan. Published by Faber & Faber Ltd. and used with permission.

Maxine Chernoff, "Lost and Found," from *Leap Year Day: New and Selected Poems*, published by Another Chicago Press. Copyright © 1990 by Maxine Chernoff. Used with permission of the author.

ACKNOWLEDGMENTS ⁓ 253

Maxine Chernoff, "Kill Yourself with an *Objet D'Art*," from *Evolution of the Bridge: Selected Prose Poems*, published by Salt Publishing. Copyright © 2004 by Maxine Chernoff. Used with permission of the author.

Chekwube O. Danladi, "Tomorrow, Chaka Demus Will Play," from *Take Me Back*, published by Akashic Books. Copyright © 2017 by Chekwube O. Danladi. Used with permission of the author.

Lydia Davis, "Letter to a Funeral Parlour," from *The Collected Stories of Lydia Davis*, published by Penguin, London. Copyright © 2013 by Lydia Davis. Used with permission of Penguin Random House, UK.

Excerpts from "Letter to a Funeral Parlor," from *The Collected Stories of Lydia Davis* by Lydia Davis. Copyright © 2009 by Lydia Davis. Reprinted by permission of Farrar, Straus and Giroux.

Raquel de Alderete, "Untitled," from *Red Blood, Black Ink*. Copyright © 2016 by Raquel de Alderete. Used with permission of the author.

Patricia Debney, "Bluebell Wood," from *How to Be a Dragonfly*, published by Smith Doorstop Books. Copyright © 2005 by Patricia Debney. Used with permission of the author.

Mike Dockins, "Eleven Gin and Tonics," from *Route Nine*, Alumni Omnibus, March 2014. Copyright © 2014 by Mike Dockins. Used with permission of the author.

"The Dummies," from *See Jack* by Russell Edson © 2009. Reprinted with permission of the University of Pittsburgh Press.

Russell Edson, excerpts from "Ape," "Erasing Amyloo," and "The Rat's Legs," from *The Tunnel: Selected Poems of Russell Edson*. Copyright © 1994 by Russell Edson. Reprinted with the permission of Oberlin College Press.

Keith Ekiss, "Into the City," originally published in *Separate City: Prose Poems, Kenyon Review* 33, no. 3. Copyright © 2013 by Keith Ekiss. Used with permission of the author.

Paul Éluard, "She Exists," translated by Mary Ann Caws. In *The Yale Anthology of Twentieth-Century French Poetry*, edited by Mary Ann Caws, page 176. Copyright © 2004 by Yale University. All rights reserved. Reproduced with permission of the Licensor through PLSclear.

Carrie Etter, "Imagined Sons 5: Reunion," from *Imagined Sons* by Carrie Etter, published by Seren Books. Copyright © 2014 by Carrie Etter. Used with permission of the author.

Sylvia Fairclough, "Unavailable," from *This Line Is Not For Turning: An Anthology of Contemporary British Prose Poetry*, edited by Jane Monson, published by Cinnamon Press. Copyright © 2011 by Sylvia Fairclough.

Robert Fitterman, excerpt from *This Window Makes Me Feel*, published by Ugly Duckling Presse. Copyright © 2018 by Robert Fitterman. Used with permission from Ugly Duckling Presse.

Charles Fort, "Darvil and Black Eyed Peas on New Year's Eve," from *Mrs. Belladonna's Supper Club Waltz*, published by Backwaters Press. Copyright © 2013 by Charles Fort. Used with permission of the author.

Jeff Friedman, "Catching the Monster," originally published in *SurVision Magazine*, issue 1. Copyright © 2017 by Jeff Friedman. Used with permission of the author.

Richard Garcia, "Diorama," in *Solstice: A Magazine of Diverse Voices*, Summer 2015. Copyright © 2015 by Richard Garcia. Used with permission of the author.

Julie Gard, "White Approach," from *Home Studies*, published by New Rivers Press. Copyright © 2015 by Julie Gard. Used with permission granted by New Rivers Press.

Amy Gerstler, excerpt from *The True Bride*, published by Lapis Press. Copyright © 1986 by Amy Gerstler. Used with permission of the author.

"The Bricklayer's Lunch Hour," by Allen Ginsberg, currently collected in *Collected Poems: 1947–1997*. Copyright © 1956, 2006 by Allen Ginsberg, used by permission of The Wiley Agency, LLC.

Excerpt of seven lines from "The Bricklayer's Lunch Hour," from *Collected Poems, 1947–1997* by Allen Ginsberg. Copyright © 2006 by The Allen Ginsberg Trust. Used by permission of HarperCollins Publishers.

Jenny Gropp, "Photo Graph Paper: American Push," in *The Hominine Egg*, published by Kore Press. Copyright © 2017 by Jenny Gropp. Used with permission of the author.

Hedy Habra, "Afterthought," in *Under Brushstrokes*. Published by Press 53. Copyright © 2015 by Hedy Habra. Used with permission of the author.

Kimiko Hahn, excerpt from *The Unbearable Heart*, published by Kaya Press. Copyright © 1995 by Kimiko Hahn. Used with permission of Kaya Press.

Oz Hardwick, "Graduation," from *Learning to Have Lost*, published by Recent Work Press. Copyright © 2018 by Oz Hardwick. Used with permission of the author.

Matthea Harvey, "The Backyard Mermaid," originally published by Poets.org. Copyright © 2011 by Matthea Harvey. Used with permission of the author.

"Yet we insist that life is full of happy chance," from *My Life and My Life in the Nineties* © 2013 by Lyn Hejinian. Published by Wesleyan University Press and reprinted with permission.

Tania Hershman, "Powers of Ten," from *Blue Fifth Review: Blue Five Notebook Series*, Broadside #51, vol. 18, no. 4. Copyright © 2018 by Tania Hershman. Used with permission of the author.

Paul Hetherington, "Antiquities," from "Broken Forms: Prose Poetry as Hybridised Genre in Australia," *Coolabah*, volume 24/25. Copyright © 2018 by Paul Hetherington. Used with permission of the author.

Jim Heynen, "The Boys Go to Ask a Neighbor for Some Apples," in *The Boys' House: Stories*, published by Minnesota Historical Society Press. Copyright © 2001 by Jim Heynen. Used with permission of the author.

Harmony Holiday, "Crisis Actor," Poetry Foundation. Copyright © 2017 by Harmony Holiday. Used with permission of the author.

Holly Iglesias, "Conceptual Art," from *Angles of Approach*, published by White Pine Press. Copyright © 2010 by Holly Iglesias. Used with permission of the author.

Brenda Iijima, "Dolly the Sheep" and "White Tigers," from *Some Simple Things Said by and about Humans*, published by BOAAT Press. Copyright © 2014 by Brenda Iijima. Used with permission of the author.

Lucy Ives, excerpt from *Orange Roses*, published by Ahsahta Press. Copyright © 2013 by Lucy Ives. Used with permission from the author.

Laura Kasischke, *Space, In Chains*, published by Copper Canyon Press. Copyright © 2011 by Laura Kasischke. Used with permission of the author.

Luke Kennard, "No Stars," from *The Migraine Hotel*, published by Salt Publishing. Copyright © 2009 by Luke Kennard. Used with permission of the author.

John Kinsella, "Graphology 300: Against 'Nature Writing,'" from *Graphology Poems, 1995–2015*, published by Five Island Press. Copyright © 2016 by John Kinsella. Used with permission of the author.

Desmond Kon, "dame de compagnie :: lady of company," from *Five Prose Poems. Asymptote Journal.* Copyright © 2012 by Desmond Kon. Used with permission of the author.

Patricia Lockwood, "Rape Joke," published by *The Awl*. Copyright © 2013 by Patricia Lockwood. Used with permission from the author.

Gian S. Lombardo, excerpt from *Machines We Have Built*, published by Quale Press. Copyright © 2014 by Gian S. Lombardo. Used with permission of the author.

Robert Lowes, "The Unity of the Paragraph," from *An Introduction to the Prose Poem*, edited by Brian Clements and Jamey Dunham, published by Firewheel Editions. Copyright © 2009 by Robert Lowes. Used with permission of the author.

Stéphane Mallarmé, excerpt from *A Roll of the Dice*, translated by Robert Bononno and Jeff Clark, published by Wave Books. Copyright © 2015 by Stéphane Mallarmé, Robert Bononno, and Jeff Clark. Used with permission from Wave Books.

Dawn Lundy Martin, *Discipline*, published by Nightboat Books. Copyright © 2011 by Dawn Lundy Martin. Used with permission of the author.

Dawn Lundy Martin, *Life in a Box Is a Pretty Life*, published by Nightboat Books. Copyright © 2014 by Dawn Lundy Martin. Used with permission of the author.

"The Prose Poem," from *No Boundaries: Prose Poems by 24 American Poets* by Campbell McGrath. Copyright © 2003 by Campbell McGrath. Courtesy of ECCO, an imprint of HarperCollins Publishers.

Erika Meitner, "A Brief Ontological Investigation," originally published on Poem-a-Day. Copyright © 2018 by Erika Meitner. Used with permission of the author.

Robert Miltner, "Québec Express," originally published in *Full Bleed: A Journal of Art and Design*, vol. 2, issue: *Crisis*. Copyright © 2018 by Robert Miltner. Used with permission of the author.

Jane Monson, excerpts from "Square of Light: The Artist is Present I" and "The Artist is Present II," from *The Shared Surface*, published by Cinnamon Press. Copyright © 2013 by Jane Monson. Used with permission of Cinnamon Press.

Margaret Moores, excerpt from *Loading the Image*, master's thesis from Massey University. Copyright © 2016 by Margaret Moores. Used with permission of the author.

Thylias Moss, "Goodness and the Salt of the Earth," in *Small Congregations: New and Selected Poems*, published by Ecco, an imprint of HarperCollins. Copyright © 1993 by Thylias Moss. Used with permission of the author.

Harryette Mullen, excerpt from *Sleeping with the Dictionary*, copyright © 2002 by Harryette Mullen, used with permission from the University of California Press.

Paul Munden, "Arthroscopy/Sports Day, 1971," in *Keys* by Paul Munden, published by Authorised Theft. Copyright © 2015 by Paul Munden. Used with permission of the author.

Mariko Nagai, excerpt from *Irradiated Cities*, published by Les Figues Press. Copyright © 2017 by Mariko Nagai. Used with permission of the author.

Maggie Nelson, excerpt from *The Argonauts*, published by Graywolf Press. Copyright © 2016 by Maggie Nelson. Used with permission of the author.

Maggie Nelson, excerpt from *Bluets*, published by Wave Books. Copyright © 2009 by Maggie Nelson. Used with permission from the author.

Aimee Nezhukumatathil, "Summer Haibun," originally published on Poets.org and Poem-a-Day. Copyright © 2017 by Aimee Nezhukumatathil. Used with permission from the author.

Kate North, "The Snow Spits," from *Bistro*, published by Cinnamon Press. Copyright © 2012 by Kate North. Used with permission from the author.

Frank O'Hara, excerpt from "The Day Lady Died," from *Lunch Poems*. Copyright © 1964 by Frank O'Hara. Reprinted with the permission of The Permissions Company, LLC on behalf of City Lights Books, www.citylights.com. All rights reserved.

Alvin Pang, "1.290270,103.851959 (2017)," originally published in *Cities: Ten Poets, Ten Cities*, edited by Paul Hetherington and Shane Strange. Copyright © 2017 by Alvin Pang. Used with permission of the author.

Elizabeth Paul, "Pianist and Still Life, 1924, Henri Matisse," from *Reading Girl*, published by Finishing Line Press. Copyright © 2016 by Elizabeth Paul. Used with permission of the author.

Pascale Petit, "My Larzac Childhood," from *The Treekeepers Tale*, published by Seren Books. Copyright © 2008 by Pascale Petit. Used with permission of the author and Seren Books.

From *Soap* by Francis Ponge, translated by Lane Dunlop. Copyright © 1967 by Editions Gallimard. English translation © 1969 by Jonathan Cape Ltd. All rights reserved.

Khadijah Queen, excerpt from *I'm So Fine: A List of Famous Men & What I Had On*, published by Sibling Rivalry Press. Copyright © 2013 by Khadijah Queen. Used with permission of the author.

Khadijah Queen, excerpt from *I'm So Fine: A List of Famous Men & What I Had On*, published by YesYes Books. Copyright © 2017 by Khadijah Queen. Used with permission of the author.

Charles Rafferty, "The Pond," originally published in *The New Yorker*. Copyright © 2018 by Charles Rafferty. Used with permission of the author.

The use of 92 (ninety-two) words and 5 (five) lines from *Citizen: An American Lyric* by Claudia Rankine published by Penguin Press, 2015. First published in the

United States of America by Graywolf Press, 2014. Text copyright © Claudia Rankine, 2014. Reproduced by permission of Penguin Books Ltd.

Claudia Rankine, excerpt from ["A friend argues . . ."], from *Citizen: An American Lyric*, page 14. Copyright © 2014 by Claudia Rankine. Reprinted with the permission of The Permissions Company, LLC on behalf of Graywolf Press, www.graywolfpress.org.

Claudia Rankine, excerpts from *Don't Let Me Be Lonely: An American Lyric*, pp. 21–23. Copyright © 2004 by Claudia Rankine. Reprinted with the permission of The Permissions Company, LLC on behalf of Graywolf Press, www.graywolfpress.org.

Tom Raworth, "Proust from the Bottom Up," from *Tottering State*, published by The Figures. Copyright © 1984 by Tom Raworth. Used with permission from Geoffrey Young, The Figures.

Arthur Rimbaud, "After the Flood" and "Cities (I)," from *Illuminations*, translated by John Ashbery. Carcanet Press Limited. Copyright © 2018 by Carcanet Press Limited.

"After the Flood" and "Cities (I)," from *Illuminations* by Arthur Rimbaud, translated by John Ashbery. Copyright © 2011 by John Ashbery. Used by permission of W. W. Norton & Company, Inc. https://wwnorton.com/books/9780393341829.

Lauren Russell, "Dream-Clung, Gone," from *What's Happening on the Hush*. Originally collected in *Dream-Clung, Gone: Poems* (Brooklyn Arts Press, 2012). Copyright © 2012, 2017 by Lauren Russell. Reprinted with the permission of The Permissions Company, LLC on behalf of Ahsahta Press, www.ahsahtapress.org.

Kristin Sanders, "Country Song of Thanks," from *Cuntry*. New Orleans, LA: Trembling Pillow Press. Copyright © 2017 by Kristin Sanders. Used with permission of the author.

Jane Satterfield, "Why I Don't Write Nature Poems," from *Apocalypse Mix*, published by Autumn House Press. Copyright © 2017 by Jane Satterfield. Used with permission of the author.

Frederich Schlegel, excerpts from *Friedrich Schlegel's "Lucinde" and the Fragments*, translated by Peter Firchow, published by the University of Minnesota Press. Copyright © 1971 by Frederich Schlegel and Peter Firchow. Used with permission of University of Minnesota Press.

Zachary Schomburg, "The Fire Cycle," from *Scary, No Scary*, published by Black Ocean. Copyright © 2009 by Zachary Schomburg. Used with permission of the author.

Ian Seed, "All Kinds of Dust," from *Anonymous Intruder*, published by Shearsman Books. Copyright © 2009 by Ian Seed. Used with permission of the author.

Ian Seed, "A Life," from *Makers of Empty Dreams*, published by Shearsman Books. Copyright © 2009 by Ian Seed. Used with permission of the author.

"my life as china," from *the new black* © 2011 by Evie Shockley. Published by Wesleyan University Press and reprinted with permission.

Ron Silliman, "You," from *The Alphabet*, published by University of Alabama Press.

Copyright © 2008 by Ron Silliman. Used with permission of University of Alabama Press.

Excerpts from "My Mother Was a Braid of Smoke" and "My Father Loved the Strange Books of André Breton," from *The World Doesn't End: Prose Poems* by Charles Simic. Copyright © 1987 by Charles Simic. Reprinted with permission of Houghton Mifflin Harcourt Publishing Company. All rights reserved.

Excerpts from "We Were So Poor," "Inside the Pot," and "We Were Stolen by the Gypsies," from *The World Doesn't End: Prose Poems* by Charles Simic. Copyright © 1987 by Charles Simic. Reprinted with permission of Houghton Mifflin Harcourt Publishing Company. All rights reserved.

Alex Skovron, "Supplication," in *Autographs*, published by Hybrid Publishers. Copyright © 2008 by Alex Skovron. Used with permission of the author.

Donna Stonecipher, "Model City [35]," from *Model City*, published by Shearsman Books. Copyright © 2015 by Donna Stonecipher. Used with permission of the author.

Excerpts from "The Cowboy," from *The Ghost Soldiers* by James Tate. Copyright © 2008 by James Tate. Used with permission of HarperCollins.

Barbara Tran, "Rosary," in *CrossXConnect*, vol. 3, no. 3. Copyright © 2005 by Barbara Tran. Used with permission of the author.

Kyle Vaughn, "Letter to My Imagined Daughter," originally appeared in *Sentence: A Journal of Prose Poetics*. Copyright © 2009 by Kyle Vaughn. Used with permission of the author.

Ocean Vuong, "Partly True Poem Reflected in the Mirror," first published in *Poetry*, London, May 2017. Copyright © Ocean Vuong. Reprinted by permission from the author.

Ocean Vuong, "Trevor," first published in *Buzzfeed News*, March 2016. Copyright © Ocean Vuong. Reprinted by permission from the author.

Samuel Wagan Watson, "There's No Place Like Home," originally published on Poetry International. Copyright © 2011 by Samuel Wagan Watson. Used with permission of the author.

Louise Wallace, "Ahakoa he iti he pounamu | Although it is small it is greenstone," from *Bad Things*, published by Victoria University Press. Copyright © 2017 by Louise Wallace. Used with permission of the author.

Ania Walwicz, "Neons," originally published in *Gangan Lit-Mag*, vol. 2. Copyright © 1996 by Ania Walwicz. Used with permission of the author.

Jen Webb, "1973," from *Sentences from the Archives*, published by Recent Work Press. Copyright © 2016 by Jen Webb. Used with permission of the author.

Tom Whalen, "The Doll's Alienation," in *Dolls: Prose Poems*, published by Caketrain. Copyright © 2007 by Tom Whalen. Used with permission of the author.

Tom Whalen, "Why I Hate the Prose Poem," in *An Introduction to the Prose Poem*, edited by Brian Clements and Jamey Dunham. Copyright © 2009 by Tom Whalen. Used with permission of the author.

"Silence," from *All at Once: Prose Poems* by C. K. Williams. Copyright © 2014 by C. K. Williams. Reprinted by permission of Farrar, Straus and Giroux.

Chloe Wilson, from "Arm's Length." Originally appeared in *Landmarks: An Anthol-*

ogy of Microlit, edited by Cassandra Atherton. Copyright © 2017 by Chloe Wilson. Used by permission of MacKenzie Wolf on behalf of the author.

Cecilia Woloch, excerpt from "Postcard to Ilya Kaminsky from a Dream at the Edge of the Sea," from *Carpathia*. Copyright © 2015 by Cecilia Woloch. Reprinted with the permission of The Permissions Company, LLC on behalf of BOA Editions, Ltd., www.boaeditions.org.

Danielle Wood, "The Hare," in *Landmarks: An Anthology of Microlit*, edited by Cassandra Atherton. Copyright © 2017 by Danielle Wood. Used with permission of the author.

Patrick Wright, "Black Square," published by *Ekphrastic Review*. Copyright © 2018 by Patrick Wright. Used with permission of the author.

Jenny Xie, excerpt from *Eye Level*, published by Graywolf Press. Copyright © 2018 by Jenny Xie. Used with permission of the author.

Gary Young, "Untitled," from *The Best of the Prose Poem* by Peter Johnson. Originally published in *Even So: New and Selected Prose Poems*, published by White Pine Press. Copyright © 2012 by Gary Young. Used with permission of the author.

Abigail Zimmer, *Child in a Winter House Brightening*, published by Tree Light Books. Copyright © 2016 by Abigail Zimmer. Used with permission of the author.

Notes

Chapter 1

1. Mark Strand's *The Monument* was recommended for the 1979 Pulitzer Prize for Poetry by two members of the three-person poetry jury but not awarded the prize because jury chairman, Louis Simpson, considered it was "prose and the terms of the award state that it is to be given for verse." See Heinz-Dietrich Fischer, *Chronicle of the Pulitzer Prize for Poetry*, 350.
2. Barker, "The Jubjub Bird," in *The Jubjub Bird, or Some Remarks on the Prose Poem and a Little Honouring of Lionel Johnson*, 1.
3. Lehman, "The Prose Poem: An Alternative to Verse," 45; Hirsch, "Prose Poem: From a Poet's Glossary," n.p.
4. P. Johnson, "Introduction," in *The Prose Poem: An International Journal*, 6.
5. At the time of publication, members of the International Prose Poetry Group include Cassandra Atherton, Lucy Alexander, Eugen Bacon, Owen Bullock, Anne Caldwell, Jennifer Crawford, Martin Dolan, Carrie Etter, Niloofar Fanaiyan, Charlotte Guest, Ross Gibson, Stephanie Green, Oz Hardwick, Dominique Hecq, Paul Hetherington, Penelope Layland, Rupert Loydell, Andrew Melrose, Paul Munden, Alvin Pang, Maggie Shapley, Lauren Slaughter, Shane Strange, Jen Webb, and Jordan Williams. Oliver Comins, Lucy Dougan, and Nigel McLoughlin are former members of the group.
6. The editors of journals and anthologies have often been able to advance discussions about prose poetry because of their immersion in the field, and we have learned from their work. Apart from the editors already mentioned, significant editorial contributors to an understanding of the form include Robert Alexander (*Spring Phantoms: Short Prose by 19th Century British & American Authors*, 2018); Robert Alexander (*Family Portrait: American Prose Poetry, 1900–1950*, 2012); Robert Alexander and Dennis Maloney (*The House of Your Dream: An International Collection of Prose Poetry*, 2008); Robert Alexander, Mark Vinz, and C. W. Truesdale (*The Party Train: A Collection of North American Prose Poetry*, 1996); Christopher Buckley and Gary Young (*Bear Flag Republic: Prose Poems and Poetics from California*, 2008); Peter H. Conners (*PP/FF: An Anthology*, 2006); Ray Gonzalez (*No Boundaries*, 2003); Gary L. McDowell and F. Daniel Rzicznek (*The Rose Metal Press Field Guide to Prose Poetry: Contemporary Poets in Discussion and Practice*, 2010); Brian Clements and Jamey Dunham (*An Introduction to the Prose Poem*, 2009); Stuart Friebert and David Young (*Models of the Universe: An Anthology of the Prose Poem*, 1995); David Lehman (*Great American Prose Poems from Poe to Present*, 2003); Peter Johnson (*Best of the Prose Poem: An International Journal*, 2000); and Rupert

M. Loydell and David Miller (*A Curious Architecture: A Selection of Contemporary Prose Poems*, 1996). There was also a special issue of the journal *TEXT* on prose poetry, edited by Monica Carroll, Shane Strange, and Jen Webb: Special Issue 46, *Beyond the Line: Contemporary Prose Poetry* (October 2017).

7. Alexander, *The American Prose Poem, 1890–1980*; Delville, *The American Prose Poem*; Murphy, *A Tradition of Subversion*; Fredman, *Poet's Prose*; Monte, *Invisible Fences*; Santilli, *Such Rare Citings*; and Monroe, *A Poverty of Objects*. Also useful are the edited collections *British Prose Poetry: The Poems Without Lines*, ed. Monson; and *The Prose Poem in France: Theory and Practice*, ed. Caws and Riffaterre.
8. Santilli, *Such Rare Citings*, 146.
9. Grosser, "The Poetic Line," 5.
10. Ibid., 3.
11. Tatarkiewicz, *A History of Six Ideas*, 86.
12. Simic, "Prose Poetry," n.p.
13. Poetry Foundation, "Glossary of Poetic Terms," n.p.
14. Turco, *The Book of Forms*, 4; emphasis in the original.
15. Santilli, *Such Rare Citings*, 22.
16. Simic, "We Were So Poor," in *The World Doesn't End*, 8.
17. Whitman, *Leaves of Grass*, 32.
18. Mirsky, "Whitman in Russia," in *Walt Whitman and the World*, 330.
19. Whitman, *Leaves of Grass*, 32.
20. Dickens, *Little Dorrit*, 15.
21. Brown, "The Emergent Prose Poem," in *A Companion to Poetic Genre*, 319.
22. Ibid.
23. Culler, *Theory of the Lyric*, 3.
24. Blasing, *Lyric Poetry*, 3.
25. Irwin, "Distortion and Disjunction in Contemporary American Poetry," 39.
26. Peacock, "The Equation of the Prose Poem," n.p.
27. Wanner, *Russian Minimalism*, 8.
28. Ibid., 7.
29. Mills, *Formal Revolution*, 84.
30. Murphy, *A Tradition of Subversion*, 90.
31. Alyan, "Oklahoma," n.p.
32. Culler, *Theory of the Lyric*, 37.
33. A. Smith, "The Mongrel," 13.
34. Fredman, *Poet's Prose*, xiii.
35. Hayes, "'Dream-Clung, Gone' by Lauren Russell," n.p.
36. Clements and Dunham, *An Introduction to the Prose Poem*, 6.
37. Noel-Tod, "Introduction: The Expansion of the Prose Poem," in *The Penguin Book of the Prose Poem*, xix.
38. Ibid., xix–xx.
39. Caldwell and Hardwick, "Introduction," in *The Valley Press Anthology of Prose Poetry*, 9.
40. Benedikt, "Introduction," in *The Prose Poem: An International Anthology*, 48–49.
41. Iglesias, *Boxing Inside the Box*, 12.

NOTES TO CHAPTER 1   263

42. Johnson and Bly, "Interview: The Art of the Prose Poem," 8–9.
43. Iglesias, *Boxing Inside the Box*, 13.
44. In Lehman, *Great American Prose Poems*, 19.
45. Spacks, *Novel Beginnings*, 276.
46. Truesdale, "Publisher's Preface," in *The Party Train*, xx.
47. Benedikt, "Introduction," in *The Prose Poem*, 47.
48. J. Taylor, "Two Cultures of the Prose Poem," 364.
49. Freud cites this definition by Schelling in his essay "The Uncanny," in *Writings on Art and Literature*, 199.
50. G. Young, "The Prose Poem," in *Bear Flag Republic*, 90.
51. G. Young, "The Unbroken Line," in *The Rose Metal Press Field Guide to Prose Poetry*, 113.
52. Murphy, *A Tradition of Subversion*, 63.
53. Monson, *This Line Is Not For Turning*, 7.
54. J. Johnson, "Introduction," *Mississippi Review*, 8.
55. J. S. Simon, quoted in Caws and Riffaterre, *The Prose Poem in France*, 40.
56. D. Young, "Introduction," in *Models of the Universe*, 18.
57. Monte, *Invisible Fences*.
58. Wall, "Questioning the Prose Poem," in *British Prose Poetry*, 167.
59. Kramer, "Sumerian Love Song," in *Ancient Near Eastern Texts*, 496.
60. Howell, "The Prose Poem: What the Hell is it?," n.p.
61. Ibid.
62. Ibid.
63. Ibid.
64. Howells, vi–vii.
65. Moore, *Prose Poems of the French Enlightenment*, 2–3.
66. Ibid., 4.
67. Marmontel, *Bélisaire*, 60.
68. Monte, *Invisible Fences*, 16.
69. Rimbaud, *Rimbaud: Complete Works, Selected Letters*, 375.
70. Catani, *Evil: A History in Modern French Literature and Thought*, 38.
71. Ibid., 38.
72. Evans, *Rhythm, Illusion and the Poetic Idea*, 113–14.
73. Ibid., 138.
74. Ibid., 139.
75. Alexander, "Richard H. Horne [1802–84] 'The Old Churchyard Tree: A Prose Poem,'" 13–14. This poem is often attributed to Charles Dickens, but it was originally published without attribution in *Household Words*. Robert Alexander makes a persuasive case for the poem being written by Horne. See his argument in *Spring Phantoms*, 181n4.
76. Monte, *Invisible Fences*, 122 and 120, respectively.
77. Lazarus, *Selected Poems and Other Writings*, 241–47.
78. Vickery, *The Prose Elegy*, 3.
79. Ibid., 1.
80. Wanner, *Russian Minimalism*, 8.

81. Carpenter, *Aesthetics of Fraudulence*, 141.
82. Kaplan, *Baudelaire's Prose Poems*, 13.
83. Hill, *New and Collected Poems, 1952–1992*, 121.
84. A. Smith, "The Mongrel," 13.
85. Horvath, "Definition," 289; Loydell, "Towards a Definition," 292; Bidart, "Borges and I," 296; and Jenkins, "The Prose Poem," 299. All of these appear in *An Introduction to the Prose Poem*, ed. Clements and Dunham.
86. McGrath, "The Prose Poem," *No Boundaries*, 207.
87. Frow, *Genre*, 11.
88. Ibid., 11 and 12.
89. Ramazani, "'To Get the News from Poems,'" in *A Companion to Poetic Genre*, 15.
90. Frow, *Genre*, 30.
91. Blanchot and Mandell, *The Book to Come*, 200.
92. Prendergast, *Nineteenth-Century French Poetry*, 6.
93. Murphy, *A Tradition of Subversion*, 198.
94. Tall and D'Agata, "The Lyric Essay," n.p.
95. Aldrich, "The Boarding School," 111.
96. Benedikt, *The Prose Poem: An International Anthology*, 544.
97. P. Johnson, *Love Poems for the Millennium*, 30.
98. Monte, *Invisible Fences*, 17.
99. Perloff, *The Poetics of Indeterminacy*, 18.
100. Simic, "From Inside the Pot," in *The World Doesn't End*, 69.

Chapter 2

1. Perkins, *The Quest for Permanence*, 3; F. Stafford, *Reading Romantic Poetry*, vii.
2. Watson, *English Poetry of the Romantic Period*, 3.
3. Allport, "The Romantic Fragment Poem," 399.
4. Harries, *The Unfinished Manner*, 1.
5. Richards, *Without Rhyme or Reason*, 15; Santilli, *Such Rare Citings*, 39.
6. Santilli, *Such Rare Citings*, 31; Monroe, *A Poverty of Objects*, 71.
7. Allport, "The Romantic Fragment Poem," 399.
8. Baudelaire, "A Joker," in *Paris Spleen*, 8.
9. Baudelaire, "Dedication: For Arsène Houssaye," in *Paris Spleen*, 3.
10. Kaplan, *Baudelaire's Prose Poems*, 9.
11. Mackenzie, "Introduction," in *Paris Spleen and La Fanfarlo*, xiii.
12. Stauffer, *Anger, Revolution and Romanticism*, 16.
13. Sadoff, *History Matters*, 39.
14. Lowenthal, *The Past Is a Foreign Country*, 171–72.
15. Thomas, *Romanticism and Visuality*, 42.
16. Fitzgerald, "Autobiographical Memory," in *Theoretical Perspectives on Autobiographical Memory*, 101.
17. Ibid.
18. Mahony, "Introduction," in *The Literature of German Romanticism*, 1.

NOTES TO CHAPTER 2   265

19. F. Moore, "Early French Romanticism," in *A Companion to European Romanticism*, 177–78.
20. Ibid., 179.
21. Partridge, *The French Romantics' Knowledge of English Literature (1820–1848)*, 325 and 323, respectively.
22. Monroe, *A Poverty of Objects*, 89.
23. Paul Davies, "German Romanticism," in *Encyclopedia of Romanticism*, 230.
24. Bode, "Europe," in *Romanticism*, 127; emphasis in the original.
25. Vigus, "The Romantic Fragment," 8.
26. Thomas, *Romanticism and Visuality*, 42.
27. Bradshaw, "Hedgehog Theory," 74.
28. Bann, *Romanticism and the Rise of History*, 90.
29. Battles, "The Antiquarian Impulse," 67.
30. Vaughan, "Turnabouts in Taste," in *Romanticism and Postmodernism*, 44.
31. Berlin, *The Crooked Timber of Humanity*, 92.
32. Coleridge, *Collected Letters of Samuel Taylor Coleridge*, 349; emphasis in the original.
33. McFarland, *Romanticism and the Forms of Ruin*, 28–29.
34. Rauber, "The Fragment as Romantic Form," 214–15.
35. Novalis, *Novalis: Philosophical Writings*, 65.
36. Ibid., 81.
37. Schlegel, *Friedrich Schlegel's "Lucinde" and the Fragments*, 155.
38. O'Brien, *Rethinking the South*, 42.
39. Coleridge, *Samuel Taylor Coleridge: The Major Works*, 102–4.
40. J. C. Robinson, "Poetic Prose and Prose Poetry," in *The Encyclopedia of Romantic Literature: A–G*, 1019.
41. Wordsworth and Coleridge, *Lyrical Ballads*, 101.
42. Keats, *John Keats: Complete Poems*, 248–69 and 361–73.
43. Levinson, *The Romantic Fragment Poem*, 50.
44. Ibid., 186.
45. McFarland, *Romanticism and the Forms of Ruin*, 25.
46. Ibid., 25 and 5, respectively.
47. McFarland, *Romanticism and the Forms of Ruin*, 25; Schlegel, *Friedrich Schlegel's "Lucinde" and the Fragments*, 164.
48. Barkan, *Unearthing the Past*, 207.
49. Spenser, *Selected Shorter Poems*, 241.
50. Pope, *The Poems of Alexander Pope*, 513.
51. Coleridge, *Collected Letters of Samuel Taylor Coleridge*, 349.
52. Lacoue-Labarthe and Jean-Luc, *The Literary Absolute*, 42–43.
53. Schlegel, *Friedrich Schlegel's "Lucinde" and the Fragments*, 175.
54. Monroe, *A Poverty of Objects*, 47.
55. Schlegel, *Friedrich Schlegel's "Lucinde" and the Fragments*, 189.
56. Innes, "On the Limits of the Work of Art," 143.
57. Bradshaw, "Hedgehog Theory," 79.

58. Schlegel, *Friedrich Schlegel's "Lucinde" and the Fragments*, 170.
59. Rosen, *The Romantic Generation*, 51.
60. Levinson, *Romantic Fragment Poem*, 49 and 50.
61. Ibid., 113.
62. Crawford, *The Modern Poet*, 67.
63. Macpherson, "A Dissertation Concerning the Antiquity," in *Works of Ossian*, xxiv–xxv.
64. Curley, *Samuel Johnson, the "Ossian" Fraud, and the Celtic Revival*, 22–23.
65. Moore, "The Reception of *The Poems of Ossian*," 35.
66. Dunn, "Introduction," in *Fragments of Ancient Poetry*, n.p.
67. Humphrey, *The English Prosody*, 21.
68. Meyerstein, "The Influence of Ossian," 96.
69. Benedikt, *The Prose Poem: An International Anthology*, 43.
70. Crawford, *The Modern Poet*, 21; Barenblat, "Prose Poems or Microfiction?," n.p.
71. Davis, "Form as Response to Doubt," in *Biting the Error*, 36.
72. Larissy, "Introduction," in *Romanticism and Postmodernism*, 1.
73. Ibid., 1.
74. Coleridge, *Collected Letters of Samuel Taylor Coleridge*, 349; emphasis in the original.
75. Wordsworth and Coleridge, *Lyrical Ballads: 1798 and 1802*, 111.
76. Satterfield, "Why I Don't Write Nature Poems," in *Apocalypse Mix*, 83; emphasis in the original.
77. Satterfield, "Why I Don't Write Nature Poems," *Beltway Poetry Quarterly*, n.p.
78. Satterfield, "Why I Don't Write Nature Poems," in *Apocalypse Mix*, 83.
79. Kinsella, "Graphology 300: Against Nature Writing," 245.
80. Bly, "Warning to the Reader," in *Great American Prose Poems*, 83.
81. Shelley, "Adonais," in *Percy Bysshe Shelley: The Major Works*, 545.
82. Alyan, "Oklahoma," n.p.
83. Ibid., n.p.
84. Ibid., n.p.
85. Keats, *John Keats: Complete Poems*, 361.
86. Woloch, "Postcard to Ilya Kaminsky," in *Carpathia*, 16.
87. Ibid.
88. Carson, "On Hedonism," in *Great American Prose Poems*, 216.
89. Keats, *John Keats: Complete Poems*, 283.
90. Caldwell, "Wild Garlic and Detours," in *The Valley Press Anthology of Prose Poetry*, 52.
91. Waldrop, "From Lawn of Excluded Middle," in *A Cast-Iron Aeroplane*, 196.
92. E. Francis, "'Conquered good and conquering ill,'" in *Romanticism and Postmodernism*, 70.
93. Murphy, *A Tradition of Subversion*, 170.
94. Santilli, *Such Rare Citings*, 22.
95. Travis, *Reading Cultures*, 6.
96. Conway, "Autobiographical Knowledge," in *Remembering Our Past*, 67.

97. J. Taylor, "The Wonder-like Lightning of Prose Poetry," in *A Little Tour through European Poetry*, 1.
98. Tanehisa, "Friedrich Schlegel and the Idea of Fragment," 61.
99. Sieburth, "Introduction," in *Hymns and Fragments*, 34.
100. Ibid., 33–34.
101. Schlegel, *Friedrich Schlegel's "Lucinde" and the Fragments*, 175.

Chapter 3

1. C. H. Webb, "How I Met the Prose Poem, and What Ensued," in *Bear Flag Republic*, 85.
2. Caddy, "Hidden Form: The Prose Poem in English Poetry," in *Stress Fractures*, 105.
3. Attridge, *The Rhythms of English Poetry*, 321.
4. Ibid., 317.
5. Ibid., 318.
6. Alexander, "Prose/Poetry," in *The Party Train*, xxxi.
7. Graham, "Introduction," in *The Best American Poetry, 1990*, xxii.
8. Noel-Tod, *The Penguin Book of the Prose Poem*, xxiv.
9. Wordsworth and Coleridge, *Lyrical Ballads*, 100.
10. Ibid., 101.
11. Newman, "'Patron of the World': Henry Thoreau as Wordsworthian Poet," in *Henry David Thoreau*, 122; Faflick, *Boarding Out*, 159–60.
12. Arnold, *Dover Beach and Other Poems*, 86–87; Wilde, "Poems in Prose," n.p.
13. Blaisdell, *Imagist Poetry*, 65.
14. Wordsworth and Coleridge, *Lyrical Ballads*, 101.
15. Clements and Dunham, *An Introduction to the Prose Poem*, 4.
16. E. Burke, *Revolutionary Writings*, 57.
17. Scott, *Translating Rimbaud*, 42.
18. Ibid., 43.
19. Ibid., 49.
20. Ibid., 43.
21. Culler, *Theory of the Lyric*, 37.
22. C. K. Williams, *All at Once*, 5.
23. Rafferty, "The Pond," 37.
24. Harmony Holiday, "Crisis Actor," n.p.
25. Berry, "Some Fears," in Noel-Tod, *Penguin Book of the Prose Poem*, 43.
26. Kozak, "Assessing Urban Fragmentation," in *World Cities and Urban Form*, 241.
27. P. Smith, *The Coral Sea*, 19.
28. Greenhaus, "Art Garfunkel," 32.
29. Garfunkel, "Poem 81," in *Still Water Prose Poems*, n.p.
30. Pang, "1.290270,103.851959 (2017)," in *Cities: Ten Poets, Ten Cities*, 31.
31. Ibid., 138.
32. Pike, *The Image of the City*, 3.
33. Blake, "London," in *The Complete Poetry and Prose of William Blake*, 26–27; Wordsworth, *The Collected Poems*, 751.

34. Browning, *Aurora Leigh*, 135.
35. Whitman, *Leaves of Grass*, 165.
36. Ibid., 165 and 160, respectively.
37. Katsaros, *New York–Paris*, 47–48.
38. Guiney, "The Lights of London," in *American Poetry*, 533.
39. Lowell, "New York at Night," in *The City that Never Sleeps*, 109–10; Eliot, *Selected Poems*, 23.
40. Eliot, *Selected Poems*, 65.
41. Spender, "After They Have Tired," in *The Faber Book of Modern Verse*, 256–57.
42. H. Smith, *Hyperscapes in the Poetry of Frank O'Hara*, 58.
43. O'Hara, *The Collected Poems of Frank O'Hara*, 325.
44. Stonecipher, "Model City [35]," 49.
45. Fitterman, *This Window Makes Me Feel*, 3.
46. Filreis, "Listening Out the Collectivist Window," n.p.
47. Fitterman, *This Window Makes Me Feel*, 4.
48. M. Berman, *All That Is Solid Melts into Air*, 171.
49. Swensen, "Poetry City," n.p.
50. Baudelaire, *Paris Spleen*, 3.
51. Benjamin, "On Some Motifs in Baudelaire," in *The Writer of Modern Life*, 183.
52. Baudelaire, *Paris Spleen*, 97.
53. Weinstein, "Fragment and Form in the City of Modernism," in *The Cambridge Companion to the City in Literature*, 138.
54. Santilli, *Such Rare Citings*, 181.
55. Weinstein, "Fragment and Form in the City of Modernism," in *The Cambridge Companion to the City in Literature*, 138–39.
56. Tandt, "Mass, Forces, and the Urban Sublime," in *The Cambridge Companion to the City in Literature*, 128.
57. Ostriker, "Waiting for the Light," n.p.
58. Stonecipher, *Prose Poetry and the City*, 4.
59. Stonecipher, "Model City: With a Critical Introduction on Prose Poetry and the City," 13.
60. Stonecipher, *Prose Poetry and the City*, 161.
61. Broome, *Baudelaire's Poetic Patterns*, 10.
62. Katasaros, *New York–Paris*, 29–30.
63. Aćamović, "Walt Whitman and the City Culture," 39.
64. E. Wilson, *The Contradictions of Culture: Cities, Culture, Women*, 78–79.
65. Janet Wolff, *Feminine Sentences*, 41–42.
66. Baudelaire, *The Painter of Modern Life*, 12.
67. Ibid., 13.
68. Ibid., 4–5.
69. Benjamin, "The Paris of the Second Empire in Baudelaire," in *The Writer of Modern Life*, 54.
70. Seigel, *Bohemian Paris*, 3.
71. Ibid., 97–98.
72. Rosemary Lloyd, *Mallarmé: The Poet and His Circle*, 192.

73. Rimbaud, *Illuminations*, 89.
74. Israel-Pelletier, *Rimbaud's Impressionist Poetics*, 95.
75. De Certeau, "Walking in the City," in *The Practice of Everyday Life*, 93.
76. Mancini, "Imagined/Remembered Londons," 1.
77. Ibid.; emphasis in the original.
78. Murphy, "Introduction," in *Family Portrait*, 23.
79. Mancini, "Imagined/Remembered Londons," 1.
80. De Quincey, *The English Opium Eater*, 100.
81. Dupeyron-Lafay, "The Art of Walking and the Mindscapes of Trauma," in *Walking and the Aesthetics of Modernity*, 158.
82. De Quincey, *Literary Reminiscences*, 281.
83. Rawnsley, *Reminiscences of Wordsworth*, 18.
84. Hazlitt, "My First Acquaintance with Poets," in *Hazlitt: Selected Essays*, 15.
85. Marc Shell, *Talking the Walk*, 11.
86. Wordsworth, *The Collected Poems of William Wordsworth*, 243.
87. Dupeyron-Lafay, "The Art of Walking," in *Walking and the Aesthetics of Modernity*, 158 and 159.
88. De Quincey, *Confessions of an English Opium-Eater*, 206.
89. Hazlitt, "My First Acquaintance with Poets," in *Hazlitt: Selected Essays*, 15.
90. Evans, *Rhythm, Illusion and the Poetic Idea*, 113.
91. Ibid., 127.
92. Santilli, "Prose Poetry and the Spirit of Jazz," in *British Prose Poetry*, 280–81.
93. Fort, *Mrs. Belladonna's Supper Club Waltz*, 29.
94. Griffin, *"Who Set You Flowin'?,"* 65.
95. Toomer, "Seventh Street," in *Cane*, n.p.
96. M. Whalan, *Race, Manhood, and Modernism in America*, 194.
97. Toomer, *A Jean Toomer Reader*, 15.
98. Garraty, *The American Nation*, 728.
99. Hutchison, "Here, There and Everywhere," 109.
100. Giscombe, *Prairie Style*, 8.
101. Ibid., 11.
102. Ibid., 31.
103. Hayes, "A Land Governed by Unkindness Reaps No Kindness," n.p.
104. Ashford, "Biography: Yusef Komunyakaa," n.p.
105. Komunyakaa, *Thieves of Paradise*, 85 and 86.
106. Murphy, "The British Prose Poem," in *British Prose Poetry*, 42.
107. Dismorr, "June Night," 67.
108. Eliot, *Selected Poems*, 23–25, 26–28; *BLAST*, no. 2 (July 1915).
109. Stein, *Tender Buttons*, 11; Knight, *The Patient Particulars*, 115.
110. Stein, *Tender Buttons*, 11.
111. Lowell, "Spring Day," in Alexander, ed., *Family Portrait*, 158–62.
112. Ibid.
113. D. R. Jones, *King of Critics*, 244.
114. Beye, "The Unremitting Stain," in Alexander, ed., *Family Portrait*, 64.
115. Borson, "City," in *The Lyric Paragraph*, 57.

116. Ekiss, "Into the City," n.p.
117. Belkhyr, "Interlude with Drug of Choice," n.p.
118. Wallace, "Ahakoa he iti he pounamu | Although it is small it is greenstone," in *Bad Things*, 63.
119. Meitner, "A Brief Ontological Investigation," n.p.
120. Mancini, "Imagined/Remembered Londons," 1.
121. Estes, "Walking and Technology in the Fiction of Jennifer Egan," in *Walking and the Aesthetics of Modernity*, 285.

Chapter 4

1. Shakespeare, *Shakespeare's Sonnets*, 147.
2. B. H. Smith, *Poetic Closure*, 26.
3. Shakespeare, *Shakespeare's Sonnets*, 193.
4. Coombs, "A Kind of Gentle Painting," in *European Visions*, 77.
5. B. H. Smith, *Poetic Closure*, 24.
6. Caws, "The Self-Defining Prose Poem," in *The Prose Poem in France*, 180–81.
7. B. H. Smith, *Poetic Closure*, 25; emphasis in the original.
8. Ibid., 25–26.
9. Ibid., 30.
10. Fredman, *Poet's Prose*, 57.
11. Ginsberg, "The Bricklayer's Lunch Hour," in *Empty Mirror*, 31.
12. Ginsberg, "The Bricklayer's Lunch Hour," in Ford, "A Little Anthology of the Poem in Prose," 342.
13. Alexander, "Prose/Poetry," in *The Party Train*, xxx.
14. Hejinian, "The Rejection of Closure," in *The Language of Inquiry*, 43.
15. Hejinian, "Continuing Against Closure," n.p.
16. M. Richards, *Without Rhyme or Reason*, 53.
17. Black, *The Son of a Shoemaker*, 39.
18. Black, "Linda Black, *Inventory*," n.p.
19. Kawakami, "Nathalie Sarraute's Accent," 511.
20. Long, "Something Like a Meditation," in *The Rose Metal Press Field Guide to Prose Poetry*, 41; and Monson, *This Line Is Not For Turning*, 7.
21. Jenkins, quoted in Freitag, ed., *Recovery and Transgression*, 110.
22. LaFemina, "A Carnival Comes to Town," in *The Rose Metal Press Guide to Prose Poetry*, 130.
23. Sooke, "Joseph Cornell," n.p.
24. Simic, *Dime Story Alchemy*, ix; Sooke, "Joseph Cornell," n.p.
25. Iglesias, *Boxing Inside the Box*, 29.
26. Ibid., 15.
27. Beckel and Rooney, "Field Notes: A Preface," in *The Rose Metal Press Guide to Prose Poetry*, xiii.
28. Ibid.
29. Santilli, "Preface," in *This Line Is Not For Turning*, 11.

30. Etter, "Poetry in the Prose," 71.
31. Sabol, "*Hotel Utopia* by Robert Miltner: Review and Interview," n.p.
32. Murphy, *A Tradition of Subversion*, 3.
33. Edson, "Portrait of the Writer as a Fat Man," in *Claims for Poetry*, 101.
34. Alexander, "Prose/Poetry," in *The Party Train*, xxv.
35. Shapcott, "Letters to the Editor," n.p.
36. Tate, "James Tate," in *Ecstatic Occasions*, 202.
37. McGookey, "Why I Write Prose Poems," in *The Rose Metal Press Field Guide to Prose Poetry*, 50.
38. Iglesias, "Prose Poetry, Point of View," n.p.
39. Larson, "The Griffin of Literature," n.p.
40. Bar-Nadav, "Who Is Flying This Plane?," in *A Broken Thing*, 44–45.
41. Price, "Hedge Sparrows," in *Lucky Day*, 27.
42. Bar-Nadav, "Who Is Flying This Plane?," in *A Broken Thing*, 45.
43. Ibid., 44.
44. Hummer, "Moravia: Postcards," in *An Introduction to the Prose Poem*, 234–36.
45. Selerie, "Casement," in *Music's Duel*, 249.
46. Adler, "Concrete Poetry," in *Encyclopedia of German Literature*, 195.
47. Simic, "We Were So Poor," in *The World Doesn't End*, 8.
48. Lehman, *Great American Prose Poems*, 125.
49. Simic, *New and Selected Poems*, 112.
50. Kinsella, *Spatial Relations*, 482.
51. Scott, *Channel Crossings*, n.p.
52. Keene, "Introduction," in *The Modern Japanese Prose Poem*, 3.
53. Watts, "Searching for a Haiku, in a Haibun," n.p.
54. Bly, *The Morning Glory*, xiii.
55. Kennard, "The Expanse," 2.
56. Nezhukumatathil, "Summer Haibun," n.p.
57. Ross, "Introduction," in *Journey to the Interior*, 16.
58. Kennard, "The Expanse," 116.
59. Greathouse, "Poetry: Burning Haibun," n.p.
60. Saito, "Peace, Bells, Cuttings," n.p.
61. Buffam, *A Pillow Book*, 55.
62. Ibid., 20.
63. Rudd, "Following Where the Brush Leads," 44.
64. Hahn, *The Unbearable Heart*, 27–28.
65. Iglesias, *Boxing Inside the Box*, 95.
66. Ibid., 82.
67. Xie, *Eye Level*, 46.
68. Ashton, "Origins of Sublime," 158–59.
69. Silliman, comments on *Rain Taxi*, *Silliman's Blog*, n.p.
70. Ashton, "Origins of Sublime," 158–59.
71. Gioia, "Thirteen Ways of Thinking about the Poetic Line," n.p.
72. Silliman, *The New Sentence*, 91.

73. Bell, "A Lifetime in Poetry: Marvin Bell," quoted in L. Glass, *Los Angeles Review of Books*.
74. Vuong, "Trevor," n.p.
75. Vuong, "Partly True Poem Reflected in a Mirror," n.p.
76. Hershman, "Powers of Ten," n.p.
77. Wrigley, review of Barbara Tran's *In the Mynah Bird's Own Words*, n.p.
78. Tran, "Rosary," n.p.
79. McMaster, review of Kasischke's "Space, in Chains," n.p.
80. Kasischke, "Memory of Grief," in *Space, in Chains*, 8.
81. Hayes, "Introduction to 'Dream-Clung, Gone,'" n.p.
82. L. Russell, *What's Hanging on the Hush*, 40.
83. Hayes and Lehman, "Sonnets and Fast Breaks," n.p.
84. Ives, *Orange Roses*, 10.
85. Agbabi, *Bloodshot and Monochrome*, 46.
86. Ibid., 45.
87. Berz, "Mapping the Contemporary Sonnet," n.p.
88. Van Dyck, "Introduction," in *Austerity Measures*, xxi–xxii.
89. Stallings, "Austerity Measures," in *Austerity Measures*, n.p.
90. Ibid.

Chapter 5

1. Lehman, *Great American Prose Poems*, 11.
2. Edson, "The Prose Poem in America," 321.
3. Delville, *The American Prose Poem*, 243.
4. Delville, "Strange Tales and Bitter Emergencies," in *An Exaltation of Forms*, 263.
5. Bruhn, *Images and Ideas*, 181.
6. Monte, *Invisible Fences*, 179.
7. Ibid., 135.
8. Baudelaire, "To Each His Chimæra," in *Paris Spleen*, 12.
9. Rimbaud, "Letter of 13 May 1871 to Georges Izambard," in *Rimbaud: Complete Works, Selected Letters*, 371; emphasis in the original.
10. Peyre, "Rimbaud's Life and Work," in *A Season in Hell; The Illuminations*, 21.
11. Quoted in McGuinness, "Symbolism," in *The Cambridge History of French Literature*, 487.
12. Ibid., 483.
13. Kennard, "The Expanse," 89.
14. Pinsky, *The Situation of Poetry*, 4; Breslin, "How to Read the New Contemporary Poem," 358.
15. Gioia, quoted in Iglesias, *Boxing Inside the Box*, 8. Henry, "'The beautiful white ruins / of America,'" 12.
16. In Caws, *The Yale Anthology of Twentieth-Century French Poetry*, 177.
17. Henry, "'The beautiful white ruins / of America,'" ii.
18. Gioia, "James Tate and American Surrealism," n.p.

NOTES TO CHAPTER 5   273

19. Tate, "The Cowboy," n.p.
20. Tate, "I sat at my desk and contemplated all that I had accomplished," in *The Government Lake*, 82.
21. Taylor, *Paths to Contemporary French Literature*, 315.
22. Tate, "The Cowboy," n.p.
23. Alexander, "The American Prose Poem, 1890–1980," 23.
24. Kennard, "The Expanse," 6–7.
25. Bradley, "If André Breton Were Alive Today," n.p.
26. Silliman, *The New Sentence*, 88.
27. Bradley, "If André Breton Were Alive Today," n.p.
28. Silliman, "You," from *The Alphabet*, n.p.
29. Silliman, *The New Sentence*, 81.
30. Kennard, " 'Man and Nature In and Out of Order' : The Surrealist Prose Poetry of David Gascoyne," 254.
31. Mullen, *Sleeping with the Dictionary*, 67.
32. Ibid.
33. Breton, *Manifesto of Surrealism*, 26.
34. Joron, *The Cry at Zero*, 100.
35. Lamantia, *The Collected Poems of Philip Lamantia*, 235.
36. Gioia, "James Tate and American Surrealism," n.p.
37. Spalding, "Charles Simic," n.p.
38. Bly, "Leaping Poetry," 1.
39. Beach, *The Cambridge Introduction to Twentieth-Century American Poetry*, 179.
40. Henry, " 'The beautiful white ruins / of America,' " 11.
41. Zweig, "The New Surrealism," in *Contemporary Poetry in America*, 316.
42. Benedikt, *The Prose Poem: An International Anthology*, 48.
43. D. Mitchell, "The Poet's Revolt," n.p.
44. Schomburg, "The Fire Cycle," in *Scary, No Scary*, 43.
45. In D. Mitchell, "The Poet's Revolt," n.p.
46. Anderson, "Thimbleism," in *Traffic: New and Selected Poems*, 14.
47. Andrews, "Editorial Letter," n.p.
48. Bateman, "Distinction," in *Clumsy*, n.p.
49. Seigel, "Urban Fantasy vs. Magical Realism: Writing Life," n.p.
50. Friedman, "Catching the Monster."
51. Lehman, *Great American Prose Poems*, 13.
52. Stevens, *Collected Poetry and Prose*, 81 and 449; Phillips, *The Poetics of the Everyday*, 1.
53. Gosetti-Ferencei, *The Ecstatic Quotidian*, 1 and 123.
54. Simic, "A Long Course in Miracles," in *Pretty Happy!*, 15.
55. Jenkins, *Nice Fish*, 1.
56. Friedman, quoted in P. Johnson, *The Best of the Prose Poem*, 11.
57. Lehman, in *Lofty Dogmas*, 266.
58. De Lautréamont, *Lautréamont's Maldoror*, 177.
59. Ponge, *Soap*, 13.

60. José Rodríguez Feo, quoted in Coyle and Filreis, eds., *Secretaries of the Moon*, 168.
61. Scottish Poetry Library, *SPL Guide to Prose Poetry*, 2.
62. Silliman, comments on Audrey Wurdemann and Joseph Auslander, *Silliman's Blog*, n.p.
63. T. Whalen, *Dolls: Prose Poems*, 10.
64. Gioia, "James Tate and American Surrealism," n.p.
65. Simic, *New and Selected Poems, 1962–2012*, 111.
66. Simic, "Seven Prose Poems," n.p.
67. Simic, *New and Selected Poems, 1962–2012*, 119.
68. Edson, "Interview: The Art of the Prose Poem," 32.
69. Ibid.
70. Edson, *The Tunnel: Selected Poems*, 118.
71. Tursi, "An Interview with Russell Edson," n.p.
72. Delville, *The American Prose Poem*, 113.
73. Ibid., 110.
74. Simic, "We Were Stolen by the Gypsies," in *The World Doesn't End*, 5.
75. Lehman, *Great American Prose Poems*, 12.
76. Ibid., 12.
77. Simic, "We Were So Poor," in *The World Doesn't End*, 8.
78. Delville, *The American Prose Poem*, 170.
79. Silliman, *The New Sentence*, 81.
80. Olson, quoted in Edson, *See Jack*, back cover; Edson, "Interview: The Art of the Prose Poem," 32.
81. Edson, "Interview: The Art of the Prose Poem," 32.
82. Edson, *The Tunnel: Selected Poems*, 180.
83. Upton, "Structural Politics: The Prose Poetry of Russell Edson," 108.
84. Edson, *The Tunnel*, 218.
85. Lehman, *Great American Prose Poems*, 12.
86. Iglesias, *Boxing Inside the Box*, 14.
87. Ibid., 15.
88. Delville, *The American Prose Poem*, 138.
89. Chernoff, "Kill Yourself with an *Objet D'art*," in *Lyrik-Line*, n.p.
90. Catalano, "Incident from a War," in *Light and Water*, n.p.
91. Skovron, "Supplication," in *Autographs*, 5.
92. Ibid.
93. Campbell, *Poetic Revolutionaries: Intertextuality & Subversion*, 185.
94. Walwicz, "Neons," n.p.
95. Manhire, "Prose Poems," in *Doubtful Sounds*, 181.
96. Ellis, "British Prose Poetry," n.p.
97. Fairclough, "Unavailable," in *This Line Is Not For Turning*, 39.
98. Caldwell and Hardwick, "Introduction," in *The Valley Press Anthology of Prose Poetry*, 9–10.
99. Seed, "A Life," in *Makers of Empty Dreams*, 53.
100. Hardwick, *Learning to Have Lost*, 2.
101. Kennard, *The Migraine Hotel*, 19.

102. Caleshu, *A Dynamic Exchange Between Us*, 13.
103. Armitage, "The Christening," in *Seeing Stars: Poems*, 3.
104. M. Atkins, *The Logic of the Stairwell*, 20.
105. Petit, "My Larzac Childhood," in *The Treekeeper's Tale*, 41.

Chapter 6

1. Wallerstein, "The Invention of TimeSpace Realities," 287–97.
2. Bemong et al., *Bakhtin's Theory of the Literary Chronotope*, 5.
3. The following discussion draws to some extent on a section of the paper by Robertson and Hetherington, "A Mosaic Patterning," in *New Writing*, 36–46.
4. Bakhtin, "Forms of Time and of the Chronotope," In *The Dialogic Imagination*, 243–49 and 252.
5. Ibid., 249.
6. Ibid.
7. Ibid., 250; emphasis in the original.
8. Barry, *Contemporary British Poetry and the City*, 55.
9. Harvey, *The Condition of Postmodernity*, 240.
10. Coles, "The Poem in Time," n.p.
11. Marvell, *The Poems of Andrew Marvell*, 81; Whitman, "Song of Myself," 83.
12. Shakespeare, *The Tragedy of Macbeth*, 203.
13. Ibid., 203–4.
14. Atherton et al., "The Prose Poetry Project," n.p.
15. Barrett Browning, *Elizabeth Barrett Browning*, 103.
16. Mallarmé, "Preface," in *A Roll of the Dice*, 1.
17. Ibid.
18. Stonecipher, *Poetry and the City*, 99.
19. Mallarmé, *A Roll of the Dice*, 20–21.
20. Derrida, "The Double Session," in *Disseminaton*, 194; emphasis in the original.
21. Ibid., 193; emphasis in the original.
22. Hoffer, *Reflets Reciproques*, 25; emphasis in the original.
23. Sartre, *Mallarmé, or the Poet of Nothingness*, 140.
24. Mallarmé, *Divagations*, 208 and 209.
25. Stonecipher, *Poetry and the City*, 76.
26. Benson, "Demeter," n.p.
27. Hoffberg, "Art People," 39.
28. Brainard, "I Remember," in *Collected Writings of Joe Brainard*, 15.
29. Wordsworth, "Home at Grasmere" in "The Recluse," in *The Collected Poems of William Wordsworth*, 884.
30. Ricks, "William Wordsworth," in *William Wordsworth's "The Prelude,"* 49.
31. Harms, "'Goodtime Jesus' and Other Sort-of Prose Poems," in *Bear Flag Republic*, 11.
32. J. S. Williams, "Lesson No. 4," n.p.
33. Oliver, *A Poetry Handbook*, 35.
34. Marcus, "Freedom, The Prose Poem & The Imagination," n.p.

35. Carver, "Will You Please Be Quiet, Please?," in *Will You Please Be Quiet, Please?*, 164.
36. Edson, "The Dummies," in *See Jack*, 15.
37. May and Thrift, *Timespace: Geographies of Temporality*, 2.
38. Harvey, *The Condition of Postmodernity*, 240; our emphasis.
39. Knowles et al., "Reading Space in Visual Poetry," 75.
40. Howell, "The Prose Poem: What the Hell is it?," n.p.
41. Lowes, "The Unity of the Paragraph," in *An Introduction to the Prose Poem*, 294.
42. Beckel, "Introduction," in the *Prose Poem Issue* of the *Beltway Poetry Quarterly*, n.p.
43. Ibid.
44. Many poets in the "Essays" sections in *Bear Flag Republic: Prose Poems and Poetics from California* (2008), *The Rose Metal Press Field Guide to Prose Poetry: Contemporary Poets in Discussion and Practice* (2010), and *A Cast-Iron Aeroplane that Can Actually Fly: Commentaries from 80 Contemporary American Poets on Their Prose Poetry* (2019) discuss their choices in deciding whether to write a prose poem or lineated poem.
45. Marcus, "In Praise of the Prose Poem," in *Bear Flag Republic*, 18.
46. Wakoski, "Looking for the New Measure," in *Bear Flag Republic*, 38.
47. Stonecipher, *Prose Poetry and the City*, 92.
48. Beckel, "Introduction," to the *Prose Poem Issue* in the *Beltway Poetry Quarterly*, n.p.
49. Dorf, "The Big Bang of Prose Poetry," n.p.
50. Monson, *This Line Is Not For Turning*, 117.
51. Alexander and Maloney, *The House of Your Dream*, n.p.
52. Clements and Dunham, "Preface," in *An Introduction to the Prose Poem*, 4.
53. Lombardo, *Machines We Have Built*, 1.
54. P. Johnson, *The Best of the Prose Poem*, 240.
55. Munden, "Playing with Time," n.p.
56. Ibid.
57. Ibid.
58. Seed, "All Kinds of Dust," in *Anonymous Intruder*, 53.
59. Black, "Begin with a Hook," 2.
60. Harvey, "The Backyard Mermaid," n.p.
61. Brophy, "The Night's Insomnia," in *Radar*, 61.
62. Longenbach, *The Art of the Poetic Line*, 88.
63. Akbar, "Calling a Wolf a Wolf (Inpatient)," n.p.
64. Danladi, *Take Me Back*, 15.
65. Culler, *Theory of the Lyric*, 37.

Chapter 7

1. Sontag, *On Photography*, 71.
2. Ibid., 95–96.
3. Rice, *Parisian Views*, 32.
4. Ibid., 51.
5. Murphy, "The British Prose Poem," in *British Prose Poetry*, 37.

NOTES TO CHAPTER 7   277

6. Ibid., 31.
7. Huyssen, *Miniature Metropolis*, 126.
8. Ibid.
9. Moores, "Loading the Image," 102.
10. Butcher-McGunnigle, *Autobiography of a Marguerite*, 84.
11. Huyssen, *Miniature Metropolis*, 127.
12. Raser, *Baudelaire and Photography*, 105.
13. Ibid., 106.
14. Weingarden, "The Mirror as a Metaphor of Baudelairean Modernity," in *Orientations*, 18.
15. Huyssen, *Miniature Metropolis*, 33.
16. Morley, *Writing on the Wall*, 19.
17. Ibid.
18. Sartre, *Baudelaire*, 22.
19. Baudelaire, "IV: A Joker," in *Paris Spleen*, 8.
20. Bernard, "Notice," in *Illuminations*, 246.
21. Robb, *Rimbaud*, 265.
22. Scott, *Translating Rimbaud's "Illuminations,"* 48.
23. Ashbery, "Preface," in *Illuminations*, 16.
24. Israel-Pelletier, *Rimbaud's Impressionist Poetics*, 87.
25. Berg, *Imagery and Ideology*, 16.
26. Rimbaud, *Illuminations*, 19.
27. A. Caldwell, "What Is Prose Poetry?," n.p.
28. A. Caldwell, "Prose Poetry and Visual Art," 28.
29. Chernoff, "Lost and Found," n.p.
30. Sanders, *This Is a Map of Their Watching Me*, 27.
31. Ibid., 22.
32. Loizeaux, *Twentieth-Century Poetry and the Visual Arts*, 2.
33. W.J.T. Mitchell, *Picture Theory*, 15 and 16.
34. Swensen, "To Writewithize," 122.
35. Paul, "Pianist and Still Life, 1924, Henri Matisse," in *Reading Girl*, n.p.
36. Miltner, "Québec Express," n.p.
37. P. Wright, "A Hybrid Form? The Ekphrastic Prose Poem," n.p.
38. P. Wright, "Black Square," n.p.
39. P. Wright, "A Hybrid Form? The Ekphrastic Prose Poem," n.p.
40. Bang, "Mask Photo," in *A Doll for Throwing: Poems*, 54.
41. Berger, *Ways of Seeing*, 10.
42. Sontag, *On Photography*, 71.
43. Murphy, "The British Prose Poem," in *British Prose Poetry*, 38.
44. Weems, "She felt monogamy had a place," n.p. (gallery display).
45. Weems, quoted in Eckardt, "Carrie Mae Weems Reflects," 1.
46. Tate Museum Collective, "Daniel Spoerri Prose Poems, 1959–60," n.p. (gallery display).
47. Gard, "White Approach," in *Threads*, n.p.
48. Habra, "Afterthought," in *Under Brushstrokes*, 23.

49. Iglesias, "Conceptual Art," in *Angles of Approach*, n.p.
50. Monson, "Square of Light: The Artist is Present I," in *The Shared Surface*, 54.
51. Ibid., 54.
52. Monson, "The Artist Is Present II," in *The Shared Surface*, 55.
53. Ibid., 55.
54. Bonomo, "Hyphen: Sketching the Bridge," in *The Rose Metal Press Field Guide to Prose Poetry*, 123–24.
55. Arnheim, *Visual Thinking*, 254.
56. Ibid., 104.
57. Ganczarek, Hünefeldt, and Belardinelli, "From 'Einfühlung' to Empathy," n.p.
58. Elliott, "Aesthetic Theory and the Experience of Art," in *Aesthetics*, 146; emphasis in the original.
59. Cohen, "Metaphor and the Cultivation of Intimacy," 8.
60. Hirsch, *How to Read a Poem*, 15.
61. Cohen, "Metaphor and the Cultivation of Intimacy," 8.
62. Downey, *Creative Imagination*, 179.
63. Lanzoni, "Empathy Aesthetics," in *Rethinking Empathy through Literature*, 34.
64. Pound, "The Serious Artist," 162.
65. P. Jones, *Imagist Poetry*, 15.
66. Rainey, *Modernism: An Anthology*, 94.
67. Flint, "Imagisme," 199; Loizeaux, *Twentieth-Century Poetry*, 3.
68. A. Berman, *Preface to Modernism*, 49.
69. Lanzoni, "Empathy Aesthetics," in *Rethinking Empathy through Literature*, 35.
70. Downey, *Creative Imagination*, 107; emphasis in the original.
71. Ibid., 145.
72. Murphy, "The British Prose Poem," in *British Prose Poetry*, 37.
73. P. Jones, *Imagist Poetry*, 14.
74. Williams, "The Red Wheelbarrow," in *Selected Poems*, 57; Eliot, "The Love Song of J. Alfred Prufrock," in *Selected Poems*, 11–16.
75. Scofield, *T. S. Eliot: The Poems*, 39.
76. Beach, *The Cambridge Introduction to Twentieth-Century American Poetry*, 179.
77. Bly, "A Caterpillar on the Desk," 34.
78. Rosenblatt, *The Reader, the Text, the Poem*, 76.
79. Gropp, "Photo Graph Paper: American Push," in *The Hominine Egg*, 16.
80. Dockins, "Eleven Gin & Tonics," n.p.
81. Brandt, "The Harbor," n.p.
82. Downey, *Creative Imagination*, 7.
83. Garcia, *Porridge: Prose Poems*, 63.
84. Garcia, "Diorama," n.p.
85. Downey, *Creative Imagination*, 176; also cited in Lanzoni, "Empathy Aesthetics," in *Rethinking Empathy through Literature*, 34.
86. Downey, *Creative Imagination*, 179.
87. Huyssen, *Miniature Metropolis*, 126.
88. Smith and Watson, *Reading Autobiography*, 277.
89. Wittgenstein, *Tractatus Logico-Philosophicus*, 68; emphasis in the original.

90. Plato, *Theaetetus*, 295; Aristotle, *On Memory*, 716; Augustine, *St. Augustine Confessions*, 185; and Locke, *An Essay Concerning Human Understanding*, 149.
91. Hume, *A Treatise on Human Nature*, 246.
92. Brewer, "Memory for Randomly Sampled," in *Remembering Reconsidered*, 86; Rubin, "Beginnings of a Theory," in *Autobiographical Memory*, 55.
93. Rubin, "Beginnings of a Theory," in *Autobiographical Memory*, 55–56.
94. Ibid., 57.
95. Albright, "Literary and Psychological Models of the Self," in *The Remembering Self*, 31.
96. Neisser, "What Is Ordinary Memory the Memory Of?," in *Remembering Reconsidered*, 367; Conway, "Autobiographical Knowledge," in *Remembering Our Past*, 67.
97. Barclay, "Autobiographical Remembering," in *Remembering Our Past*, 99.
98. A. Berman, *Preface to Modernism*, 67.
99. Ibid.
100. Abrantes, *Meaning and Mind*, 161.
101. Mar and Oatley, "The Function of Fiction," 173.
102. Ross, *Remembering the Personal Past*, vii.
103. Munden, "Arthroscopy/Sports Day, 1971," in *Keys*, 21.
104. Huyssen, *Miniature Metropolis*, 127.
105. Monson, "Introduction," in *British Prose Poetry*, 7.
106. Murphy, "The British Prose Poem," in *British Prose Poetry*, 37.
107. Monte, *Invisible Fences*, 212.
108. Kosslyn, Thompson, and Ganis, *The Case for Mental Imagery*, 4.
109. Bond, "Empathy and the Poetic Imagination," n.p.

Chapter 8

1. Greene, Cushman, and Cavanagh, *Princeton Encyclopedia of Poetry and Poetics*, 876.
2. Brown, "The Emergent Prose Poem," in *A Companion to Poetic Genre*, 325.
3. Radden and Kövecses, "Towards a Theory of Metonymy," in *Metonymy in Language and Thought*, 20.
4. Littlemore, *Metonymy*, 13.
5. Glucksberg, *Understanding Figurative Language*, v.
6. Nowottny, *Language Poets Use*, 67.
7. Barcelona, "Introduction: The Cognitive Theory," in *Metaphor and Metonymy at the Crossroads*, 9.
8. Dickinson, "I dwell in Possibility," in *The Poems of Emily Dickinson*, 483–84.
9. Barcelona, "Introduction: The Cognitive Theory," in *Metaphor and Metonymy at the Crossroads*, 10.
10. Ibid., 11.
11. Yoon, "Productivity of Spanish Verb-Noun Compounds," in *Metaphor and Metonymy Revisited*, 104.
12. Brittan, *Poetry, Symbol and Allegory*, x.
13. B. H. Smith, *Poetic Closure*, 85–86.
14. Caws, "The Self-Defining Prose Poem," in *The Prose Poem in France*, 181.

15. Clements and Dunham, "Prose Poems about Prose Poems," in *An Introduction to the Prose Poem*, 287.
16. T. Whalen, "Why I Hate the Prose Poem," in *An Introduction to the Prose Poem*, 300.
17. Edson, "The Prose Poem as a Beautiful Animal," in *An Introduction to the Prose Poem*, 302; Loydell, "Towards a Definition," in *An Introduction to the Prose Poem*, 292.
18. Bly, "The Prose Poem as an Evolving Form," in *Selected Poems*, 199–204; P. Johnson, "Introduction," *The Best of the Prose Poem*, 11.
19. Vico, *The New Science of Giambattista Vico* (404), 129.
20. Merwin, "Humble Beginning," in *An Introduction to the Prose Poem*, 135.
21. Vaughn, "Letter to My Imagined Daughter," in *An Introduction to the Prose Poem*, 45.
22. Ibid.
23. Heynen, "The Boys Go to Ask a Neighbor," in *The Boys' House: Stories*, 28–29.
24. Ibid.
25. Ibid.
26. Preminger, ed., *Princeton Encyclopedia of Poetics*, 664.
27. Santilli, *Such Rare Citings*, 138.
28. T. Atkins, *Koto Y Yo*, 44.
29. Aldama, *Formal Matters in Contemporary Latino Poetry*, 22.
30. Stein, *Tender Buttons*, 13.
31. Delville, *The American Prose Poem*, 76.
32. J. Webb, "1973," in *Sentences from the Archive*, 38.
33. R. Robinson, "1 Minute Lecture: On Prose Poems," n.p.
34. Kristeva, "Word, Dialogue and Novel," in *The Kristeva Reader*, 85; emphasis in the original.
35. Lehman, "Poem in the Manner of Charles Baudelaire," in *Poems in the Manner Of*, 36.
36. M. Riffaterre, "On the Prose Poem's Formal Features," in *The Prose Poem in France*, 119.
37. Scheele, "The Wake of Plenty," in *Models of the Universe*, 248.
38. Proust, "The Captive," in *Marcel Proust: Remembrance of Things Past*, 657.
39. Scheele, "The Wake of Plenty," in *Models of the Universe*, 248.
40. Santilli, "Prose Poetry and the Spirit of Jazz," in *British Prose Poetry*, 286.
41. Ibid., 287.
42. Rushdie, "The Empire Writes Back," n.p.
43. Ashcroft, Griffiths, and Tiffin, *The Empire Writes Back*, 32.
44. Thieme, *Postcolonial Con-texts*, 1.
45. Chanan, "Revisiting Rocha's 'Aesthetics of Violence,'" in *Killer Images*, 92.
46. Atherton, *Pre-Raphaelite*, 13.
47. Ibid.
48. Hemingway, "Hills Like White Elephants," in *The Essential Hemingway*, 406.
49. Hetherington, "Antiquities," 122.
50. Austen, *Emma*, 51.

51. K. Miller, "Things," n.p.
52. Hetherington, "Antiquities," 122.
53. Ramazani, *The Cambridge Companion to Postcolonial Poetry*, 1.
54. McCooey, "Postcolonial Poetry," in *The Cambridge Companion to Postcolonial Poetry*, 77.
55. Wagan Watson, "There's No Place Like Home," n.p.
56. Zhicheng-Mingdé Kon, "dame de compagnie :: lady of company," n.p.
57. Ibid.
58. Atwood, "In Love with Raymond Chandler," in *Great American Prose Poems*, 131.
59. Shumate, *The Floating Bridge*, 4.
60. Ibid., 4.
61. Ibid., 9.
62. Shumate, *High Water Mark*, 3.
63. Bar-Nadav, "And Leaves the Shreds Behind," 45; Dickinson, "She Sweeps," in *The Poems of Emily Dickinson*, 335–37.
64. Rodríguez, "A Weekend in the Country," 176.
65. Ibid.
66. Burns, "Out There," 145.
67. Russell, *What's Hanging on the Hush*, 69.
68. Shapiro, "Richard M. Nixon," 121.
69. Ibid.
70. Strand, "Chekhov: A Sestina," in *Great American Prose Poems*, 114.
71. I. A. Richards, *The Philosophy of Rhetoric*, 94; emphasis in the original.
72. Brown, "I Went Disguised in It," in *British Prose Poetry*, 184.
73. Murphy, *A Tradition of Subversion*, 170.

Chapter 9

1. Iglesias, *Boxing Inside the Box*, 3–4.
2. Griffin, *Women and Nature*, xiii.
3. Iglesias, *Boxing Inside the Box*, 98.
4. Moorman Robbins, *American Hybrid Poetics*, 103–4.
5. Chernoff, "Maxine Chernoff: In Conversation," n.p.
6. McGrath Smith, "Gendre: Women's Prose Poetry," 257.
7. Iglesias, *Boxing Inside the Box*, 14.
8. Ibid.
9. Monte, *Invisible Fences*, 62.
10. Staff, "Reading Anne Carson's Reissued *Short Talks*," n.p.; Bass, "Claudia Rankine's *Citizen*," n.p.
11. Fehr, "Female Desire in Prose Poetry," 2.
12. Ibid., 4–8.
13. Ibid., 6.
14. Ibid., 4.
15. Ibid., 16.
16. Ibid., 17.

17. Markotic, "Narrotics," n.p.
18. Ibid.
19. Ibid.
20. Delville, *The American Prose Poem*, 140.
21. Ibid., 142.
22. Ibid., 148–49.
23. Monson, "The Prose Poem in England Today," n.p.
24. Debney, *How to Be a Dragonfly*, 61.
25. Andrews and Bernstein, "Repossessing the Word," in *The L=A=N=G=U=A=G=E Book*, ix.
26. Pallant, "Yonder Zongs," in *An Introduction to the Prose Poem*, 262–63.
27. Bartlett, "What is 'Language Poetry'?," 742.
28. Bernstein and Aryal, "Interview with Charles Bernstein," 56.
29. Ibid.
30. Staff and Silliman, "Ron Silliman Redefines Language Poetry," n.p.
31. Silliman, "Disappearance of the Word," in *The L=A=N=G=U=A=G=E Book*, 125.
32. Ibid., 130.
33. Silliman, "Wise Guys Meet in La Jolla," *Silliman's Blog*, n.p.
34. Lerner, "Beyond 'Lyric Shame,'" n.p.
35. Balkun, "Review of Human-Ghost Hybrid Project by Carol Guess and Daniela Olszewska," n.p.
36. Lundy Martin, *Discipline*, i–ii.
37. Iglesias, "Perishables," in *A Cast-Iron Aeroplane*, 101.
38. Silliman, "Boxing Inside the Box," n.p.
39. Delville, *The American Prose Poem*, 1.
40. Hinton, "An Introduction to Reading Carla Harryman," n.p.
41. Silliman, *The New Sentence*, 91 and 92.
42. Perloff, "Marjorie Perloff: On 'The Chinese Letter,'" n.p.
43. Perloff, "Language Poetry and the Lyric Subject," 415–16.
44. Delville, *The American Prose Poem*, 210.
45. Hejinian, *My Life and My Life in the Nineties*, 62–63.
46. Ibid., 62.
47. Hejinian, *The Language of Inquiry*, 48.
48. Ibid., 43.
49. Hejinian, *My Life*, 62.
50. McLane, "Anne Boyer's 'Garments Against Women,'" n.p.
51. Boyer, "Not Writing," 41.
52. Boyer, *Garments Against Women*, 47.
53. Ibid., 58.
54. Ibid., 46.
55. Huntsperger, "Objectivist Form," in *Procedural Form in Postmodern American Poetry*, 131.
56. Boyer, *Garments Against Women*, 2.
57. Schoonebeek, "Three Questions," n.p.
58. Lundy Martin, *Life in a Box*, 7.
59. Ibid., 29.

60. Lundy Martin, *Discipline*, 38.
61. Slings, "The I in Personal Archaic Lyric," in *The Poet's I in Archaic Greek Lyric*, 12.
62. Lerner, "Beyond 'Lyric Shame,'" n.p.
63. Carson, *Autobiography in Red*, 141.
64. Talei, "The Claim of Fragmented Self," 5.
65. Carson, *Red doc>*, 14.
66. Ibid., 6.
67. Carson, *Nox*, n.p.
68. Carson, *Short Talks*, 27.
69. Chaisson, "Color Codes," n.p.
70. Lerner, "Beyond 'Lyric Shame,'" n.p.
71. Rankine, *Don't Let Me Be Lonely*, 131.
72. Ibid., 62.
73. Ibid., 104.
74. K. Caldwell, "*Citizen: An American Lyric* by Claudia Rankine," n.p.
75. Rankine, *Citizen*, 14.
76. Pierce et al., "An Experiment in Racism: TV Commercials," in *Television and Education*, 66.
77. Nelson, *The Argonauts*, 13.
78. G. Francis, "*Bluets* by Maggie Nelson Review," n.p.
79. Larson, "Now, Where Was I? On Maggie Nelson's *Bluets*," n.p.
80. Nelson, *Bluets*, 46.
81. Nelson, *Argonauts*, 5–6.
82. Lerner, "Beyond 'Lyric Shame,'" n.p.
83. De Alderete, "Untitled," n.p.
84. Ibid.
85. HuffPost, "Patricia Lockwood's Sext Poems Will Make You LOL," n.p.
86. Plunkett, "Patricia Lockwood's Crowd-Pleasing Poetry," n.p.
87. Burt, "Not Quite the End of the World," in *American Poetry since 1945*, 240.
88. Lichtenstein, "The Smutty-Metaphor Queen," n.p.
89. Lanphier, "The Internet," n.p.
90. Lockwood, "Rape Joke," n.p.
91. Ibid.
92. Lanphier, "The Internet," n.p.
93. Moss, "Goodness," 291.
94. Sanders, "Country Song of Thanks," in *Cuntry*, 38–39.
95. Ibid.
96. Wabuke, "Dispatches from Rape Culture," n.p.
97. Queen, *I'm So Fine: A List of Famous Men & What I Had On* (Sibling Rivalry Press), 10.
98. Four years later this chapbook was republished as part of a full collection entitled *I'm So Fine: A List of Famous Men & What I Had On; A Narrative* by YesYes Books, without the bold font and the vertical lines.
99. Queen, *I'm So Fine: A List of Famous Men & What I Had On* (Sibling Rivalry Press), 18.
100. Ibid., 69.

101. Ibid., 71.
102. Ibid.
103. Auden, *Collected Poems*, 246.

Chapter 10

1. Nelles, "Microfiction: What Makes a Very Short Story Very Short?," 87–88.
2. Ibid., 87.
3. Botha, "Microfiction," in *The Cambridge Companion to the English Short Story*, 202.
4. Trimarco, "Short Shorts," in *Teaching the Short Story*, 13–27.
5. Delville, *The American Prose Poem*, 104.
6. Ibid., 107.
7. Stohlman, "Ask a Flash Fiction Editor?," n.p.
8. Loveday, "Interview with Carrie Etter," n.p.
9. Seed, on BBC Radio 3, "New Towns," n.p.
10. Stohlman, "Ask a Flash Fiction Editor?," n.p.; Hummel and Lenox, *Short-Form*, xvii; and Botha, "Microfiction," in *The Cambridge Companion to the English Short Story*, 202.
11. Booten, Freedman, and Hull, "The Internet's Concept of Story," in *English Language Arts Research and Teaching*, 151.
12. Ibid., 140.
13. Botha, "Microfiction," in *The Cambridge Companion to the English Short Story*, 201.
14. Ibid.
15. Byrd, "I Cannot Escape the Prose Poem," in *The Rose Metal Press Field Guide to Poetry*, 33.
16. Mullen, *Recyclopedia: Trimmings, S*PeRM**K*T, Muse & Drudge*, x.
17. Ibid., ix.
18. Ibid.
19. Perloff, "Postmodernism/*Fin de siècle*," in *Romanticism and Postmodernism*, 186.
20. LaFemina, "The Text as Richard Serra Sculpture: On Reading the Prose Poem," n.p.
21. Clements and Dunham, "Structural Analogies," in *An Introduction to the Prose Poem*, 233.
22. Simic, "The Poetry of Village Idiots," 8; Zawacki, "Accommodating Commodity," 303.
23. Vas Dias, "The Flourishing," in *British Prose Poetry*, 49.
24. Moorman Roberts, "Amy Gerstler (1956–)," in *Contemporary American Women Poets*, 139.
25. Axelrod and Axelrod, "Amy Gerstler's Rhetoric of Marriage," 96.
26. Gerstler, *The True Bride*, 45–46.
27. Diggory, *Encyclopedia of the New York School Poets*, 478.
28. Ibid.
29. Vas Dias, "The Flourishing," in *British Prose Poetry*, 46.
30. Axelrod and Axelrod, "Amy Gerstler's Rhetoric of Marriage," 103.
31. Ibid.

32. Shockley, "my life as china," in *The New Black*, 5.
33. Richee, "Evie Shockley's 'my life as china.'"
34. Andrews, "Southern Culture," in *Miss August*, 31.
35. Iijima, "White Tigers," in *Some Simple Things Said by and about Humans*, 16.
36. Iijima, "Dolly the Sheep," in *Some Simple Things Said by and about Humans*, 42.
37. Ziegler, "Introduction," in *Short: An International Anthology*, xxx.
38. Barenblat, "Prose Poems or Microfiction?," n.p.
39. Ibid.
40. Ziegler, "Introduction," in *Short: An International Anthology*, xxxii.
41. Owlcation, "The Tragic Carnival: A Reflection on 'The Hanging of the Mouse,'" n.p.
42. Duhamel, quoted in Tony Leuzzi, "Response and Bio," n.p.
43. Wood, "Hare," in *Landmarks*, 31.
44. C. Wilson, "Arm's Length," in *Landmarks*, 33.
45. Alexander, "September," in *Richmond Burning*, 35.
46. Alexander, "Like Our Shadow-Selves," in *Richmond Burning*, 33.
47. Booten, Freedman, and Hull, "The Internet's Concept of Story," in *English Language Arts Research and Teaching*, 142.
48. Lehman, "Introduction," in *Great American Prose Poems*, 15.
49. Murphy, *A Tradition of Subversion*, 64.
50. Balog, *The Mirror that Lied*, n.p.
51. Ziegler, "Introduction," in *Short: An International Anthology*, xxxii.
52. James, "Review of Christopher Merrill's *Boat*," n.p.
53. Darling, "'This goes back to vision,'" n.p.
54. Strange, "Formless Form," 4.
55. D. Young, "Introduction," in *Models of the Universe*, 18.
56. Lehman, *Great American Prose Poems*, 23–24.
57. Alexander, "Prose/Poetry," in *The Party Train*, xxi–xxii.
58. Beckel, "Introduction," in the *Prose Poem Issue* in the *Beltway Poetry Quarterly*, n.p.
59. De Pree, *The Ravishment of Persephone*, 67.
60. A. Jones, "Reply," in *A Cast-Iron Aeroplane*, 111.
61. E. Miller, *The Ear Is an Organ Made for Love*, 93.
62. In *An Introduction to the Prose Poem*, editors Clements and Dunham also include Geraldine Monk, Eunice Odio, William Matthews, and Steve Wilson in the section entitled "Poems of Address/Epistolary Poems."
63. De Pree, *Ravishment of Persephone*, 13.
64. McGookey, "Ordinary Emotions, Extraordinary Emotions," in *A Cast-Iron Aeroplane*, 153.
65. Davis, "Letter to a Funeral Parlor," in *The Collected Stories of Lydia Davis*, 380.
66. Skidelsky, "Lydia Davis: 'My style is a reaction to Proust's long sentences,'" n.p.
67. Sadoff, *History Matters*, 34.
68. Bradley, *The Party Train*, n.p.
69. Similarly, Pulitzer Prize–winning poet C. K. Williams's *All at Once* (2014) contains prose poems, while some of the other writing in this book may be read as personal essays or even as dramatic monologues.

70. Zimmer, *Child in a Winter House Brightening*, n.p.
71. Collins, "Whiteness Shops for a Prayer," n.p.
72. Nagai, *Irradiated Cities*, 129.
73. Upward, "Scented Leaves," n.p.
74. Also see Francesca Rendle-Short's sequence referencing Carson, "Towards Poetic Address: Anne Carson Slag" (2019).
75. Other examples include Julia Bloch's *Letters to Kelly Clarkson* (2012), *Valley Fever* (2015), *Hollywood Forever* (2015), and *Like Fur* (2017); Suzanne Buffam's *The Irrationalist* (2010); Anne Carson's *Red doc>* (2013); Lisa Ciccarello's *At Night* (2015); Elizabeth J. Colen's *What Weaponry* (2016); Adam Craig's *Year W* (2015); Gregoire Pam Dick's *Metaphysical Licks* (2014); Jenny Drai's *The New Sorrow Is Less than the Old Sorrow* (2015); Martina Evans's *Through the Glass Mountain* (1997) and *Petrol* (2012); Adam Fitzgerald's "Riverboat" (2014); John Fuller's *A Skin Diary* (1997) and *The Dice Cup* (2014); Sarah Goshal's *The Pine Tree Experiment* (2015); Danny Hayward's *Pragmatic Sanction* (2015); Lyn Hejinian's *Saga/Circus* (2008); Paul Hetherington's *Gallery of Antique Art* (2016) and *Íkaros* (2017); Lisa Jarnot's *Sea Lyrics* (1996), *Black Dog Songs* (2003), and *Night Scenes* (2008); Harryette Mullen's *Broken Glish: Five Prose Poems* (2013); Alice Oswald's *Dart* (2002); Brynne Rebele-Henry's *Fleshgraphs* (2016); and Liz Rosenberg's *17: A Novel in Prose Poems* (2002).
76. Seaton, "Moving Violations: The Prose Poem as Fast Car," in *The Rose Metal Press Field Guide to Prose Poetry*, 141.
77. Dreyer, "'Getting Over Our Selves': Elegy and Rhetoric," 16 and 15, respectively.
78. Etter, "Imagined Sons 5: Reunion," in *Imagined Sons*, 14.
79. Capildeo, *Measures of Expatriation*, 110–11.
80. Noel-Tod, "Immeasurable as One," in *British Prose Poetry*, 211.
81. Ibid.
82. Fredman, *Poet's Prose*, quotes on 114 and 102, respectively.
83. Monte, *Invisible Fences*, 188; Murphy, *A Tradition of Subversion*, 170.
84. Jeremy Noel-Tod, *The Penguin Book of the Prose Poem*, xxx.
85. Ashbery, *Three Poems*, 3.
86. Herd, *John Ashbery and American Poetry*, 128.
87. Pearson and Petelinsek, *Prose Poems (Poetry Party)*; Heiden and Huntington, *Penelope and Pip Build a Prose Poem*.
88. Clancy, *England: Poems from a School*.
89. M. Riffaterre, "On the Prose Poem's Formal Features," in *The Prose Poem in France*, 117.
90. Caldwell and Hardwick, "Introduction," in *The Valley Press Anthology of Prose Poetry*, 10–11.
91. Chan, *Flèche*, 43.
92. Hussain, "A Mastery of English: A Conversation with Mary Jean Chan," n.p.
93. Yeats, *The Collected Works of W. B. Yeats*, 356.

Bibliography

Abbott, Helen. *Between Baudelaire and Mallarmé: Voice, Conversation and Music*. London: Routledge, 2009.

Aćamović, Bojana. "Walt Whitman and the City Culture: The Poet as a Flâneur and a Bohemian." In *Selected Papers from the Third International Conference English Language and Anglophone Literatures Today* (ELALT 3), edited by Bojana Vujin and Mirna Radin-Sabadoš, 29–40. Novi Sad, Serbia: University of Novi Sad, 2016.

Adler, Jeremy D. "Concrete Poetry." In *Encyclopedia of German Literature*, edited by Matthias Konzett, 195–97. Chicago, IL: Fitzroy Dearborn, 2000.

Agbabi, Patience. *Bloodshot Monochrome*. London: Cannongate, 2008.

Akbar, Kaveh. "Calling a Wolf a Wolf (Inpatient)." *Adroit Journal* 17 (2017): n.p. http://www.theadroitjournal.org/issue-seventeen-kaveh-akbar-the-adroit-journal/.

Albright, Daniel. "Literary and Psychological Models of the Self." In *The Remembering Self: Construction and Accuracy in the Self-Narrative*, edited by Ulric Neisser and Robyn Fivush, 19–40. Cambridge: Cambridge University Press, 1994.

Aldama, Frederick Luis. *Formal Matters in Contemporary Latino Poetry*. New York: Palgrave Macmillan, 2013.

Aldrich, Marcia. "The Boarding School." *Seneca Review* 37, no. 2 (2007): 106–11.

Alexander, Robert. "The American Prose Poem, 1890–1980." PhD thesis. University of Wisconsin-Milwaukee, 1982.

———, ed. *Family Portrait: American Prose Poetry, 1900–1950*. Buffalo, NY: White Pine Press, 2012.

———. "Prose/Poetry." In *The Party Train: A Collection of North American Prose Poetry*, edited by Robert Alexander, Mark Vinz, and C. W. Truesdale, xxiv–xxxiii. Minneapolis: New Rivers Press, 1996.

———. "Richard H. Horne (1802–1884): The Old Churchyard Tree; A Prose Poem." In *Spring Phantoms: Short Prose by 19th Century British & American Authors*, edited by Robert Alexander, 13–14. Marie Alexander Poetry Series. Buffalo, NY: White Pine Press, 2018.

———. *Richmond Burning*. Northfield, MN: Red Dragonfly Press, 2017.

———, ed. *Spring Phantoms: Short Prose by 19th Century British & American Authors*. Marie Alexander Poetry Series. Buffalo, NY: White Pine Press, 2018.

Alexander, Robert, and Dennis Maloney, eds. *The House of Your Dream: An International Collection of Prose Poetry*. Marie Alexander Poetry Series, no. 11. Buffalo, NY: White Pine Press, 2008.

Allen, R.E.N., and Grant Loewen. *Sudden Fictions*. 2nd edition. Quebec: Livres DC Books, 2006.

Allport, Andrew. "The Romantic Fragment Poem and the Performance of Form." *Studies in Romanticism* 51, no. 3 (2012): 399–417.
Alyan, Hala. "Oklahoma." *Poetry*. July/August 2017. https://www.poetryfoundation.org/poetrymagazine/poems/142865/oklahoma.
Anderson, Jack. *Traffic: New and Selected Prose Poems*. Minneapolis: New Rivers Press, 1998.
Andrews, Bruce. *Paradise and Method: Poetry & Praxis*. Evanston, IL: Northwestern University Press, 1996.
Andrews, Bruce, and Charles Bernstein. "Repossessing the Word." In *The L=A=N=G=U=A=G=E Book*, edited by Bruce Andrews and Charles Bernstein, ix–x. Carbondale: Southern Illinois University Press, 1983.
Andrews, Nin. "Editorial Letter." *New Flash Fiction Review: Prose Poetry Issue* 7 (Summer 2016): n.p. http://newflashfiction.com/prose-poetry-issue-2016/.
———. "Southern Culture." In *Miss August*. New Jersey: CavanKerry Press, 2017.
An-hwei Lee, Karen. *Ardor*. North Adams, MA: Tupelo Press, 2008.
———. *In Media Res*. Louisville, KY: Sarabande Books, 2004.
Apollinaire, Guillaume. *Calligrammes: Poems of Peace and War (1913–1916)*. Translated by Anne Hyde Greet. Berkeley: University of California Press, 2004.
Aristotle. *On Memory*. Translated by J. I. Beare. In *The Complete Works of Aristotle*, edited by Jonathan Barnes, 714–20. Volume 1 [sixth printing with corrections]. Princeton, NJ: Princeton University Press, 1991.
Armitage, Simon. "The Christening." In *Seeing Stars: Poems*, 3. London: Faber & Faber, 2010.
Arnheim, Rudolph. *Visual Thinking*. Berkeley: University of California Press, 1997.
Arnold, Matthew. *Dover Beach and Other Poems*. Edited by Candace Ward. New York: Dover Publications, 1994.
Ashbery, John. *Three Poems*. New York: Elizabeth Sifton Books/Penguin Books, 1986.
———. "Two Prose Poems." In *London Review of Books* 22, no. 14 (July 20, 2000): n.p. https://www.lrb.co.uk/v22/n14/john-ashbery/two-prose-poems.
Ashcroft, Bill, Gareth Griffiths, and Helen Tiffin. *The Empire Writes Back: Theory and Practice in Post-Colonial Literatures*. New York: Routledge, 2002.
Ashford, Tomeiko. "Biography: Yusef Komunyakaa." *Internet Poetry Archive*. n.d. https://www.ibiblio.org/ipa/poems/komunyakaa/biography.php.
Ashton, Sally. "Origins of Sublime." *Sentence: A Journal of Prose Poetics* 2 (2004): 158–59.
Atherton, Cassandra, and Paul Hetherington, eds. *Anthology of Australian Prose Poetry*. Melbourne: Melbourne University Press, 2020.
Atherton, Cassandra. *Pre-Raphaelite*. Adelaide, SA: Garron Press, 2018.
———. "Rapunzel." In *Exhumed*, 76–77. Melbourne: Grand Parade Poets, 2015.
Atherton, Cassandra, Owen Bullock, Jen Crawford, Paul Munden, Shane Strange, and Jen Webb. "The Prose Poetry Project." *Axon Capsule 1: Poetry on the Move* (2015): n.p. http://www.axonjournal.com.au/issue-c1/prose-poetry-project.
Atkins, Marc. *The Logic of the Stairwell and Other Images*. Exeter, UK: Shearsman Books, 2011.
Atkins, Tim. *Koto Y Yo [Koto & I]*. New Malden: Crater 34, 2016.

Attridge, Derek. *The Rhythms of English Poetry*. New York: Routledge, 2014.
Atwood, Margaret. "In Love with Raymond Chandler." In *Great American Prose Poems: From Poe to the Present*, edited by David Lehman, 131. New York: Scribner Poetry, 2003.
Auden, W. H. *Collected Poems*. Edited by Edward Mendelson. London: Faber, 2007.
Augustine. *Confessions*. Translated by Henry Chadwick. London: Oxford University Press, 1991.
Austen, Jane. *Emma*. London: Penguin, 2003.
Axelrod, Mark. "The Poetics of Prose Poetry in Elizabeth Smart's *By Grand Central Station I Sat Down and Wept*." In *The Poetics of Novels: Fiction and Its Executions*, by Mark Axelrod, 171–86. London: Macmillan Press, 1999.
Axelrod, Rise B., and Steven Gould Axelrod. "Amy Gerstler's Rhetoric of Marriage." *Twentieth Century Literature* 50, no. 1 (2004): 88–105.
Bagoo. Andre. *Pitch Lake*. Leeds, UK: Peepal Tree Press, 2018.
Bakhtin, Mikhail M. "Forms of Time and of the Chronotope in the Novel: Notes towards a Historical Poetics." In *The Dialogic Imagination: Four Essays*, edited by Michael Holquist, 84–258. Translated by Caryl Emerson and Michael Holquist. Austin: University of Texas Press, 1981.
Balakian, Anna. *Surrealism: The Road to the Absolute*. Chicago: University of Chicago Press, 1986.
Balkun, Stacey. "Review of Human-Ghost Hybrid Project by Carol Guess and Daniela Olszewska." *The Bind*, December 7, 2017, n.p. https://www.thebind.net/blog/human-ghost-guess-olszewska.
Balog, Amy. *The Mirror that Lied (A Prose Poem)*. Kindle edition. Seattle: Amazon Digital Services, 2017.
Bang, Mary Jo. *A Doll for Throwing: Poems*. Minneapolis: Graywolf Press, 2017.
Bann, Stephen. *Romanticism and the Rise of History*. New York: Twayne; Toronto: Maxwell Macmillan, 1995.
Barcelona, Antonio. "Introduction: The Cognitive Theory of Metaphor and Metonymy." In *Metaphor and Metonymy at the Crossroads: A Cognitive Perspective*, edited by Antonio Barcelona, 1–28. New York: Mouton de Gruyter, 2003.
Barclay, Craig R. "Autobiographical Remembering: Narrative Constraints." In *Remembering Our Past: Studies in Autobiographical Memory*, edited by David C. Rubin, 94–125. Cambridge: Cambridge University Press, 1996.
Bardes, Charles. *Diary of Our Fatal Illness*. Chicago: University of Chicago Press, 2017.
Barenblat, Rachel. "Prose Poems or Microfiction?" In *Posse Review* 3, no. 1 (1999): n.p. http://www.webdelsol.com/InPosse/barenblat.htm.
Barkan, Leonard. *Unearthing the Past: Archaeology and Aesthetics in the Making of Renaissance Culture*. New Haven: Yale University Press, 1999.
Barker, George. "The Jubjub Bird, or Some Remarks on the Prose Poem." In *The Jubjub Bird, or Some Remarks on the Prose Poem and a Little Honouring of Lionel Johnson*, edited by George Barker, 1–21. Warwick: Greville Press, 1985.
Bar-Nadav, Hadara. "And Leaves the Shreds Behind." *Sentence: A Journal of Prose Poetry and Poetics* 10 (2015): 45.
———. "Who Is Flying This Plane? The Prose Poem and the Life of the Line." In *A Bro-*

ken Thing: Poets on the Line, edited by Emily Rosko and Anton Vander Zee, 44–47. Iowa City: University of Iowa Press, 2011.

Barry, Peter. *Contemporary British Poetry and the City*. New York: Manchester University Press, 2000.

Bartlett, Lee. "What is 'Language Poetry'?" *Critical Inquiry* 12, no. 4 (Summer 1986): 741–52.

Bass, Holly. "Claudia Rankine's *Citizen*." *New York Times*, December 24, 2014. https://www.nytimes.com/2014/12/28/books/review/claudia-rankines-citizen.html.

Bateman, Claire. "Distinction." In *Clumsy*, 24. Kalamazoo, MI: New Issues Press, 2003.

Battles, Kelly Eileen. "The Antiquarian Impulse: History, Affect, and Material Culture in Eighteenth- and Nineteenth-Century British Culture." PhD diss., Michigan University, 2008. UMI No.: 3312662.

Baudelaire, Charles. *The Flowers of Evil*. Translated with notes by James McGowan. Oxford: Oxford University Press, 1993.

———. *The Painter of Modern Life and Other Essays*. Translated by Jonathan Mayne. London: Phaidon, 1964.

———. *Paris Spleen: Little Poems in Prose*. Translated by Keith Waldrop. Middletown, CT: Wesleyan University Press, 2009.

BBC Radio 3. "New Towns." *The Verb*. Podcast, 2016.

Beach, Christopher. *The Cambridge Introduction to Twentieth-Century American Poetry*. Cambridge: Cambridge University Press, 2003.

Beachy-Quick, Dan. *Of Silence and Song*. Minneapolis: Milkweed Editions, 2017.

Beckel, Abigail. "Introduction." *Prose Poem Issue* of the *Beltway Poetry Quarterly* 14, no. 4 (Fall 2013): n.p. http://www.beltwaypoetry.com/prose-poem-issue-introduction/.

Beckel, Abigail, and Kathleen Rooney. "Field Notes: A Preface." In *The Rose Metal Press Field Guide to Prose Poetry: Contemporary Poets in Discussion and Practice*, edited by Gary L. McDowell and F. Daniel Rzicznek, xi–xiv. Brookline, MA: Rose Metal Press, 2010.

Belkhyr, Yasmin. "Interlude with Drug of Choice." *Pinwheel* (Spring 2016): n.p. http://pinwheeljournal.com/poets/yasmin-belkhyr/.

Bemong, Nele, Pieter Borghart, Michel De Dobbeleer, Kristoffel Demoen, Koen De Temmerman, and Bart Keunen, eds. *Bakhtin's Theory of the Literary Chronotope: Reflections, Applications, Perspectives*. Belgium: Academia Press, 2010.

Benjamin, Walter. "On Some Motifs in Baudelaire." In *The Writer of Modern Life: Essays on Charles Baudelaire*, 170–212. Cambridge, MA: Belknap Press of Harvard University Press, 2006.

———. "The Paris of the Second Empire in Baudelaire." In *The Writer of Modern Life: Essays on Charles Baudelaire*, 46–133. Cambridge, MA: Belknap Press of Harvard University Press, 2006.

Benedikt, Michael. *The Poetry of Surrealism: An Anthology*. Boston: Little, Brown, 1974.

———. *The Prose Poem: An International Anthology*. New York: Dell, 1976.

Benis White, Allison. *Small Porcelain Head*. New York: Four Way Books, 2013.

Benson, Fiona. "Demeter." *Granta* 126 (2014): n.p. https://granta.com/demeter/.

Berg, William J. *Imagery and Ideology: Fiction and Painting in Nineteenth-Century France*. Cranbury, NJ: Rosemont, 2007.

Berger, John. *Ways of Seeing.* London: Penguin, 1972.
Berlin, Isaiah. *The Crooked Timber of Humanity: Chapters in the History of Ideas.* London: Random House, 2003.
Berman, Art. *Preface to Modernism.* Champaign: University of Illinois Press, 1994.
Berman, Marshall. *All That Is Solid Melts into Air: The Experience of Modernity.* New York: Verso, 1983.
Bernard, Suzanne, ed. "Notice." In *Illuminations*, by Arthur Rimbaud. In *Oeuvres*, 246. Paris: Garnier, 1960.
Bernstein, Charles, and Yubraj Aryal. "Interview with Charles Bernstein on Language Poetry." *Journal of Philosophy: A Cross-Disciplinary Inquiry* 3, no. 7 (Fall 2007): 56–58.
Berry, Emily. "Some Fears." In *The Penguin Book of the Prose Poem: From Baudelaire to Anne Carson*, edited by Jeremy Noel-Tod, 43. London: Penguin Books, 2018.
Berz, Carole Birkan. "Mapping the Contemporary Sonnet in Mainstream and Linguistically Innovative Late 20th- and Early 21st-Century British Poetry." *Études britanniques contemporaines* 46 (2014): n.p. https://journals.openedition.org/ebc/1202.
Bidart, Frank. "Borges and I." In *An Introduction to the Prose Poem*, edited by Brian Clements and Jamey Dunham, 296–98. Newtown, CT: Firewheel Editions, 2009.
Bird, Hera Lindsay. *Hera Lindsay Bird.* Wellington: Victoria University Press, 2016.
Black, Linda. "Begin with a Hook." *Magma* 54 (2012): 2.
———. *Inventory.* Exeter: Shearsman Books, 2008.
———. "Linda Black, *Inventory*." Commentary on Shearsman Books website. Shearsman Books, n.d., n.p. https://www.shearsman.com/store/-p102838543.
———. *The Son of a Shoemaker.* London: Hearing Eye, 2012.
———. "Three Prose Poems: With a Brief Afterword." *Fortnightly Review*, February 7, 2019. https://fortnightlyreview.co.uk/2019/02/black-prose-poems/.
Blaisdell, Bob, ed. *Imagist Poetry: An Anthology.* Mineola, NY: Dover Publications, 1999.
Blake, William. "London." In *The Complete Poetry and Prose of William Blake*. Revised edition. Edited by David V. Erdman, 26–27. Berkeley: University of California Press, 2008.
Blanchot, Maurice, and Charlotte Mandell. *The Book to Come.* Stanford, CA: Stanford University Press, 2003.
Blasing, Mutlu Konuk. *Lyric Poetry: The Pain and the Pleasure of Words.* Princeton, NJ: Princeton University Press, 2007.
Bletsoe, Elisabeth. "Birds of the Sherborne Missal." In *Landscape from a Dream*, by Elisabeth Bletsoe. Exeter, UK: Shearsman Books, 2008.
Bloch, Julia. *Hollywood Forever.* Houston, TX: Little Red Leaves Textile Series, 2015.
———. *Letters to Kelly Clarkson.* Portland, OR: Sidebrow Books, 2012.
———. *Like Fur.* Oakland, CA: Essay Press, 2017.
———. *Valley Fever.* Portland, OR: Sidebrow Books, 2015.
Bly, Robert. "A Caterpillar on the Desk." *Poetry* (1971): 34. Poetry Foundation. https://www.poetryfoundation.org/poetrymagazine/browse?contentId=31850.
———. *Leaping Poetry: An Idea with Poems and Translations.* Boston: Beacon Press, 1975.
———. *The Morning Glory.* New York: Harper & Row, 1975.

Bly, Robert. *Point Reyes Poems*. Half-Moon Bay, CA: Mudra, 1974.

———. "The Prose Poem as an Evolving Form." In *Selected Poems*, 199–204. New York: Harper, 1986.

———. *Silence in the Snowy Fields: Poems*. Middletown, CT: Wesleyan University Press, 1962.

———. "Warning to the Reader." In *Great American Prose Poems: From Poe to the Present*, edited by David Lehman, 83. New York: Scribner, 2003.

Bode, Christoph. "Europe." In *Romanticism: An Oxford Guide*, edited by Nicholas Roe, 126–36. Oxford: Oxford University Press, 2005.

Bond, Bruce. "Empathy and the Poetic Imagination." *Coldfront*, September 10, 2014. http://coldfrontmag.com/empathy-and-poetic-imagination/.

Bonomo, Joe. "Hyphen: Sketching the Bridge with Invisible Ink." In *The Rose Metal Press Field Guide to Prose Poetry: Contemporary Poets in Discussion and Practice*, edited by Gary L. McDowell and F. Daniel Rzicznek, 121–26. Brookline, MA: Rose Metal Press, 2010.

———. *Installations*. National Poetry Series. New York: Penguin Books, 2008.

Booten, Kyle, with Sarah Warshauer Freedman and Glynda A. Hull. "The Internet's Concept of Story." In *English Language Arts Research and Teaching: Revisiting and Extending Arthur Applebee's Contributions*, edited by Russell K. Durst, George E. Newell, and James D. Marshall, 138–53. New York: Routledge, 2017.

Borges, Jorge Luis. *The Book of Imaginary Beings*. New York: E. P. Dutton, 1969. [Originally published in Spanish in 1967 by Editorial Kier, Buenos Aires.]

Borson, Roo. "City." In *The Lyric Paragraph: A Collection of Canadian Prose Poems*, edited by Robert Allen, 13–15. Montreal: DC Books, 1987.

Botha, Marc. "Microfiction." In *The Cambridge Companion to the English Short Story*, edited by Ann-Marie Einhaus, 201–20. Cambridge: Cambridge University Press, 2016.

Boyer, Anne. *Garments Against Women*. Boise, ID: Ahsahta Press, 2015.

———. "The Two Thousands." *Free Poetry* 5, no. 1 (2009): 3–5. https://freepoetrycom.files.wordpress.com/2017/09/anne-boyer-_the-two-thousands_.pdf.

Bradley, John. "If André Breton Were Alive Today He'd Be Spinning in His Grave: Surrealism and Contemporary Prose Poetry." *Turnrow: The Biannual Journal of the University of Louisiana at Monroe* 4, no. 2 (Winter 2005): n.p. http://turnrow.ulm.edu/view.php?i=10&.

———. "Review of *The Party Train: A Collection of North American Prose Poetry; A Curious Architecture: A Selection of Contemporary Prose Poetry; Models of the Universe: An Anthology of the Prose Poem*." In *The Prose Poem: An International Journal* 6 (1997): n.p. https://digitalcommons.providence.edu/cgi/viewcontent.cgi?article=1458&context=prosepoem.

Bradshaw, Michael. "Hedgehog Theory: How to Read a Romantic Fragment Poem." *Literature Compass* 5, no. 1 (2007): 74.

Brainard, Joe. "I Remember." In *Collected Writings of Joe Brainard*, edited by Ron Padgett, 15. New York: Library of America, 2012.

Brand, Dionne. *The Blue Clerk: Ars Poetica in 59 Versos*. Toronto: McClelland and Stewart, 2018.

Brandt, Emily. "The Harbor." *Literary Hub*, August 10, 2016. https://lithub.com/the-harbor/.

Breslin, Paul. "How to Read the New Contemporary Poem." *American Scholar* 47, no. 3 (Summer 1978): 357–70. https://www.jstor.org/stable/41210436?seq=1#page_scan_tab_contents.

Breton, André. "Manifesto of Surrealism" (1924). In *Manifestoes of Surrealism*, edited by Richard Seaver and Helen R. Lane, 2–47. Ann Arbor: University of Michigan Press, 1972.

Brewer, William F. "Memory for Randomly Sampled Autobiographical Events." In *Remembering Reconsidered: Ecological and Traditional Approaches to the Study of Memory*, edited by Ulric Neisser and Eugene Winograd, 21–90. Cambridge: Cambridge University Press, 1988.

Briante, Susan. *Utopia Minus*. Boise, ID: Ahsahta Press, 2011.

Brittan, Simon. *Poetry, Symbol and Allegory: Interpreting Metaphorical Language from Plato to the Present*. Charlottesville: University of Virginia Press, 2003.

Broome, Peter. *Baudelaire's Poetic Patterns: The Secret Language of "Les fleurs du mal."* Atlanta, GA: Rodopi, 1999.

Brophy, Kevin. "The Night's Insomnia." In *Radar*, by Kevin Brophy and Nathan Curnow, 61. Tasmania, Australia: Walleah Press Poetry, 2012.

Brown, Andy. "The Emergent Prose Poem." In *A Companion to Poetic Genre*, edited by Eric Martiny, 318–29. West Sussex: John Wiley and Sons, 2012.

———. "I Went Disguised in It: Re-evaluating Seamus Heaney's *Stations*." In *British Prose Poetry: The Poems Without Lines*, edited by Jane Monson, 177–92. Cham, Switzerland: Palgrave Macmillan, 2018.

Brown, Richard Danson. "'Your Thoughts Make Shape like Snow': Louis MacNeice on Stephen Spender." *Twentieth Century Literature* 48, no. 3 (Autumn 2002): 292–323.

Browne, Laynie. *The Desires of Letters*. Denver: Counterpath Press, 2010.

———. *The Scented Fox*. Seattle, WA: Wave Books, 2007.

Browning, Elizabeth Barrett. *Aurora Leigh*. New York: C. S. Francis, 1857.

———. *Elizabeth Barrett Browning: Key Women's Writers*. Edited by Angela Leighton. Bloomington: Indiana University Press, 1986.

Bruhn, Siglind. *Images and Ideas in Modern French Piano Music: The Extra-Musical Subtext in Piano Works by Ravel, Debussy and Messiaen*. Stuyvesant, NY: Pendragon Press, 1997.

Buckley, Christopher, and Gary Young, eds. *Bear Flag Republic: Prose Poems and Poetics from California*. Santa Cruz, CA: Greenhouse Review Press/Alcatraz Editions, 2008.

Buffam, Suzanne. *The Irrationalist*. Toronto: House of Anansi Press, 2010.

———. *A Pillow Book*. Toronto: House of Anansi Press; Marfa, TX: Canarium Books, 2016.

Burke, David. *Writers in Paris: Literary Lives in the City of Light*. 2nd edition. New York: Paris Writers Press, 2008.

Burke, Edmund. *Revolutionary Writings: Reflections on the Revolution in France and the First Letter on a Regicide Peace*. Edited by Iain Hampsher-Monk. New York: Cambridge University Press, 2014.

Burns, Suzanne. "Out There." *Sentence: A Journal of Prose Poetry and Poetics* 10 (2013): 145.

Burt, Stephen. "Not Quite the End of the World: American Poetry since 2000." In *American Poetry since 1945*, edited by Eleanor Spencer, 222–44. New York: Palgrave Macmillan, 2017.

Butcher-McGunnigle, Zarah. *Autobiography of a Marguerite*. Auckland: Hue and Cry Press, 2014.

Byrd, Brigitte. "I Cannot Escape the Prose Poem." In *The Rose Metal Press Field Guide to Prose Poetry: Contemporary Poets in Discussion and Practice*, edited by Gary L. McDowell and F. Daniel Rzicznek, 31–35. Brookline, MA: Rose Metal Press, 2010.

Caddy, David. "Hidden Form: The Prose Poem in English Poetry." In *Stress Fractures: Essays on Poetry*, edited by Tom Chivers, 103–14. London: Penned in the Margins, 2016.

Caldwell, Anne. "Prose Poetry and Visual Arts." *Writing in Education* 68 (Spring 2016): 27–30.

———. "What Is Prose Poetry?" *Prose Poetry UK: About Prose Poetry*, 2018. https://www.prose-poetry.uk/about.

———. "Wild Garlic and Detours." In *The Valley Press Anthology of Prose Poetry*, edited by Anne Caldwell and Oz Hardwick, 52. Scarborough, UK: Valley Press, 2019.

Caldwell, Anne, and Oz Hardwick. "Introduction." In *The Valley Press Anthology of Prose Poetry*, edited by Anne Caldwell and Oz Hardwick, 9–11. Scarborough, UK: Valley Press, 2019.

Caldwell, Kelly. "*Citizen: An American Lyric* by Claudia Rankine." *MAKE Literary Magazine*, February 6, 2018. http://www.makemag.com/review-citizen-an-american-lyric/.

Caleshu, Anthony. *A Dynamic Exchange between Us*. Bristol, UK: Shearsman Books, 2019.

Calvino, Italo. *Invisible Cities*. Translated by William Weaver. London: Vintage Digital, 2010.

Campbell, Marion May. *Poetic Revolutionaries: Intertextuality & Subversion*. Amsterdam: Rodopi, 2014.

Capildeo, Vahni. *Measures of Expatriation*. Manchester, UK: Carcanet, 2016.

Carpenter, Scott. *Aesthetics of Fraudulence in Nineteenth-Century France: Frauds, Hoaxes, and Counterfeits*. New York: Routledge, 2016.

Carroll, Amy Sara. *Fannie + Freddie: The Sentimentality of Post-9/11 Pornography*. New York: Fordham University Press, 2013.

Carroll, Monica, Shane Strange, and Jen Webb. *TEXT*, Special Issue 46, *Beyond the Line: Contemporary Prose Poetry* (October 2017).

Carson, Anne. *The Albertine Workout*. New York: New Directions, 2014.

———. *Autobiography in Red: A Novel in Verse*. New York: Alfred A. Knopf, 1998.

———. *Nox*. New York: New Directions, 2010.

———. "On Defloration." In *Plainwater: Essays and Poetry*, 33. London: Vintage Books, 2000.

———. "On Hedonism." In *Plainwater: Essays and Poetry*, 44. London: Vintage Books, 2000.

———. *Red doc>*. New York: Knopf, 2013.
Carver, Raymond. *Will You Please Be Quiet, Please?* London: Vintage Books, 2003.
Catalano, Gary. "Incident from a War." In *Light and Water*, n.p. Braidwood, NSW: Finlay Press, 2002.
Catani, Damian. *Evil: A History in Modern French Literature and Thought*. London: Bloomsbury, 2013.
Caws, Mary Ann. "The Self-Defining Prose Poem: On Its Edge." In *The Prose Poem in France: Theory and Practice*, edited by Mary Ann Caws and Hermine Riffaterre, 180–97. New York: Columbia University Press, 1983.
———, ed. *The Yale Anthology of Twentieth-Century French Poetry*. New Haven: Yale University Press, 2008.
Caws, Mary Ann, and Michel Delville, eds. *The Edinburgh Companion to the Prose Poem*. Edinburgh: Edinburgh University Press, forthcoming.
Chaisson, Dan. "Color Codes: A Poet Examines Race in America." *New Yorker*, October 27, 2014. https://www.newyorker.com/magazine/2014/10/27/color-codes.
Chan, Mary Jean. *Flèche*. London: Faber & Faber, 2019.
Chanan, Michael. "Revisiting Rocha's 'Aesthetics of Violence.'" In *Killer Images: Documentary Film, Memory and the Performance of Violence*, edited by Joram ten Brink and Joshua Oppenheimer, 80–94. New York: Wallflower Press, 2012.
Chernoff, Maxine. "Kill Yourself with an *Objet D'art*." *Lyrik-Line*, n.p. Originally published in *Evolution of the Bridge: Selected Prose Poems*. Cromer, UK: Salt, 2004. https://www.lyrikline.org/en/poems/kill-yourself-iobjet-darti-6416.
———. "Lost and Found." Poetry Foundation, 1990. Originally published in *Leap Year Day: New and Selected Poems*. Chicago: Another Chicago Press, 1990. https://www.poetryfoundation.org/poems/50987/lost-and-found.
Christle, Heather. *The Trees The Trees*. London: Octopus Books, 2011.
Ciccarello, Lisa. *At Night*. Boston: Black Ocean, 2015.
Clancy, Kate. *England: Poems from a School*. London: Picador, 2018.
Clements, Brian, and Jamey Dunham, eds. *An Introduction to the Prose Poem*. Newtown, CT: Firewheel Editions, 2009.
———. "Preface." In *An Introduction to the Prose Poem*, edited by Brian Clements and Jamey Dunham, 1–8. Newtown, CT: Firewheel Editions, 2009.
———. "Prose Poems about Prose Poems." In *An Introduction to the Prose Poem*, edited by Brian Clements and Jamey Dunham, 287–88. Newtown, CT: Firewheel Editions, 2009.
———. "Structural Analogues." In *An Introduction to the Prose Poem*, edited by Brian Clements and Jamey Dunham, 233. Newtown, CT: Firewheel Editions, 2009.
Cohen, Ted. "Metaphor and the Cultivation of Intimacy." *Critical Inquiry* 5, no.1 (Autumn 1978): 3–12.
Colen, Elizabeth J. *What Weaponry: A Novel in Prose Poems*. New York: Black Lawrence Press, 2016.
Coleridge, Samuel Taylor. *Collected Letters of Samuel Taylor Coleridge*. Volume 1, edited by Earl Leslie Griggs. Oxford: Clarendon Press, 1966.
———. *Samuel Taylor Coleridge: The Major Works*. Edited by H. J. Jackson. Oxford: Oxford University Press, 2008.

Coles, Katharine. "The Poem in Time." *Axon: Creative Explorations* 7, no. 2 (December 2017): n.p. http://www.axonjournal.com.au/issue-13/poem-time.

———. "Sonnet in Prose." Unpublished prose poem.

Collings, Simon. "Typesetter's Delight." A Review of *British Prose Poetry: The Poems Without Lines*, edited by Jane Monson. *Fortnightly Review*, December 6, 2018. https://fortnightlyreview.co.uk/2018/12/modern-british-prose-poetry/.

Collins, Donte. "Whiteness Shops for a Prayer." *Vinyl Poetry and Prose*, January 1, 2017. https://vinylpoetryandprose.com/2017/01/donte-collins/.

Conners, Peter H. *PP/FF: An Anthology*. Buffalo, NY: Starcherone Books, 2006.

Conway, Martin A. "Autobiographical Knowledge and Autobiographical Memories." In *Remembering Our Past: Studies in Autobiographical Memory*, edited by David C. Rubin, 67–93. Cambridge: Cambridge University Press, 1999.

Coombs, Katherine. "'A Kind of Gentle Painting': Limning in 16th-Century England." In *European Visions: American Voices*, edited by Kim Sloan, 77–84. British Museum Research Publication 172. London: British Museum, 2009.

Coyle, Beverly, and Alan Filreis, eds. *Secretaries of the Moon: The Letters of Wallace Stevens and José Rodríguez Feo*. Durham, NC: Duke University Press, 1986.

Craig, A. *Year W*. Blaenau Ffestiniog, Wales: Cinnamon Press, 2015.

Crawford, Robert. *The Modern Poet: Poetry, Academia, and Knowledge since the 1750s*. Oxford: Oxford University Press, 2001.

Crewe, Sarah. *Floss*. Llangattock, UK: Aquifer Books, 2018.

Crosby, Henry. *Seeing with Eyes Closed: The Prose Poems of Harry Crosby*. Edited by Gian Lombardo. Boston, MA: Quale Press, 2019.

Culler, Jonathan. *Theory of the Lyric*. Princeton, NJ: Princeton University Press, 2015.

Curley, Thomas M. *Samuel Johnson, the "Ossian" Fraud, and the Celtic Revival in Great Britain and Ireland*. Cambridge: Cambridge University Press, 2009.

Danladi, Chekwube O. "Tomorrow, Chaka Demus Will Play." In *Take Me Back*. Brooklyn, NY: Akashic Books, 2017.

Darling, Kristina Marie. "'This goes back to vision': A Conversation with Joshua Edwards of Canarium Books, Curated by Kristina Marie Darling." *Tupelo Quarterly*, June 14, 2018. http://www.tupeloquarterly.com/this-goes-back-to-vision-a-conversation-with-joshua-edwards-of-canarium-books-curated-by-kristina-marie-darling/.

Davies, Paul. "German Romanticism." In *Encyclopedia of Romanticism: Culture in Britain, 1780s–1830s*, edited by Laura Dabundo, 226–31. London: Routledge, 2014.

Davis, Lydia. *The Collected Stories of Lydia Davis*. London: Penguin, 2013.

———. "Form as Response to Doubt." In *Biting the Error: Form as a Response to Narrative*, edited by Mary Burger, Robert Glück, Camille Roy, and Gail Scott, 35–37. Toronto: Coach House Books, 2004.

———. "Letter to a Funeral Parlor." In *The Collected Stories of Lydia Davis*, by Lydia Davis, 380. London: Penguin, 2013.

De Alderete, Raquel. "Untitled." *Red Blood, Black Ink*, July 30, 2016. https://bust.com/feminism/17105-laundry-prose-poem.html.

Debney, Patricia. *How to Be a Dragonfly*. Huddersfield, UK: Smith|Doorstop, 2005.

De Certeau, Michel. "Walking in the City." In *The Practice of Everyday Life*. Volume 1,

translated by Steven F. Rendall, 91–110. Berkeley: University of California Press, 1984.
De Lautréamont, Comte. *Lautréamont's Maldoror*. Translated by Alexis Lykiard. New York: Thomas Y. Crowell, 1972.
Delville, Michel. *The American Prose Poem: Poetic Form and the Boundaries of Genre*. Gainesville: University Press of Florida, 1998.
———. "Review of Stephen Fredman's *Poet's Prose: The Crisis in American Verse*." *The Prose Poem: An International Journal* 7 (1998): n.p. http://digitalcommons.providence.edu/cgi/viewcontent.cgi?article=1525&context=prosepoem.
———. "Strange Tales and Bitter Emergencies: A Few Notes on the Prose Poem." In *An Exaltation of Forms: Contemporary Poets Celebrate the Diversity of Their Art*, edited by Annie Finch and Kathrine Varnes, 262–71. Ann Arbor: University of Michigan Press, 2002.
Den Tandt, Christophe. "Mass, Forces, and the Urban Sublime." In *The Cambridge Companion to the City in Literature*, edited by Kevin R. McNamara, 126–37. New York: Cambridge University Press, 2014.
De Pree, Julia K. *The Ravishment of Persephone: Epistolary Lyric in the Siècle des Lumières*. Chapel Hill: University of North Carolina Press, 1998.
De Quincey, Thomas. *Literary Reminiscences: From the Autobiography of an English Opium Eater*. Boston: James R. Osgood, 1873.
———. *The Works of Thomas De Quincey, "The English Opium Eater": Including All His Contributions to Periodical Literature*. Edinburgh: Adam and Charles Black, 1863.
Derrida, Jacques. "The Double Session." In *Disseminaton*, by Jacques Derrida, 187–316. Translated by Barbara Johnson. New York: Continuum, 2004.
Dick, Gregoire Pam. *Metaphysical Licks*. Toronto, Ontario: Book Thug, 2014.
Dickens, Charles. *Little Dorrit*. Edited by Harvey Peter Sucksmith. Oxford: Oxford University Press, 2012.
Dickinson, Emily. *The Poems of Emily Dickinson*. Edited by R. W. Franklin. Variorum Edition. Cambridge, MA: Belknap Press of Harvard University Press, 1998.
Diggory, Terence. *Encyclopedia of the New York School Poets*. New York: Infobase, 2009.
Dismorr, Jessie. "June Night." *BLAST* 2 (July 1915), edited by Wyndham Lewis, 67–68.
Dockins, Mike. "Eleven Gin & Tonics." *Route Nine*, Alumni Omnibus (March 2014). http://route9litmag.com/post/80857647350/two-poems.
Dorf, Carol. "The Big Bang of Prose Poetry." *Talking Writing*, January 14, 2013. http://talkingwriting.com/the-big-bang-of-prose-poetry.
Downey, June E. *Creative Imagination: Studies in the Psychology of Literature*. London: Routledge, 1999. [Originally published in 1929 by Kegan Paul, London.]
Drai, Jenny. *The New Sorrow Is Less Than the Old Sorrow*. New York: Black Lawrence Press, 2015.
Dreyer, Cathy. "'Getting Over Our Selves': Elegy and Rhetoric in Ted Hughes's *Birthday Letters* and Carrie Etter's *Imagined Sons*." *Journal of Writing in Creative Practice* 12, nos. 1 & 2 (April 2019): 9–27.
Dunn, John J. "Introduction." In *Fragments of Ancient Poetry, 1760*, by James Macpherson, ix. Reprinted edition. Berkeley: University of California, William Andrews Clark Memorial Library, 1966.

Dupeyron-Lafay, Françoise. "The Art of Walking and the Mindscapes of Trauma in Thomas De Quincey's Autobiographical Works: The Pains of Wandering, the Pains of Remembering." In *Walking and the Aesthetics of Modernity: Pedestrian Mobility in Literature and the Arts*, edited by Klaus Benesch and François Specq, 157–72. New York: Palgrave Macmillan, 2016.

Eckardt, Stephanie. "Carrie Mae Weems Reflects on Her Seminal, Enduring *Kitchen Table Series*." *W Magazine*, April 7, 2016. https://www.wmagazine.com/story/carrie-mae-weems-kitchen-table-series-today-interview.

Edson, Russell. "Interview: The Art of the Prose Poem." *The Prose Poem: An International Journal* 8 (1999). http://digitalcommons.providence.edu/cgi/viewcontent.cgi?article=1596&context=prosepoem.

———. "Portrait of the Writer as a Fat Man: Some Subjective Ideas or Notions on the Care and Feeding of Prose Poems, 1975." In *Claims for Poetry*, edited by Donald Hall, 95–103. Ann Arbor: University of Michigan Press, 1983.

———. "The Prose Poem as a Beautiful Animal." In *An Introduction to the Prose Poem*, edited by Brian Clements and Jamey Dunham, 303. Newtown, CT: Firewheel Editions, 2009.

———. "The Prose Poem in America." *Parnassus: Poetry in Review* 5, no. 1 (Fall/Winter 1976): 321–25.

———. *See Jack*. Pittsburgh: University of Pittsburgh Press, 2009.

———. *The Tunnel: Selected Poems*. Field Poetry Series. Ohio: Oberlin College Press, 1994.

Eichler, Charlotte. "The Coffin Calendars." In *The Valley Press Anthology of Prose Poetry*, edited by Anne Caldwell and Oz Hardwick, 45. Scarborough, UK: Valley Press, 2019.

Eiselen, Gregory. "*Leaves of Grass*, 1860 Edition." In *The Routledge Encyclopedia of Walt Whitman*, edited by J. R. LeMaster and Donald D. Kummings, 362–65. New York: Routledge, 1998.

Ekiss, Keith. "Into the City." *Separate City: Prose Poems, Kenyon Review* 35, no. 3 (Summer 2013): n.p. https://www.kenyonreview.org/journal/summer-2013/selections/keith-ekiss/.

Eliot, T. S. "The Borderline of Prose." *New Statesman* 9 (May 1917): 157–59.

———. *Selected Poems*. London: Faber & Faber, 1976.

Elliott, R. K. "Aesthetic Theory and the Experience of Art." In *Aesthetics*, edited by Harold Osborne, 145–57. Oxford: Oxford University Press, 1972.

Ellis, Beverly. "British Prose Poetry: Recovering a Neglected Form." *Ink Sweat and Tears: The Poetry and Prose Webzine* (April 2012): n.p. http://www.inksweatandtears.co.uk/pages/?p=2091.

Estes, A. "Walking and Technology in the Fiction of Jennifer Egan: Moving Towards the Posthuman." In *Walking and the Aesthetics of Modernity: Pedestrian Mobility in Literature and the Arts*, edited by Klaus Benesch and François Specq, 279–95. New York: Palgrave Macmillan, 2016.

Etter, Carrie. *Imagined Sons*. Bridgend, Wales: Seren Books, 2014.

———. "Poetry in the Prose: Getting to Know the Prose Poem." *Poetry Review* 102, no. 2 (Summer 2012): 69–71.

Evans, David. *Rhythm, Illusion and the Poetic Idea: Baudelaire, Rimbaud, Mallarmé.* New York: Rodopi, 2004.

Evans, Martina. *Petrol.* London: Anvil Press Poetry, 2012.

———. *Through the Glass Mountain.* London: Sinclair-Stevenson, 1997.

Faflick, David. *Boarding Out: Inhabiting the American Urban Literary Imagination, 1840–1860.* Evanston, IL: Northwestern University Press, 2012.

Fanuzzi, Robert. "Thoreau's Urban Imagination." *American Literature* 68, no. 2 (June 1996): 321–46.

Faris, Wendy B. *Ordinary Enchantments: Magical Realism and the Remystification of Narrative.* Nashville, TN: Vanderbilt University Press, 2004.

Fehr, Joy. "Female Desire in Prose Poetry: Susan Holbrook's 'as thirsty as' and Hilary Clark's 'Tomato.'" *Thirdspace: A Journal of Feminist Theory and Culture* 1, no. 1 (July 2001): 3–10.

Filreis, Al. "Listening Out the Collectivist Window: 'Okay, my name is so-and-so. . . .'" *Jacket 2* (April 30, 2018): n.p.

Fischer, Heinz-Dietrich, ed. *Chronicle of the Pulitzer Prizes for Poetry: Discussions, Decisions and Documents.* Volume 23. Boston: De Gruyter Saur, 2010.

Fitterman, Robert. *This Window Makes Me Feel.* New York: Ugly Duckling Presse, 2018.

Fitzgerald, Adam. "Riverboat." *Boston Review: A Political and Literary Forum*, August 25, 2014. http://bostonreview.net/poetry/adam-fitzgerald-riverboat.

Fitzgerald, J. M. "Autobiographical Memory and Conceptualizations of the Self." In *Theoretical Perspectives on Autobiographical Memory*, edited by M. A. Conway, David C. Rubin, Hans Spinnler, and Willem A. Wagenaar, 99–114. Dordrecht: Kluwer Academic, 2002.

Flint, F. S. "Imagisme." *Poetry: A Magazine of Verse* 1, no. 6 (March 1913): 198–200.

Ford, Charles Henri. "A Little Anthology of the Poem in Prose." In *New Directions in Prose and Poetry*, edited by C. H. Ford, 329–407. Volume 14. New York: New Directions, 1953.

Fort, Charles. *Mrs. Belladonna's Supper Club Waltz: New and Selected Prose Poems.* Omaha, NE: Backwaters Press, 2013.

Fowler, Alastair. *Kinds of Literature: An Introduction to the Theory of Genres and Modes.* Oxford: Clarendon Press, 1985.

Francis, Emma. "'Conquered good and conquering ill': Femininity, Power and Romanticism in Emily Brontë's Poetry." In *Romanticism and Postmodernism*, edited by Edward Larrissy, 47–72. Cambridge: Cambridge University Press, 1999.

Francis, Gavin. "Bluets by Maggie Nelson Review: Heartbreak and Sex in 240 Turbocharged Prose Poems." *Guardian*, June 9, 2017. https://www.theguardian.com/books/2017/jun/08/bluets-maggie-nelson-review-heartbreak-sex.

Fredman, Stephen. *Poet's Prose: The Crisis in American Verse.* 2nd edition. Cambridge: Cambridge University Press, 1990.

Freitag, Kornelia, ed. *Recovery and Transgression: Memory in American Poetry.* Newcastle-upon-Tyne: Cambridge Scholars, 2015.

Freud, Sigmund. "The Uncanny." In *Writings on Art and Literature*, by Sigmund Freud. Foreword by Neil Hertz, 193–233. Stanford, CA: Stanford University Press. [Originally published in 1919 as *Das Unheimliche* in *Imago* 5 (5–6).]

Friebert, Stuart, and Donald Young, eds. *Models of the Universe: An Anthology of the Prose Poem*. Oberlin, OH: Oberlin College Press, 1995.

Friedman, Jeff. "Catching the Monster." *Survision Magazine* 1 (2017): n.p. http://survisionmagazine.com/Issue1/jefffriedman.htm.

Frow, John. *Genre: The New Critical Idiom*. 2nd edition. Oxford: Routledge, 2014.

Fuller, John. *The Dice Cup*. London: Chatto and Windus, 2014.

———. *A Skin Diary*. London: Chatto and Windus, 1997.

Gailey, Amanda. "Walt Whitman and the King of Bohemia: The Poet in the *Saturday Press*." In *Whitman among the Bohemians*, edited by Joanna Levin and Edward Whitley, 19–36. Iowa City: University of Iowa Press, 2014.

Ganczarek, Joanna, Thomas Hünefeldt, and Marta Olivetti Belardinelli. "From 'Einfühlung' to Empathy: Exploring the Relationship between Aesthetic and Interpersonal Experience." *Cognitive Processing* 19, no. 2 (2018): 141–45.

Garcia, Richard. "Diorama." *Solstice: A Magazine of Diverse Voices* (Summer 2015): n.p. https://solsticelitmag.org/content/finalistdiorama/.

———. *Porridge: Prose Poems*. Winston-Salem, NC: Press 53, 2016.

Gard, Julie. "White Approach." In *Threads: A Photography and Prose Poetry Collaboration*. Exhibition of photographs by Heidi Mae Niska and prose poems by Julie Gard. Virginia, MN: Lyric Centre for the Arts, 2018.

Garfunkel, Art. "Poem 81." In *Still Water Prose Poems*. Art Garfunkel.com, 2018. https://www.artgarfunkel.com/stillwater/poem81.html.

Garraty, John A. *The American Nation: A History of the United States since 1865*. Volume 2. 7th edition. New York: HarperCollins, 1991.

Geczy, Adam. "Between Virtue and Innocence: In Defence of Prose Poetry." *Cordite Poetry Review* (February 2001). http://cordite.org.au/essays/between-virtue-and-innocence/3/.

Gerstler, Amy. *The True Bride*. Culver City, CA: Lapis Press, 1986.

Ghoshal, Sarah. *The Pine Tree Experiment*. Berkeley, CA: Lucky Bastard Press, 2015.

Gibbs, Raymond W., ed. *The Cambridge Handbook of Metaphor and Thought*. New York: Cambridge University Press, 2008.

Ginsberg, Allen. "The Bricklayer's Lunch Hour." In *Empty Mirror: Early Poems*, 31. New York: Totem Press/Corinth Books, 1961.

———. "The Bricklayer's Lunch Hour." In "A Little Anthology of the Poem in Prose," by Charles Henri Ford. In *New Directions in Poetry and Prose*, edited by C. H. Ford, 329–407. New York: New Directions, 1953.

Gioia, Dana. *Can Poetry Matter? Essays on Poetry and American Culture*. Saint Paul, MN: Graywolf Press, 1992.

———. "James Tate and American Surrealism." *Dana Gioia*, n.d. http://danagioia.com/essays/reviews-and-authors-notes/james-tate-and-american-surrealism/.

———. "Meaningful Dreamscapes." *Jacket* 2, 33 (July 2007): n.p. http://jacketmagazine.com/33/arrieu-king-schomburg.shtml.

———. "Thirteen Ways of Thinking about the Poetic Line." *Dana Gioia*, n.d. http://danagioia.com/essays/writing-and-reading/thirteen-ways-of-thinking-about-the-poetic-line/.

Giscombe, G. S. *Prairie Style*. McLean, IL: Dalkey Archive Press, 2008.

Glass, Emma. *Peach*. New York: Bloomsbury, 2018.
Glass, Loren. "A Lifetime in Poetry: Marvin Bell on Iowa and the 'Dead Man' Poems." *Los Angeles Review of Books*, August 17, 2017. https://lareviewofbooks.org/article/a-lifetime-in-poetry-marvin-bell-on-iowa-and-the-dead-man-poems/.
Glucksberg, Sam. *Understanding Figurative Language: From Metaphor to Idioms*. New York: Oxford University Press, 2001.
Gonzalez, Ray, ed. *No Boundaries*. North Adams, MA: Tupelo Press, 2003.
Gosetti-Ferencei, Jennifer Anna. *The Ecstatic Quotidian: Phenomenological Sightings in Modern Art and Literature*. University Park: Pennsylvania State University Press, 2007.
Graham, Jorie. "Introduction." In *The Best American Poetry 1990*, edited by Jorie Graham, xv–xxvi. New York: Scribner, 1990.
Greathouse, Torrin A. "Poetry: Burning Haibun by Torrin A. Greathouse." *Frontier Poetry* (June 16, 2017): n.p. https://www.frontierpoetry.com/2017/06/16/poetry-burning-haibun-torrin-greathouse/.
Greenberg, Arielle. "Ticking the Box: The Rules and Permissions of the Prose Poem Form." In *The Rose Metal Press Field Guide to Prose Poetry: Contemporary Poets in Discussion and Practice*, edited by Gary L. McDowell and F. Daniel Rzicznek, 69–73. Brookline, MA: Rose Metal Press, 2010.
Greene, Roland, Stephen Cushman, and Clare Cavanagh, eds. *The Princeton Encyclopedia of Poetry and Poetics*. 4th edition. Princeton, NJ: Princeton University Press, 2012.
Greenhaus, Mike. "Art Garfunkel." Interview. *Relix* 285 (January/February 2018): 32–33.
Griffin, Farah Jasmine. *"Who Set You Flowin'?" The African-American Migration Narrative*. New York: Oxford University Press, 1995.
Griffin, Susan. *Women and Nature: The Roaring Inside Her*. San Francisco: Sierra Club Books, 1978.
Gropp, Jenny. *The Hominine Egg*. Tucson, AZ: Kore Press, 2017.
Gros, Frédéric. *A Philosophy of Walking*. Translated by John Howe. London: Verso, 2014.
Grosser, Emmylou J. "The Poetic Line as Part and Whole: A Perception-Oriented Approach to Lineation of Poems in the Hebrew Bible." PhD diss., University of Wisconsin-Madison, 2013. http://www.academia.edu/3731763/DISSERTATION_The_poetic_line_as_part_and_whole_A_perception-oriented_approach_to_lineation_of_poems_in_the_Hebrew_Bible.
Guess, Carol, and Daniela Olszewska. *Human-Ghost Hybrid Project*. New York: Black Lawrence, 2017.
Guiney, Louise Imogen. "The Lights of London." In *American Poetry: The Nineteenth Century, Volume Two: Melville to Stickney, American Indian Poetry, Folk Songs and Spirituals*, edited by John Hollander, 533. New York: Literary Classics of the United States, 1993.
Habra, Hedy. *Under Brushstrokes*. Winston-Salem, NC: Press 53, 2015.
Hahn, Kimiko. *A Field Guide to the Intractable*. Brooklyn, NY: Small Anchor Press, 2009. http://smallanchorpress.blogspot.com/2010/01/field-guide-to-intractable-by-kimiko.html.
———. *The Narrow Road to the Interior*. New York: W. W. Norton, 2006.

Hahn, Kimiko. *The Unbearable Heart*. New York: Kaya Press, 1995.
Hall, Donald. "On Russell Edson's Genius." *American Poetry Review* 6, no. 5 (September/October 1977): 12–13.
Halter, Peter. *The Revolution in the Visual Arts and the Poetry of William Carlos Williams*. New York: Cambridge University Press, 1994.
Hamilton, Lucy. *Stalker*. Bristol, UK: Shearsman Books, 2012.
Hardwick, Oz. *An Eschatological Bestiary*. Manchester, UK: Dog Horn, 2013.
———. *Learning to Have Lost*. Kambah, Australian Capital Territory: Recent Work Press, 2018.
Harmon, William. *Handbook to Literature*. 12th edition. Boston, MA: Longman, 2012.
Harms, James. "'Goodtime Jesus' and Other Sort-of Prose Poems." In *Bear Flag Republic: Prose Poems and Poetics from California*, edited by Christopher Buckley and Gary Young, 6–12. Santa Cruz, CA: Greenhouse Review Press/Alcatraz Editions, 2008.
Harries, Elizabeth Wanning. *The Unfinished Manner: Essays on the Fragment in the Later Eighteenth Century*. Charlottesville: University Press of Virginia, 1994.
Harris, Claire. *She*. Fredericton, New Brunswick: Goose Land Editions, 2000.
Harsent, David. *In Secret: Versions of Yannis Ritsos*. London: Enitharmon Press, 2012.
Harvey, David. *The Condition of Postmodernity: An Enquiry into the Origins of Cultural Change*. Oxford: Blackwell, 1990.
Harvey, Matthea. "The Backyard Mermaid." Poets.org, 2011. https://www.poets.org/poetsorg/poem/backyard-mermaid.
Hayes, Terrance. "Introduction to 'Dream-Clung, Gone' by Lauren Russell." *New York Times Magazine*, October 13, 2017. https://www.nytimes.com/2017/10/13/magazine/poem-dream-clung-gone.html.
———. "A Land Governed by Unkindness Reaps No Kindness." *McSweeney's Internet Tendency*, May 7, 2018. https://www.mcsweeneys.net/articles/a-land-governed-by-unkindness-reaps-no-kindness.
Hayes, Terrance, and David Lehman. "Sonnets and Fast Breaks: A Conversation between David Lehman and Terrance Hayes about *The Best American Poetry 2014*." *Best American Poetry*, December 11, 2014. https://blog.bestamericanpoetry.com/the_best_american_poetry/2014/12/a-conversation-between-david-lehman-and-terrance-hayes-.html.
Hayward, Danny. *Pragmatic Sanction*. London: Materials, 2015.
Hazlitt, William. "My First Acquaintance with Poets." In *Hazlitt: Selected Essays*, edited by George Sampson, 1–20. Cambridge: Cambridge University Press, 1958.
Hecq, Dominique. "The Borderlines of Poetry." *Margins and Mainstreams: Refereed Conference Papers of the 14th Annual AAWP Conference*. 2009. http://d3n8a8pro7vhmx.cloudfront.net/theaawp/pages/84/attachments/original/1385080755/Hecq.pdf?1385080755.
Heiden, Pete, and Amy Huntington. *Penelope and Pip Build a Prose Poem*. Chicago: Norwood House Press, 2011.
Hejinian, Lyn. "Continuing Against Closure." *Jacket* 14, coproduced with *Salt* 13 (July 2001): n.p. http://jacketmagazine.com/14/hejinian.html.
———. *The Language of Inquiry*. Berkeley: University of California Press, 2000.

———. *My Life and My Life in the Nineties*. Middletown, CT: Wesleyan University Press, 2013.

———. *Saga/Circus*. Richmond, CA: Omnidawn, 2008.

Hemingway, Ernest. "Hills Like White Elephants." In *The Essential Hemingway*, by Ernest Hemingway, 402–7. London: Vintage Books, 2004.

———. *In Our Time*. New York: Boni & Liveright, 1925.

Henry, Peter. "'The beautiful white ruins / of America': Surrealist Poetry and the Cold War." PhD diss., University of Virginia, 2013. https://doi.org/10.18130/V39003.

Herd, David. *John Ashbery and American Poetry*. Manchester, UK: Manchester University Press, 2000.

Hershman, Tania. *Nothing Here Is Wild, Everything Is Open*. Cork, Ireland: Southword Editions, 2016.

———. "Powers of Ten." In *Blue Fifth Review: Blue Five Notebook Series*. Broadside #51, vol. 18, no. 4 (Summer 2018): n.p. https://bluefifthreview.wordpress.com/2018/08/15/broadside-51-summer-2018-18-4/.

Hetherington, Paul. "Antiquities." Quoted in "Broken Forms: Prose Poetry as Hybridised Genre in Australia," by Paul Hetherington and Cassandra Atherton. *Coolabah* 24–25 (2018): 112–126.

———. *Gallery of Antique Art*. Kambah, Australian Capital Territory: Recent Work Press, 2016.

———. *Ikaros*. Kambah, Australian Capital Territory: Recent Work Press, 2017.

———. *Palace of Memory*. Kambah, Australian Capital Territory: Recent Work Press, 2019.

Hetherington, Paul, and Cassandra Atherton. "Broken Forms: Prose Poetry as Hybridised Genre in Australia." *Coolabah* 24/25 (2018): 112–26. Observatori: Centre d'Estudis Australians I Transnacionals/Observatory: Australian and Transational Studies Centre, Universitat de Barcelona. http://revistes.ub.edu/index.php/coolabah/article/view/22076/23611.

———. "'Unconscionable Mystification'? Rooms, Spaces and the Prose Poem." *New Writing: The International Journal for the Practice and Theory of Creative Writing* 12, no. 3 (2015): 265–81.

Heynen, Jim. "The Boys Go to Ask a Neighbor for Some Apples." In *The Boys' House: Stories*, by Jim Heynen, 28–29. Saint Paul: Minnesota Historical Society Press, 2001.

Hicok, Bob. "Prose Poem Essay on the Prose Poem." In *The Rose Metal Press Field Guide to Prose Poetry: Contemporary Poets in Discussion and Practice*, edited by Gary L. McDowell and F. Daniel Rzicznek, 1. Brookline, MA: Rose Metal Press, 2010.

Hill, Geoffrey. *New and Collected Poems, 1952–1992*. Boston: Houghton Mifflin Harcourt, 2000.

Hilson, Jeff. *Bird Bird*. Norwich, UK: Landfill Press, 2009.

Hinton, Laura. "An Introduction to Reading Carla Harryman." *How 2 Online Journal* 3, no. 3: n.d. https://www.asu.edu/piper/how2journal/vol_3_no_3/harryman/.

Hirsch, Edward. *How to Read a Poem: And Fall in Love with Poetry*. New York: Harcourt, 1999.

———. "Prose Poem: From a Poet's Glossary." Poets.org, 2014. https://www.poets.org/poetsorg/text/prose-poem-poets-glossary.

Hoang, Lily. *Changing.* Tuscon, AZ: Fairy Tale Review Press, 2008.

Hoffberg, Judith A. "Art People." *Umbrella* 17, no. 2 (1994): 38–41.

Hoffer, Pamela Marie. *Reflets Reciproques: A Prismatic Reading of Stéphane Mallarmé and Hélène Cixous.* New York: Peter Lang, 2006.

Holiday, Harmony. "Crisis Actor." Poetry Foundation, 2017. https://www.poetry foundation.org/poetrymagazine/poems/144386/crisis-actor-59bc02272653c.

Hollander, John. "Swan and Shadow." In *Types of Shape*, 35. New expanded edition. New Haven: Yale University Press, 1991.

Horvath, Brooke. "Definition." In *An Introduction to the Prose Poem*, edited by Brian Clements and Jamey Dunham, 289. Newtown, CT: Firewheel Editions, 2009.

Howe, Sarah. *Loop of Jade.* London: Chatto & Windus, 2015.

Howell, Anthony. "The Prose Poem: What the Hell is it?" *Fortnightly Review*, April 1, 2016. https://fortnightlyreview.co.uk/2016/04/prose-poetry/.

Howells, W. D. "Introduction." In *Pastels in Prose.* Translated by Stuart Merrill, with illustrations by Henry W. McVickar, and an introduction by William Dean Howells. New York: Harper & Brothers, Franklin Square, 1890. https://archive.org/details/pastelsinprose00merriala/page/n8/mode/2up.

HuffPost. "Patricia Lockwood's Sext Poem Will Make You LOL." January 24, 2012. https://www.huffingtonpost.com/2012/01/24/patricia-lockwoods-sext-p_n_1228606.html.

Hume, David. *A Treatise on Human Nature.* London: Dent, 1911.

Hummel, H. K., and Stephanie Lenox. *Short-Form Creative Writing: A Writer's Guide and Anthology.* London: Bloomsbury Academic, 2019.

Hummer, Theo. "Moravia: Postcards." In *An Introduction to the Prose Poem*, edited by Brian Clements and Jamey Dunham, 234–36. Newtown, CT: Firewheel Editions, 2009.

Humphrey, Asa. *The English Prosody: With Rules Deduced from the Genius of Our Language, and the Examples of the Poets.* Boston: Crocker & Brewster, 1847.

Huntsperger, David W. "Objectivist Form and Feminist Materialism in Lyn Hejinian's *My Life*." In *Procedural Form in Postmodern American Poetry: Berrigan, Antin, Silliman, and Hejinian*, by David W. Hunstperger, 131–63. New York: Palgrave Macmillan, 2010.

Hussain, Hamzah M. "A Mastery of English: A Conversation with Mary Jean Chan." *Dundee University Review of the Arts*, 2019. https://dura-dundee.org.uk/2019/06/25/a-mastery-of-english-a-conversation-with-mary-jean-chan/.

Hutchison, Coleman. "Here, There and Everywhere: C. S. Giscombe's Poetics of Race and Place." *Global South* 9, no. 1 (Spring 2015): 107–23.

Huyssen, Andreas. *After the Great Divide: Modernism, Mass Culture, Postmodernism.* Bloomington: Indiana University Press, 1986.

———. *Miniature Metropolis: Literature in an Age of Photography and Film.* Cambridge, MA: Harvard University Press, 2015.

Iglesias, Holly. *Boxing Inside the Box: Women's Prose Poetry.* Florence, MA: Quale Press, 2004.

———. "Conceptual Arts." In *Angles of Approach*. Buffalo, NY: White Pine Press, 2010.

Retrieved from *Blue Ridge Journal*, 2010. http://www.blueridgejournal.com/poems/hi-conceptual.htm.

———. "Perishables." In *A Cast-Iron Aeroplane that Can Actually Fly: Commentaries from 80 Contemporary American Poets on Their Prose Poetry*, edited by Peter Johnson, 101–2. Asheville, NC: Madhat Press, 2019.

———. "Prose Poetry, Point of View, and Personal Archives." *North Carolina Writers' Network*, September 20, 2011. https://www.ncwriters.org/2014-01-07-18-35-09/network-news/4860-prose-poetry-point-of-view-and-personal-archives.

———. *Sleeping Things: Prose Poems*. Winston-Salem, NC: Press 53, 2018.

Iijima, Brenda. *Some Simple Things Said by and about Humans*. Amherst, MA: BOAAT Press, 2014.

Innes, Randy Norman. "On the Limits of the Work of Art: The Fragment in Visual Culture." PhD diss., University of Rochester, New York, 2008. https://search.proquest.com/openview/0c5201c458956eda1cdd85372922fe95/1?pq-origsite=gscholar&cbl=18750&diss=y.

Iredell, Jamie. *Prose. Poems. A Novel.* St. Charles, IL: Orange Alert Press, 2009.

Irwin, Mark. "Distortion and Disjunction in Contemporary American Poetry." *American Poetry Review* 40, no. 6 (2011): 39–42.

Israel-Pelletier, Aimée. *Rimbaud's Impressionist Poetics: Vision and Visuality*. Cardiff: University of Wales Press, 2012.

Ives, Lucy. *Orange Roses*. Boise, ID: Ahsahta Press, 2013.

Jakobson, Roman. "The Metaphoric and Metonymic Poles." In *Metaphor and Metonymy in Comparison and Contrast*, edited by René Dirven and Ralf Pörings, 41–48. Berlin: Mouton D. Gruyter, 2002.

James, Sonya. "Review of Christopher Merrill's *Boat*." North Adams, MA: Tupelo Press, 2013. https://www.tupelopress.org/product/boat-christopher-merrill/.

Jarnot, Lisa. *Black Dog Songs*. Chicago: Flood Editions, 2003.

———. *Night Scenes*. Chicago: Flood Editions, 2008.

———. *Sea Lyrics*. New York: Situations, 1996.

Jastrzebska, Maria. *The True Story of Cowboy Hat and Ingénue*. Blaenau Ffestiniog, Wales: Cinnamon Press, 2018.

Jenkins, Louis. *Nice Fish: New and Selected Poems*. Duluth, MN: Holy Cow! Press, 1995.

———. "The Prose Poem." In *An Introduction to the Prose Poem*, edited by Brian Clements and Jamey Dunham, 299. Newtown, CT: Firewheel Editions, 2009.

Jobson, Liesl. *100 Papers: A Collection of Prose Poems and Flash Fiction*. Braamfontein, South Africa: Botsotso, 2008.

Johnson, Julia. "Introduction." *Mississippi Review* 34, no. 3 (Fall 2006): 7–9.

Johnson, Peter, ed. *The Best of the Prose Poem: An International Journal*. Buffalo, NY: White Pine Press, 2000.

———, ed. *A Cast-Iron Aeroplane that Can Actually Fly: Commentaries from 80 Contemporary American Poets on Their Prose Poetry*. Asheville, NC: Madhat Press, 2019.

———. "An Interview with Russell Edson." *Writer's Chronicle* 31, no. 6 (May/Summer 1999): 30–36.

———. "Introduction." In *The Best of the Prose Poem: An International Journal*, 10–18. Buffalo, NY: White Pine Press; Providence, RI: Providence College, 2000.

Johnson, Peter. *Love Poems for the Millennium*. Niantic, CT: Quale Press, 1998.

———. "Preface." In *A Cast-Iron Aeroplane that Can Actually Fly: Commentaries from 80 Contemporary American Poets on Their Prose Poetry*, edited by Peter Johnson, xi–xii. Asheville, NC: Madhat Press, 2019.

Johnson, Peter, and Robert Bly. "Interview: The Art of the Prose Poem." *Prose Poem: An International Journal* 7 (1998): n.p. https://digitalcommons.providence.edu/prosepoem/vol7/iss1/52/.

Jones, Alice. "Reply." In *A Cast-Iron Aeroplane that Can Actually Fly: Commentaries from 80 Contemporary American Poets on Their Prose Poetry*, edited by Peter Johnson, 111–12. Asheville, NC: Madhat Press, 2019.

Jones, Dorothy Richardson. *"King of Critics": George Saintsbury, 1845–1933, Critic, Journalist, Historian, Professor*. Ann Arbor: University of Michigan Press, 1992.

Jones, Peter. *Imagist Poetry*. London: Penguin, 1976.

Joron, Andrew. *The Cry at Zero: Selected Prose*. Denver, CO: Counterpath Press, 2007.

Joseph, Eve. *Quarrels*. Vancouver: Anvil Press, 2018.

Kafka, Franz. *Parables and Paradoxes*. Berlin: Schocken Books, 1961.

Kapil, Bhanu. *Humanimal: A Project for Future Children*. Berkeley, CA: Kelsey Street Press, 2009.

Kaplan, Edward K. *Baudelaire's Prose Poems: The Esthetic, the Ethical, and the Religious in the Parisian Prowler*. Athens: University of Georgia Press, 2009.

Kasischke, Laura. *Space, in Chains*. Port Townsend, WA: Copper Canyon Press, 2011.

Katsaros, Laure. *New York–Paris: Whitman, Baudelaire, and the Hybrid City*. Ann Arbor: University of Michigan Press, 2012.

Kawakami, Akane. "Nathalie Sarraute's Accent: The Poetry of *Tropismes*." *French Studies* 86, no. 4 (October 2004): 499–512.

Keats, John. *John Keats: Complete Poems*. Edited by Jack Stillinger. Cambridge, MA: Belknap Press of Harvard University Press, 2003.

Keene, Dennis. "Introduction." In *The Modern Japanese Prose Poem: An Anthology of Six Poets*. Translated and with an introduction by Dennis Keene, 3–54. Princeton, NJ: Princeton University Press, 1980.

Kennard, Luke. *Cain: Poems*. London: Penned in the Margins, 2017.

———. "The Expanse: Self-Consciousness and the Transatlantic Prose Poem." PhD diss., University of Exeter, 2008. https://ethos.bl.uk/OrderDetails.do;jsessionid=C689DB024B612893C3EDADFABB63012F?uin=uk.bl.ethos.496112.

———. "'Man and Nature In and Out of Order': The Surrealist Prose Poetry of David Gascoyne." In *British Prose Poetry: The Poems Without Lines*, edited by Jane Monson, 249–64. Cham, Switzerland: Palgrave Macmillan, 2018.

———. *The Migraine Hotel*. Cambridge, UK: Salt, 2009.

———. *The Solex Brothers (Redux): And Other Prose Poems; Now with Explanatory Notes*. Cambridge, UK: Salt, 2010.

Kinsella, John. "Graphology 300: Against 'Nature Writing.'" In *Graphology Poems: 1995–2015*. Volume 1, 245–46. Parkville, Australia: Five Islands Press, 2016.

———. *Spatial Relations: Essays, Reviews, Commentaries and Chorography*. Volume 1, edited by Gordon Collier. Amsterdam: Rodopi, 2013.

Knight, Christopher J. *The Patient Particulars: American Modernism and the Technique of Originality*. Lewisburg, PA: Bucknell University Press, 1995.

Knowles, Kim, Anna Katharina Schaffner, Ulrich Weger, and Andrew Michael Roberts. "Reading Space in Visual Poetry: New Cognitive Perspectives." *Writing Technologies* 4 (2012): 75–106.

Komunyakaa, Yusef. *Thieves of Paradise*. Middleton, CT: Wesleyan University Press; Hanover: University Press of New Hampshire, 1998.

Kosslyn, Stephen M., William L. Thompson, and Giorgio Ganis. *The Case for Mental Imagery*. Oxford: Oxford University Press, 2006.

Kozak, Daniel. "Assessing Urban Fragmentation: The Emergence of New Typologies in Central Buenos Aires." In *World Cities and Urban Form: Fragmented, Polycentric, Sustainable?* Edited by Mike Jenks, Daniel Kozak, and Pattaranan Takkanon, 239–58. New York: Routledge, 2008.

Kramer, S. N., trans. "Sumerian Love Song." In *Ancient Near Eastern Texts Relating to the Old Testament*. 3rd edition with supplement, edited by James B. Pritchard, 496. Princeton, NJ: Princeton University Press, 1992.

Kristeva, Julia. "Word, Dialogue and Novel." In *The Kristeva Reader: Julia Kristeva*, edited by Toril Moi, 34–61. New York: Columbia University Press, 1986.

Kukuljevic, Alexi. *Liquidation World: On the Art of Living Absently*. Cambridge, MA: MIT Press, 2017.

Lacoue-Labarthe, Phillipe, and Jean-Luc Nancy. *The Literary Absolute: The Theory of Literature in German Romanticism*. Translated by Philip Barnard and Cheryl Lester. Albany: State University of New York Press, 1988.

LaFemina, Gerry. "A Carnival Comes to Town: Showing Prose Poems at the County Fair." In *The Rose Metal Press Guide to Prose Poetry: Contemporary Poets in Discussion and Practice*, edited by Gary L. McDowell and F. Daniel Rzicznek, 127–33. Brookline, MA: Rose Metal Press, 2010.

———. "The Text as Richard Serra Sculpture: On Reading the Prose Poem." *TEXT: The Journal of the Australian Association of Writing Programs* 7, no. 1 (2003): n.p. http://www.textjournal.com.au/april03/lafemina.htm.

Lagamarsino, Nancy. *Light from an Eclipse*. Buffalo, NY: White Pine Press, 2005.

Lamantia, Philip. *The Collected Poems of Philip Lamantia*. Berkeley: University of California Press, 2013.

Lanphier, Elizabeth. "The Internet as Spectator Disclosure: Consent, Community, and Responsibility in Patricia Lockwood's Viral Poem 'Rape Joke.'" *American Studies Journal* 61 (2016): n.p. http://www.asjournal.org/61-2016/internet-spectator-disclosure-consent-community-responsibility-patricia-lockwoods-viral-poem-rape-joke/.

Lanzoni, Susan. "Empathy Aesthetics: Experimenting Between Psychology and Poetry." In *Rethinking Empathy through Literature*, edited by Meghan Marie Hammond and Sue J. Kim, 34–46. New York: Routledge, 2014.

Larissy, Edward. "Introduction." In *Romanticism and Postmodernism*, edited by Edward Larissy, 1–12. Cambridge: Cambridge University Press, 1999.

Larson, Thomas. "The Griffin of Literature: Three New Books of Prose Poetry." *TriQuar-*

terly, January 31, 2014. http://www.triquarterly.org/reviews/griffin-literature-three-new-books-prose-poetry.

Larson, Thomas. "Now, Where Was I? On Maggie Nelson's *Bluets*." *TriQuarterly*, January 24, 2011. http://www.triquarterly.org/craft-essays/now-where-was-i-maggie-nelson's-bluets.

Lawrence, D. H. *Lady Chatterley's Lover*. Camberwell, Victoria: Penguin, 2008.

Lazarus, Emma. *Selected Poems and Other Writings*, edited by Gregory Eiselein. Orchard Park, NY: Broadview Press, 2002.

Lehman, David. "David Lehman." In *Lofty Dogmas: Poets on Poetry*, edited by Deborah Brown, Annie Finch, and Maxine Kumin, 265–69. Fayetteville: University of Arkansas Press, 2005.

———, ed. *Great American Prose Poems: From Poe to the Present*. New York: Scribner, 2003.

———. "Introduction." In *Great American Prose Poems: From Poe to the Present*, edited by David Lehman, 11–26. New York: Scribner, 2003.

———. *Poems in the Manner Of*. New York: Scribner, 2007.

———. "The Prose Poem: An Alternative to Verse." *American Poetry Review* 32, no. 2 (March/April 2003): 45–49. https://www.jstor.org/stable/20682182?seq=1#page_scan_tab_contents.

Lempert, Benjamin R. "Harryette Mullen and the Contemporary Jazz Voice." *Callaloo* 33, no. 4 (Fall 2010): 1059–78.

Lerner, Ben. "Beyond 'Lyric Shame': Ben Lerner on Claudia Rankine and Maggie Nelson." *Literary Hub*, November 29, 2017. https://lithub.com/beyond-lyric-shame-ben-lerner-on-claudia-rankine-and-maggie-nelson/.

Leuzzi, Tony. "Response and Bio." *Double Room: A Journal of Prose Poetry and Flash Fiction* 2 (2003): n.p. https://doubleroomjournal.com/issue_two/TL_ResBio.html.

Levin, Joanna. *Bohemia in America, 1858–1920*. Stanford, CA: Stanford University Press, 2009.

Levinson, Marjorie. *The Romantic Fragment Poem: A Critique of a Form*. Chapel Hill: University of North Carolina Press, 1986.

Levy, Deborah. *Black Vodka: Ten Stories*. New York: Bloomsbury, 2014.

Li, Bella. *Argosy*. Newtown, NSW: Vagabond Press, 2017.

———. *Lost Lake*. Newtown, NSW: Vagabond Press, 2018.

Lichtenstein, Jesse. "The Smutty-Metaphor Queen of Lawrence, Kansas." *New York Times*, May 28, 2014. https://www.nytimes.com/2014/06/01/magazine/the-smutty-metaphor-queen-of-lawrence-kansas.html.

Littlemore, Jeannette. *Metonymy: Hidden Shortcuts in Language, Thought and Communication*. Cambridge: Cambridge University Press, 2015.

Lloyd, Rosemary. *Mallarmé: The Poet and His Circle*. New York: Cornell University Press, 2005.

Locke, John. *An Essay Concerning Human Understanding*, edited by Peter H. Nidditch. Oxford: Oxford at the Clarendon Press, 1975.

Lockwood, Patricia. "Rape Joke." *Awl*, July 25, 2013. https://www.theawl.com/2013/07/patricia-lockwood-rape-joke/.

Loizeaux, Elizabeth Bergmann. *Twentieth-Century Poetry and the Visual Arts*. Cambridge: Cambridge University Press, 2010.

Lombardo, Gian S. *Machines We Have Built*. Niantic, CT: A Clear Sound Book of Quale Press, 2014.

Long, Alexander. "Something Like a Meditation." In *The Rose Metal Press Field Guide to Prose Poetry: Contemporary Poets in Discussion and Practice*, edited by Gary L. McDowell and F. Daniel Rzicznek, 41–47. Brookline, MA: Rose Metal Press, 2010.

Longenbach, James. *The Art of the Poetic Line*. Minneapolis: Graywolf Press, 2008.

Loveday, Michael. "Interview with Carrie Etter." *Page Chatter: Conversations about Flash Fiction, Prose Poetry and Poetry*, April 21, 2018. https://pagechatter.org/2018/04/21/interview-with-carrie-etter/.

Lowell, Amy. "New York at Night." In *The City that Never Sleeps: Poems of New York*, edited by Shawkat M. Toorawa, 109–10. Albany: State University of New York Press, 2015.

Lowenthal, David. *The Past Is a Foreign Country*. 11th printing. Cambridge: Cambridge University Press, 2003.

Lowes, Robert. "The Unity of the Paragraph." In *An Introduction to the Prose Poem*, edited by Brian Clements and Jamey Dunham, 293–95. Newtown, CT: Firewheel Editions, 2009.

Loydell, Rupert. "Towards a Definition." In *An Introduction to the Prose Poem*, edited by Brian Clements and Jamey Dunham, 292. Newtown, CT: Firewheel Editions, 2009.

Lundy Martin, Dawn. *Discipline*. Brooklyn, NY: Nightboat Books, 2011.

———. *Life in a Box Is a Pretty Life*. Callicoon, NY: Nightboat, 2014.

Mackenzie, Raymond. "Introduction." In *Paris Spleen and La Fanfarlo*, by Charles Baudelaire. Translated by Raymond Mackenzie, xii–xxxiv. Indianapolis, IN: Hackett, 2008.

Macpherson, James. "A Dissertation Concerning the Antiquity &c of the Poems of Ossian the son of Fingal." In *Works of Ossian*, by James Macpherson. Volume 1, xxiv–xxv. Leipzig: LG Fleischer, 1783.

Mahony, Dennis F. "Introduction." In *The Literature of German Romanticism*, edited by Dennis F. Mahony and James N. Hardin, 1–24. Rochester, NY: Cambden House, 2004.

Mallarmé, Stéphane. *Divagations*. Translated by Barbara Johnson. Cambridge, MA: Belknap Press of Harvard University Press, 2007.

———. *A Roll of the Dice*. Translated by Robert Bononno and Jeff Clark. Seattle: Wave Books, 2015.

Mancini, C. Bruna. "Imagined/Remembered Londons." *Literary London: Interdisciplinary Studies in the Representation of London* 2, no. 2 (September 2004): n.p. http://literarylondon.org/the-literary-london-journal/archive-of-the-literary-london-journal/issue-2-2/imaginedremembered-londons/.

Manhire, Bill. "Prose Poems." In *Doubtful Sounds: Essays and Interviews*, by Bill Manhire, 180–82. Wellington, NZ: Victoria University Press, 2000.

Mar, Raymond A., and Keith Oatley. "The Function of Fiction Is the Abstraction and

Simulation of Social Experience." *Perspectives on Psychological Science* 2, no. 3 (2008): 173–92.

Marcus, Morton. "Freedom, The Prose Poem & The Imagination." *Caesura* (Winter 2000): n.p. https://docs.wixstatic.com/ugd/05e4cd_ab1991cf95b042acb52ad74b3ea28ba2.pdf.

———. "In Praise of the Prose Poem: An Interview with Morton Marcus." In *Bear Flag Republic: Prose Poems and Poetics from California*, edited by Christopher Buckley and Gary Young, 17–18. Santa Cruz, CA: Greenhouse Review Press/Alcatraz Editions, 2008.

Markotic, Nicole. "Narrotics: New Narrative and the Prose Poem." *Narrativity: A Critical Journal of Innovative Narrative* 1 (2000): n.p. https://www.sfsu.edu/~newlit/narrativity/issue_one/markotic.html.

Marmontel, Jean-François. *Bélisaire*. Paris: Chez Merlin, 2009. [Originally published 1767.]

Martens, Amelia. *Purgatory*. New York: Black Lawrence Press, 2012.

Marvell, Andrew. "To His Coy Mistress." In *The Poems of Andrew Marvell*, edited by Nigel Smith, 81–84. Revised edition. Harlow, UK: Pearson Longman, 2007.

May, Jon, and Nigel Thrift, eds. *Timespace: Geographies of Temporality*. New York: Routledge, 2001.

Mayer, Bernadette. *The Desires of Mothers to Please Others in Letters*. West Stockbridge, MA: Hard Press, 1994.

McCooey, David. "Postcolonial Poetry of Australia and Aotearoa/New Zealand." In *The Cambridge Companion to Postcolonial Poetry*, edited by Jahan Ramazani, 72–84. Cambridge: Cambridge University Press, 2017.

McFarland, Thomas. *Romanticism and the Forms of Ruin: Wordsworth, Coleridge, the Modalities of Fragmentation*. Princeton, NJ: Princeton University Press, 1981.

McGookey, Kathleen. "Ordinary Emotions, Extraordinary Emotions." In *A Cast-Iron Aeroplane that Can Actually Fly: Commentaries from 80 Contemporary American Poets on Their Prose Poetry*, edited by Peter Johnson, 152–53. Asheville, NC: Madhat Press, 2019.

———. "Why I Write Prose Poems." In *The Rose Metal Press Field Guide to Prose Poetry: Contemporary Poets in Discussion and Practice*, edited by Gary L. McDowell and F. Daniel Rzicznek, 48–51. Brookline, MA: Rose Metal Press, 2010.

McGrath, Campbell. "The Prose Poem." In *No Boundaries: Prose Poems by 24 American Poets*, edited by Ray González, 207. Dorset, VT: Tupelo Press, 2003.

McGrath Smith, Ellen. "Gendre: Women's Prose Poetry in the 1980s." *Sentence: A Journal of Prose Poetics* 10 (2013): 207.

McGuinness, Patrick. "Symbolism." In *The Cambridge History of French Literature*, edited by William Burgwinkle, Nicholas Hammond, and Emma Wilson, 479–87. Cambridge: Cambridge University Press, 2011.

McLane, Maureen N. "Anne Boyer's 'Garments Against Women.'" *New York Times*, December 24, 2015. https://www.nytimes.com/2015/12/27/books/review/anne-boyers-garments-against-women.html.

McLees, Ainslie Armstrong. *Baudelaire's Argot Plastique: Poetic Caricature and Modernism*. Athens: University of Georgia Press, 2010.

McMaster, Arthur. "Space, in Chains." *Poet's Quarterly* (Winter 2013): n.p. http://www.poetsquarterly.com/2013/01/space-in-chains-by-laura-kasischke.html.
Meitner, Erika. "A Brief Ontological Investigation." Poets.org, 2018. https://www.poets.org/poetsorg/poem/brief-ontological-investigation.
Merrill, Christopher. *Boat*. North Adams, MA: Tupelo Press, 2013.
Merwin, W. S. "Humble Beginning." In *An Introduction to the Prose Poem*, edited by Brian Clements and Jamey Dunham, 135. Newtown, CT: Firewheel Editions, 2009.
Meyerstein, E.H.W. "The Influence of Ossian." In *English* 7 (1948): 95–98.
Miller, E. Ethelbert. *The Ear Is an Organ Made for Love*, 2010. http://www.eethelbertmiller.com/THE_EAR_IS_AN_ORGAN_MADE_FOR_LOVE.pdf.
Miller, Karl. "Things." *London Review of Books* 9, no. 7 (April 2, 1987): n.p. https://www.lrb.co.uk/v09/n07/karl-miller/things.
Mills, Kathryn Oliver. *Formal Revolution in the Work of Baudelaire and Flaubert*. Newark: University of Delaware Press, 2012.
Miltner, Robert. *Hotel Utopia*. Moorhead, MN: New Rivers Press, 2011.
———. "Québec Express." *Full Bleed: A Journal of Art and Design* 2, issue: *Crisis* (Summer 2018): n.p. https://www.full-bleed.org/a-series-by-robert-miltner/.
Mirsky, D. S. "Whitman in Russia: D. S. Mirsky." In *Walt Whitman and the World*, edited by Gay Wilson Allen and Ed Folsom, 320–32. Iowa City: University of Iowa Press, 1995.
Mitchell, Danielle. "The Poet's Revolt: A Brief Guide to the Prose Poem." *DIY MFA*, April 30, 2014. https://diymfa.com/writing/poets-revolt-brief-guide-prose-poem.
Mitchell, W.J.T. *Picture Theory: Essays on Verbal and Visual Representation*. Chicago: University of Chicago Press, 1995.
Monroe, Jonathan. *A Poverty of Objects: The Prose Poem and the Politics of Genre*. Ithaca, NY: Cornell University Press, 1987.
Monson, Jane, ed. *British Prose Poetry: The Poems Without Lines*. Cham, Switzerland: Palgrave Macmillan, 2018.
———. "Introduction." In *British Prose Poetry: The Poems Without Lines*, edited by Jane Monson, 1–16. Cham, Switzerland: Palgrave Macmillan, 2018.
———. "The Prose Poem in England Today: A Poet's View." *Extract: Newsletter* 26, no. 5 (June 2005), University of Kent. http://www.webdelsol.com/Double_Room/issue_six/Jane_Monson.htm.
———. *The Shared Surface*. Blaenau Ffestiniog, Wales: Cinnamon Press, 2013.
———. *Speaking without Tongues*. Blaenau Ffestiniog, Wales: Cinnamon Press, 2010.
———, ed. *This Line Is Not For Turning: An Anthology of Contemporary British Prose Poetry*. Blaenau Ffestiniog, Wales: Cinnamon Press, 2011.
Monte, Steven. *Invisible Fences: Prose Poetry as a Genre in French and American Literature*. Lincoln: University of Nebraska Press, 2000.
Moore, Dafydd R. "The Critical Response to Ossian's Romantic Bequest." In *English Romanticism and the Celtic World*, edited by Gerard Carruthers and Alan Rawes, 38–53. Cambridge: Cambridge University Press, 2003.
———. "The Reception of *The Poems of Ossian* in England and Scotland." In *The Reception of Ossian in Europe*, edited by Howard Gaskill, 21–39. New York: Thoemmes, 2004.

Moore, Fabienne. "Early French Romanticism." In *A Companion to European Romanticism*, edited by Michael Ferber, 172–91. Malden, MA: Blackwell, 2005.

———. *Prose Poems of the French Enlightenment: Delimiting Genre*. Farnham, UK: Ashgate, 2009.

Moores, Margaret Ruth. "Loading the Image." Master's thesis. Massey University, 2016. https://mro.massey.ac.nz/handle/10179/11193.

Moorman Robbins, Amy. *American Hybrid Poetics: Gender, Mass Culture, and Form*. New Brunswick, NJ: Rutgers University Press, 2014.

———. "Amy Gerstler (1956–)." In *Contemporary American Women Poets: An A-to-Z Guide*, edited by Catherine Cucinella, 138–41. Westport, CT: Greenwood, 2002.

Morley, Simon. *Writing on the Wall: Word and Image in Modern Art*. Berkeley: University of California Press, 2003.

Moss, Thylias. "Goodness and the Salt of the Earth." In *Models of the Universe: An Anthology of the Prose Poem*, edited by Stuart Friebert and David Young, 291. Oberlin, OH: Oberlin College Press, 1995.

Mullen, Harryette. *Broken Glish: Five Prose Poems* [chapbook]. New York: Centre for Book Arts, 2013.

———. *Recyclopedia: Trimmings, S*PeRM*K*T, Muse & Drudge*. Minneapolis: Graywolf Press, 2006.

———. *Sleeping with the Dictionary*. Berkeley: University of California Press, 2002.

———. *Trimmings*. New York: Tender Buttons Press, 2002.

Munden, Paul. "Arthroscopy/Sports Day, 1971." In *Keys*, by Paul Munden. Canberra: Authorised Theft, 2015.

———. "Playing with Time: Prose Poetry and the Elastic Moment." *TEXT*, Special Issue 46, *Beyond the Line: Contemporary Prose Poetry* (October 2017): 1–13. http://www.textjournal.com.au/speciss/issue46/Munden.pdf.

Murphy, Margueritte S. "The British Prose Poem and 'Poetry' in Early Modernism." In *British Prose Poetry: The Poems Without Lines*, edited by Jane Monson, 29–45. Cham, Switzerland: Palgrave Macmillan, 2018.

———. "Introduction." In *Family Portrait: American Prose Poetry, 1900–1950*, edited by Robert Alexander, 19–39. Buffalo, NY: White Pine Press, 2012.

———. *A Tradition of Subversion: The Prose Poem in English from Wilde to Ashbery*. Amherst: University of Massachusetts Press, 1992.

———. "What Titles Tell Us: The Prose Poem in the Little Magazines of Early Modernism." *TEXT*, Special Issue 46, *Beyond the Line: Contemporary Prose Poetry* (October 2017): 1–15. http://www.textjournal.com.au/speciss/issue46/Murphy.pdf.

Myers, Steve. "Haibun for Smoke and Fog." In *An Introduction to the Prose Poem*, edited by Brian Clements and Jamey Dunham, 221–23. Newtown, CT: Firewheel Editions, 2009.

Nagai, Mariko. *Irradiated Cities*. Los Angeles: Les Figues Press, 2017.

Nakagawa, Jane Joritz, and Maxine Chernoff. "Maxine Chernoff: In Conversation with Jane Joritz-Nakagawa." *Jacket* 39 (2009): n.p. http://jacketmagazine.com/38/iv-chernoff-ivb-nakagawa.shtml.

Neisser, Ulric. "What Is Ordinary Memory the Memory Of?" In *Remembering Reconsidered: Ecological and Traditional Approaches to the Study of Memory*, edited by Ulric

Neisser and Eugene Winograd, 356–73. Cambridge: Cambridge University Press, 1988.
Nelles, William. "Microfiction: What Makes a Very Short Story Very Short?" *Narrative* 20, no. 1 (2012): 87–104.
Nelsen, Julia. "Modernist Laboratories: The Prose Poem and the Little Magazines." *Letteratura e letterature* 4 (2010): 47–65.
Nelson, Maggie. *The Argonauts*. Minneapolis: Graywolf Press; Melbourne: TEXT, 2016.
———. *Bluets*. Seattle: Wave Press, 2009.
———. *Women, the New York School, and Other True Abstractions*. Iowa City: University of Iowa Press, 2007.
Newman, Lance. "'Patron of the World': Henry Thoreau as Wordsworthian Poet." In *Henry David Thoreau*, edited by Harold Bloom, 107–25. Updated edition. New York: Blooms Literary Criticism, 2007.
Nezhukumatathil, Aimee. "Summer Haibun." Poets.org, 2017. https://www.poets.org/poetsorg/poem/summer-haibun.
Noel-Tod, Jeremy. "'Immeasurable as One': Vahni Capildeo's Prose Poetics." In *British Prose Poetry: The Poems Without Lines*, edited by Jane Monson, 211–25. Cham, Switzerland: Palgrave Macmillan, 2018.
———. "Introduction: The Expansion of the Prose Poem." In *The Penguin Book of the Prose Poem: From Baudelaire to Anne Carson*, edited by Jeremy Noel-Tod, xix–xliv. London: Penguin Books, 2018.
———, ed. *The Penguin Book of the Prose Poem: From Baudelaire to Anne Carson*. London: Penguin Books, 2018.
North, Kate. *Bistro*. Blaenau Ffestiniog, Wales: Cinnamon Press, 2011.
Novalis. *Novalis: Philosophical Writings*, edited and translated by Margaret Mahony Stoljar. Albany: State University of New York Press, 1997.
Nowottny, Winifred. *The Language Poets Use*. London: Althone Press, 1965.
O'Brien, Michael. *Rethinking the South: Essays in Intellectual History*. Athens: University of Georgia Press, 1993.
O'Hara, Frank. *The Collected Poems of Frank O'Hara*. Edited by Donald Allen. New York: Knopf, 1979.
Oliver, Mary. *A Poetry Handbook: A Prose Guide to Writing and Understanding Poetry*. San Diego: Harcourt Brace, 1994.
Olson, Ray. "Commentary on Russell Edson." In *See Jack*, by Russell Edson, backcover. Pittsburgh: University of Pittsburgh Press, 2009.
Orah Mark, Sabrina. *The Babies*. Ardmore, PA: Saturnalia Books, 2004.
Ostriker, Alicia Suskin. "Waiting for the Light." Poets.org, 2017. https://www.poets.org/poetsorg/poem/waiting-light.
Oswald, Alice. *Dart*. London: Faber, 2002.
Owlcation. "The Tragic Carnival: A Reflection on 'The Hanging of the Mouse.'" September 30, 2016. https://owlcation.com/humanities/The-Tragic-Carnival-A-Reflection-on-The-Hanging-of-the-Mouse.
Pallant, Cheryl. "Brian Clements Interview." *Argotist Online*, n.d. http://www.argotistonline.co.uk/Clements%20interview.htm.

Pallant, Cheryl. "Yonder Zongs." In *An Introduction to the Prose Poem*, edited by Brian Clements and Jamey Dunham, 262–63: Newtown, CT: Firewheel Editions, 2009.

Pang, Alvin. "1.290270,103.851959 (2017)." In *Cities: Ten Poets, Ten Cities*, edited by Paul Hetherington and Shane Strange. Canberra: Recent Work Press, 2017.

Partridge, Eric. *The French Romantics' Knowledge of English Literature (1820–1848)*. Genève, Switzerland: Slatkine Reprints, 1974.

Paul, Elizabeth. "Pianist and Still Life, 1924, Henri Matisse." In *Reading Girl*, by Elizabeth Paul. Georgetown, KY: Finishing Line Press, 2016.

Peacock, Molly. "The Equation of the Prose Poem." *Poetry Magazine* (2014). https://www.poetryfoundation.org/harriet/2014/12/the-equation-of-the-prose-poem-.

Pearson, Yvonne, and Kathleen Petelinsek. *Prose Poems (Poetry Party)*. Mankato, MN: Child's World, 2015.

Perkins, David. *The Quest for Permanence: The Symbolism of Wordsworth, Shelley and Keats*. Cambridge, MA: Harvard University Press, 1959.

Perloff, Marjorie. "Language Poetry and the Lyric Subject: Ron Silliman's *Albany*, Susan Howe's *Buffalo*." *Critical Inquiry* 25, no. 3 (Spring 1999): 405–34. See also http://writing.upenn.edu/epc/authors/perloff/langpo.html.

———. "Marjorie Perloff: On 'The Chinese Letter.'" *Modern American Poetry* 27 (October 2014): n.p. http://www.modernamericanpoetry.org/criticism/marjorie-perloff-chinese-notebook.

———. *The Poetics of Indeterminacy: Rimbaud to Cage*. Princeton, NJ: Princeton University Press, 1981.

———. "Postmodernism/*Fin de siècle*: Defining 'Difference' in Late Twentieth-Century Poetics." In *Romanticism and Postmodernism*, edited by Edward Larrissy, 179–209. Cambridge: Cambridge University Press, 1999.

Petit, Pascale. "My Larzac Childhood." In *The Treekeeper's Tale*, 41. Bridgend, UK: Seren Books, 2008.

Peyre, Henri. "Rimbaud's Life and Work." In *A Season in Hell; The Illuminations*, by Arthur Rimbaud, 3–33. Translated by Enid Rhodes Peschel. London: Oxford University Press, 1974.

Philip, Marlene NourbeSe. *She Tries Her Tongue, Her Silence Softly Breaks*. Middletown, CT: Wesleyan University Press, 2015.

Phillips, Siobhan. *The Poetics of the Everyday: Creative Repetition in Modern American Verse*. New York: Columbia University Press, 2009.

Pierce, Chester M., Jean V. Carew, Diane Pierce-Gonzalez, and Deborah Wills. "An Experiment in Racism: TV Commercials." In *Television and Education*, edited by C. Pierce, 62–88. Beverly Hills, CA: Sage, 1978.

Pike, Burton. *The Image of the City in Modern Literature*. Princeton, NJ: Princeton University Press, 1981.

Pinsky, Robert. *The Situation of Poetry: Contemporary Poetry and Its Traditions*. Princeton, NJ: Princeton University Press, 1976.

Plato. *Theaetetus*. In *The Dialogues of Plato*, 191–319. Translated by B. Jowett. Volume 3. 4th edition. Oxford: Oxford at the Clarendon Press, 1953.

Plunkett, Adam. "Patricia Lockwood's Crowd-Pleasing Poetry." *New Yorker*, May 29,

2014. https://www.newyorker.com/books/page-turner/patricia-lockwoods-crowd-pleasing-poetry.

Poe, Edgar Allan. *Selected Prose, Poetry and Eureka*. New York: Holt, Rinehart and Winston, 1970. [Originally published 1848.]

Poetry Foundation. "Glossary of Poetic Terms." https://www.poetryfoundation.org/learn/glossary-terms/genre.

Ponge, Francis. *Soap*. Translated by Lane Dunlop. Stanford, CA: Stanford University Press, 1998.

Pope, Alexander. *The Poems of Alexander Pope*. Edited by John Butt. London: Methuen, 1963.

Pound, Ezra. "The Serious Artist." *New Freewoman* 1, no. 9 (1913): 161–63 [2013 edition]. https://library.brown.edu/cds/repository2/repoman.php?verb=render&id=1303308737203252&view=pageturner.

Preminger, Alex, ed. *Princeton Encyclopedia of Poetics*. Enlarged edition. Princeton, NJ: Princeton University Press, 1974.

Prendergast, Christopher. "Introduction." In *Nineteenth-Century French Poetry: Introductions to Close Reading*, edited by Christopher Prendergast, 1–28. New York: Cambridge University Press, 1990.

Price, Richard. "Hedge Sparrows." In *Lucky Day*, by Richard Price, 27. Manchester, UK: Carcanet Press Limited, 2005.

Proust, Marcel. "The Captive." In *Marcel Proust: Remembrance of Things Past*. Volume 2. Translated by C. K. Scott Moncrieff and Stephen Hudson, 449–605. Hertfordshire, UK: Wordsworth Editions, 2006.

Queen, Kahdijah. *Black Peculiar*. Las Cruces, NM: Noemi Press, 2011.

———. *I'm So Fine: A List of Famous Men & What I Had On*. E-book. Little Rock, AR: Sibling Rivalry Press, 2013.

———. *I'm So Fine: A List of Famous Men & What I Had On*. Portland, OR: YesYes Books, 2017.

Radden, Günter, and Zoltán Kövecses. "Towards a Theory of Metonymy." In *Metonymy in Language and Thought*, edited by Kaus-Uwe Panther and Günter Radden, 17–59. Amsterdam: John Benjamins, 1999.

Rafferty, Charles. "The Pond." *New Yorker*, July 30, 2018, 37.

Rainey, Lawrence, ed. *Modernism: An Anthology*. Oxford: Blackwell, 2005.

Ramazani, Jahan, ed. *The Cambridge Companion to Postcolonial Poetry*. Cambridge: Cambridge University Press, 2017.

———. "'To Get the News from Poems': Poetry as Genre." In *A Companion to Poetic Genre*, edited by Eric Martiny, 3–16. West Sussex: John Wiley and Sons, 2012.

Rankine, Claudia. *Citizen: An American Lyric*. Minneapolis: Graywolf Press, 2014.

———. *Don't Let Me Be Lonely: An American Lyric*. Minneapolis: Graywolf Press, 2004.

Raser, Timothy. *Baudelaire and Photography: Finding the Painter of Modern Life*. Abingdon, Oxford: Modern Languages Research Association and Routledge, 2015.

Rauber, D. F. "The Fragment as Romantic Form." *Modern Language Quarterly* 30, no. 2 (1969): 212–21. https://read.dukeupress.edu/modern-language-quarterly/article-abstract/30/2/212/17496/The-Fragment-as-Romantic-Form?redirectedFrom=fulltext.

Rawnsley, Hardwicke Drummond. *Reminiscences of Wordsworth among the Peasantry of Westmoreland*. London: Dillon's University Bookshop, 1969.

Rebele-Henry, Brynne. *Autobiography of a Wound*. Pittsburgh: University of Pittsburgh Press, 2018.

———. *Fleshgraphs*. Brooklyn, NY: Nightboat Books, 2016.

Rendle-Short, Francesca. "*Towards* Poetic Address: Anne Carson Slag." *Overland Journal* 235 (July 25, 2019): n.p. https://overland.org.au/2019/07/towards-poetic-address-anne-carson-slag/.

Rice, Shelley. *Parisian Views*. Cambridge, MA: MIT Press, 2000.

Richards, I. A. *The Philosophy of Rhetoric*. New York: Oxford University Press, 1936.

Richards, Marvin. *Without Rhyme or Reason: "Gaspard de la Nuit" and the Dialectic of the Prose Poem*. Lewisburg, PA: Bucknell University Press, 1998.

Richee, Clarissa. "Evie Shockley's 'my life as china.'" *Cultural Front: A Notebook on Literary Art, Digital Humanities, and Emerging Ideas*, October 11, 2011. http://www.culturalfront.org/2011/10/evie-shockleys-my-life-as-china.html.

Ricks, Christopher. "William Wordsworth: 'A Pure Organic Pleasure from the Lines.'" In *William Wordsworth's "The Prelude": A Casebook*, edited by Stephen Gill, 43–72. Oxford: Oxford University Press, 2006.

Riffaterre, Hermine. "Reading Constants: The Practice of the Prose Poem." In *The Prose Poem in France: Theory and Practice*, edited by Mary-Ann Caws and Hermine Riffaterre, 98–116. New York: Columbia University Press, 1984.

Riffaterre, Michael. "On the Prose Poem's Formal Features." In *The Prose Poem in France: Theory and Practice*, edited by Mary-Ann Caws and Hermine Riffaterre, 117–32. New York: Columbia University Press, 1984.

Riley, A. *Analysis of Poetry: An Attempt to Develop the Elements of Figurative Language, with a View to Facilitate the Study of Poetical Criticism*. London: S. Robinson and G. B. Whitaker, 1827.

Rimbaud, Arthur. *Illuminations*. Translated by John Ashbery. Revised edition. Manchester, UK: Carcanet, 2018.

———. *Rimbaud: Complete Works, Selected Letters; A Bilingual Edition*. Edited and translated by Wallace Fowlie; updated and revised by Seth Whidden. Chicago: University of Chicago Press, 2005.

Robb, Graham. *Rimbaud*. London: Picador, 2001.

Robertson, Rachel, and Paul Hetherington. "A Mosaic Patterning: Space, Time and the Lyric Essay." *New Writing: The International Journal for the Practice and Theory of Creative Writing* 14, no. 1 (2017): 36–46.

Robinson, Gregory. *All Movies Love the Moon: Prose Poems on Silent Film*. Brookline, MA: Rose Metal Press, 2014.

Robinson, Jeffrey C. "Poetic Prose and Prose Poetry." In *The Encyclopedia of Romantic Literature: A–G*. Volume 1, edited by Frederick Burwick, 1019. West Sussex, UK: Blackwell, 2012.

Robinson, Roger. "1 Minute Lecture: On prose poems." Cited in "The Prose Poem as Igel: A Reading of Fragmentation and Closure in Prose Poetry," by Cassandra Atherton and Paul Hetherington. *Axon Capsule 1: Poetry on the Move*. https://www.axonjournal.com.au/issue-c1/prose-poem-igel.

Rodríguez, Alicita. "A Weekend in the Country." *Sentence: A Journal of Prose Poetry and Poetics* 10 (2013): 176.

Rombauer, Irma S., and Marion Rombauer Becker. *The Joy of Cooking*. New York: Simon and Schuster, 1975.

Rosen, Charles. *The Romantic Generation*. Cambridge, MA: Harvard University Press, 1998.

Rosenberg, Liz. *17: A Novel in Prose Poems*. Chicago: Cricket Books, 2002.

Rosenblatt, Louise R. *The Reader, the Text, the Poem: The Transactional Theory of the Literary Work*. Carbondale: Southern Illinois University Press, 1994.

Ross, Bruce. "Introduction." In *Journey to the Interior: American Versions of Haibun*, edited by Bruce Ross, 13–84. North Clarendon, VT: Tuttle, 1998.

Ross, Bruce M. *Remembering the Personal Past: Descriptions of Autobiographical Memory*. New York: Oxford University Press, 1991.

Rubin, David C. "Beginnings of a Theory of Autobiographical Remembering." In *Autobiographical Memory: Theoretical and Applied Perspectives*, edited by Charles P. Thompson, Douglas J. Herrmann, Darryl Bruce, J. Don Read, and David G. Payne, 47–68. Mahwah, NJ: Lawrence Erlbaum Associates, 1998.

Rudd, Amanda. "Following Where the Brush Leads: The Potential of the Zuihitsu in American Postmodernist Literature." *Plaza: Dialogues in Language and Literature* 1, no. 1(2011): 42–49. https://journals.tdl.org/plaza/index.php/plaza/article/view/2094.

Rushdie, Salman. "The Empire Writes Back with a Vengeance." *London Times*, July 3, 1982.

Russell, Lauren. *What's Hanging on the Hush*. Boise, ID: Ahsahta Press, 2017.

Sabol, Barbara. "*Hotel Utopia* by Robert Miltner: Review and Interview." *Poetry Matters: Poetry Book Reviews and Interviews*, August 9, 2012. http://readwritepoetry.blogspot.com/2012/08/hotel-utopia-by-robert-miltner.html.

Sadoff, Ira. *History Matters: Contemporary Poetry on the Margins of American Culture*. Iowa City: University of Iowa Press, 2009.

Saito, Brynn. "Peace, Bells, Cuttings: Bravery, Energy, and Emotion in Poetry." *Anomaly*, September 26, 2016. https://medium.com/anomalyblog/peace-bells-cuttings-e01f0f85e996.

Sanders, Kristin. "Country Song of Thanks." In *Cuntry*. New Orleans, LA: Trembling Pillow Press, 2017.

———. *This Is a Map of Their Watching Me*. Jackson, NJ: BOAAT Press, 2015.

Santilli, Nikki. "Foreword." In *This Line Is Not For Turning: An Anthology of Contemporary British Prose Poetry*, edited by Jane Monson, 9–11. Blaenau Ffestiniog, Wales: Cinnamon Press, 2011.

———. "Prose Poetry and the Spirit of Jazz." In *British Prose Poetry: The Poems Without Lines*, edited by Jane Monson, 279–98. Cham, Switzerland: Palgrave Macmillan, 2018.

———. *Such Rare Citings: The Prose Poem in English Literature*. Cranbury, NJ: Associated University Presses, 2002.

Saphra, Jacqueline, and Mark Andrew Webber. *If I Lay on My Back I Saw Nothing but Naked Women*. Wokingham, UK: Emma Press, 2014.

Sartre, Jean-Paul. *Baudelaire*. Translated by Martin Turnell. New York: New Directions, 1967.

———. *Mallarmé, or the Poet of Nothingness*. Translated by Ernest Sturm. University Park: Pennsylvania State University Press, 1991.

Satterfield, Jane. "Why I Don't Write Nature Poems." In *Apocalypse Mix*, 83. Pittsburgh, PA: Autumn House Press, 2017.

———. "Why I Don't Write Nature Poems." *Prose Poem Issue* in the *Beltway Poetry Quarterly* 14, no. 4 (Fall 2013): n.p. http://www.beltwaypoetry.com/why-i-dont-write-nature-poems/.

Saunders, George. *The Tenth of December: Stories*. New York: Random House, 2013.

Scheele, Roy. "The Wake of Plenty." In *Models of the Universe: An Anthology of the Prose Poem*, edited by Stuart Friebert and David Young, 248. Oberlin, OH: Oberlin College Press, 1995.

Schlegel, Frederich. *Friedrich Schlegel's "Lucinde" and the Fragments*. Translated by Peter Firchow. Minneapolis: University of Minnesota Press, 1971.

Schmitt, Kate. *Singing Bones*. Clarksville, TN: Zone 3 Press, 2014.

Schomburg, Zachary. "The Fire Cycle." In *Scary, No Scary*, 43. Boston, MA: Black Ocean, 2009.

Schoonebeek, Danniel. "Three Questions with Dawn Lundy Martin." *PEN America*, September 23, 2015, n.p. https://pen.org/three-questions-with-dawn-lundy-martin/.

Scofield, Martin. *T. S. Eliot: The Poems*. Cambridge: Cambridge University Press, 1997.

Scott, Clive. *Channel Crossings: French and English Poetry in Dialogue, 1550–2000*. New York: Routledge, 2017.

———. *Translating Rimbaud's "Illuminations."* Exeter, UK: University of Exeter Press, 2006.

Seaton, Maureen. "Moving Violations: The Prose Poem as Fast Car." In *The Rose Metal Press Field Guide to Prose Poetry: Contemporary Poets in Discussion and Practice*, edited by Gary L. McDowell and F. Daniel Rzicznek, 140–45. Brookline, MA: Rose Metal Press, 2010.

Sebald, W. G. *After Nature*. Translated by Michael Hamburger. New York: Random House, 2011.

Seed, Ian. *Anonymous Intruder*. Bristol, UK: Shearsman Books, 2009.

———. *Makers of Empty Dreams*. Bristol, UK: Shearsman Books, 2014.

———. *New York Hotel*. Bristol, UK: Shearsman Books, 2018.

Seigel, Jerrold. *Bohemian Paris: Culture, Politics, and the Boundaries of Bourgeois Life, 1830–1930*. Baltimore: Johns Hopkins University Press, 1986.

Seigel, Rachel. "Urban Fantasy vs. Magical Realism: Writing Life." *Pub Crawl*, November 7, 2012. http://www.publishingcrawl.com/2012/11/07/urban-fantasy-vs-magical-realism/.

Selerie, Gavin. "Casement." In *Music's Duel: New and Selected Poems, 1972–2008*, by Gavin Selerie, 249. Exeter, UK: Shearsman Books, 2009. https://irp-cdn.multiscreensite.com/12e499a6/files/uploaded/gavin-selerie-musics-duel-SAMPLE.pdf.

Shakespeare, William. *Shakespeare's Sonnets*. Edited by Katherine Duncan-Jones. Revised edition. London: Methuen Drama, 2010.

———. *The Tragedy of Macbeth*. Edited by Nicholas Brooke. Oxford: Oxford University Press, 1998.

Shapard, Robert. "The Remarkable Reinvention of Very Short Fiction." *World Literature Today* 86, no. 5 (September 2012): n.p. https://www.worldliteraturetoday.org/2012/september/remarkable-reinvention-very-short-fiction-robert-shapard.

Shapcott, Thomas. "Letters to the Editor." *TEXT: Journal of Writing and Writing Courses* 6, no. 2 (October 2002): n.p. http://www.textjournal.com.au/oct02/letters.htm.

Shapiro, Daniel M. "Richard M. Nixon Attends *Star Wars* Premiere, Brea Mann Theatre, 5/25/77." *Sentence: A Journal of Prose Poetry and Poetics* 10 (2013): 121.

Shapiro, Karl. *The Bourgeois Poet*. New York: Random House, 1964.

Sheehan, Hilda. *Frances and Martine*. Chicago: Dancing Girl Press, 2014.

Shell, Marc. *Talking the Walk & Walking the Talk: A Rhetoric of Rhythm*. New York: Fordham University Press, 2015.

Shelley, Percy Bysshe. "Adonais." In *Percy Bysshe Shelley: The Major Works, Including Poetry, Prose, and Drama*, edited by Zachary Leader and Michael O'Neill, 529–45. New York: Oxford University Press, 2009.

Shin, Sun Yung. *Unbearable Splendor*. Minneapolis: Coffee House Press, 2016.

Shockley, Evie. "my life as china." In *The New Black* by Evie Shockley, 5. Middleton, CT: Wesleyan University Press, 2011.

Shumate, David. *The Floating Bridge: Prose Poems*. Pittsburgh, PA: University of Pittsburgh Press, 2008.

———. *High Water Mark: Prose Poems*. Pittsburgh, PA: University of Pittsburgh Press, 2004.

Sieburth, Richard. "Introduction." In *Hymns and Fragments*, by Friedrich Hölderlin, 3–43. Translated and introduced by Richard Sieburth. Princeton, NJ: Princeton University Press, 1984.

Silliman, Ron. "The Alphabet" [excerpt]. *Jacket 2* 6 (January 1999): n.p. http://jacketmagazine.com/06/silliman.html.

———. "Boxing Inside the Box: Women's Prose Poetry by Holly Iglesias." *Silliman's Blog: A Weblog Focused on Contemporary Poetry and Poetics*, January 23, 2006. https://ronsilliman.blogspot.com/2006/01/angry-book-on-history-st.html.

———. Comments on Audrey Wurdemann and Joseph Auslander. *Silliman's Blog: A Weblog Focused on Contemporary Poetry and Poetics*, November 23, 2009. https://ronsilliman.blogspot.com/2009/11/she-was-youngest-winner-ever-of.html.

———. Comments on *Rain Taxi*. *Silliman's Blog: A Weblog Focused on Contemporary Poetry and Poetics*, June 2003. https://ronsilliman.blogspot.com/2003_06_15_archive.html.

———. "Disappearance of the Word, Appearance of the World." In *The L=A=N=G=U=A=G=E Book*, edited by Bruce Andrews and Charles Bernstein, 121–32. Carbondale: Southern Illinois University Press, 1984.

———. *The New Sentence*. New York: Roof Books, 1989.

———. "Wise Guys Meet in La Jolla." *Silliman's Blog: A Weblog Focused on Contempo-

rary Poetry and Poetics, May 30, 2012. https://ronsilliman.blogspot.com/2012/05/wise-guys-meet-in-la-jolla-clockwise.html.

Simic, Charles. *Dime-Story Alchemy: The Art of Joseph Cornell*. New York: New York Review of Books, 1992.

———. "A Long Course in Miracles." In *Pretty Happy!*, edited by Peter Johnson, 15–17. Fredonia, NY: White Pine Press, 1997.

———. *New and Selected Poems, 1962–2012*. Boston: Houghton Mifflin Harcourt, 2013.

———. "Seven Prose Poems." *The Café Irreal* 13 (2005): n.p.

———. "The Poetry of Village Idiots." *Verse* 13, no. 1 (1996): 7–8.

———. "Prose Poetry." Poetry International, June 2010. https://www.poetryinternational.org/pi/poet/17369/Editorial-1-June-2010/en/tile.

———. *The World Doesn't End; Prose Poems*. New York: Harcourt, Brace, 1989.

Singh, Jessica. *When Love Lived Alone*. Chennai, India: Notion Press, 2017.

Skidelsky, William. "Lydia Davis: 'My style is a reaction to Proust's long sentences.'" *Observer*, August 1, 2010. https://www.theguardian.com/books/2010/aug/01/lydia-davis-interview-reaction-proust.

Skovron, Alex. *Autographs*. Ormond, Australia: Hybrid, 2008.

Slings, S. R. "The I in Personal Archaic Lyric: An Introduction." In *The Poet's I in Archaic Greek Lyric: Proceedings of a Symposium Held at the Vrije Universiteit Amsterdam*, edited by S. R. Slings, 1–30. Amsterdam: Vrije Universiteit University Press, 1990.

SPL Guide to Prose Poetry. Scottish Poetry Library, n.d. https://www.scottishpoetrylibrary.org.uk/sites/default/files/FORM%20prose%20poems.pdf.

Smart, Elizabeth. *By Grand Central Station I Sat Down and Wept*. London: Editions Poetry, 1945.

Smith, Ali. "The Mongrel: Australian Prose Poetry." *Australian Poetry Journal* 4, no. 1 (2014): 7–14.

Smith, Barbara Herrnstein. *Poetic Closure: A Study of How Poems End*. Chicago: University of Chicago Press, 1968.

Smith, Hazel. *Hyperscapes in the Poetry of Frank O'Hara: Difference / Homosexuality / Topography*. Liverpool: Liverpool University Press, 2000.

Smith, Patti. *The Coral Sea*. New York: W. W. Norton, 2012.

Smith, Sidonie, and Julia Watson. *Reading Autobiography: A Guide for Interpreting Life Narratives*. 2nd edition. Minneapolis: University of Minnesota Press, 2010.

Sontag, Susan. *On Photography*. London: Penguin, 1977.

Sooke, Alistair. "Joseph Cornell: The Man Who Put the World in a Box." *BBC Culture*, October 23, 2015. http://www.bbc.com/culture/story/20151023-joseph-cornell-the-man-who-put-the-world-in-a-box.

Spacks, Patricia Meyer. *Novel Beginnings: Experiments in Eighteenth-Century English Fiction*. New Haven: Yale University Press, 2006.

Spalding, J. M. "Charles Simic." *Cortland Review* 4 (August 1998): n.p.

Spender, Stephen. "After They Have Tired." In *The Faber Book of Modern Verse*, edited by Michael Roberts, 256–57. Revised by Donald Hall. London: Faber, 1965.

Spenser, Edmund. *Selected Shorter Poems*. London: Longman, 1995.

Staff, Harriet. "Reading Anne Carson's Reissued *Short Talks*." Poetry Foundation, July 28, 2016. https://www.poetryfoundation.org/harriet/2016/07/reading-anne-carsons-reissued-short-talks.

Staff, Harriet, and Ron Silliman. "Ron Silliman Redefines Language Poetry in Light of Community, Conceptualism, Time. . . ." Poetry Foundation, May 30, 2012. https://www.poetryfoundation.org/harriet/2012/05/ron-silliman-redefines-language-poetry-in-light-of-community-conceptualism-time.

Stafford, Fiona. *Reading Romantic Poetry*. Oxford: Wiley Blackwell, 2012.

Stafford, William. *The Way It Is: New and Selected Poems*. Minneapolis: Graywolf Press, 1998.

Stallings, A. E. *Like*. New York: Farrar, Straus and Giroux, 2018.

———. "Austerity Measures." In *Austerity Measures: The New Greek Poetry*, edited by Karen Van Dyck, n.p. New York: New York Review of Books, 2016.

———. "Austerity Measures." In "Greece, Getting By on the Brink of a Financial Meltdown" by Rachel Martin. *Weekend Edition Sunday*, NPR.org, April 5, 2015. https://www.npr.org/2015/04/05/397560140/in-greece-getting-by-on-the-brink-of-a-financial-meltdown.

Stauffer, Andrew M. *Anger, Revolution and Romanticism*. Cambridge: Cambridge University Press, 2005.

Stein, Gertrude. *Tender Buttons: The Corrected Centennial Edition*. Edited, with a note on the text by Seth Perlow and afterword by Juliana Spahr. San Francisco: City Lights Books, 2014.

Stepanchev, Stephen. "Whitman in Russia." In *Whitman and the World*, edited by Gay Wilson Allen and Ed Folsom, 300–38. Iowa City: University of Iowa Press, 1995.

Stevens, Wallace. *Collected Poetry and Prose*. New York: Library of America, 1997.

Stock, Jon. "Man Booker International Prize 2013: Lydia Davis Wins." *Telegraph*, May 22, 2013. https://www.telegraph.co.uk/culture/books/10074108/Man-Booker-International-Prize-2013-Lydia-Davis-wins.html.

Stohlman, Nancy. "Ask a Flash Fiction Editor: Is This Flash Fiction or a Prose Poem?" *Nancy Stohlman*, April 28, 2013. https://nancystohlman.com/2013/04/28/ask-a-flash-fiction-editor-is-this-flash-fiction-or-a-prose-poem/.

Stonecipher, Donna. "Model City [35]." In *Model City*, 49. Bristol, UK: Shearsman Books, 2015.

———. "Model City: With a Critical Introduction on Prose Poetry and the City." PhD diss., University of Georgia, 2011. https://getd.libs.uga.edu/pdfs/stonecipher_donna_201105_phd.pdf.

———. *Prose Poetry and the City*. Illuminations: A Series on American Poetics. Anderson, SC: Parlor Press, 2017.

———. *Transaction Histories*. Iowa: University of Iowa Press, 2018.

Story, Julia. *Post Moxie*. Louisville, KY: Sarabande Books, 2010.

Strand, Mark. "Chekhov: A Sestina." In *Great American Prose Poems: From Poe to the Present*, edited by David Lehman, 114. New York: Scribner, 2003.

Strange, Shane. "Formless Form, or the Return of Form? Prose Poetry in Practice and Theory." *TEXT*, Special Issue 46, *Beyond the Line: Contemporary Prose Poetry* (2017): 1–11.

Strub, Alison. *Lillian, Fred.* Jackson, NJ: BOAAT Press, 2016.

"Sumerian Love Song." Translated by S. N. Kramer. In *Ancient Near Eastern Texts Relating to the Old Testament.* 3rd edition with supplement, edited by James B. Pritchard, 496. Princeton, NJ: Princeton University Press, 1992.

Swensen, Cole. "Poetry City." *Identity Theory*, October 26, 2004, n.p. http://www.identitytheory.com/poetry-city/.

———. "To Writewithize." *American Letters and Commentary* (Winter 2001): 122–27.

Talei, Leila. "The Claim of Fragmented Self in *Autobiography of Red* by Anne Carson." *eTopia: Canadian Journal of Cultural Studies*, "Thresholds: Presence and Territory, Intersections|Cross-Sections" (2005): 1–8.

Tall, Deborah, and John D'Agata. "The Lyric Essay." *Seneca Review*, n.d. https://www.hws.edu/senecareview/lyricessay.aspx.

Tanehisa, Otabe. "Friedrich Schlegel and the Idea of Fragment: A Contribution to Romantic Aesthetics." *Aesthetics* 13 (2009): 59–68.

Tatarkiewicz, Wladyslaw. *A History of Six Ideas: An Essay in Aesthetics.* Warsaw, Poland: PWN/Polish Scientific, 1980.

Tate, James. "The Cowboy." Poetry Foundation, 2008. https://www.poetryfoundation.org/poems/53691/the-cowboy.

———. "I sat at my desk and contemplated all that I had accomplished." In *The Government Lake*, 82. New York: Ecco, an imprint of HarperCollins, 2019.

———. "James Tate." In *Ecstatic Occasions, Expedient Forms: 85 Leading Contemporary Poets Select and Comment on Their Poems*, edited by David Lehman, 201–3. 2nd edition. Ann Arbor: University of Michigan Press, 1996.

Tate Museum Collective. "Daniel Spoerri Prose Poems, 1959–60." Display caption. August 2004. https://www.tate.org.uk/art/artworks/spoerri-prose-poems-t03382.

Taylor Carlisle, Wendy. *The Mercy of Traffic.* New Orleans, LA: Unlikely Books, 2019.

Taylor, John. *A Little Tour through European Poetry.* New York: Routledge, 2017.

———. *Paths to Contemporary French Literature.* Volume 2. New Brunswick, NJ: Transaction, 2009.

———. "Two Cultures of the Prose Poem." *Michigan Quarterly Review* 44, no. 22 (Spring 2005): 362–38.

———. "The Wonder-like Lightning of Prose Poetry." In *A Little Tour through European Poetry.* New York: Routledge, 2017.

Tejada, Robert. *Exposition Park.* Middleton, CT: Wesleyan University Press, 2010.

Thieme, John. *Postcolonial Con-texts: Writing Back to the Canon.* New York: Continuum, 2001.

Thomas, Sophie. *Romanticism and Visuality: Fragments, History and Spectacle.* New York: Routledge, 2008.

Thornton, Naoko Fuwa. "Robert Bly's Poetry and the Haiku." *Comparative Literature Studies* 20, no. 1 (1983): 1–13.

Toomer, Jean. *A Jean Toomer Reader: Selected Unpublished Writings*, edited by Frederik L. Rusch. New York: Oxford University Press, 1993.

———. "Seventh Street." In *Cane*, by Jean Toomer. New York: Liveright, 1993. Poetry Foundation. https://www.poetryfoundation.org/poems/52945/seventh-street.

Tran, Barbara. *In the Mynah Bird's Own Words.* North Adams, MA: Tupelo Press, 2002.

———. "Rosary." *CrossXConnect* 3, no. 3 (2005): n.p. http://ccat.sas.upenn.edu/xconnect/v3/i3/g/tran.html.

Travis, Molly Abel. *Reading Cultures: The Construction of Readers in the Twentieth Century*. Carbondale: Southern Illinois University Press, 1998.

Trimarco, Paola. "Short Shorts: Exploring Relevance and Filling in Narratives." Abstract. In *Teaching the Short Story*, edited by Ailsa Cox, 13–27. New York: Palgrave Macmillan, 2011.

Truesdale, C. W. "Publisher's Preface." In *The Party Train: A Collection of North American Prose Poetry*, edited by Robert Alexander, Mark Vinz, and C. W. Truesdale, xix–xxiii. Minneapolis: New Rivers Press, 1996.

Turco, Lewis. *The Book of Forms: A Handbook of Poetics*. 3rd edition. Hanover, NH: University Press of New England, 2000.

Tursi, Mark. "An Interview with Russell Edson." *Double Room* 4 (Spring/Summer 2004): n.p. http://www.webdelsol.com/Double_Room/issue_four/Russell_Edson.html.

Upton, Lee. "Structural Politics: The Prose Poetry of Russell Edson." *South Atlantic Review* 58 (1993): 101–15.

Upward, Allen. "Scented Leaves: From a Chinese Jar." *Poetry: A Magazine of Verse II*, no. 6 (September 1913): n.p. Poetry Foundation. https://www.poetryfoundation.org/poetrymagazine/issue/70329/september-1913.

Van Dyck, Karen, ed. *Austerity Measures: The New Greek Poetry*. New York: New York Review of Books, 2016.

———. "Introduction." In *Austerity Measures: The New Greek Poetry*, edited by Karen Van Dyck, xxi–xxii. New York: New York Review of Books, 2016

Vas Dias, Robert. "The Flourishing of the Prose Poem in America and Britain." In *British Prose Poetry: The Poems Without Lines*, edited by Jane Monson, 47–70. Cham, Switzerland: Palgrave Macmillan, 2018.

Vaughn, Kyle. "Letter to My Imagined Daughter." In *An Introduction to the Prose Poem*, edited by Brian Clements and Jamey Dunham, 45. Newtown, CT: Firewheel Editions, 2009.

Vaughan, William. "Turnabouts in Taste: The Case of Late Turner." In *Romanticism and Postmodernism*, edited by Edward Larrissy, 29–46. Cambridge: Cambridge University Press, 1999.

Vickery, John B. *The Prose Elegy: An Exploration of Modern American and British Fiction*. Baton Rouge: Louisiana State University Press, 2009.

Vico, Giambattista. *The New Science of Giambattista Vico: Unabridged Translation of the Third Edition (1744) with the Addition of "Practice of the New Science."* Translated by Thomas Goddard Bergin and Max Harold Fisch. New York: Cornell University Press, 1984.

Vigus, James. "The Romantic Fragment and the Legitimation of Philosophy: Platonic Poems of Reason." Leopardi Centre, University of Birmingham, 2011. http://www.birmingham.ac.uk/Documents/college-artslaw/lcahm/leopardi/fragments/leopardi/paper-vigus.pdf.

Vuong, Ocean. *Night Sky with Exit Wounds*. London: Jonathan Cape, 2017.

———. "On Earth We Are Briefly Gorgeous." Poetry Foundation, 2014.

Vuong, Ocean. "Partly True Poem Reflected in a Mirror." *Poetry London*, May 29, 2017. http://poetrylondon.co.uk/partly-true-poem-reflected-in-a-mirror-ocean-vuong/.

———. "Trevor." *Buzzfeed News*, March 24, 2016. https://www.buzzfeednews.com/article/oceanvuong/poem-trevor-by-ocean-vuong#.glNe1eMNnr.

Wabuke, Hope. "Dispatches from Rape Culture: The Prescient Vision of Khadijah Queen's *I'm So Fine: A List of Famous Men & What I Had On*." *Medium*, February 7, 2017. https://medium.com/anomalyblog/dispatches-from-rape-culture-the-prescient-vision-of-khadijah-queens-i-m-so-fine-a-list-of-91d1b80d452e.

Wagan Watson, Samuel. "There's No Place Like Home." Poetry International, 2011. https://www.poetryinternational.org/pi/poem/19584/auto/0/0/Samuel-Wagan-Watson/Theres-No-Place-Like-Home/en/nocache.

Wakoski, Diane. "Looking for the New Measure." In *Bear Flag Republic: Prose Poems and Poetics from California*, edited by Christopher Buckley and Gary Young, 36–42. Santa Cruz, CA: Greenhouse Review Press/Alcatraz Editions, 2008.

Waldman, Anne. *Marriage: A Sentence*. New York: Penguin Books, 2000.

———. *Voice's Daughter of a Heart Yet to Be Born*. Minneapolis: Minneapolis Coffee House Press, 2016.

Waldrop, Rosmarie. "From Lawn of Excluded Middle." In *A Cast-Iron Aeroplane that Can Actually Fly: Commentaries from 80 Contemporary American Poets on Their Prose Poetry*, edited by Peter Johnson, 195–96. Asheville, NC: Madhat Press, 2019.

———. *The Reproduction of Profiles*. New York: New Directions, 1987.

Wall, Alan. "Questioning the Prose Poem: Thoughts on Geoffrey Hill's *Mercian Hymns*." In *British Prose Poetry: The Poems Without Lines*, edited by Jane Monson, 167–76. Cham, Switzerland: Palgrave Macmillan, 2018.

Wallace, Louise. "Ahakoa he iti he pounamu | Although it is small it is greenstone." In *Bad Things*, 63. Wellington, NZ: Victoria University Press, 2017.

Wallerstein, Immanuel. "The Invention of TimeSpace Realities: Towards an Understanding of Our Historical System." *Geography* 73, no. 4 (October 1988): 287–97.

Wallschlaeger, Nikki. *Houses*. Providence, RI: Horse Less Press, 2015.

Walwicz, Ania. *Horse*. Perth: UWA, 2018.

———. "Neons." *Gangan Lit-Mag* 2 (1996): n.p. https://www.gangan.at/02/ania-walwicz/.

———. *Palace of Culture*. Glebe, NSW: Purcher and Wattmann, 2014.

Wanner, Adrian. *Russian Minimalism: From the Prose Poem to the Anti-Story*. Evanston, IL: Northwestern University Press, 2003.

Watson J. R. *English Poetry of the Romantic Period, 1789–1830*. 2nd edition. London: Routledge, 1996.

Watts, Lew. "Searching for a Haiku, in a Haibun." *Contemporary Haibun Online: A Quarterly Journal of Contemporary English Language Haibun* 14, no. 1 (2018): n.p. https://contemporaryhaibunonline.com/pages141/Article_Watts_Searching.html.

Webb, Charles Harper. "How I Met the Prose Poem, and What Ensued." In *Bear Flag Republic: Prose Poems and Poetics from California*, edited by Christopher Buckley and Gary Young, 84–86. Santa Cruz, CA: Greenhouse Review Press/Alcatraz Editions, 2008.

Webb, Jen. "1973." In *Sentences from the Archive*, by Jen Webb, 38. Canberra: Recent Work Press, 2016.

Webb, Jen, Paul Hetherington, Jordan Williams, Paul Munden, and Cassandra Atherton. *Prosody: Stanza, Line, Metre, Rhyme, Enjambment*. Kambah, Australian Capital Territory: Authorised Theft, 2018.

Weems, Carrie Mae. "Framed by Modernism" Series [gallery archive]. *Carrie Mae Weems*, 1996. http://carriemaeweems.net/galleries/framed.html.

———. "She felt monogamy had a place but invested it with little value." Screenprint on paper. National Gallery of Art, 1990, printed 2003. https://www.nga.gov/collection/art-object-page.211447.html.

Weingarden, Lauren S. "The Mirror as a Metaphor of Baudelairean Modernity." In *Orientations: Space/Time/Image/Word*, edited by Claus Clüver, Véronique Plesch, and Leo Hoek, 17–36. Amsterdam: Rodopi, 2005.

Weinstein, Arnold. "Fragment and Form in the City of Modernism." In *The Cambridge Companion to the City in Literature*, edited by Kevin R. McNamara, 138–52. New York: Cambridge University Press, 2014.

Whalan, Mark. *Race, Manhood, and Modernism in America: The Short Story Cycles of Sherwood Anderson and Jean Toomer*. Knoxville: University of Tennessee Press, 2007.

Whalen, Tom. *Dolls: Prose Poems*. Pittsburgh: Caketrain [a journal and press], 2007.

———. "Why I Hate the Prose Poem." In *An Introduction to the Prose Poem*, edited by Brian Clements and Jamey Dunham, 300. Newtown, CT: Firewheel Editions, 2009.

White, Michael. *Narrative Practice and Exotic Lives: Resurrecting Diversity in Everyday Life*. Adelaide, SA: Dulwich Centre, 2004.

Whitman, Walt. *Leaves of Grass: Authoritative Texts, Prefaces, Whitman on His Art, Criticism*. Edited by Sculley Bradley and Harold W. Blodgett. A Norton Critical Edition. New York: W. W. Norton, 1973.

Wilde, Oscar. "Poems in Prose." *Fortnightly Review*, September 2014. http://fortnightlyreview.co.uk/2014/09/wilde-poems-in-prose/.

Williams, C. K. *All at Once*. New York: Farrar, Straus and Giroux, 2014.

Williams, Diane. *Vicky Swanky Is a Beauty*. San Francisco: McSweeney's, 2012.

Williams, John Sibley. "Lesson No. 4: Untangling the Prose Poem with John Sibley Williams." *Doctor T. J. Eckleburg Review*, 2018. https://www.eckleburg.org/lessons/lesson-no-4-untangling-the-prose-poem-with-john-sibley-williams-2/.

Williams, William Carlos. *Kora in Hell: Improvisations*. San Francisco: City Lights Books, 1957.

———. *Selected Poems*. Edited by Charles Tomlinson. Harmondsworth, UK: Penguin, 1976.

Wilson, Chloe. "Arm's Length." In *Landmarks: An Anthology of Microlit*, edited by Cassandra Atherton, 33. Strawberry Hills, NSW: Spineless Wonders, 2017.

Wilson, Elizabeth. *Bohemians: The Glamorous Outcasts*. London: Tauris Parke, 2003.

———. *The Contradictions of Culture: Cities, Culture, Women*. London: Sage, 2001.

Wilson, Sugar Magnolia. *Because a Woman's Heart Is Like a Needle at the Bottom of the Ocean*. Auckland, NZ: Auckland University Press, 2019.

Wisher, Yolanda. "west of philly." Poets.org, 2018. https://www.poets.org/poetsorg/poem/west-philly.

Wittgenstein, Ludwig. *Tractatus Logico-Philosophicus*. Translated by D. F. Pears and B. F. McGuinness, 68 (5.6). New York: Routledge, 2013.

———. *Zettel*. Translated by G.E.M. Anscombe. Oxford: Basil Blackwell, 1981.

Wolff, Janet. *Feminine Sentences: Essays on Women and Culture*. Berkeley: University of California Press, 1990.

Wollstonecraft, Mary, Anne Kostelanetz Mellor, and Noelle Chao. *Mary Wollstonecraft's "A Vindication of the Rights of Woman; and, the Wrongs of Woman, or Maria."* New York: Pearson Longman, 2007 [originally published 1798].

Woloch, Cecilia. "Postcard to Ilya Kaminsky from a Dream at the Edge of the Sea." In *Carpathia*, by Cecilia Woloch, 16. Rochester, NY: BOA Editions, 2009.

Wood, Danielle. "Hare." In *Landmarks: An Anthology of Microlit*, edited by Cassandra Atherton, 31. Strawberry Hills, NSW: Spineless Wonders, 2017.

Wordsworth, William. *The Collected Poems of William Wordsworth*. Hertfordshire, UK: Wordsworth Editions, 2006.

Wordsworth, William, and Samuel Taylor Coleridge. *Lyrical Ballads: 1798 and 1802*, edited by Fiona Stafford. Oxford: Oxford University Press, 2013.

Wright, C. D. *Deepstep Come Shining*. Port Townsend, WA: Copper Canyon Press, 1998.

Wright, James. *The Shape of Light*. Companions for the Journey Series. New York: White Pine Press, 2007.

Wright, Patrick. "Black Square." *Ekphrastic Review*, April 17, 2018. http://www.ekphrastic.net/ekphrastic/black-square-by-patrick-wright.

———. "A Hybrid Form? The Ekphrastic Prose Poem." Unpublished paper delivered at Leeds Trinity International Prose Poetry Symposium, July 13, 2019.

Wrigley, Robert. "Tupelo Press web page review for Barbara Tran's *In the Mynah Bird's Own Words*." n.d. https://www.tupelopress.org/product/mynah-birds-words-barbara-tran/.

Xie, Jenny. *Eye Level*. Minneapolis: Graywolf Press, 2018.

Yeats, W. B. *The Collected Works of W. B. Yeats: Volume 1: The Poems*, edited by Richard J. Finneran. 2nd edition. New York: Scribner, 1997.

Yoon, Jiyoung. "Productivity of Spanish Verb-Noun Compounds: Patterns of Metonymy and Metaphor." In *Metaphor and Metonymy Revisited beyond the Contemporary Theory of Metaphor: Recent Developments and Applications*, edited by Francisco Gonzálvez-García, María Sandra Peña Cervel, and Lorena Pérez Hernández, 85–108. Philadelphia: Jon Benjamins, 2013.

Young, David. "Introduction." In *Models of the Universe: An Anthology of the Prose Poem*, edited by Stuart Friebert and David Young, 17–20. Oberlin, OH: Oberlin College Press, 1995.

Young, Gary. *Even So: New and Selected Prose Poems*. Buffalo, NY: White Pine Press, 2012.

Young, Gary. "The Prose Poem." In *Bear Flag Republic: Prose Poems and Poetics from California*, edited by Christopher Buckley and Gary Young, 47–51. Santa Cruz, CA: Greenhouse Review Press/Alcatraz Editions, 2008.

———. "The Unbroken Line." In *The Rose Metal Press Field Guide to Prose Poetry:*

Contemporary Poets in Discussion and Practice, edited by Gary L. McDowell and F. Daniel Rzicznek, 112–14. Brookline, MA: Rose Metal Press, 2010.

Zawacki, Andrew. "Accommodating Commodity: The Prose Poem." *Antioch Review* 58, no. 3 (2000): 286–303.

———. *Masquerade*. Sydney, Australia: Vagabond Press, 2001.

Zhicheng-Mingdé Kon, Desmond. "dame de compagnie :: lady of company." In *Five Prose Poems*. *Asymptote Journal* (October 2012): n.p. https://www.asymptotejournal.com/special-feature/desmond-kon-zhichengmingde-five-prose-poems/.

Ziegler, Alan, ed. "Introduction." In *Short: An International Anthology of Five Centuries of Short-Short Stories, Prose Poems, Brief Essays, and Other Short Prose Forms*, edited by Alan Ziegler, xxv–xxiv. New York: Persea Books, 2014.

———. *Short: An International Anthology of Five Centuries of Short-Short Stories, Prose Poems, Brief Essays, and Other Short Prose Forms*. New York: Persea Books, 2014.

Zimmer, Abigail. *Child in a Winter House Brightening*. Chicago: Tree Light Books, 2016.

Zweig, Paul. "The New Surrealism." In *Contemporary Poetry in America*, edited by Robert Boyers, 314–29. New York: Schocken, 1974.

Index

"1.290270,103.851959 (2017)" (Pang), 59
100 Papers (Jobson), 231
"1973" (Webb), 186–87

Abbott, Helen, 20–21
"A Box" (Stein), 185–86
Abramović, Marina, 163–64
Abrantes, Ana Margarida, 173
"A Brief Ontological Investigation" (Meitner), 74
absence, 197; and ambiguity, 197; fragments and expression of, 37, 48–50, 99, 148; vacancy within the text, 48; white space as, 133–35. *See also* gaps
abstraction, 47
Aćamović, Bojana, 65
"A Carafe, that is a Blind Glass" (Stein), 72
A Cast Iron Aeroplane that Can Actually Fly (Johnson, ed.), 4
"A Caterpillar on the Desk" (Bly), 168
"A City Sunset" (Hulme), 167
A Curious Architecture (Loydell and Miller, eds.), 124
A Doll for Throwing (Bang), 161–62
A Field Guide to the Intractable (Hahn), 93
"Afro-Prairie" (Giscombe), 71
After Nature (Sebald), 90–91
"After the Flood" (Rimbaud), 157–58
After the Great Divide (Huyssen), 228
"Afterthoughts" (Habra), 163
"Afterwards" (Atkins), 126
Agbabi, Patience, 100–101, 203
"Ahahoa he iti he pounamu | Although it is small it is greenstone" Wallace, Louise, 74
"A.I." (Kennard), 124
Akbar, Kaveh, 148
"A Land Governed by Unkindness Reaps No Kindness" (Hayes), 71
"Albatross" (Atherton), 190–91, 196
The Albertine Workout (Carson), 241

Albright, Daniel, 173
Alderete, Raquel de, 218
Aldington, Richard, 167
Aldrich, Martha, 25
Alexander, Robert, 5, 52, 81, 85–86, 107, 143, 233–34, 237
"A Life" (Seed), 125
"A Linnet" (Ashbery), 243–44
"A Little Anthology of Prose Poems" (Ford), 81
Allen, R.E.N., 231
"All Kinds of Dust" (Seed), 145–46
"All Movies Love the Moon" (Robinson), 175
Allport, Andrew, 28
allusion, 44, 85, 143, 183–84, 190–91; intertextuality and, 187–88; metonymy and intertextuality or, 183–84, 187–95
"All Your Houses: Notebook Including a Return" (Capildeo), 242–43
"A Long Course in Miracles" (Simic), 114
The Alphabet (Silliman), 108
Alyan, Hala, 11, 45–46
ambiguity, 14, 85; and absence, 197; and fragments, 37; and gaps, 96; and lack of closure, 79, 85–87, 196; and metonymy, 186, 196–97; and TimeSpace, 128
The American Prose Poem (Delville), 102, 202, 205
"Amoretti 33" (Spenser), 37–38
analogy, 14–15, 157, 179, 197, 245; surrealism and, 105, 110–12
"And Leaves the Shreds Behind" (Bar-Nadav), 87, 194
Andrews, Bruce, 203–4
Andrews, Nin, 103, 112, 203, 205, 230
An Eschatological Bestiary (Hardwick), 240
A New Language for Falling Out of Love (Privitello), 239
An Introduction to the Prose Poem (Clements and Dunham, eds.), 95, 180–81, 236

Anthology of Australian Prose Poetry (Atherton and Hetherington, eds.), 4
"Antiquities" (Hetherington), 191
A Pillow Book (Buffam), 92–94, 203, 241
A Poverty of Objects (Monroe), 29
Apollinaire, 89
Archilochus, 211
Ardor (Lee), 239
The Argonauts (Nelson), 216–17
Argosy (Li), 240
Aristotle, 224–25
Armantrout, Rae, 205
Armitage, Simon, 125, 126
"Arm's Length" (Wilson), 232
Arnheim, Rudolph, 165
Arnold, Matthew, 53
A Roll of the Dice (Mallarmé), 133–35, 137, 150
Aronofsky, Darren, 200
"Arthroscopy/Sports Day, 1971" (Munden), 174
A Season in Hell (Rimbaud), 18, 104
Ash, John, 91
Ashbery, John, 25, 157, 243
Ashcroft, Bill, 189
"as thirsty as" (Holbrook), 201
Aston, Sally, 95
A Test of Solitude (Hocquard), 100
Athenaeum Fragment (Schlegel), 37
Atherton, Cassandra, 4, 89, 190–91, 193
Atkins, Marc, 126–27
Atkins, Tim, 184–85, 187
Attridge, Derek, 51
Atwood, Margaret, 193–94, 202
Aurora Leigh (Browning), 60
"Austerity Measures" (Stallings), 101
Australian prose poetry, 4, 122–24, 189–93, 231–32
autobiography, 24, 206; autobiographical memory, 49, 172–73, 176
Autobiography of a Marguerite (Butcher-McGunnigle), 155, 240
Autobiography of a Wound (Rebele-Henry, Brynne), 241
Autobiography of Red (Carson), 212
"Autumn" (Hulme), 53–54, 167
awards, 105–6, 225, 239
"A Weekend in the Country" (Rodríguez), 194

Axelrod, Rise B., 229
Axelrod, Steven Gould, 229

The Babies (Mark), 239
"The Backyard Mermaid" (Harvey), 146–47
Bagoo, Andre, 241
Bakhtin, Mikhail, 129–30
Balog, Amy, 234
Bang, Mary Jo, 161–62
Bann, Stephen, 34
"Barbarian" (Rimbaud), 157
Barclay, Craig R., 173
Barenblat, Rachel, 42, 232
Barkan, Leonard, 28
Barker, George, 3–4
Bar-Nadav, Hadara, 87–88, 89, 194
Barry, Peter, 129
Barthes, Roland, 154, 155, 217
Bashō, Matsuo, 91–92
Bateman, Claire, 112–13, 120
"Battle of Plataea: Aftermath" (Stallings), 86
Battles, Kelly Eileen, 34
Baudelaire, Charles, 8, 10, 64–65, 155–56
Beach, Christopher, 110
Beachy-Quick, Dan, 231
Beckel, Abigail, 84, 142, 237
Belkhyr, Yasmin, 73
Bell, Marvin, 96
Beltway Poetry Quarterly, 142
Benedikt, Michael, 12–15, 25, 42, 103, 110, 200
Benjamin, Walter, 63, 66
Benson, Fiona, 135
Berg, William, 157
Berger, John, 162
Berlardinelli, Marta Olivetti, 165
Berlin, Isaiah, 34
Berman, Art, 167, 173
Bernard, Suzanne, 13
Bernstein, Charles, 25–26, 203–4
Berry, Emily, 58
Berssenbrugge, Mei-mei, 205
Bertrand, Aloysius, 18, 22, 29, 102
Berz, Carole Birkan, 100–101
The Best American Poetry (annual), 52, 219
Beye, Holly, 72–73
Bird, Bird (Hilson), 241
Bishop, Elizabeth, 232
Bitch's Maldoror (Boyer), 208–9

INDEX   331

Black, Linda, 82, 124–25, 146, 203, 240
Black Square (Malevich), 161
"Black Square" (Wright), 161
Black Vodka (Levy), 226–27
Blanchet, Maurice, 24
Blasing, Mutlu Konuk, 10
BLAST magazine, 72
Bletsoe, Elisabeth, 203
Block, Julia, 237–38
"Bluebell Wood" (Debney), 203
The Blue Clerk (Brand), 241
Bluets (Nelson), 216–17, 241
Bly, Robert, 13, 45, 91, 109–10, 168, 181
Boat (Merrill), 235
"The Bobinski Brothers" (Ashbery), 243–44
Bode, Christoph, 33
Bond, Bruce, 176
Bonomo, Joe, 164, 241
"Book II, Anagrams" (Kennard), 124
Booten, Kyle, 226
Borson, Roo, 73
Botha, Marc, 225–26, 227
Boxing Inside the Box (Iglesias), 84, 199, 205
"box" of prose poetry, 58, 87–89, 91, 95–98, 100, 110, 114, 142–43, 153, 163; and compression, 83–88; and concrete poetry, 89; and containment, 83–85, 145, 150, 199, 219–20; and readerly expectation, 27, 85–87, 114, 141, 201. *See also* photography
"The box this comes in: (a deviation on poetry)" (Wright), 199
Boyer, Anne, 205, 208–10, 239
"The Boys Go Ask a Neighbor for Some Apples" (Heynen), 183, 187
Bradley, John, 108, 239
Bradshaw, Michael, 34
Brainard, Joe, 136–37, 140
Brand, Dionne, 203, 241
Brandt, Emily, 170–71
"Breakfast Table" (Lowell), 72
Breslin, Paul, 105
Breton, André, 104–5, 108, 109, 115, 116–17, 126
Brewer, William, 172
Briante, Susan, 237
"The Bricklayer's Lunch" (Ginsberg), 81
British Prose Poems: The Poems Without Lines (Monson), 4
British prose poetry, 4, 84, 124–25, 124–27

Brittan, Simon, 180
Broome, Peter, 64–65
Brophy, Kevin, 147–48
Brouwer, Joel, 101, 103
Brown, Andy, 9, 177, 180, 196–97
Browne, Laynie, 203, 238, 239
Browning, Elizabeth Barrett, 60, 132–33
Buffam, Suzanne, 92–93, 203, 241
Burke, Edmund, 54–55
Burn, Jane, 124
Burnett, Constance Buel, 82
"Burning Haibun" (greathouse), 92
burns, joanne, 203
Burns, Suzanne, 194
Butcher-McGunnigle, Zarah, 155, 203, 239–40
Byrd, Brigitte, 227
"By the Waters of Babylon" (Lazarus), 21

Caddy, David, 51
Cain Poems (Kennard), 124
Caldwell, Anne, 4, 12, 47–48, 124, 158, 246
Caldwell, Kelly, 215
Caleshu, Anthony, 125–26
Calligrames (Apollinaire), 89
"Calling a Wolf a Wolf (Inpatient)" (Akbar), 148
Calvino, Italo, 67
The Cambridge Companion to Postcolonial Poetry (Ramazani, ed.), 192
Cane (Toomer), 70
"Cannes" (Johnson), 25
canon, Western literary: prose poetry and "writing back" to, 189–95
Capildeo, Vahni, 203, 242–43
Carjat, Étienne, 156
Carlisle, Wendy Taylor, 203
Carpenter, Scott, 22
Carroll, Amy Sara, 239
Carson, Anne, 47, 104, 201, 211–14, 217
Carver, Raymond, 139
"Casement" (Selerie), 89
Catalano, Gary, 122–24
Catani, Damian, 20
"Catching the Monster" (Friedman), 113
Caws, Mary Anne, 4, 80, 180, 199
Centuries (Brouwer), 101
Chan, Mary Jean, 83–84, 148, 203, 239, 246–47

Chanan, Michael, 190
Chandler, Raymond, 193–94
Changing (Hoang), 89, 241
Char, René, 91
Chariot of the Sun (Crosby), 158
"Chekhov: A Sestina" (Strand), 195, 236–37
Chernoff, Maxine, 103, 121–22, 158–59, 200, 202, 205, 210
Child in a Winter House Brightening (Zimmer), 240
"The Christening" (Armitage), 126
Christle, Heather, 148
Chromatic (Munden), 100
chronotopes, 129–30
cities, 20–21; "alternative city" created by art, 67; and Baudelaire's *flaneur,* 64–67; and fragmentation, 60, 62–64; as incomprehensible, 66; and memorialization, 63–64; photography and, 154; and postmodernity, 58, 61; prose poetry as ontologically urban, 64; rhythm and, 52, 59, 67–75; urban fantasy, 105, 112–13, 115, 123; urbanization and the city as poetic subject, 60
Cities: Ten Poets, Ten Cities, 4
Citizen: An American Lyric (Rankine), 3, 89, 211–12, 214–16, 224–25, 239
"City" (Borson), 73
Clark, Hillary, 201
Clary, Killarney, 203
Clements, Brian, 54, 95, 144, 180–81, 228, 236
Clive, Scott, 55
closure: absence and indeterminacy, 197; ambiguity in prose poetry, 79, 85–87, 196; and completeness, 80; and completion of fragmentary works, 37–38; compression and, 86–87; disjunction and lack of, 208; enclosure (*See* containment); figurative language and resistance to, 195; Hejinian on "open text," 81–82; and infinity or perfection, 35–36; the open and the inconclusive, 35–38; prose poems as unresolved or in process, 87; resistance to, 245; revision and, 81–82, 206; Romanticism and aversion to, 34; "thoroughness" of prose, 141; and visual containment of text, 83–87 (*See also* "box" of prose poetry)
"The Coffin Calendars" (Eichler), 89
Cohen, Ted, 166

Coleridge, Samuel Taylor, 33–34, 33–38, 40, 43, 46, 190
Coles, Katharine, 100, 130–31
The Collected Stories of Lydia Davis (Davis), 238–39
Collins, Donte, 240
colloquial language, 12, 25, 26, 114, 120, 183
"The Colonel" (Forché), 199
colonialism. *See* postcolonial prose poems
colons, 229–30, 240
"Coming to Prose Poetry" (Gross), 202
commas, 58, 133, 144–45, 147, 186
"Companions in the Garden" (Char), 91
compression, 6, 10, 13, 14; allusion and condensed meaning, 190; and ambiguity, 86–87; and box of text, 83–88; as characteristic of prose poetry, 245; and compounds, 59; and containment, 168–69; and docupoetry, 185; and exclusion or elision of information, 48–49; and expansion, 16, 205–6; and free-lines, 97–98; and "friction of distance," 128; and intensity of reading experience, 164; length as feature of prose poetry, 16–17; and memory, 55–56, 174; and metaphor, 184; and metonymy, 184; and neo-surrealism, 119; and reading, 130–31, 140; and sentence as poetic unit, 84; and style, 6; and TARDIS-like expansion, 16, 85; and velocity, 140, 147; and visual imagery, 168–69
"Conceptual Art" (Iglesias), 163
concrete poetry (shape poetry), 89, 161
connotation, 14–15, 26, 108–9, 139, 153, 165, 177–82, 184, 196–97, 238, 245, 248
containment: and "box" of prose poetry, 83–85, 150, 199, 219–20; and claustrophobic TimeSpace, 143–44; compression and visual imagery in, 168–69; and expansion, 83, 85, 149, 150; margins as boundaries, 58, 88, 110–11; OULIPOian techniques and, 109, 203; and paragraph as unit, 86; photograph as container (*See* photography); poem as "cage," 110–11; reader expectations and, 86–87, 163–64; and reading experience, 142; and rooms or houses, 85; space as boundary to text, 141; and TARDIS-like dilation, 16, 85; visual, 83 (*See also* margins); visual containment and closure, 83–87 (*See also* "box" *under this heading*);

of women within patriarchal conventions, 121, 199–202
"Continuing Against Closure" (Hejinian), 82
Conway, Martin, 173
Cornell, Joseph, 83
"Country Song of Thanks" (Sanders), 221
"The Cowboy" (Tate), 106–7
Crawford, Jen, 132
Crawford, Robert, 40–41, 42
Crewe, Sarah, 203
"Crisis Actor" (Holiday), 57–58
"Crisis of Verse" (Mallarmé), 135
Critical Fragments (Schlegel), 28, 29, 36
Crosby, Harry, 103, 158
"Crossing Brooklyn Ferry" (Whitman), 60
Culler, Jonathan, 9, 11, 55, 149
Curley, Thomas M., 41
"Cutting" (Hahn), 93–94

D'Agata, John, 24–25
"dame de compagnie :: lady of company" (Zhicheng-Mingdé), 193
Danladi, Chekwube O., 149
Darling, Kristina Marie, 235
Darraugh, Tina, 205
"Darvil and Black Eyed Peas on New Year's Eve" (Fort), 70
dashes, 95–96, 97, 136–37, 191
Davis, Lydia, 43, 225, 236–39
Davis, Paul, 33
Dear Editor: Poems (Newman), 237
"Dear Sister" series (Wilson), 238
"Debriefing Ghosts" (Hayes), 71
de Certeau, Michel, 66–67
de Chirico, Giorgio, 18
"The Deck" (Hayes), 71
Deep Image poetry, 102, 109–10, 168
Deepstep Come Shining (Wright), 241
defamiliarization, 15, 105, 108, 114–15, 141, 188
definitions of prose poetry, *vii–viii*, 3–7, 12
Delville, Michel, 4, 5, 12, 28, 102, 118, 186, 205–6, 225; on Chernoff, 121, 202; on Edson, 118; on Simic, 119
Demeny, Paul, 20
"Demeter" (Benson), 135
Den Tandt, Christophe, 64
De Pree, Julia K., 237–38
DeQuincey, Thomas, 68, 69

The Desires of Mothers to Please Others in Letters (Mayer), 205, 238
The Desires of Letters (Browne), 238
dialogue, 39, 83, 115, 120, 141, 145, 156, 216, 233; formatting and, 139
Dickens, Charles, 8–9
diction: "elevated" language of poetry, 8, 25, 52, 247; prose poetry and colloquial, 12, 52, 114, 183
diction, everyday speech, 30
Diggory, Terence, 229
digital media, 140, 153, 205, 226, 234
dilation, 16–17, 132; TARDIS-like expansion, 16, 85
"Dime-Story Alchemy" (Simic), 83
"Diorama" (Garcia), 171
Discipline (Martin), 210–11
discursive prose, 8, 9, 11, 16–17, 25, 47, 55, 141, 206, 228, 236
Dismorr, Jane, 71–72
"Distinction" (Bateman), 113, 120
Divagations or *Wanderings* (Mallarmé), 18, 66, 224
Dockins, Mike, 170
"The Doll's Alienation" (Whalen), 115–16
"Dolly the Sheep" (Iijima), 231
"Don Quixote" (Shumate), 194
Don't Let Me Be Lonely (Rankine), 211, 214–15, 217, 239
Doolittle, Hilda, 162, 167
"Dover Beach" (Arnold), 53
Downey, June, 166–67, 171–72
"Dream-Clung, Gone" (Russell), 12, 99
Dreamlife of a Philanthropist (Kaplan), 100
Dreyer, Lynne, 205
"The Dummies" (Edson), 139–40
Dunham, Jamey, 54, 95, 144, 180–81, 228, 236
Dunn, John J., 42
Dupeyron-Lafey, Françoise, 68–69

"Early Poem" (Ives), 10
The Edinburgh Companion to the Prose Poem (Caws and Delville), 4
Edson, Russell, 13, 52, 56, 86, 139–40, 181, 200–201; neo-surrealism and, 102, 103, 110, 116–21
Edwards, Joshua, 235
Eichler, Charlotte, 89

Ekiss, Keith, 73
ekphrastic poems, *viii,* 155, 159–64, 237
elegies, 21
"Eleven Gin and Tonics" (Dockins), 170
Eliot, T. S., 40–41, 61, 72, 168, 245
Elliot, R. K., 166
ellipses, 45, 57, 120, 210
Éluard, Paul, 106–7, 115
Emerson, Ralph Waldo, 100
empathy, aesthetic, 164–70, 176; imagery as "empathy conductor," 168–69; and subjectivity, 168–70
"The Empire Writes Back with a Vengeance" (Rushdie), 189
Empty Mirror: Early Poems (Ginsberg), 81
England: Poems from a School (Clancy, ed.), 244
enjambment, 87–88, 132, 135–36, 142, 222
epistolary prose poems, 4, 100, 237–39, 238
"Erasing Amyloo" (Edson), 120
An Eschatological Bestiary (Hardwick), 240
Estes, Andrew, 74
Etter, Carrie, 84, 199, 226, 242
Evans, David, 20, 69
the everyday, 32; colloquial language, 7, 12, 26, 30, 44, 52, 106, 113, 114, 115–16, 119–20, 228, 245; defamiliarization of, 15, 105, 108, 114–15, 141, 188; democratization of literature and, 37; and humor, 114; poetry's responsibility to, 10, 86, 197; and surrealism, 106–16, 118–19
Eye Level (Xie), 94–95, 239

fables, 13, 102, 117, 119, 181, 208; metaphors as, 181
Faflick, David, 53
"The Fall of Hyperion" (Keats), 37, 46
Fanaiyan, Niloofar, 59
Fannie + Freddie: The Sentimentality of Post-9/11 Pornography (Carroll), 239
Fehr, Joy, 201
feminism: ecofeminism, 199–200; and prose poetry as means of expression, 199–200; prose poetry as subversive form, 223
Fenollosa, Ernest, 89
Feo, José Rodríguez, 115
The Fictional Letters of Don Millo…(Miller), 237
film, 175–76. *See also* photography

"The Fire Cycle" (Schomburg), 110–11
"fire prose," 13
Fitterman, Rob, 62
Fitzgerald, J. M., 32
flaneurism, 64–68, 209
flash fiction, 225–26, 231–33
Flèche (Chan), 83–84, 239
Flowers of Evil (Les Fleurs du mal) (Baudelaire), 64–65, 104, 156
"Flowers" (Rimbaud), 157
Forché, Carolyn, 199
Ford, Charles Henri, 81
form of prose poetry, *vii,* 7, 9–10, 11, 21–24; as "box" (*See* "box" of prose poetry); and concrete or shape poetry, 89; as container (*See* containment); as democratic and non-hierarchical, 15, 37, 214; as fluid or flexible, 13, 23, 83, 100, 105, 162–63, 226, 228, 231, 236; and genre, 23; and horizontal trajectory, 15, 132, 138; and hybridity (*See* hybridity); and innovation, 13–14; as inviting to the reader, 3, 83, 87; and margins (*See* margins); and poems as objects, 83; as process rather than product, 69; and readerly expectations, 228; and reading experience, 83; as "rooms," 15, 23, 83–85, 143–44, 165–66; and surreal content, 110; and typography, 15, 82–84; variations or types of, 236–37
Fort, Charles, 70
Fragments of Ancient Poetry, Collected in the Highlands of Scotland (Macpherson), 41
fragments or fragmentation, 10–11, 246; and absence, 37, 48–50, 99, 148; of antiquities or ruins, 31–32, 37, 43; the city and, 60, 62–64; Coleridge's "Kubla Khan," 36; and compression, 228; and exclusion or elision of information, 48–49; and expansion, 38; and gaps, 48, 86, 148; and hybridity, 227–28; and infinity or perfection, 35–36; integrity of, 80; intertextuality and, 187–88; and lack of closure, 34; lived experience as fragmented or incoherent, 49; and metonymy, 39, 43, 197, 247–48; postmodernism and, 35, 48–50, 58, 229; quotations as, 187–88; as ripe or complete, 49; Romantic interest in, 28–32, 34–37, 43; Schlegel on, 28–29, 34, 36, 37, 38–40, 49–50; and subjectiv-

ity, 49, 93–94, 227–28; white space and visual, 148
"Framed by Modernism" series, (Weems), 210
Francis, Emma, 48
Fredman, Stephen, 5, 12, 28, 80–81, 101, 110, 205–6, 243
Freedman, Sarah Warshauer, 226
"free lines," 17, 44–45, 95–98, 101, 214–15, 219–20
free verse, 4, 6–8, 11–12, 21, 42, 51–53, 71–73, 86–87; prose poetry as form of, 96; as "proto-prose" poetry, 81; rhythm of prose poetry contrasted with, 51
French poetry: "fire prose," 13; and fragmentation, 29, 30–31; as influence on American neo-surrealism, 102–8, 112; *poème en prose,* 19–20, 22, 102; and prose poetry as innovative form, 11, 18–22, 29, 91, 133, 245 (*See also* Baudelaire, Charles); and Romanticism, 11, 28, 29, 33–34; and subversion, 18–19, 24–26, 30; and surrealism, 30, 116–17; and Symbolism, 12, 104–5, 133, 156, 167, 245; and urban life, 62–67; and visual imagery, 156–57
Fried, Michael, 157
Friedman, Bruce Jay, 114
Friedman, Jeff, 112–13
"FROM AFRICA SINGING" (Agbabi), 100–101
Frow, John, 23

Gallery of Antique Art (Hetherington), 164
Ganczarek, Joanna, 165
gaps: and ambiguity, 96; and ellipses, 120; and erasure, 129; and expansion, 84, 148; fragmentation and, 48, 86, 148; and free lines, 96; as "ghostings" of lineation, 148; informational gaps and reader engagement, 81–82, 130, 173, 185, 197, 210, 226–27; within lines, 136, 137, 148; paralipsis and, 209; punctuation and, 120, 137, 210; and resistance to closure, 96, 201, 208; as shocks or torquing moment, 96, 157–58; and tension, 96; vacancy within text, 48; and velocity, 148. *See also* white space
Garcia, Richard, 171
Gard, Julie, 162–63
Garfunkel, Art, 58–59
Garments Against Women (Boyer), 208–10, 239

Gaspard de la nuit (Bertrand), 18, 29, 102
"The Gender of Genre" (Delville), 202
"Gendre: Women's Prose Poetry in the 1980s" (Smith), 200
Gerstler, Amy, 205, 228–29, 236
"Ghost Video" (Hayes), 71
Ginsberg, Allen, 81
Gioia, Dana, 96, 105–6, 109, 116
Giscombe, C. S., 70–71
Glass, Emma, 241
Goldberg, Arielle, 111
"Good Dogs" (Baudelaire), 63
"Goodness and the Salt of the Earth" (Moss), 220–21
Gosetti-Ferencei, Jennifer Anna, 114
The Government Lake (Tate), 106–7
Gracián, Baltasar, 18
"Graduation" (Hardwick), 125
Graham, Jorie, 52
"Graphology 300: Against Nature Writing" (Kinsella), 44–45
Great American Prose Poems (Lehman), 89–90
"The Great Autumn Rains" (Atkins), 184–85, 187
greathouse, torrin a., 92
Grief Sequence (Sharma), 231
Griffin, Farah Jasmine, 70
Griffin, Susan, 199–200
Griffiths, Gareth, 189
Gropp, Jenny, 169–70
Gross, Philip, 202
Grosser, Emmylou, 5
Guess, Carol, 204
Guiney, Louise Imogen, 61

Habra, Hedy, 163
Hahn, Kimiko, 93–94, 203, 239
haibun, 17–18, 91–93, 94
"Haibun for Smoke and Fog" (Myers), 92
haiku, 18, 91–92, 224
Hamilton, Lucy, 203
"The Hanging of the Mouse" (Bishop), 232
"Happy" (Phillips), 232
The Harbour Beyond the Movie (Kennard), 125
"The Harbour" (Brandt), 170–71
Hardwick, Oz, 4, 124, 125, 240, 246
"Hare" (Wood), 232
Harmon, Claire Louise, 218
Harms, James, 138

Harris, Claire, 203
Harris, Marie, 205
Harryman, Carla, 205, 206
Harvey, David, 130, 140
Harvey, Matthea, 146–47
Haussmann, Georges-Eugene, 66
Hayes, Terrance, 12, 71, 99, 100
Hazlitt, William, 68
H.D. (Hilda Doolittle), 162, 167
Heaney, Seamus, 196–97
Hebdomeros (Chirico), 18
hedgehogs, garlanded, 39–40, 49
"Hedge Sparrows" (Price), 88
Hejinian, Lyn, 81–82, 205–9, 208, 239, 241
Hendrix, Jimi, 71
Henry, Peter, 105–6
Herd, David, 244
Hershman, Tania, 97–98, 239
Hetherington, Paul, 4, 164, 191–92, 193, 241
Heynen, Jim, 183, 187
Hill, Geoffrey, 22, 51
Hilson, Jeff, 241
Hinton, Laura, 206
"Historic Evening" (Rimbaud), 157
Hoang, Lily, 89, 241
Hocquard, Emmanuel, 100
Hoffberg, Judith A., 136–37
Hoffer, Pamela Marie, 133
Holbrook, Susan, 201
Hölderlin, Friedrich, 49–50, 224
Holiday, Harmony, 57–58, 71
"Home at Grasmere" (Wordsworth), 137
Horne, Richard H., 21
Horse (Walwicz), 241
Hotel Utopia (Miltner), 85
The House of Your Dream (Alexander and Maloney, eds.), 143
Houses (Wallschlaeger), 85
"The House that Jack Built" (Seed), 124
"How Do I Love Thee" (Browning), 132–33
Howe, Fanny, 205
Howe, Sarah, 239
Howell, Anthony, 18, 141
Howells, W. D., 18
Hull, Glenda A., 226
Hulme, T. E., 53–54, 162, 167
Human-Ghost Hybrid Project (Guess and Olszewska), 204–5
"Humble Beginnings" (Merwin), 181

Hummel, H. K., 226
Hummer, Theo, 89
humor, 12, 107, 119; cultural differences in, 123–24; and gender, 200–201, 219–20; as subversive, 141–42
Humphrey, Asa, 42
Hünefeldt, Thomas, 165
Hunt, Erica, 205
Huyssen, Andreas, 154–56, 172, 228
hybridity, 4–5, 13–14, 19, 22, 82, 136–37; and categorization, 235–36; and fragments, 28, 227–28; and free-line form, 95; and innovation, 224; juxtaposed and combined forms, 92; and labeling of works, 101; Macpherson's *Ossian* as hybrid work, 40; mixed forms in poems, 239, 242–43; multimedia works, 4, 211, 213; and reading experience, 241; and rhythm, 70–71
Hyperion (Hölderlin), 37
"Hyperion" (Keats), 37
"Hysteria" (Eliot), 245

"I discovered a journal in the children's ward...." (Young), 144–45
If I Lay on My Back I Saw Nothing but Naked Women (Saphra and Webber), 240
Iglesias, Holly, 13, 84, 87, 94, 121, 163, 199–201, 203, 205
Ignatow, David, 13, 103, 200
Illuminations (Rimbaud), 18, 30, 55, 66, 103–4, 157–58, 243
Imagined Sons (Etter), 242
Imagism, 53–54, 71, 153, 157, 162, 167–68, 169, 171–72
"Imagisme" (Pound as Flint), 167
"Immigrant Haibun" (Vuong), 92
impressionism, 156–57
I'm So Fine (Queen), 221–22, 239
"In a Station of the Metro" (Pound), 167
"Incident From a War" (Catalano), 122
"In Love with Raymond Chandler" (Atwood), 193–94
In Media Res (Lee), 239
Innes, Randy Norman, 39
Installations (Bonomo), 164, 241
"Interlude with Drug of Choice" (Belkyhr), 73
International Poetry Studies Institute, University of Canberra, 4

International Prose Poetry Group, 4
intertextuality, *viii*, 10, 163, 175, 184, 187–91, 193–94, 197, 209, 216, 217
In the Mynah Bird's Own Words (Tran), 98, 239
"Into the City" (Ekiss), 73
An Introduction to the Prose Poem (Clements and Dunham), 54, 95, 180–81, 236
Inventory (Black), 240
Invisible Cities (Calvino), 67
Invisible Fences (Monte), 103
"I Remember" (Brainard), 136, 140
Irigaray, Luce, 201
"Irony is Not Enough" (Carson), 104
Irradiated Cities (Nagai), 240
Irwin, Mark, 10
Israel-Pelletier, Aimée, 157
Ives, Lucy, 10
"I was stolen" (Simic), 118
Izambard, Georges, 103

Jacob, Max, 118
Jaireth, Subhash, 59
Jakobson, Roman, 5
Japanese poetic traditions, 17–18, 90–94
Jastrzebska, Maria, 203, 239
jazz, 69–71
Jenkins, Louis, 83, 103, 114
Jobson, Liesl, 231
Johnson, Julia, 16
Johnson, Peter, 4, 13, 25, 103, 114, 121, 181
Jones, Alice, 237
Jones, Dorothy Richardson, 72
Jones, Peter, 168
Joron, Andrew, 109
Joseph, Eve, 3
"June Night" (Dismorr), 71–72
juxtaposition, 8, 88; parataxis, 72

"Kafka" (Shumate), 194
Kansas City Spleen (Boyer), 209
Kant, Immanuel, 34, 129
Kapil, Bhanu, 203
Kaplan, Edward, 22, 29–30
Kaplan, Janet, 100
Kasischke, Laura, 98–99
Katsaros, Laure, 60–61, 65
Kawakami, Akane, 82
Keats, John, 34, 37, 46, 47
Keene, Dennis, 91

Kennard, Luke, 3, 83, 91–92, 104, 107–8, 124–26
Kennedy, Christopher, 103
"Kill Yourself with an *Objet D'art*" (Chernoff), 121
Kinsella, John, 44–45, 90–91
Kitchen Table Series (Weems), 162
"KNEW WHITE SPEECH" (Agbabi), 100–101
Knight, Christopher, 72
Knott, Bill, 110
Knowles, Kim, 141
Komunyakaa, Yusef, 71
Koncel, Mary A., 203
Kora in Hell: Improvisations (Williams), 241
Kosslyn, Stephen M., 176
Kracauer, Siegfried, 155
Kristeva, Julia, 187
"Kubla Kahn" (Coleridge), 36, 40

LaFemina, Gerry, 83, 228
Laforgue, Jules, 66
Lagomarsino, Nancy, 231
"Lake" (Bagoo), 241
Lamantia, Philip, 109
Landmarks: An Anthology of Microlit (Atherton, ed.), 232
L=A=N=G=U=A=G=E, 203–4
language poetry, 25–26, 42, 82, 107, 203–12
Lanphier, Elizabeth, 220
Lanzoni, Susan, 167, 171
Larissy, Edward, 43
Larson, Thomas, 87, 216
Lazarus, Emma, 21
"Leaping Poetry" (Bly), 109–10
Leaves of Grass (Whitman), 7–8, 53, 63
Lee, Karen An-hwei, 203, 239
Lehman, David, 89–90, 102, 114–15, 187, 234, 236
Lemieux, Jean-Paul, 160–61
Lempert, Benjamin, 71
length: Aristotle's aesthetic "magnitude," 224–25; brevity as characteristic of prose poetry, 16–17, 25–26, 245; and compression of prose poetry, 16–17, 141–42, 146; and division into sections, 241–44; and labeling or nomenclature, 91, 225, 231–36; line length, 213 (*See also* margins); page as limit to, 16–17, 91, 205; and reading

length (*cont.*)
  experience, 130–31; of sentence units, 146–47, 149, 206; stigmatization of short works, 224–25; and visual rhythm, 206
Lenox, Stephanie, 226
Le Rapide (Lemieux), 160–61
Lerner, Ben, 204, 211–12, 217
Le Symbolisme (Symbolism) Moreas, 104
Letters to Kelly Clarkson (Bloch), 237–38
"Letter to a Funeral Parlor" (Davis), 236–39
"Letter to My Imagined Daughter" (Vaughn), 181–83, 196
Levinson, Marjorie, 37, 40
Levis, Larry, 110
Levy, Deborah, 124, 226–27
Li, Bella, 240
Life in a Box Is a Pretty Life (Martin), 210
Light from and Eclipse (Lagomarsino), 231
"The Lights of London" (Guiney), 61
"Like Our Shadow-Selves" (Alexander), 233
Like (Stallings), 86
lineated poetry, 3, 9; and attention to formal elements, 80; and closure, 79–80; contrasted with prose poetry, 132, 141; disenjambment, 87–88; "lineated prose poems," 90–91; and line break decisions, 84; prose poems contrasted with, 97; and stanzas, 7, 132; and vertical trajectory, 132
lineation, 7–8, 10, 12
line breaks, 84; as editorial decision, 89–90; punctuation and, 240; rhythm and, 54; and rupture, 212; and silence, 132; typography and attention to, 88; and white space, 137–38
"Lines Composed a Few Miles above Tintern Abbey" (Wordsworth), 68–69
Little Dorrit (Dickens), 8–9
The Lives They Left Behind (exhibition), 163
Lockwood, Patricia, 218, 219–20
Loewen, Grant, 231
Logic of the Stairwell and Other Images (Atkins), 126
Logological Fragments (Novalis), 35–36
Loizeaux, Elizabeth Bergmann, 159, 167
Lombardo, Gian, 144
Longenbach, James, 148
Loop of Jade (Howe), 239
"Lost and Found" (Chernoff), 158–59
Loveday, Michael, 226

Love Poems for the Millenium (Johnson), 241
"The Love Song of J. Alfred Prufrock" (Eliot), 168
Lowell, Amy, 61, 72, 167, 245
Lowes, Robert, 141
Loydell, Rupert, 124, 181
Lyotard, Jean François, 48, 197–98
lyric essays, 4, 24–25, 94, 201, 244
lyric prose poetry, 211–17

Machines We Have Built (Lombardo), 144
Mackenzie, Raymond, 30
Macpherson, James, 40–42
magical realism, 105, 112–13, 115, 117, 119
Mallarmé, Stephane, 18–21, 24, 66, 104, 133–35, 137–38, 150, 224, 243
Maloney, Dennis, 143
Mancini, C. Bruna, 67, 74
Manhire, Bill, 124
Manifesto of Surrealism (Breton), 104–5, 109, 115
Marcus, Morton, 103, 138, 142
margins, 22, 48, 58, 222; and "boxes" of text, 213; and containment, 58, 88, 110–11; ignored during typesetting of prose poems, 88; as "invisible fence," 17; justified vs. ragged, 58, 85–86, 89–90, 110–11, 132, 161; and reader experience, 138; and visual containment, 83; as visual cue to reader, 86; and white space, 212. *See also* white space
Mark, Sabrina Orah, 239
Markotic, Nicole, 202
Marriage: A Sentence (Waldman), 241
Martens, Amelie, 85, 120
Martin, Dawn Lundy, 205, 210
Marvell, Andrew, 131
Marville, Charles, 154
"Mask Photo" (Bang), 161–62
Masquerade (Zawacki), 241
Maxims and Moral Reflections (Rochefoucauld), 18
May, Jon, 140
Mayer, Bernadette, 205, 216, 238
McFarland, Thomas, 35, 37
McGookey, Kathleen, 83, 87, 238
McGrath, Campbell, 22
McGuiness, Patrick, 104
Measures of Expatriation (Capildeo), 242–43
Mehta, Shivani, 112

Meitner, Erika, 74
memory: autobiographical memory, 49, 172–73, 176; compression and, 55–56, 174; poets access to, 173–74; and selfhood, 172–73; visual imagery and activation of, 172–73
"The Memory of Grief" (Kasischke), 98–99
Mercian Hymns (Hill), 22, 51
Merrill, Christopher, 235
Merwin, W. S., 181
metaphor, 14; and empathic aesthetic experience, 166–67; as fables in brief, 181; and human thought, 179; and metonymy, 179–84, 195; reading and metaphorical transitions, 181–83; thought as, 195–96
"Meta" (Russell), 194–95
metered verse, 51, 68–69
metonymy: and absence, 39, 247–48; and allusion or intertextuality, 183–84, 187–95; and ambiguity, 186, 196–97; as characteristic of prose poetry, *viii*, 14, 185–86, 196–98, 245; and compression, 184; defined, 177–78; and expansion, 196–97; and fragments, 39, 43, 197, 247–48; and human thought, 178–79; and memory retrieval, 174, 186; and metaphor, 179–84, 195; and reader engagement, 196–97
metropolis, 29
Meyerstein, E. H. W., 42
Michell, Danielle, 110–11
microfiction, 4, 26, 202, 225–27, 232
"Midday and Afternoon" (Lowell), 72
Miller, E. Ethelbert, 237
Mills, Kathryn Oliver, 10
Miltner, Robert, 85, 160–61, 162
The Mirror that Lied (Balog), 234
Mirsky, D. S., 8
Miss August (Andrews), 230
Mitchell, W. J. T., 159
Model City (Stonecipher), 61–62
Models of the Universe (Friebert and Young, eds.), 61–62, 220–21, 236
modernism, prose poetry and, 62–63, 71, 154, 167–68, 226, 228, 241
Monroe, Harriet, 53
Monroe, Jonathan, 5, 28–29, 33, 39, 53, 85–86
Monson, Jane, 4, 16, 83, 124, 163–64, 175, 199, 202–3

Monte, Steven, 5, 17, 19, 21, 25, 103, 175, 201, 243
The Monument (Strand), 3
Moore, Dafydd, 41–42
Moore, Fabienne, 19, 33
Moores, Margaret, 155
The Moralist of Bananas (Benedikt), 25
"Moravia: Postcards" (Hummer), 89
Moréas, Jean, 104, 156
Moriarty, Laura, 205
Morley, Simon, 156
The Morning Glory (Bly), 91
Moss, Thylias, 218, 220
"The Most Exciting Beliefs Could Be Written in Verse" (Black), 82
"Mrs. Belladonna's Supper Club Waltz" (Fort), 70
Mullen, Harryette, 71, 108–9, 203, 205, 227–28, 241
multilingual poetry, 74, 246
Munden, Paul, 100, 145, 174–76
Murphy, Margueritte S., 5, 10, 48, 162, 167, 197–98, 199, 234; and fragmentation of urban life, 67, 71, 154; and length as characteristic of prose poetry, 16–17, 24–25, 243, 245; on reading, 175; on relationship of photography to prose poetry, 154; as subversive, 85–86
music or musicians, 58–59, 69–71
Myers, Steve, 92
"My Larzac Childhood" (Petit), 127
My Life and My Life in the Nineties (Hejinian), 82, 205–9, 241
"my life as china" (Shockley), 229
"My Mother is Locked in a Jar of Ginger" (Black), 123

Nagai, Mariko, 203, 240
Nansi, Pooja, 59
narrative, 27, 232–33, 237, 246, 247; closure, 149–50; gaps or perturbations in, 145–46, 149–50, 197; subversion of traditional, 201
"narrative digression," 80–81
narrative prose, 225–26
"Narrotics: New Narrative and Prose Poem" (Markotic), 202
The Narrow Road (Hahn), 93
"Neighborhood? Proximities change on you sooner or later" (Giscombe), 71

Neisser, Ulric, 173
Nelles, William, 224, 227
Nelson, Maggie, 201, 211–12, 216–17, 241
"Neons" (Walwicz), 123–24
neo-surrealism, 15; in Australia, 122–24; French influence on American, 102–8; as male-centered tradition, 121; and poetic logic, 117; and postmodernism, 105; women poets and, 121, 125, 200
New and Selected Poems, 1962–2012 (Simic), 90
Newman, Amy, 237
Newman, Lance, 53
"The New Sentence" (Silliman), 96, 107–8, 203, 206
"The New Spirit" (Ashbery), 243–44
"New York at Night" (Lowell), 61
Nezhukumatathil, Aimee, 92
Niépce, Nicéphore, 154
"Night and Sleep" (Lowell), 72
"The Night's Insomnia" (Brophy), 147–48
Night Sky with Exit Wounds (Vuong), 92, 239
"Nights of Dreaming" (O'Sullivan), 91
"1973" (Webb), 186–87
Niska, Heidi Mae, 162–63
Noel-Tod, Jeremy, 4, 12, 17, 52, 243
nonfiction, 9, 231, 237
North, Kate, 143
"No Stars" (Kennard), 125–26
Nothing Here is Wild, Everything is Open (Hershman), 239
Novalis, 28, 33–36
Nox (Carson), 213

"Obituary" (Moores), 240
"Ode on a Grecian Urn" (Keats), 47
Of Silence and Song (Beachy-Quick), 231
"Oklahoma" (Alyan), 11, 45–46
"The Old Churchyard Tree" (Horne), 21
Olson, Ray, 119
Olszewska, Daniela, 204–5
1.290270,103.851959 (2017) (Pang), 59
"On Earth We Are Briefly Gorgeous" (Vuong), 97
100 Papers (Jobson), 231
"On Hedonism" (Carson), 47
openness. *See* closure
The Oracle (Gracián), 18
Orange Roses (Ives), 10

"Ordinary Objects, Extraordinary Emotions" (McGookey), 238
"Origins of the Sublime" (Ashton), 95–96
Orr, Greg, 106, 110
Ostriker, Alice, 64
O'Sullivan, Vincent, 91
"Out There" (Burns), 194

Page Chatter (website), 226
pages: page turns, 48; single-page length, 16–17, 91, 205
Palace of Culture (Walwicz), 241
Palace of Memory (Hetherington), 241
"Palaver" (Giscombe), 71
Pallant, Cheryl, 203
Pang, Alvin, 59
paragraphs as unit, 51, 84, 141, 206; and compression, 121; and organization from within, 180; as rooms, 85; as stanzas, 85. *See also* "box" of prose poetry
parallelism, 88
"Parallel Oz" (Wagan Watson), 192–93
Paris Spleen (Baudelaire), 8, 18, 20–21, 29–30, 53, 63–65, 69–70, 103, 154, 156–57, 209
"Partly True Poem Reflected in a Mirror" (Vuong), 97
Partridge, Eric, 33
The Party Train (Alexander, Vinz, and Truesdale, eds.), 81, 237
Pastels in Prose (Howells), 18
Paul, Elizabeth, 160, 162
Peach (Glass), 241
Peacock, Molly, 10
Penelope and Pip Build a Prose Poem (Heiden and Huntington), 244
The Penguin Book of the Prose Poem (Noel-Tod, ed.), 4, 12, 17, 243
Perkins, David, 28
Perloff, Marjorie, 25–26, 206, 228
Petit, Pascale, 125, 127
Peyre, Henri, 103
Philip, NourbeSe Marlene, 203
Phillips, Jayne Anne, 232
Phillips, Siobhan, 113–14
"Photo Graph Paper: American Push" (Gropp), 169–70
photography: and "captioning" as poetry, 162; and ekphrastic poems, *viii*, 155, 159–64, 240; and image as "box," 153; and intrusion

of image into verbal media, 156–58; poetry image composition and like photographic development, 158; as quotation, 153; stills or frames as fragments, 175
"Photoheliograph" (Crosby), 158
"*Pianist and Still-Life,* 1929, Henri Matisse" (Paul), 160
"Picture of the Dead Woman as a Bride" (Burn), 124
Pierce, Chester, 216
Pike, Burton, 60
Pillow Book (Sei Shōnagon), 9, 92, 93–94
Pinsky, Robert, 105
Pitch Lake (Bagoo), 241
play, as characteristic of prose poetry, 22, 43–44, 82, 101, 126, 148, 238–39, 246. *See also* humor
Plowes, Winston, 124
poème en prose tradition, 19–20, 22, 102
"Poem in the Manner of Baudelaire" (Lehman), 187
Poems in Prose (Wilde), 53
Poems in the Manner Of (Lehman), 187
The Poems of Ossian (Macpherson), 40–42
poetic prose, 58–59, 62–63, 67, 82; as distinct from prose poetry, *vii,* 6–9, 12, 16–17, 137, 235; and hybridity, 222, 224; language poets and, 25–26, 41–42, 206; Macpherson's *Ossian,* 41–42. *See also poème en prose* tradition
"Poetry City" (Swenson), 62–63
The Poetry Foundation, 6
Poetry (magazine), 53
"poet's prose," 12, 101, 206
Point Reyes Poems (Bly), 91
"The Pond" (Rafferty), 56–57, 58
Ponge, Francis, 13, 115
Pope, Alexander, 38
"Postcard to Ilya Kaminsky" (Woloch), 46–47
postcolonial prose poems, 189–95, 197
postmodernism, 29, 31; and compression, 130; and fragmentation, 35, 48–50, 58, 197, 229; and hybridity, 13–14; and neo-surrealism, 105; and prose poem form, 50; and prose poetry, 140–41, 197–98; and Romanticism, 43–45; and short forms, 226–28; and surrealism, 105, 109; and urban life, 58, 61, 64; and very short forms, 245–46

Pound, Ezra, 40–41, 53, 89, 162, 167–68
"Powers of Ten" (Hershman), 97–98
Preface to Lyrical Ballads (Wordsworth), 52–53
"Preludes" (Eliot), 61, 71–72
"The Prelude" (Wordsworth), 32
Prendergast, Christopher, 24
Price, Richard, 88
"Primacy and Preference" (Russell), 194–95
Princeton Encyclopedia of Poetics, 184
Privitello, Meghan, 239
The Prose Poem: An International Anthology (Benedikt), 12, 200
The Prose Poem: An International Journal (Johnson), 4
"The Prose Poem as a Beautiful Animal" (Edson), 181
"The Prose Poem as An Evolving Form" (Bly), 181
"The Prose Poem" (Bly), 181
Prose Poem Issue, Beltway Poetry Quarterly, 142
Prose Poem Issue, Mississippi Review, 16
"The Prose Poem" (McGrath), 22
Prose Poems and Sudden Fiction (Allen and Loewen, eds.), 231
Prose Poems (Poetry Party) (Pearson and Petelinsek), 237, 244
"Prose Poetry and the Spirit of Jazz" (Santilli), 188
Prosody (chapbook collection), 101
Proust, Marcel, 188–89
"Proust from the Bottom Up" (Raworth), 188–89
publication of poetry: and categorization of works, 231–33, 235; on digital or online platforms, 153, 175, 205, 217–19, 226, 234, 246; formatting choices and, 89–90, 171; photographic technology and changes in, 156
Pulitzer Prize, 3, 5, 225
Pulse: Prose Poems, 4
punctuation, 44; colons, 229–30, 240; commas, 58, 133, 144–45, 147, 186; dashes, 95–96, 97, 136–37, 191; ellipses, 45, 57, 120, 210; em dashes, 95–96; and rhythm, 58, 186; slashes, 96–97, 149, 240
Purgatory (Martens), 85

Quarrels (Joseph), 3
"Quebec Express" (Miltner), 160–61

Queen, Khadijah, 203, 218, 221–22, 239
the quotidian. *See* the everyday

Rafferty, Charles, 55–56
"The Rain" (Shumate), 194
Ramazani, Jahan, 23
Rankine, Claudia, 3, 89, 201, 211–12, 214–16, 217, 224–25, 239
"Rape Joke" (Lockwood), 219–20
"Rapunzel" (Atherton), 89
"The Rat's Legs" (Edson), 120–21
Rauber, D. F., 35
Raworth, Tom, 188–89
reading, 16, 26–27, 31; as archaeological, 174; brevity and experience of reader, 121; compression and, 130; destabilization of readerly expectations, 15, 27, 85–87, 114–15, 141, 185, 201, 206–7, 239; direct address to reader, 45; empathic aesthetics and, 164–69, 176; entry into the poem, 163–66, 170–72, 174; and figurative language, 180; and fragmentation of experience, 227; and genre or form categorization, 231–36; hybrid texts, 241; and identification with the poet, 176; informational gaps and reader engagement, 81–82, 130, 173, 185, 197, 210, 226–27; intensity of experience, 164–66, 238; interpretation and engagement with prose poetry, 166; intimacy and intensity of prose poetry, 164–66; Levinson's "reading protocol," 40; memory and projection during, 173; and metaphorical transitions, 181–83; multilingual texts, 246–47; new media and changes in, 175, 244; and "open text," 81–83; orientation on the page and, 15; and processing of visual imagery, 165; prose poetry for younger readers, 244; reception of innovative poems, 53; rereading, 174–75; satisfaction, 226; seduction of the reader, 85–87, 174, 202; and subjectivity, 169; typography and, 86; velocity of, 132–33, 138, 140–42, 144, 241; and vertical trajectory of prose poems, 15, 132, 138–39; visual cues and, 85–87, 111–12; as voyeuristic, 176; white space and, 132–36, 138, 139, 144
realism, 156
"The Recital" (Ashbery), 244
recursion, 128–29, 146, 149

Recyclopedia (Mullen), 227, 241
Red doc> (Carson), 213
"The Red Wheelbarrow" (Williams), 168
"Regulator, I Married Him" (Russell), 194–95
"The Rejection of Closure" (Hejinian), 81–82, 208
repetition, 137, 143, 171
"Reply" (Jones), 237
The Reproduction of Profiles (Waldrop), 241
"Rhapsody of a Windy Night" (Eliot), 71–72
rhythm, 16; and Baudelaire's concept of the flaneur, 64–67; "dancing" prosody, 72; free verse and, 51, 73; improvisation and, 55, 70; irregular meter and prose, 54–55; lineated poetry and, 73, 96; line breaks and, 54; metered verse, 51, 68–69; musician-poets and, 58–59; prose poetry as "ghosted" by meter, 56; of prose poetry *vs.* metered or free verse, 51; punctuation and, 186; and repetition, 55, 58, 71; and sentence as poetic unit, 56, 186; staccato or disrupted, 57, 69–70, 72–74, 124; syncopated, 69–71, 131; of urban life, 52, 67–75; visual rhythm, 206; "walking" pace and, 67–69
Rice, Shelley, 154
"Richard M. Nixon Attends 'Star Wars' Premiere, Brea Mann Theatre, 5/25/77" (Shapiro), 195
Richee, Clarissa, 230
Richmond Burning (Alexander), 233
Richter, Jean Paul Friedrich, 18
Ricks, Christopher, 137
Riffaterre, Michael, 187–88
Rimbaud, Arthur, 13, 30, 33, 41, 55, 62, 66; and history of prose poetry, 18–24, 28; as protosurrealist, 103–4; visual arts and emphasis on images, 156–57
Robbins, Amy Moorman, 200
Robinson, Gregory, 175, 186
Robinson, Jeffrey C., 36
Robinson, Roger, 186
Rochefoucauld, François VI, Duc de La, 18
Rodríguez, Alicita, 194
Romanticism, 33–34, 60; and appeal of abstraction, 47; contemporary subversions of, 42–43; and dreams or surreal images, 30, 46–47; and fragments, 28–32, 34–37, 43; and incompleteness (lack of closure),

34; prose poets and rejection of, 20; as subversive or oppositional, 30–31, 34–35, 36, 49. *See also* specific poets
"The Rooms Behind the Eyes" (Plowes), 124
"rooms," prose poems as, 15, 23, 83–85, 143–44, 165–66
Rooney, Kathleen, 84
"Rosary" (Tran), 98
Rosen, Charles, 39–40
Rosenblatt, Louise, 169
Ross, Bruce M., 174
Rossetti, Christina, 53
Rubin, David C., 172–73
Rushdie, Salman, 189
Russell, Lauren, 12, 99, 194

sacred texts, 5, 9, 183–84
Sadoff, Ira, 31, 239
Saintsbury, George, 72
Sanders, Kristin, 159, 218, 221
Santilli, Nikki, 5–6, 28–29, 48, 63, 69–70, 84, 184, 188–89, 196–97, 199
Saphra, Jaqueline, 240
Sappho, 211
Sartre, Jean-Paul, 133–35
Satterfield, Jane, 44
Saunders, George, 225
Scalapino, Leslie, 205, 230, 239
The Scented Fox (Browne), 239
"Scented Leaves—From a Chinese Jar" (Upward), 241
Scheele, Roy, 188
Schlegel, Friedrich, 28–29, 34, 36, 37, 38–40, 49–50
Schmitt, Kate, 231
Schomburg, 110–11
Scofield, Martin, 168
Scott, Clive, 91, 157
Seam: Prose Poems, 4
Seaton, Maureen, 241–42
Sebald, W. G., 90–91
Seed, Ian, 124, 226
Sei Shōnagon, 9, 92–94
Seigel, Jerrold, 66
Selerie, Gavin, 89
sentence as poetic unit, 51, 53–54, 80, 83, 206; and compression, 84, 121; contrasted with lines, 101; and free line form, 95–96; juxtaposition and interaction of, 144; "The

New Sentence" and late surrealism, 107–8; and prose fiction, 138–39; and rhythm of poem, 56, 186; structure and rhythm, 186; and velocity of poem, 147
"September" (Alexander), 233
sequences of prose poems, 17, 241–43
"Seven Prose Poems" (Simic), 116–17
Shakespeare, William, 37, 79–80, 131, 192
Shapard, Robert, 226
Shapcott, Thomas, 86–87
Shapiro, Daniel M., 195
"She Exists" (Éluard), 106–7
Shell, Marc, 68
Shelley, Mary, 209
Shelley, Percy Bysshe, 34, 37, 45
Shockley, Evie, 229
Short: An International Anthology (Ziegler, ed.), 2321
"Short Talk on Defloration" (Carson), 214
Short Talks (Carson), 213–14, 241
Shumate, David, 194
Sieburth, Richard, 49–50
"Silence" (Williams), 55–56, 58
Silesky, Barry, 239
Silliman, Ron, 95–96, 107–8, 115, 119; and language poetry, 203–6
Simic, Charles, 3, 27, 83, 89–90; neo-surrealism and, 106, 109, 110, 114, 116–21
Singh, Jessica, 240
Singing Bones (Schmitt), 231
Skovron, Alex, 123–24
slashes, 96–97, 149, 240
Sleeping with the Dictionary (Mullen), 108–9, 203
Small Porcelain Head (White), 231
Smith, Ali, 11, 22
Smith, Barbara Herrnstein, 79–80, 180–81
Smith, Ellen McGrath, 200
Smith, Hazel, 61
Smith, Patti, 11–12, 58–59
Smith, Sidonie, 172
"The Snow Spits" (North), 143
Soap (Ponge), 115
The Solex Brothers (Kennard), 3
"Some Fears" (Berry), 58
Some Simple Things Said by and about Humans (Iijima), 230–31
"Song of Myself" (Whitman), 7, 8, 9, 131
"Sonnet in Prose" (Coles), 100

sonnets, 38, 61, 64–65, 79–80, 100–101, 132–33, 145, 236–37
The Son of a Shoemaker (Burnett), 82
Sontag, Susan, 153
space. *See* gaps; TimeSpace; white space
Space, in Chains (Kasischke), 98–99
Spacks, Patricia Meyer, 13–14
Spenser, Edmund, 37–38
S*PeRM**K*T (Mullen), 227, 241
Spineless Wonders publishing, 231–32
Spoerri, David, 162
"Spring Day" (Lowell), 72
"Square of Light: The Artist is Present" (Monson), 163–64
Stallings, A. E., 86, 101
Stanford, Frank, 110
stanzas, 7, 15, 85, 86, 137
"Stations" (Heaney), 196–97
Stauffer, Andrew M., 30
Stein, Gertrude, 72, 185–86, 199, 226–27
Stevens, Wallace, 114
Still Water Prose Poems (Garfunkel), 59
Stohlman, Nancy, 225–26
Stonecipher, Donna, 61–62, 64, 133–35, 142, 241
Story, Julia, 203
Strand, Mark, 3, 103, 106, 110, 116–17, 195, 236–37
Strange, Shane, 235
Strich, Fritz, 35
subjectivity, 40, 43–44, 47, 156–57, 247; and aesthetic empathy, 168–70; and autobiographical memories, 172–76; and fragmentation, 49, 93–94, 227–28; prose poetry and expression of, 197–98; reading and, 169; Romanticism and, 32; voicing and, 202
subversion, 12, 15–16, 24–26, 201, 231, 245; destabilization of readerly expectation, 85–86; of genre, 86; language poetry and political resistance, 204; Macpherson's *Ossian* and, 40; of narrative, 201, 246; neo-surrealism and contemporary relevance, 107; postcolonial poets and "writing back" to the canon, 189–95; prose poetry as form of resistance, 15, 70, 71, 210; prose poetry as subversive form, *viii*, 18–19, 24–26, 31, 223; and racial identity or voice, 71; Romanticism and, 30–31, 34–35; of "rules" of poetry, 18; and surrealism, 106; women and resistance to patriarchal strictures, 208
Such Rare Citings (Santilli), 29, 63
sudden fiction, 225, 231
"Summer Haibun" (Nezhukumatathil), 92
"Supplication" (Skovron), 123–24
surrealism, 15; and the everyday, 105–16; poetic prose and dream images, 41–42; Romanticism and, 30, 46–47; and symbolism, 104–5. *See also* neo-surrealism
Suspira de Profundis (De Quincey), 69
Swenson, Cole, 62–63, 159–60
Symbolism, 12, 104–5, 156
"The System" (Ashbery), 175–76, 244
Szirtes, Georges, 124–25

Talei, Leila, 212
Tall, Deborah, 24–25
Tanehisa, Otabe, 49–50
Tatarkiewicz, Wladyslaw, 5
Tate, James, 87, 103, 106–7, 110
Taylor, John, 15, 49, 107
Tender Buttons (Stein), 72, 185–86
The Tenth of December (Saunders), 225
Thelwall, John, 35, 38, 43
"There's No Place Like Home" (Wagan Watson), 192–93
"Thimbleism" (Anderson), 112
"This is a Map of Their Watching Me" (Sanders), 159
This Line Is Not For Turning (Monson, ed.), 4, 84, 124
This Window Makes Me Feel (Fitterman), 62
Thomas, Sophie, 32
Thoreau, Henry David, 53
Threads: A Photography and Prose Poetry Collaboration (Niska and Gard), 162–63
Three Poems (Ashbery), 25, 243–44
Thrift, Nigel, 140
Tiffin, Helen, 189
TimeSpace: Bakhtin's chronotope concept, 130; compression and velocity, 140, 147; dilation or expansion of, 85, 129, 145–49; the ephemeral or transitory, 65; and fragments as becoming or ongoing, 50; in literary theory, 128–31; "present time of discourse" and prose poetry, 11–12, 26–27, 55, 146; dilation of, 129; rhythm and

cyclical time, 55; and sequences of prose poems, 241–43; TARDIS-like expansion of, 16, 85; visual imagery and dilation of, 164–65
"To Each His Chimæra" (Baudelaire), 103
"To His Coy Mistress" (Marvell), 131
Tolstoy, Leo, 129
"Tomato" (Clark), 201
"Tomorrow, Chaka Demus Will Play" (Danladi), 149
Toomer, Jane, 70
"Towards A Definition" (Loydell), 181
"To Writewithize" (Swenson), 159–60
Tract: Prose Poems, 4
Traherne, Thomas, 18
Tran, Barbara, 98, 239
translation, 211, 235; as influence on form, 91; Macpherson's *Ossian* "translations," 40–42; and multilingual poetry, 46, 74, 245–46; and rhythm, 55
Travis, Molly Abel, 48–49
Treat, Jessica, 103
The Trees The Trees (Christle), 148
"Trevor" (Vuong), 96–97
Trimmings (Mullen), 227, 241
"The True Bride" (Gerstler), 228–29
Truesdale, C. W., 14, 237
Tupelo Press, 235
Turco, Lewis, 6
Turgenev, Ivan, 10
"Twelve Dark Passages No. 6" (Szirtes), 124
"TWO LOVES I HAVE" (Agbabi), 100–101
The Two Thousands (Boyer), 205
Types of Shape (Hollander), 89
typography, 83–84, 234, 245; and attention to line breaks, 88; and dialogue, 83; font choice, 222; and form, 15, 89; italics, 44, 233; margins and meaning, 22; as visual cues to the reader, 15, 86–87. *See also* white space

The Unbearable Heart (Hahn), 93
Under Brushstrokes (Habra), 163
"The Unity of the Paragraph" (Lowes), 141
The Unremitting Stain (Beye), 72–73
Upton, Lee, 120
Upward, Allen, 241
urban fantasy, 105, 112–13, 115, 123
Utopia Minus (Briante), 237

The Valley Press Anthology of Prose Poetry (Caldwell and Hardwick), 4, 12, 124
Vas Dias, Robert, 228–29
Vaughn, Kyle, 181–83
Vaughn, William, 34
Verlaine, Paul, 157
Vickery, John B., 21
Vicky Swanky Is a Beauty (Williams), 31, 239
Vico, Giambattista, 181
Vinz, Mark, 237
visual cues, 85–87
visual imagery, *viii,* 109, 162, 176, 245; and empathy, 169, 170; memory activation and, 172–73; photographs as "boxes," 153, 175; reading and, 164–65; and thought, 164–65. *See also* Imagism; photography
"Visual Orders" (Xie), 94
voice, 103, 197; first-person, 3, 57 (*See also* Lyric "I" *under this heading*); flânerie and ironic or detached, 22; lyric "I," 3, 211–14, 247; polyphony, 10–11, 230; third-person, 57; ventriloquism, 161–62
Voice's Daughter of a Heart Yet to Be Born (Waldman), 241
Vuong, Ocean, 92, 96–97, 239

Wabuke, Hope, 221–22
Wagan Watson, Samuel, 192–93
"Waiting for the Light" (Ostriker), 64
"The Wake of Plenty" (Scheele), 188
Wakoski, Diane, 110, 142
Walden (Thoreau), 53
Waldman, Anne, 92, 241
Waldrop, Rosmarie, 48, 100, 200, 205, 239
"Walk" (Lowell), 72
Wall, Alan, 17
Wallace, Louise, 74
Wallerstein, Immanuel, 128
Wallschlaeger, Nikki, 85, 203
Walser, Robert, 162
Walwicz, Ania, 123–24, 241
Wanner, Adrian, 10, 11
Wanning, Elizabeth, 28
Ward, Diane, 205
"Warning to the Reader" (Bly), 45
"The Waste Land" (Eliot), 61, 168
Watson, Julia, 172
Webb, Jen, 186–87, 193
Webber, Mark Andrews, 240

Weems, Carrie, 162, 210
Weiner, Hannah, 205
Weinstein, Arnold, 63–64
"We Were So Poor" (Simic), 90, 118–19
Whalen, Tom, 112, 115–16, 181
What's Hanging on the Hush (Russell), 194–95
When Love Lived Alone (Singh), 240
White, Allison Benis, 231
White, Gillian, 212
"White Approach" (Gard), 162–63
"White House" (Wallschlaeger), 85
white space, 207; and absence, 133–35, 137–38, 150, 214–15; as border or enclosure, 80, 138, 143, 150, 161, 222; dialogue and, 139–40; free-lines, 17, 44–45, 95–98, 101, 214–15, 219–20; gaps or spaces within lines, 136, 148; interaction with text, 137; and isolation, 214–15; lack of, 144–45; lineated poetry and, 128, 132, 137, 141; and line breaks, 137–38; in prose fiction, 137–39; and reading experience, 128, 132–36, 138, 139, 144; and "reverberation," 128; and shaped poems, 89; and silence, 132, 150; and visual fragmentation, 148. *See also* gaps; margins
"White Tigers" (Iijima), 230–31
Whitman, Walt, 7–9, 53, 60–61, 65, 75, 131, 136, 245
"Who Is Flying This Plane? The Prose Poem and The Life of the Line" (Bar-Nadav), 87–88
"Why I Don't Write Nature Poems" (Satterfield), 44
"Why I Hate the Prose Poem" (Whalen), 181
Wilde, Oscar, 42, 53
"Wild Garlic and Detours" (Caldwell), 47–48
Williams, C. K., 55–56, 58
Williams, Diane, 239
Williams, John Sibley, 138
Williams, William Carlos, 168, 200, 224, 241
"Will You Please Be Quiet, Please" (Carver), 139
Wilson, Chloe, 232
Wilson, Sugar Magnolia, 238
"With Your Permission, Allow Me To Perform Exemplary Surgery on Your Brian" (Caleshu), 125–26

Wollstonecraft, Mary, 209
Woloch, Cecilia, 46–47
Women, the New York School, and Other True Abstractions (Nelson), 216
Women and Nature (Griffin), 199–200
women poets, 13; Baudelaire and visibility of women, 65; containment within patriarchal conventions, 201–2; and disruption, 205; and humor, 219–20; and male "template" as default, 200–201; and prose poetry as subversive form, 223; rape narratives in works, 217–22; women and the pillow book tradition, 93–94
Wood, Danielle, 232
"Woods: A Prose Sonnet" (Emerson), 100
"Word, Dialogue, and Novel" (Kristeva), 187
Wordsworth, William, 32, 34, 36–37, 40, 44, 60, 137; "bumming" and composition while walking, 68–69; and poetic diction, 52–54
"The World Doesn't End" (Simic), 116
The World Doesn't End (Simic), 3, 5–7, 89–90, 225
Wright, C. D., 199, 203, 205
Wright, James, 13, 103, 106, 109–10, 168
Wright, Patrick, 161–62
"Written in a Historically White Place (I)" (Chan), 246–47

Xie, Jenny, 92, 94–95, 203, 239
"XLIV: Photographs: The Old Days" (Carson), 212

"Yet we insist that life is full of happy chance" (Hejinian), 207
"Yonder Zongs" (Pallant), 203
Young, David, 236
Young, Gary, 15, 144–45
"You" (Silliman), 108

Zawacki, Andrew, 228, 241
Zhicheng-Mingdé, Desmond Kon, 193
Ziegler, Alan, 231–32, 235
Zimmer, Abigail, 240
zuihitsu, 92–94
Zweig, Paul, 110